Computational Practices and Applications for Digital Art and Crafting

Shalin Hai-Jew
Hutchinson Community College, USA

A volume in the Advances in Multimedia and Interactive Technologies (AMIT) Book Series

IGI Global
PUBLISHER of TIMELY KNOWLEDGE

Published in the United States of America by
IGI Global
Information Science Reference (an imprint of IGI Global)
701 E. Chocolate Avenue
Hershey PA, USA 17033
Tel: 717-533-8845
Fax: 717-533-8661
E-mail: cust@igi-global.com
Web site: http://www.igi-global.com

Library of Congress Cataloging-in-Publication Data

CIP DATA PROCESSING

2024 Information Science Reference
ISBN(hc) 9798369329276 | ISBN(sc) 9798369351055 | eISBN 9798369329283

British Cataloguing in Publication Data
A Cataloguing in Publication record for this book is available from the British Library.

For electronic access to this publication, please contact: eresources@igi-global.com.

Advances in Multimedia and Interactive Technologies (AMIT) Book Series

Joel J.P.C. Rodrigues
Senac Faculty of Ceará, Fortaleza-CE, Brazil; Instituto de Telecomunicações, Portugal

ISSN:2327-929X
EISSN:2327-9303

Mission

Traditional forms of media communications are continuously being challenged. The emergence of user-friendly web-based applications such as social media and Web 2.0 has expanded into everyday society, providing an interactive structure to media content such as images, audio, video, and text.

The **Advances in Multimedia and Interactive Technologies (AMIT) Book Series** investigates the relationship between multimedia technology and the usability of web applications. This series aims to highlight evolving research on interactive communication systems, tools, applications, and techniques to provide researchers, practitioners, and students of information technology, communication science, media studies, and many more with a comprehensive examination of these multimedia technology trends.

Coverage

- Digital Communications
- Digital Watermarking
- Multimedia Services
- Social Networking

IGI Global is currently accepting manuscripts for publication within this series. To submit a proposal for a volume in this series, please contact our Acquisition Editors at Acquisitions@igi-global.com or visit: http://www.igi-global.com/publish/.

The Advances in Multimedia and Interactive Technologies (AMIT) Book Series (ISSN 2327-929X) is published by IGI Global, 701 E. Chocolate Avenue, Hershey, PA 17033-1240, USA, www.igi-global.com. This series is composed of titles available for purchase individually; each title is edited to be contextually exclusive from any other title within the series. For pricing and ordering information please visit http://www.igi-global.com/book-series/advances-multimedia-interactive-technologies/73683. Postmaster: Send all address changes to above address.

Titles in this Series

For a list of additional titles in this series, please visit: www.igi-global.com/book-series

The Rise of Over-the-Top (OTT) Media and Implications for Media Consumption and Production
Nithin Kalorth (Mahindra University, India)
Information Science Reference • copyright 2024 • 297pp • H/C (ISBN: 9798369301166) • US $245.00 (our price)

Transformed Communication Codes in the Mediated World A Contemporary Perspective
Hasan Gürkan (Girona University, Spain) and Aybike Serttaş (Istinye University, Turkey)
Information Science Reference • copyright 2024 • 407pp • H/C (ISBN: 9798369308967) • US $240.00 (our price)

Examining Multimedia Forensics and Content Integrity
Sumit Kumar Mahana (National Institute of Technology, Kurukshetra, India) Rajesh Kumar Aggarwal (National Institute of Technology, Kurukshetra, India) and Surjit Singh (Thapar Institute of Engineering and Technology, India)
Information Science Reference • copyright 2023 • 301pp • H/C (ISBN: 9781668468647) • US $225.00 (our price)

Handbook of Research on Advanced Practical Approaches to Deepfake Detection and Applications
Ahmed J. Obaid (University of Kufa, Iraq) Ghassan H. Abdul-Majeed (University of Baghdad, Iraq) Adriana Burlea-Schiopoiu (University of Craiova, Romania) and Parul Aggarwal (Jamia Hamdard, India)
Information Science Reference • copyright 2023 • 379pp • H/C (ISBN: 9781668460603) • US $295.00 (our price)

Dynamics of Dialogue, Cultural Development, and Peace in the Metaverse
Swati Chakraborty (GLA University, India)
Information Science Reference • copyright 2023 • 236pp • H/C (ISBN: 9781668459072) • US $240.00 (our price)

Handbook of Research on New Media, Training, and Skill Development for the Modern Workforce
Dominic Mentor (Teachers College, Columbia University, USA)
Business Science Reference • copyright 2022 • 439pp • H/C (ISBN: 9781668439968) • US $295.00 (our price)

IGI Global
PUBLISHER of TIMELY KNOWLEDGE

701 East Chocolate Avenue, Hershey, PA 17033, USA
Tel: 717-533-8845 x100 • Fax: 717-533-8661
E-Mail: cust@igi-global.com • www.igi-global.com

Table of Contents

Detailed Table of Contents

With the rapidly developing technology, the use of digital art applications in the visual art education process is becoming widespread as a new field of study. When the literature was examined, no study was found that investigated the digital art applications that can be used in early childhood and the views of preschool teachers on these applications and evaluated them as a visual art education tool in early childhood. In this context, this study aims to identify digital art applications and tools that can be used in the early childhood visual arts education process, to examine these applications in terms of scope and content, and to examine the knowledge and opinions of teachers about the digital supported art education applications/tools.

There is an important value in human-machine collaborations using artmaking generative AI tools: that is, the preservation of the human hand (the human mental-emotional-embodied manual contribution) in the artwork. One way to ensure the original look-and-feel involves using multimodal prompts—both text and visual—with a twist. The visual may be one that is human-generated—either born-analog (and then digitized) or born-digital (such as imagery created on tablets or laptops, on digital drawing systems)—in a way that is unrelated or only peripherally related to the text prompt. This chapter explores how to craft seeding imagery for use in artmaking generative AI tools for innovations in color, color blends, textures, layouts, various perspectives, style blends, and others. This work describes some early ways to introduce human-touch novelty in seeding imagery from analog and digital approaches.

Athos Bulcão is a renowned Brazilian artist recognized for his outstanding surface work with tiles on murals of Brasília's buildings, the 1960s-designed modern capital of Brazil, and other localities. The beauty of his work can be expressed by how it has become part of the city landscape and people's everyday encounters. It is also very contemporaneous regarding how he used logic to organize his tiles, using rotation and pattern distribution, allowing chance and error while architectural surfaces are assembled. Explaining logic and making it into tile distribution is difficult to explain to students; using paper prototypes helps, but Common Digital Art coding takes it a step further in the complexity of tiling

Preface

Recently, I came across an impassioned posting on a social generative AI website. The named artist (who went by a handle instead of an actual name) was frustrated that others on and off the website were using her prompts but removing her name from the prompts. (The inclusion of her name on the prompt with a © symbol showed up in the visual and served as a watermark, to prevent others from easily using the output images.) She felt that the artworks were hers (even though they were machine generated for the most part), and she felt that the use of the prompting text through a feature of the website contravened her rights as a common artist. The copyright symbol was applied even though works created by machine are not seen as generally copyrightable since they were not created by a human person. Since then, some have suggested that if a person puts in a certain amount of work, even in collaboration with a generative AI tool, that they may be credited. Current practice is that images by GAIs are not generally copyright-able. That said, I found the posting to be gauche but also touching: the individual clearly valued the images that she made with the use of the GAI tool, and she felt possessive enough that she appealed to her fellow common "artists" to lay off using her text prompts without giving her credit, either in the image itself or in the notes about the image.

The opening anecdote shows something of the sense of ownership that people have over their digital artworks. Even if their investment is "merely" thinking up a prompt, their sense of authorship is strong.

I have long had a level of affection for the topic of digital art and digital craft. I so enjoyed common art that I edited and wrote much of *Common Visual Art in a Social Digital Age* (2022), which appeared with a different press. Especially alluring is the idea of "art" and "computation" and "sociality." Those elements are resonant in this collection also. There is affection for the topic and respect for the contributing researchers and research teams.

Figure 1. Deconstructed Scissors

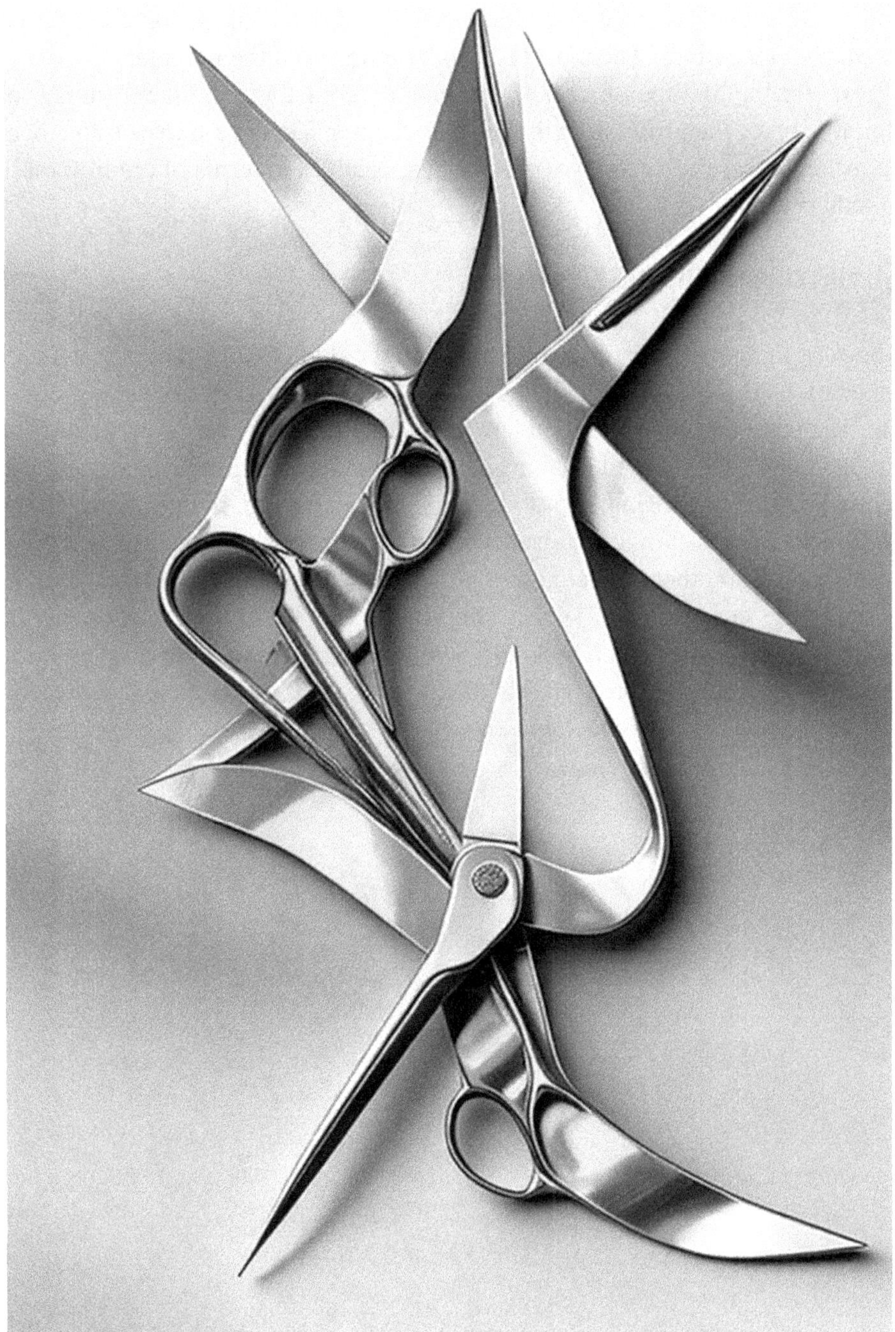

A former colleague of mine (from graduate school) went onto a social fundraising site to ask for moneys to write a book. I think she raised several thousand dollars, but that was many years ago, and no book ever appeared in any publicly available way, whether print or electronic or both. Another colleague, a fellow college professor, applied for an internal grant to write a chapter proposal. I never saw any publicly available chapter. Without the internal drive to actually do the work, external incentives are rarely motivating enough to encourage the work. A book has to be something a person would do regardless of external incentives. The work itself is grueling, and the monetary payoff is the equivalent of a day's wages…for the lifetime of a book. For chapter contributors, the return is even less, with the payment a digital copy of the professionally laid-out chapter. That is a transaction a person would have to be a fool to make, unless they got payoffs elsewhere, such as in terms of credit for tenure or personal satisfaction in other ways.

About Digital Art and Digital Crafting

Why this book at this time? For the public, this is the golden age of generative AI (GAI), especially art-making generative AI (A-GAI), which has changed both digital artmaking and digital craft-making fundamentally. The technologies are only a few years old, at least in terms of some of the forms of the large language models (LLMs) based on machine learning and training through neural network means. From the user experience, the technologies are fiddly. There are challenges with "hallucinations" (the making up of false source citations and false facts) and "memory" (the regurgitation of works verbatim based on the prompts), and other challenges.

Societally, there are concerns that such technologies will harm human jobs, particularly those in the creative space. The advent of such technologies are not only changing how artworks are made but perhaps how people see and interpret what is artful. The standards of visual representation may also change with exemplars of machine precision entering the arts and crafts space.

Figure 2. Digital Cocoon

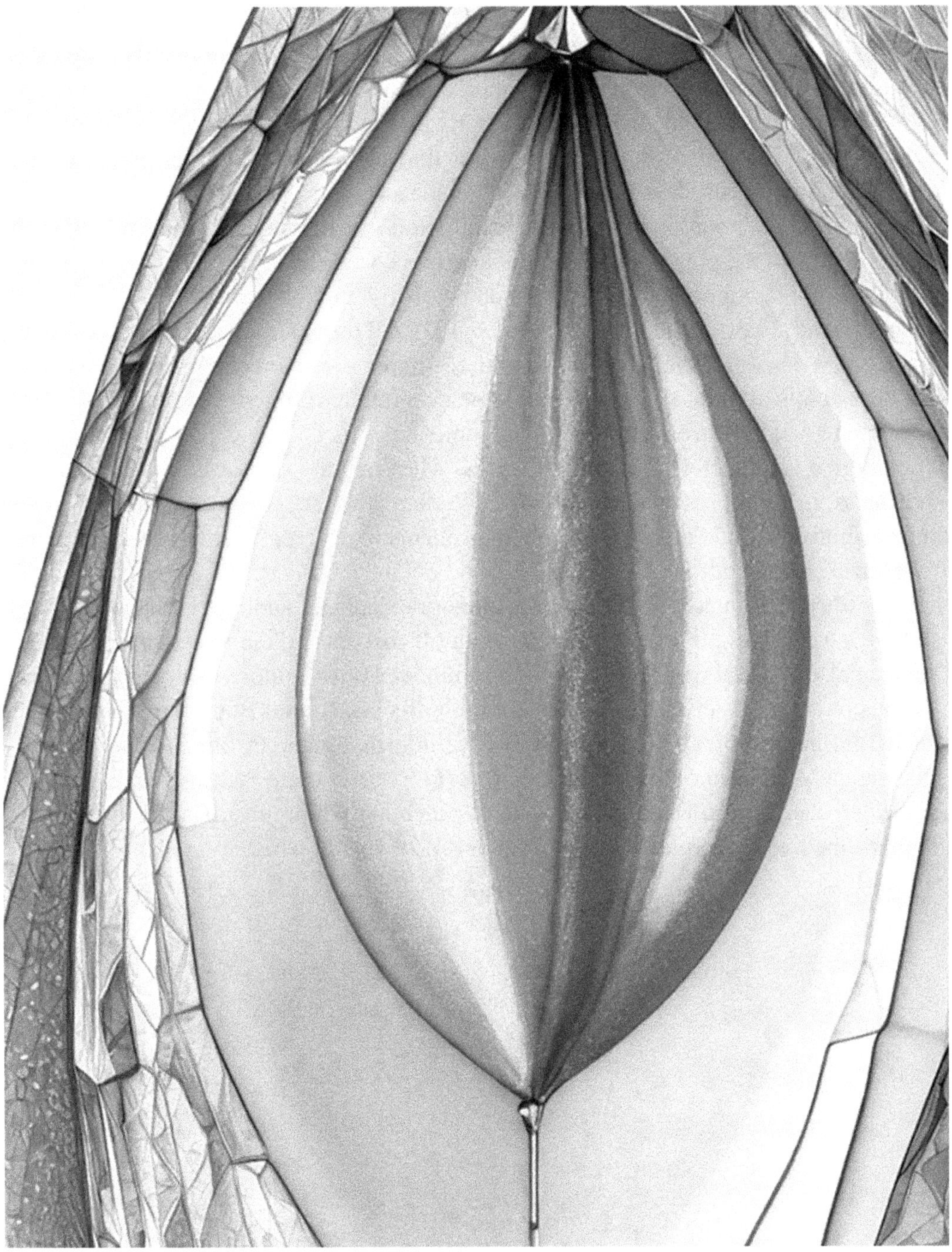

There are rare occasions when works of nature are so jaw-droppingly astounding and beautiful that one is left speechless. I have experienced that once at the Bellevue College campus. I turned a corner to see a tree in bright red-orange leafage that left me dumbstruck. Twice, I saw men who had that handsomeness that left me awestruck. Once, a child. Those are rare experiences. However, in terms of A-GAI tools, these, too, may create works that are awe-inspiring, jaw-dropping, and so potent as to leave one unable to speak.

Digital art and digital craft rely in part on digital means for their creation and existence. Digital art tends towards informal or common art, in terms of practice. Here, people use various technologies to work ideas and materials to an outcome that may be wholly digital, a mix of physical (analog) and digital, or wholly analog. Digital craft may also result in works that are wholly digital (born digital and delivered digitally), computational (based on computer-generated patterns), physical (analog, but built using some computational digital intervention in part), and technocraft ("craft with technological objects"). There is much transcoding from the physical to the digital and vice versa. This point brings to mind a question: What material is more common and low-cost than pixels (picture elements)?

At a recent art fair, I saw welded artworks that were based on an automated bandsaw. So, too, organic jewelry boxes carved and polished from wood with the hyper precision of a machine and computational patterning. At a booth later on, I saw beautiful large decorative rocks polished using machines, and the carvings looked to originate from computational templates.

How do "digital arts" differ from "digital crafts"? Perhaps the first has more formal origins, more high-mindedness, more expression and big ideas. Perhaps the latter is more based on items that may have home decorative use and practical use. Perhaps there are different markets for the different objects. Perhaps human experimentation and skill and experimental dabbling are important for both. Perhaps the first is more aesthetic-oriented, and the latter is more practical and applied. Perhaps the first is more *ex* nihilo, and the latter is more tradition-based, formed off models and templates, in some cases. Perhaps art is for personal and social pleasure and conversation, and craft is more fit to particular practical purposes. Various physical materialities are seen in both arts and crafts. Both digital art and digital craft are somewhat influenced by DIY culture. Both have informal markets, both offline (various markets, arts events, garage sales) and online (digital shops). [Of course, there is the scourge of micropayments on various video-sharing and image-sharing sites, which are wholly insufficient to making a survival wage.] Perhaps the maker or future owner of a work may decide whether a work is "art" or "craft" or both ("art-craft").

Figure 3. Digital Crafting

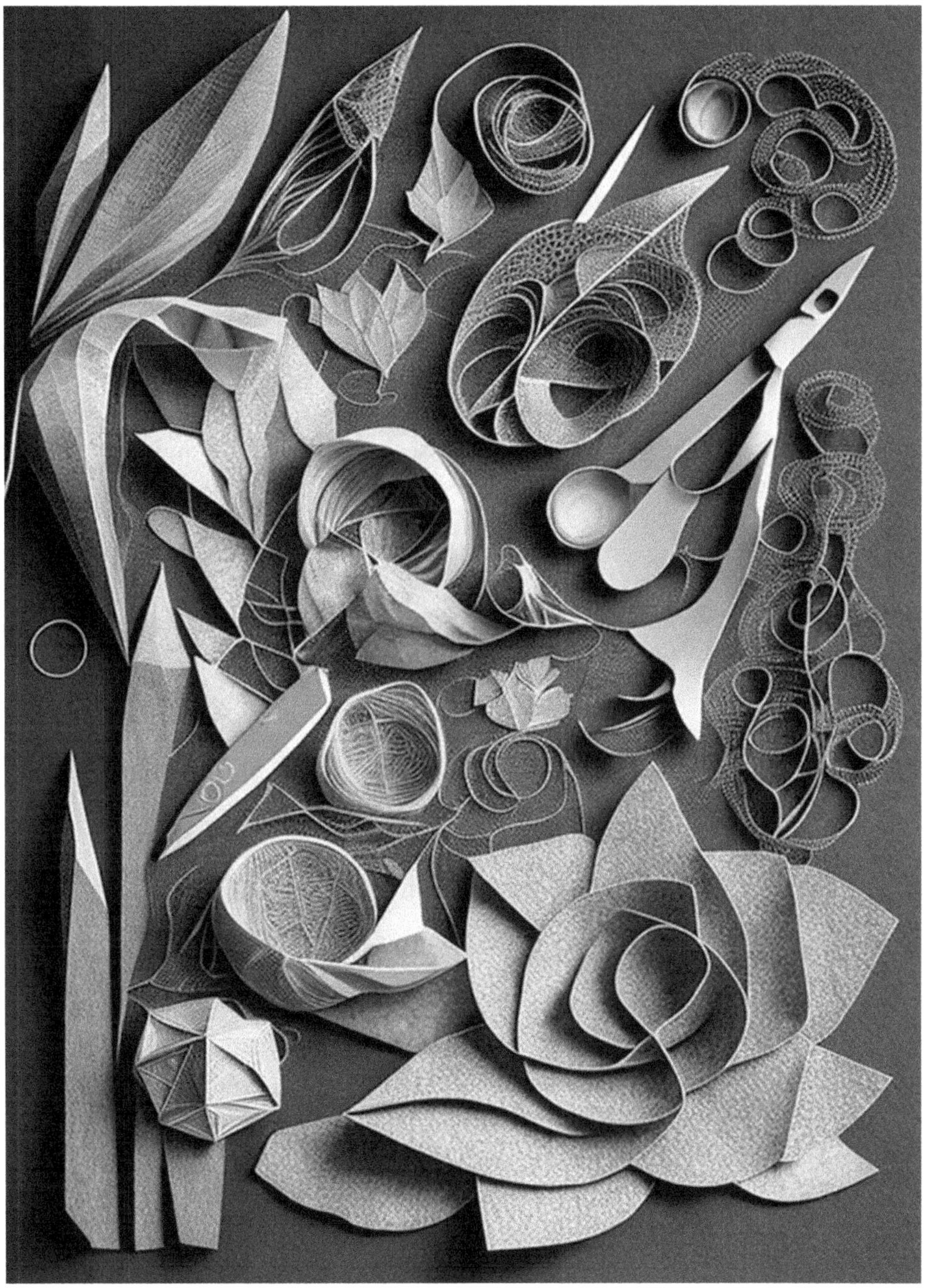

Humanity and Making Traditions

A core part of human identity involves "making," the generation of an idea, a process, a product, and /or a solution (ideally to an unsolved problem, and ideally a practical and low-cost solution). Making can be done physically with analog materials, digitally with pixels and equations and texts, and in mixed physical-digital approaches. The work may be done in standalone individual ways but also in the company of others, in teams of various sizes and mix of talents. Part of making requires not only the end-state product but something of style, efficiency, speed, and design. This book explores a wide range of computational (and computer-supported) practices used for digital art-making and digital crafting, for personal, commercial, educational, and other purposes and contexts. How are "common digital art" and "digital crafting" harnessed? What technologies are used? What techniques? What sorts of problems have been solved using these approaches? What sorts of innovations have been created? How are people entranced and entertained and taught?

Further, based on the technologies and the arts and crafts practices, where do the rewards accrue? For artists and consumers, how can they avoid being too easily pleased with simple visuals from generative AI? How can they avoid a world where the world is all Picasso and all cubist?

Figure 4. A Pixel Art Toy Display

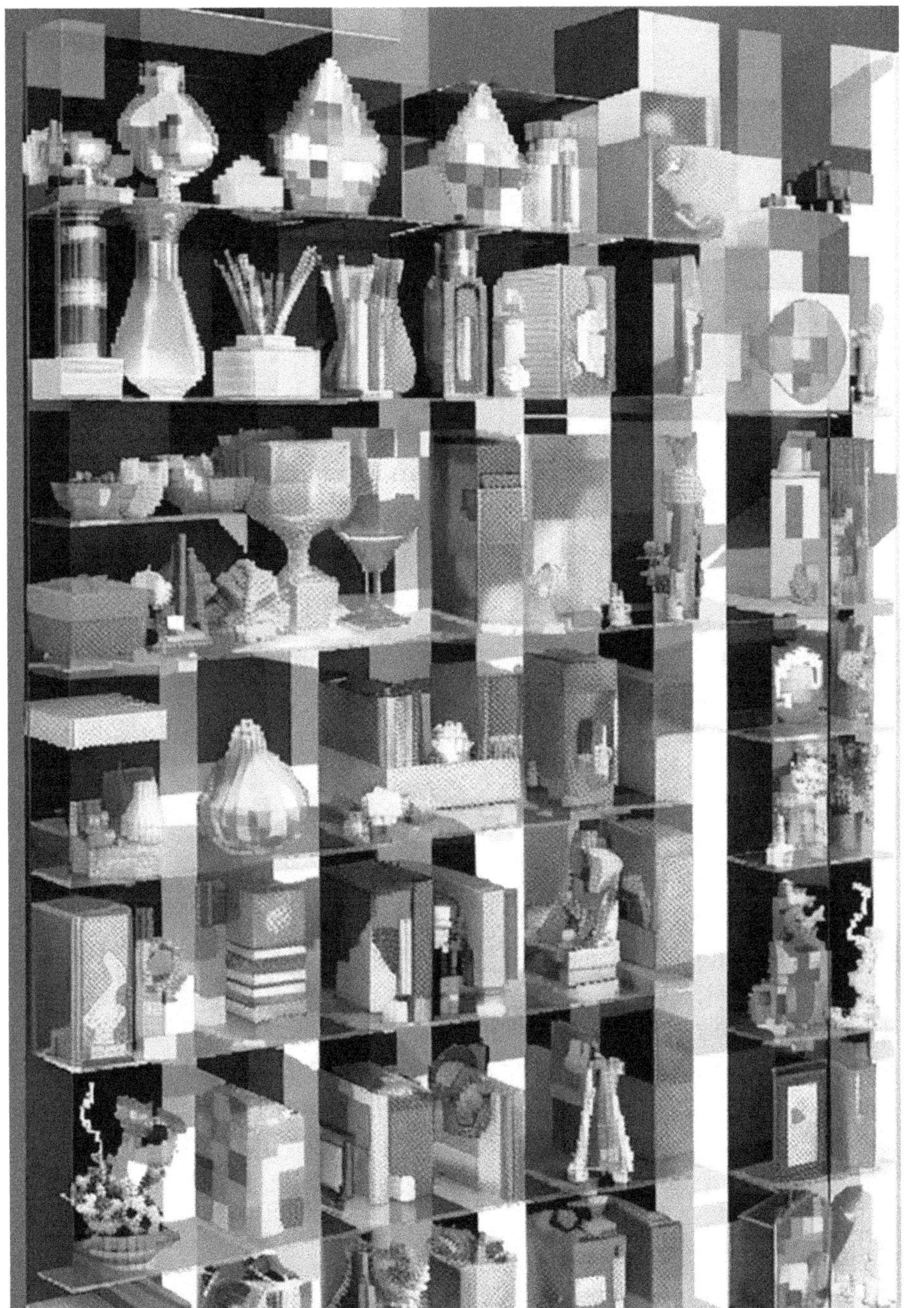

Some Early Proposed Topics

Every edited text is a journey, requiring a year of weekend work and weekday nights (and some weekday work). Each experience is also different in its own way. *Computational Practices and Applications for Digital Art and Crafting*, for example, went through a book title change midstream, with more of a focus on technologies and techniques. And now, drafting the Preface is one of those milestones. At every milestone, one looks forwards but also backwards.

I always enjoy looking back at some of the early proposed topics. A list of these follow:

Common digital art
Common digital art practices
Markets for common digital art, price setting, sales events
Customer bases
Social media, sales platforms, social and other marketing to reach customers
Practitioners of common digital art, common digital art communities online and offline
Hobbyist digital crafting
Work-based (professional) digital crafting
Digital and analog tools for digital crafting
Markets for digital crafting, object pricing
Practitioners of digital crafting, digital crafting communities online and offline
Analog crafting transcoded to digital crafting; digitization
Transcoding from digital crafting to analog materials
2d objects
3d objects
Motion objects
Digital designs for real and practical life
Direct experiences of digital crafting (case studies)
Direct experiences of digital making (case studies)
Digital experiences in 2d, 3d, and 4d spaces
Inventing and creating in maker / fabrication / hacker spaces
Innovating and bringing to market in maker / fabrication / hacker spaces
Transfer learning from maker / fabrication / hacker spaces to other domains

Acquired skills in being a "super maker" with analog and digital skills

Tools and techniques for no-code making
Tools and techniques for low-code making
Tools and techniques for high-code making
Materiality of making
Materials re-use
Immateriality (virtuality, digital aspects) of making
Digital fabrication
Kits for making
3d printing

Machinima
Animation / motion design
Rotoscoping
Generative AI
Motion capture
Artificial intelligence (AI)
Illustrating and making with data
Showcases for common digital art
Showcases for digital crafts
Fans and aficionados and built user bases for common digital art
Fans and aficionados and built user bases for digital crafts
Online and offline markets for digital crafts
Online and offline markets for makerspace objects
Aesthetics in digital crafting and making
Comparing analog and digital made objects
Histories of digital making
Histories of digital crafting
Standards for digital-made objects
Standards for digital-made crafts
Harnessing "making spaces" and "making labs" for teaching and learning
Hands-on embodied experiential learning
Using analog/physical tools for embodied learning
Materiality in making spaces
Virtualized learning in digital "making spaces" and "making labs" for teaching and learning
Hands-on embodied virtual experiential learning
Using digital tools for embodied learning
Virtuality in making spaces
Designs of making spaces and labs for teaching, learning, practice, experimentation, and innovation
Trainings for making spaces and labs
Pedagogies in fabrication spaces and labs
Technologies and techniques for making spaces and labs
Aesthetics in digital arts
Aesthetics in digital crafts
Case studies in common digital art
Cases studies in common digital crafting
Design journeys with common art
Design journeys with digital crafting
Future of digital common art and crafting
Singleton projects in the digital arts
Singleton projects in digital crafts
Teamwork in digital (common) arts
Teamwork in digital crafts
Digital crafting to new insights, perspectives, worldviews
Documenting, showcasing, and displaying digital works

Anticipated futures of digital making
Anticipated futures of digital crafting
Mass-scale making, with molds, designs, templates, patterns, and references
Variations on themes
And others

I still think that many of these ideas are valid and interesting. But a call for chapter proposals may go out to the "world" on the Web and Internet, but the siren call messages are really only to a handful of people, and of that handful, only a smaller number will ultimately respond. And of those who express interest, an even smaller number will follow through with actual work. These works go through a gauntlet of review. Works are revised and edited, and these works make it into print.

An Overview of the Parts and the Table of Contents (TOC)

The book is organized into four parts. They are the following:
Part 1: Common Digital Art, Digital Crafting: Techniques and Technologies
Part 2: Computational Exploration of Art and Culture
Part 3: Conducive Physical Spaces for Making
Part 4: Boundaries in the Digital Art and Crafting Spaces

Part 1: Common Digital Art, Digital Crafting: Techniques and Technologies

Applications for Digital Art and Crafting: Digital Supported Visual Art Applications in Early Childhood
Crafting Seeding Imagery for Artmaking Generative AI Tools

Part 2: Computational Exploration of Art and Culture

Athos Bulcão's Tile Distribution Logic Using Common Digital Art (Bergamo)
The Concept Digital Art and Refik Anadol

Part 3: Conducive Physical Spaces for Making

Setting up a Home "Making Space" After Professional and Academic-Based Ones Built for Everyday Learning, Creativity, and Innovation

Part 4: Boundaries in the Digital Art and Crafting Spaces

Making Original 2D Visual Deepfakes With a Generative AI Tool
Generative AI and the Expansion of the Solitary Human Imagination: An Experiential Case
Multimodal Outputs for the Workplace From Generative AI: Effective or Not?

THE FOLLOWING SECTION INCLUDES THE ABSTRACTS FOR EACH CHAPTER.

Part 1: Common Digital Art, Digital Crafting: Techniques and Technologies

Applications for Digital Art and Crafting: Digital Supported Visual Art Applications in Early Childhood

With the rapidly developing technology, the use of digital art applications in the visual art education process is becoming widespread as a new field of study. When the literature was examined, no study was found that investigated the digital art applications that can be used in early childhood and the views of preschool teachers on these applications and evaluated them as a visual art education tool in early childhood. In this context, this study aims to identify digital art applications and tools that can be used in the early childhood visual arts education process, to examine these applications in terms of scope and content, and to examine the knowledge and opinions of teachers about the digital supported art education applications/tools.

Crafting Seeding Imagery for Artmaking Generative AI Tools

There is an important value in human-machine collaborations using artmaking generative AI tools: that is, the preservation of the human hand (the human mental-emotional-embodied manual contribution) in the artwork. One way to ensure the original look-and-feel involves using multimodal prompts—both text and visual—with a twist. The visual may be one that is human-generated—either born-analog (and then digitized) or born-digital (such as imagery created on tablets or laptops, on digital drawing systems)—in a way that is unrelated or only peripherally related to the text prompt. This chapter explores how to craft seeding imagery for use in artmaking generative AI tools for innovations in color, color blends; textures; layouts; various perspectives; style blends; and others. This work describes some early ways to introduce human-touch novelty in seeding imagery from analog and digital approaches.

Part 2: Computational Exploration of Art and Culture

Athos Bulcão's Tile Distribution Logic Using Common Digital Art (Bergamo)

Athos Bulcão is a renowned Brazilian artist recognized for his outstanding surface work with tiles on murals of Brasília's buildings, the 1960s-designed modern capital of Brazil and other localities. The beauty of his work can be expressed by how it has become part of the city landscape and people's everyday encounters. It is also very contemporaneous regarding how he used logic to organize his tiles, using rotation and pattern distribution, allowing chance and error while architectural surfaces are assembled. Explaining logic and making it into tile distribution is difficult to explain to students; using paper prototypes helps, but Common Digital Art coding takes it a step further in the complexity of tiling art. This chapter proposes a method for students to learn those skills and also to learn to develop their logic if they intend to create authorial tiling works in murals.

The Concept Digital Art and Refik Anadol

Humanity is moving forward in a process of evolution where technology and art intersect. In the modern era, the spread of computers and the Internet has enabled works of art to reach a wider audience and has brought innovations in the way art is created and exhibited. Digital Art has emerged as a product of this transformation and has become a developing discipline using the aesthetic and creative potentials of computers and the Internet. With the spread of the Internet, fundamental changes have been experienced in the media and communication order, and digital media and encodings have created new forms of communication. Refik Anadol, one of the leading names of digital art in Turkey, has built bridges between the physical and digital worlds through the use of data and artificial intelligence, and has taken art to a new dimension. Dec. Anadol's works have transformed the perception of space and presented alternative realities to the audience. These works change and expand the way art is perceived by making the audience active participants.

Part 3: Conducive Physical Spaces for Making

Setting up a Home "Making Space" After Professional and Academic-Based Ones Built for Everyday Learning, Creativity, and Innovation

Common artists, crafters, artisans, and DIY (do-it-yourself) makers need spaces to explore their inspirations and creativity and to advance their making skills. They need a place to set up their equipment. They need a physical location to store their supplies and reference materials and incomplete works. They may need a virtual space to create, too, to harness the power of computation They need a market for their goods. They need a community, in the real and the virtual, for emotional support, ideas, and camaraderie. There is little known in the way of how these at-home making spaces may be set up for the best outcomes, broadest ranges of possibilities, and ultimate creativity, but it is thought that some insights from professional maker spaces and the academic literature may inform on this challenge. This exploratory work offers some initial ideas from the literature review and applied action research in a case.

Part 4: Boundaries in the Digital Art and Crafting Spaces

Making Original 2D Visual Deepfakes With a Generative AI Tool

In the research and popular literature, there are many concerns about the deepfakes that may be generated using generative AI and other tools, to mislead people and to compromise them in various ways through deception. This work explores the nature of deepfakes, generative AI, and manual and computational and combined means to identify (and neutralize) potential deepfakes, as described in the academic literature. Deepfakes may have positive effects as well, to enhance human creativity and to expand the toolkit for digital making. This work also explores how to create a credible (non-malicious) 2D visual deepfake using a popular generative AI tool to understand some affordances and constraints for this particular "use case". For this basic work, the idea is only to trick the eyes, not the more in-depth detection methods based on computation.

Generative AI and the Expansion of the Solitary Human Imagination: An Experiential Case

The affordances of generative AI—in its ability to provide feedback on human-made (or human-machine made, or computer-made) works, its ability to create text / audio / video / still imagery / multimedia—enables powerful augmentations to the solitary human imagination. To wit, such technologies enable human-machine collaboration in terms of (1) human-directed non-neutral culture-informed feedback on created works (for original texts), and (2) digital informational content generation (for inspiration, for reference, for comparison, for learning, for hands-on image editing, and other applications). Generative AI may enable pathways to grow skillsets, and perhaps, even courage and strength in the expression of an individual voice.

Multimodal Outputs for the Workplace From Generative AI: Effective or Not?

Workplace documents are a combination of genre (form) and topic (content), and there are a variety of standards they must meet to be usable. Most such files are also multimodal, consisting of both text and still imagery. When outputting multimodal digital works for the workplace from multimodal generative AI (GAI) tools, their usability depends on various factors. This work explores some elicited multimodal outputs (text + imagery) from a popular multimodal generative AI tool to assess the respective quality based on practical dimensions. This work offers an early assessment for just how useful multimodal generative AIs are for this broad use case. And this work offers a checklist of factors to evaluate for multimodal file output quality for the workplace. Some initial observations are made about the practical usability of the multimodal GAI for outputs for professional workplace usage, based on this light prompt-response-analysis exploration.

CONCLUSION

I am deeply grateful to each of the contributors to this edited collection. So many hours of human thought, research, and labor have gone into their respective works. Thanks also to the makers of various technologies, from generative AIs to digital image editing tools to machining tools, that make such works and such human creative expressions possible.

It is with appreciation that I ready for the handover to the professional folks at IGI Global for the next phases in the making of a research book. I know such moments are not arrived at without much prior effort and good fortune.

Note: The visuals were created using seeding imagery (alcohol ink paintings) and the Deep Dream Generator.

Shalin Hai-Jew
Hutchinson Community College, USA
2024

Section 1
Common Digital Art, Digital Crafting: Techniques and Technologies

Chapter 1
Applications for Digital Art and Crafting:
Digital Supported Visual Art Applications in Early Childhood

Duygu Mutlu Demir
http://orcid.org/0009-0004-2369-3740
Gazi University, Turkey

Ilkay Ulutaş
http://orcid.org/0000-0002-2234-0773
Gazi University, Turkey

ABSTRACT

With the rapidly developing technology, the use of digital art applications in the visual art education process is becoming widespread as a new field of study. When the literature was examined, no study was found that investigated the digital art applications that can be used in early childhood and the views of preschool teachers on these applications and evaluated them as a visual art education tool in early childhood. In this context, this study aims to identify digital art applications and tools that can be used in the early childhood visual arts education process, to examine these applications in terms of scope and content, and to examine the knowledge and opinions of teachers about the digital supported art education applications/tools.

INTRODUCTION

Visual art education in early childhood improves children's cognitive, emotional, and motor skills by activating many lobs of the brain and helps them discover and develop their creative artistic talents. They develop visual perception, hand-eye coordination, and problem-solving skills and regulate emotions through drawing and art-making (Edward, 1997; Ulutaş & Demiriz, 2019). Winner (2008) emphasized that students' work in the field of art develops valuable mental abilities that children can use throughout their lives and that skills such as observation, imagination, and innovation obtained through art education also help students develop different ways of thinking. In addition, it has been observed that art

DOI: 10.4018/979-8-3693-2927-6.ch001

positively affects students' general development by strengthening their problem-solving, creativity, and communication skills. Since art requires manipulative materials, it also contributes to developing daily life skills (Winner & Hetland, 2008).

Educating children in a way that ensures their cognitive and socio-emotional development in early childhood has a significant place in determining their behaviors and skills. These skills form the basis of their future lives (Wentzel & Watkins, 2002). Research states that the positive increase in learning behaviors in early childhood increases children's academic success and social-emotional well-being (McDermott, Goldberg, Watkins, Stanley, & Glutting, 2006; Rouse & Fantuzzo, 2008; Hyson, 2008). Children grow up surrounded by digital tools from birth. This makes the role and impact of technology even more critical in the education and development of children. Digital games, interactive applications, and online resources enrich children's learning experiences and shape their thinking skills.

For this reason, school programs are expected to adapt children to 21st-century digital skills. In recent years, the usage of digital tools has increased considerably daily with the gradual increase in technology activities of early childhood (Canbek & Sağıroğlu, 2007). Due to the rapid progress of technology, traditional methods are preferred in education and training in this period when children are referred to as "screen generations" may be insufficient in the process of adaptation of children to the digital world (Jenkins, 2009; Tapscott, 2009; Taylor, 2007, Wesch, 2007). Integrating technology and digital applications into art education offers excellent opportunities to support and develop students' creativity, ensure the acquisition of their artistic skills, and allow them to discover their talents in digital art. This also allows children to have safer digital experiences.

When the studies are analyzed, the advantages of using technology in art education are:

1. *Encouraging students' creativity:* Digital tools and software offer students a wide range of possibilities to create and express works of art differently (Browning, 2008, p. 213).
2. *Supporting learning with visual and auditory stimuli:* Technology can make learning more effective by providing students with rich visual and aural experiences (Jenkins, 2009; Tapscott, 2009; Taylor, 2007; Wesch, 2007).
3. *Developing students' digital skills:* Digital arts education can provide students with the ability to use digital tools effectively, which can help them to be successful in the digital age by developing their digital skills (Browning, 2008; Nisenholt, 2007). This can assist students in the digital age in being equipped with the age requirements.
4. *Possibility to exhibit and share artworks on digital platforms:* Technology allows students to show and share their artworks to reach a wider audience.

Purpose of the Study

Integrating digital art in early childhood education is becoming widespread as a new field of study. When the research is examined, there are no studies in which current digitally supported art applications are reviewed and evaluated as a tool for art activities in early childhood. In this context, this study aims to determine the applications, platforms, and Web 2.0 tools that can be used in the process of digitally supported art activities in early childhood and to examine the content, supported areas, and functionality of these applications. The following questions were sought to be answered in the research.

- What are the characteristics of applications/tools/platforms that can be used for digital art education in early childhood?

- What are the early childhood teachers' practices on digital art education applications/tools/platforms?

METHOD

The study was designed using a basic qualitative research design. Basic qualitative research design categorizes theoretical concepts explained in detail as a result of research (Caeli et al., 2003). Within the scope of the study, online application stores and search engines related to digital art were scanned, and the features of suitable applications/platforms for early childhood were listed. Then, interviews were conducted with preschool teachers to determine practices about digital art applications/tools. In this direction, teachers were asked which digital art applications/platforms they use and the content and frequency of the digital art activities.

Study Group

Two study groups were created for the research. The first study group was a digital applications/tools group built among Web 2.0 tools and digital art applications in smartphone application stores and various search engines. The digital applications and tools were determined by criterion sampling. According to Patton (2014), criterion sampling criteria are to study and review situations that meet some essential criteria that have been previously defined. The researcher can prepare these criteria or criteria before the analysis, or a previously prepared list of criteria can be taken as criteria (Yıldırım & Şimşek, 2006). Digital applications for preschool-aged children, with free access and creative art styles, were included in the study group.

The second study group comprised 23 early childhood teachers working in state kindergartens affiliated with the Ministry of National Education in Istanbul. The "snowball sampling" method was used to reach the teachers. The snowball sampling method is based on the growth of the sample with the snowball effect by reaching other people through the person selected to be appropriate for the subject of the study (Biernacki & Waldorf, 1981). The researchers started interviewing teachers they knew and reached out to other teachers through the references given by these teachers.

Table 1. Demographic information of the teachers

Teacher	Gender	Age	Educational Level	Graduation	Years of Service
T1	Woman/Female	31-35	Master d.	Preschool Teacher	10
T2	Woman/Female	20-25	Bachelor d.	Preschool Teacher	1
T3	Woman/Female	26-30	Bachelor d.	Preschool Teacher	2
T4	Woman/Female	26-30	Bachelor d.	Preschool Teacher	2
T5	Woman/Female	36+	Bachelor d.	Preschool Teacher	15
T6	Woman/Female	26-30	Master d.	Preschool Teacher	2
T7	Woman/Female	31-35	Bachelor d.	Preschool Teacher	5
T8	Woman/Female	26-30	Bachelor d.	Preschool Teacher	2
T9	Woman/Female	26-30	Bachelor d.	Preschool Teacher	9

Table 1 continued

Teacher	Gender	Age	Educational Level	Graduation	Years of Service
T10	Woman/Female	26-30	Bachelor d.	Preschool Teacher	2
T11	Woman/Female	26-30	Bachelor d.	Child Development and Education	3
T12	Woman/Female	26-30	Bachelor d.	Preschool Teacher	3
T13	Woman/Female	26-30	Bachelor d.	Preschool Teacher	3
T14	Woman/Female	31-35	Bachelor d.	Preschool Teacher	10
T15	Woman/Female	20-25	Bachelor d.	Preschool Teacher	3
T16	Woman/Female	26-30	Bachelor d.	Preschool Teacher	2
T17	Woman/Female	31-35	Master d.	Preschool Teacher	9
T18	Woman/Female	31-35	Bachelor d.	Preschool Teacher	8
T19	Woman/Female	26-30	Bachelor d.	Preschool Teacher	4
T20	Woman/Female	36+	Bachelor d.	Preschool Teacher	18
T21	Woman/Female	26-30	Bachelor d.	Preschool Teacher	9
T22	Woman/Female	31-35	Bachelor d.	Child Development And Education	12
T23	Woman/Female	31-35	Bachelor d.	Preschool Teacher	11

All teachers participating in the research are women; nine of them are thirty-one years old or older, most of them graduated from a preschool education undergraduate program, only three of them completed a master's program, and four of them have been working for ten years or more.

Data Collection Tools

Digital Art Application/Tools Record Form *and* Teacher Interview Form *used for data collection.*

Digital Art Application/Tools Record Form

The researcher prepared this form to record the characteristics of the Digital Art Applications/Platforms evaluated within the study's scope. This form includes the name of the application/Tools, aim, target age, content, and the opportunities it provides its users for art education for preschool children. Each application/tool was recorded in this form, allowing comparisons, and the applications that serve the purpose were selected.

Teacher Interview Form

The teacher interview form is a semi-structured interview form prepared by the researchers to identify early childhood teachers' experiences with digital art applications/tools. After the preparation of the form, it was presented to three experts in early childhood education. According to their suggestions, revisions were made, and content validity was ensured.

The first four teachers were also used as a pilot study. Thus, the comprehensibility of the questions in the form and the problems that may be encountered in the interviews were tested in advance (Kümbetoğlu, 2005).

Teacher Interview Form includes open-ended questions about digital applications/tools they use for visual art, which types of art activities they use these applications/tools more frequently, and their preferences for participation in digitally supported visual art education in the preschool period. The researchers collected the data by taking written and audio recordings with the participants' permission during the interview.

Data Collection

The researchers searched mobile phone stores for the reach data on the applications/tools. The applications/tools were asked with the keywords "digital art applications," "visual art applications," and "art applications," and what achieved was saved and listed. They classified those who met the first "being free of charge" criterion according to their **"age"** levels. The applications that were not suitable for the age of preschool children were deleted from the phone (although the Google Art& Culture application appeals to users aged 12 and above, it was not deleted because it has a vast range of applications that can guide both parents and preschool teachers to guide children and form the foundations of digital art in children). In the next stage, the experts classified the applications according to their **"content suitable for preschool children."** The applications unsuitable for children's developmental levels were removed from the list. Then, applications/tools were classified according to their "**usability in digital art activities in preschool education,"** and unsuitable applications for visual art were deleted. Afterward, the researchers entered the most widely preferred Google and Safari search engines and repeated the same process. They selected the ones suitable for the criteria determined by many Web 2.0 tools and included them in the list. The applications included in the list were paid attention to have content, especially for art education, and 7 applications were included in the list with the consensus. And 7 web 2.0 tools were decided to be included in the scope of the research.

The data collected with the Teacher Interview Form were by making an appointment on the appropriate day and time and using the semi-structured interview technique in an environment where they would feel comfortable.

Data Analyses

Data were analyzed using the content analysis method. Digital art applications/tools were examined to meet criteria such as target age (3-6 years old), the aim, being free of charge, content, and addressing art education in the preschool period. A total list of 14 applications/tools, including 7 digital applications and 7 Web 2.0 tools, was defined by consensus.

In the content analysis of the teacher interviews, codes and frequencies were determined. Findings were listed as tables, and a consensus was reached among the researchers.

FINDINGS

The contents of the digital art applications/tools, how they will be applied, and teachers' opinions on this issue are of great importance in providing an effective and efficient digitally supported art education environment. In this direction, the findings obtained from the research are presented under two sub-headings: *1. the characteristics of the digital art applications/tools that can be used* in digital-supported art education in early childhood and 2. *Teachers' practices on digital art applications/tools.*

1. Features of applications/tools that can be used in digitally supported art activities in early childhood.

The characteristics of the 14 applications/tools accessed to answer the first question of the research, "What are the characteristics of applications/tools that can be used for digitally supported art education in early childhood?" are given in Table 2.

Table 2. Applications/tools that can be used in digital supported art activities

Application Name	Age Group	Operating System	Application Content and Gain for Art Education
Google Arts and Culture	+12 year age	IOS/ Android Application	It can be used by children under the guidance oi an adult and allows its users to explore artwork: from around the world.
Quiver 3D Colouring	+4 year age	IOS/ Android Application	This application offers children the opportunity tc colour interactively and see the coloured picture in 3D. The application, which has more than 15C colouring pages, appeals to all age groups especially preschool children.
Canva	+4 years old	IOS/ Android Application	It can be easily used by children with drag anc drop feature. With a wide range of applications children can create their own art projects.
Tayasui Sketches	+4 year age	IOS/ Android Application	With a wide palette of colours and various tools such as pens, brushes and pencils, children car draw as they wish and store these drawings.
Kids Doodle	+4 year age	IOS/ Android Application	It contains easy-to-use drawing tools and dozen: of effects, enables children to draw colorful anc creative drawings with fun.
Chatter Pix Kids	+4 year age	IOS/ Android Application	It allows children to use their imagination tc create their own stories and bring their pictures tc life.
Voila AI Artist	+4 year age	IOS/ Android Application	Children can create avatars/portraits by uploading photos of themselves and family members choosing styles such as caricature, pencil
Paint	+4 year age	Web 2.0 tool	Children can use primary and secondary hues in different styles, explore the tonal differences between colors with a wide range of color gradation alternatives, and create creative drawings with color combinations.

Table 2 conitnued

Application Name	Age Group	Operating System	Application Content and Gain for Art Education
Animated Drawingshttps://sketch.metademolab.com	+4 year age	Web 2.0 Tool	It offers the opportunity to transform the pictures/characters that children have drawn on paper into fun animations very easily.
Funny Pho.to https://funny.pho.to/tr/	+4 years old	Web 2.0 Tool	In addition to different alternatives such as converting captured photos into drawings, choosing a wide variety of frames for the drawn picture or captured photo, or placing the photo on money, creating a magazine cover, it also offers extraordinary design opportunities such as turning captured photos into animal faces.
Blabberize https://edu.blabberize.com	--	Web 2.0 Tool	It is a fun web 2.0 tool that adds a mouth to the photos taken or pictures drawn by children, making the pictures talk and animated.
360 Cities https://www.360cities.net)	+4 year age	Web 2.0 Tool	It is a web 2.0 tool that allows users to explore 360-degree panoramic pictures or videos of various cities or places. It offers access to images from many parts of the world as well as images of the moon and mars.
Turn Drawings into Music with Kandinsky https://musiclab.chromeexperiments.com	+4 year age	Web 2.0 Tool	Based on Kandinsky drawings, the web tool is an artificial intelligence tool that offers users the opportunity to turn Kandinsky drawings into music. The site is very easy to use.
Draw to Art https://artexperiments.withgoogle.com	+4 year age	Web 2.0 Tool	It is a web 2.0 tool that finds the artistic equivalent of random pictures created by selecting / dragging the geometric shapes at the top of the page with the help of the mouse and shows these pictures to its users.

When the art applications/tools included in the scope of the research were examined (n=14), it was seen that there were sample applications for art education in the introductions of the applications/tools, and these sample applications mainly included three-dimensional geometric shapes. In addition, it was observed that most of the applications (n=7) were designed for both IOS and Android operating systems.

Detailed information about these platforms and tools, which are fun and user-friendly for preschool children to step into the world of digital art, is given below:

1. Google Arts and Culture (iOS/Android)

It is an application that allows users to explore artworks worldwide. The application offers a variety of digital art content suitable for the developmental levels of preschool children. The digital art content that can be accessed through the Google Art and Culture application for preschool children can be analyzed under the following sub-headings:

√ **Artwork Images:** The application contains high-quality images of artworks by world-famous painters that have come to life worldwide. For example, when children open the application via tablet and phone, they can closely examine Vincent van Gogh's "Starry Nights" painting in high resolution. Images of different types of artwork can help children explore different types and styles of art.

√ **Stories and Information of Artworks:** After searching for artworks in the application, it can effortlessly access other works of the artist by using the "Discover this artist" tab. It also provides stories, information, and exciting details about each artwork. This can help children learn and understand the stories behind the artworks.

√ **Interactive Art Experiences:** The application offers a variety of experiences that will enable children to explore works of art interactively. Through the app, children can also visit the virtual museum where the artwork is located. For example, children can closely examine a work of art, look at it from different perspectives, or highlight specific details. Children can also use the application to add fun to art by placing their photograph on the "Girl with a Pearl earring" painting.

√ **Art Education Resources:** Google Arts & Culture also has educational resources to help preschoolers learn about and understand art. These resources can teach children basic art techniques or introduce them to art history.

√ **Art Games and Activities:** The application offers art-oriented games and activities that children can learn while having fun. Thus, it is mediated for children to develop their creativity and interact with art. For example, when children click on the title "What if you could hear the colors?" they can click on each element in Kandinsky's work, hear different sounds from each component, and create their own music.

Figure 1. Examples from Google arts and culture

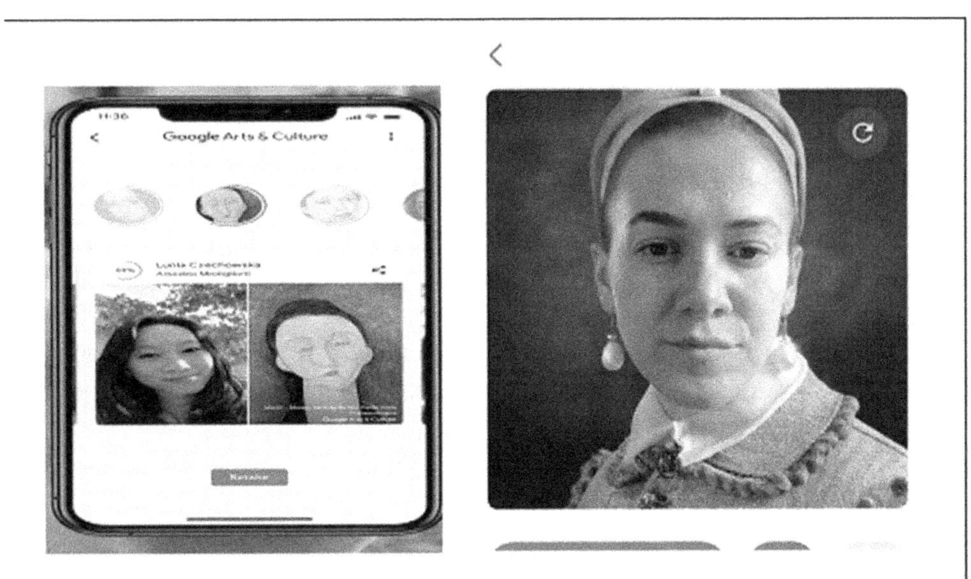

2. Quiver: 3D Colouring App (iOS/Android)

This application allows children to color interactively and see the colored picture in 3D. The application, which has over 150 coloring pages, appeals to all age groups, especially preschool children. For example, children are likely to have pleasant moments when they see the dinosaur pictures; they have colored them to come to life in 3D by reading the QR codes with the application.

Figure 2. Examples from Quiver -3D coloring

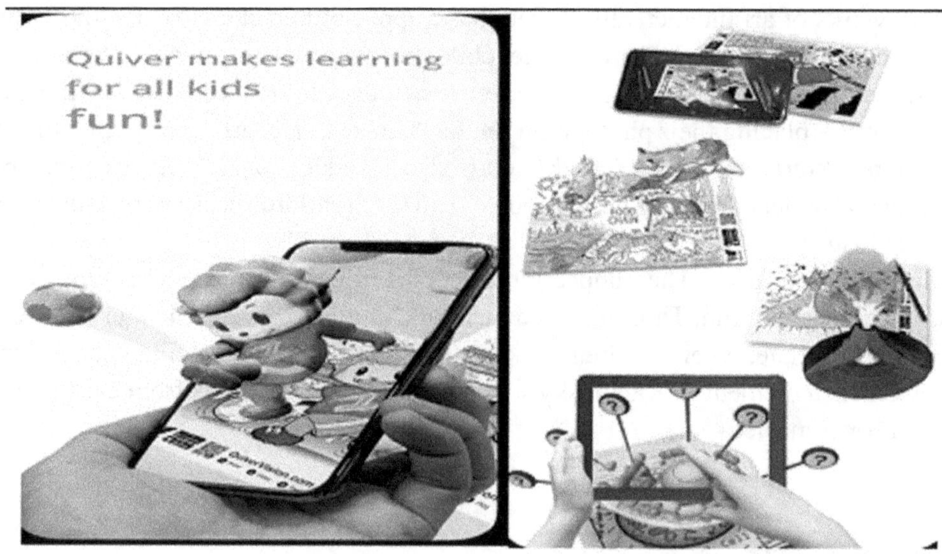

3. Canva (iOS/Android)

Some of the digitally supported art works and techniques that children can perform using the application are as follows:

√ **Digital Artworks**: Canva is a platform where children can create and save digital artworks. Using the toolkit in the application, children can make drawings, create pictures, and design digital artworks that align with their creativity.

√ **Collages**: Using the different letter styles in the app, children can create manipulative shapes, pictures, or exciting collages. For example, they can make a collage of the equivalent food they eat during the day in their imagination.

√ **Character Design**: Children can design their characters using simple drawing tools in Canva. These characters can be animals, fantastic beings, or characters they create themselves.

√ **Story Books**: Canva offers a platform where children can create their storybooks. Children can write stories supported with pictures and edit these stories in Canva.

- √ **Color Pages and Coloring Books: Children can create their drawings by creating colored pages or designing colo**ring books in Canva. This helps children develop their color knowledge and express their creativity.
- √ **Basic Graphic Design Exercises**: Children can do simple graphic design work in Canva. For example, they can design their own t-shirt or birthday invitation.

Figure 3. Examples from Canva

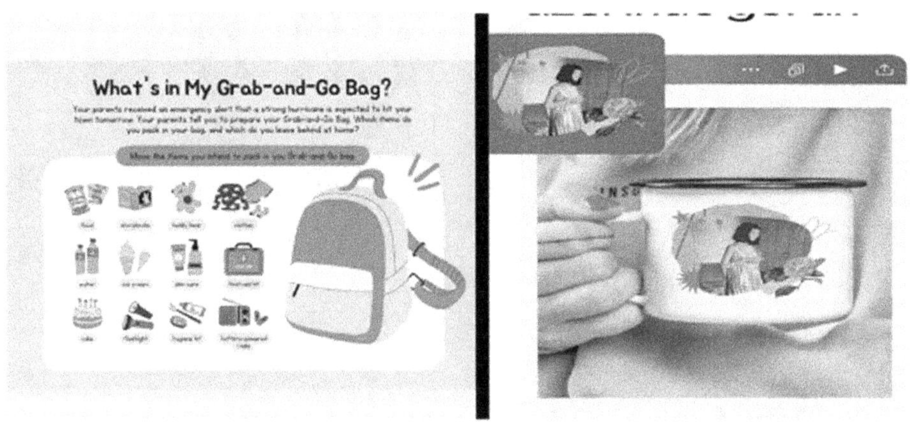

4. Tayasui Sketches (iOS/Android)

This application allows creative and fun digital artwork; children can make simple or colorful drawings through imagination. It is a good alternative for preschool children because it has a straightforward interface. It also allows drawing with different brushes, coloring, or adding patterns to the work. Through these features, the application is the chance to do art activities at a basic level, such as painting, helping children develop their color knowledge and creativity.

Figure 4. Examples from Tayasui sketches

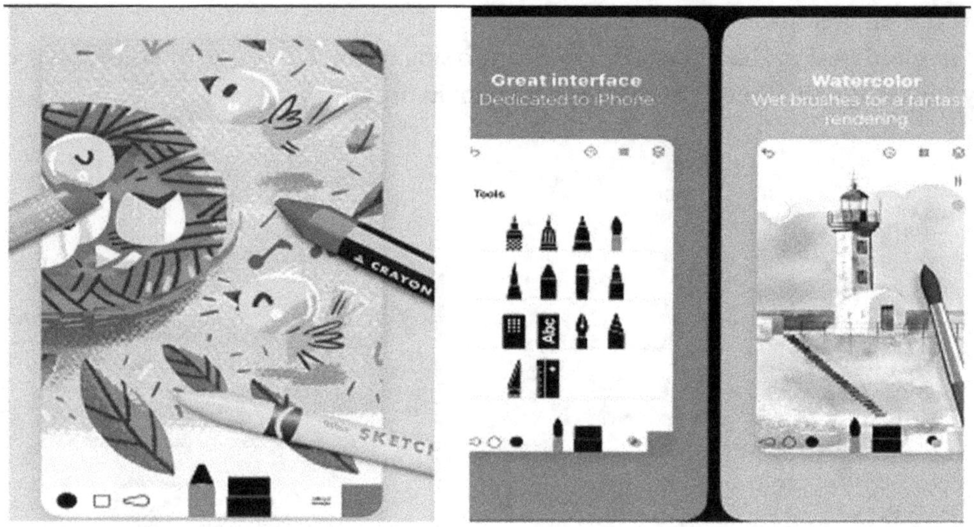

5. Kids Doodle: Draw Sketch (iOS/Android)

This application contains easy-to-use drawing tools and dozens of effects, enabling children to draw fun, colorful, creative drawings. This process will be more enjoyable since children can draw using their fingers in this application.

Figure 5. Examples From Kids Doodle: Draw Sketch

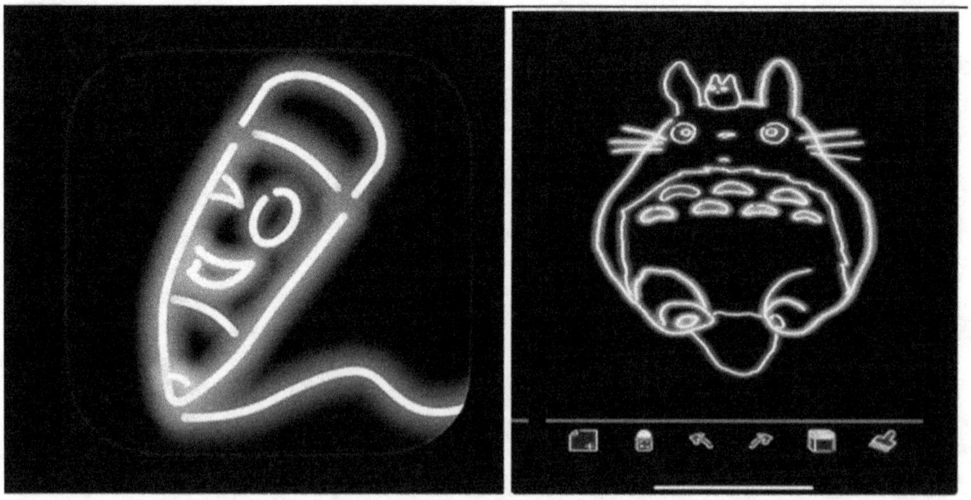

6. Chatter Pix-Kids (iOS/Android)

Chatterpix allows children to use their imagination to create stories and animate pictures. Users can record the speech or sound effects they want to record on the image, so they can add a speech effect to the mouth of a picture or draw in line with their creativity.

Figure 6. Examples from Chatter Pix-Kids

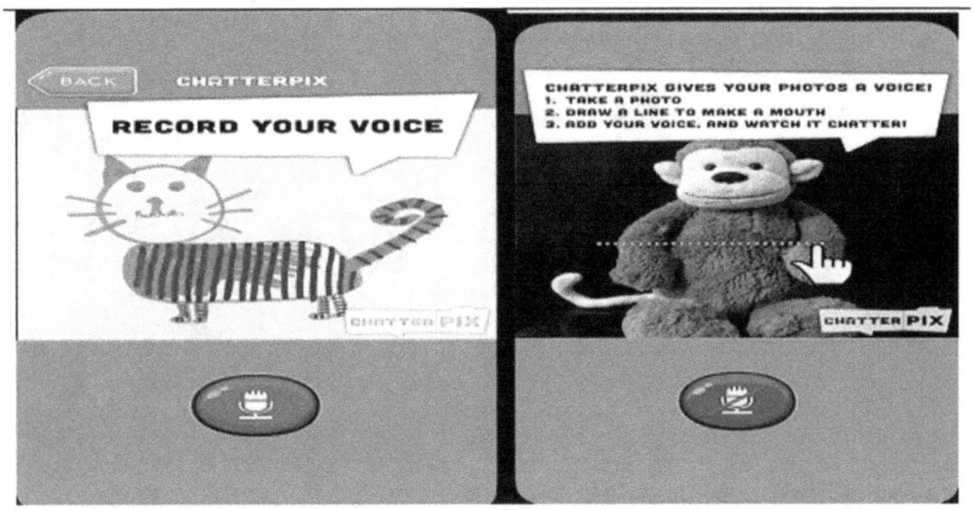

7. Voila AI Artist (iOS/Android)

Children can create avatars/portraits by uploading photos of themselves and family members and choosing styles such as caricatures and pencil drawings. It also allows children to lay the foundations of their artistic style by trying different filters and effects on the photos. In general, these applications help children develop their art and creativity skills while at the same time providing a fun and interactive experience.

Figure 7. Examples from Voila Al Artist

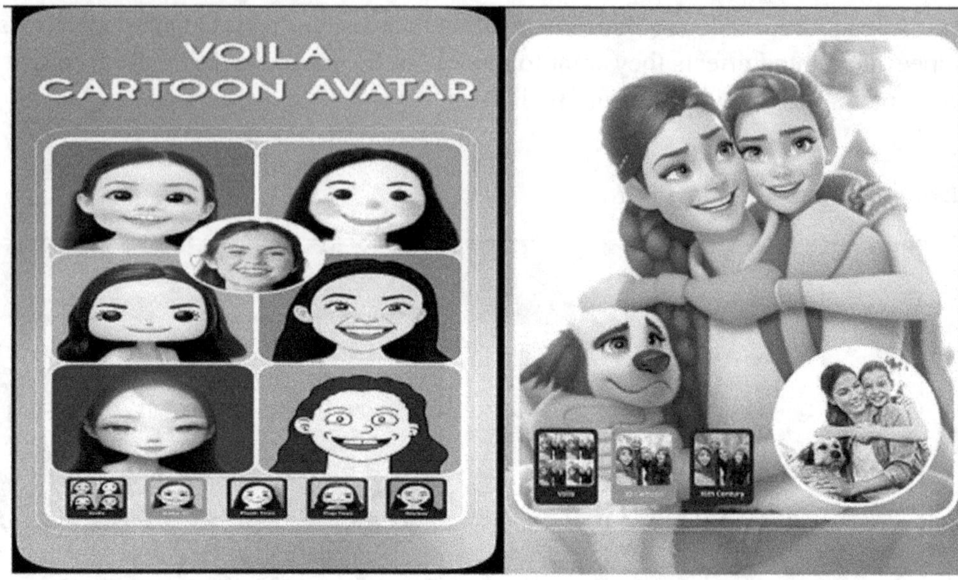

8. Paint (Application and Web 2.0 Tool)

Due to its ease of use, it is one of the most preferred applications worldwide. For preschool children, the importance and usage areas of Paint in digital art can be summarized under the following headings:

√ Children can develop skills such as drawing accurate lines and recognizing shapes by drawing with a mouse or touch screen.
√ Children can use primary and secondary shades in different styles to explore the tonal differences between colors with various color gradation alternatives and combinations.
√ It is thought that children are progressing with the mouse or touch screen they will use during the application, which will help them develop their hand-eye coordination.
√ In the 21st century, with the spread of digital technologies, children's adaptation process to the digital world is critical. Therefore, easy-to-use digital art tools like Paint help children develop digital skills and interact with technology more comfortably.

9. Animated Drawings (https://sketch.metademolab.com)

The online tool can be used without requiring any membership and offers the opportunity to quickly transform the pictures/characters drawn by children into fun animations.

To create an animation, upload the picture drawn by the child from the gallery of your electronic device, such as a phone, etc., to the given site. By following the next steps, fun animations of the drawn picture appear.

10. Funny Pho.To (https://funny.pho.to/tr/)

With the online tool, children can create their own collages and greeting cards using face montage, filters, and effects (monster, character, etc.) on the photos they have taken. The tool also offers alternatives such as converting the taken photos into drawings, choosing different frames for the drawn picture or photo or placing the photo on the money, creating a magazine cover, and extraordinary design opportunities such as transforming the photos into animal faces.

11. Blabberize (https://edu.blabberize.com)

It is a fun Web 2.0 tool that adds a mouth to the photos or drawings taken by children, making the pictures talk and animate. It is a platform that requires membership after logging in to the site. After the image you upload to the platform, you can record a voice with the help of a microphone, and by following the forward commands, you can witness the sounds recorded by the children turn into a fun animation on the picture they draw. Preschool children can also create interactive stories using their photographs or drawings with Web 2.0 tools. Such activities will help children develop their imagination and language skills while increasing their interaction with technology.

12. 360 Cities (https://www.360cities.net)

It is a web 2.0 tool that allows users to explore 360-degree panoramic pictures or videos of various cities or places. The site can be used with VR glasses and other electronic devices. It offers images from many parts of the world and pictures of the moon and Mars. Such a platform for preschool children will help them explore the world and improve their visual perception, especially in the space theme, to concretize the subject.

13. Turn Drawings Into Music With Kandinsky (https://musiclab.chromeexperiments.com)

Based on Kandinsky's drawings, the web tool is an artificial intelligence tool that allows users to turn Kandinsky's drawings into music. The site is straightforward to use. After clicking the link, each line turns into a note when the play button at the bottom is clicked after the circles are drawn with the help of the mouse or finger on the open page. Unfortunately, the site does not offer the possibility to download the music created. It is a good application for preschool teachers to concretize the subject while working on Kandinsky, who emphasizes that seeing and hearing are equal at every opportunity.

14. Draw to Art (https://artexperiments.withgoogle.com)

It is a web 2.0 tool that finds the artistic equivalent of random pictures created by selecting/dragging the geometric shapes at the top of the page with the help of the mouse and shows these pictures to its users. The imprint information, such as the photograph's name automatically found by artificial intelligence and the year it was drawn, is also included below the picture.

The applications/tools analyzed can provide an interactive and fun environment for children to explore and learn about art. This increases preschool children's interest in art and encourages them to think creatively.

Teachers' Practices on Digital Applications/Tools

Teachers' experiences with digital art practices included the digital applications/tools they used and the content and frequency of the digital art activities.

Table 3. Digital applications/tools of teachers in art education

Digital Applications/Tools	Frequency(n)
Canva	18
Paint	11
Chatterkids	1
Adobe	1
Powerpoint	2
Sketch	1

According to Tablo 10, the teacher reported they use Canva, Paint, PowerPoint, Chatterkids, Adobe, and Sketch to create digital art activities with children. Among the applications/tools, most teachers use Canva and Paint, and fewer teachers use PowerPoint, Chatterkids, Adobe, and Sketch.

Table 4. Content and frequency of the digital art activities carried out by teachers

	Frequency					
Content	1 (the less)	2	3	4	5	6 (the most)
Color	4	3	6	3	1	6
Lines and Patterns	1	7	4	4	1	6
Artists	3	3	7	3	3	4
Museums	2	1	6	4	3	7
Doodle	3	2	3	1	1	13
Picture animation	4	1	4	2	4	8

As seen in Table 4, teachers planned digital art activities on colors, lines, patterns, artists, museums, mandalas, and picture animation. The most frequently chosen activity was the mandala, followed by painting, animation, museum examination, colors, lines and patterns, and artists.

DISCUSSION AND RESULTS

At the end of this study which was conducted to determine the characteristics of applications/tools that can be used for digitally supported art education in early childhood and to examine the practices of teachers, who are the most important stakeholders of this education, regarding digitally supported art education applications/tools, it was seen that there are 7 applications in total on Android and Apple stores (Google Art &Culture, Canva, Quiver 3D Coloring App, Tayasui Sketches, Kids Doodle, Chatter Pix-Kids and Voila Al Artist) and 7 Web 2.0 tools that can be used in preschool digital supported art activities. Considering the general characteristics of these applications/tools, they were evaluated as applications that offer opportunities to children in the early childhood period, such as painting, drawing, creating effects, panoramic pictures, 3D vision, virtual tours, and animation.

Digital art applications/tools enable children to develop their creativity, experience basic art concepts such as color-pattern-tone, strengthen feelings of curiosity and discovery, and create artwork. The fact that the applications are accessible, free, and open to sharing is also a positive gain. Browning (2008, p. 213) stated in his study that digital tools and software to be used in students' art education offer students a wide range of opportunities to create and express artworks differently. The richness, ease, and diversity of experience gained through digital art applications increase students' interest and attitudes toward art (Avcı 2015; Dilmaç 2019; Patton, 2013).

Although there are many application/tool alternatives for digital art in early childhood education, when teachers were asked about the applications/tools they know and use for digital art, they mainly stated Canva and Paint. These applications support children's digital art skills and have child-friendly features; they are mostly teacher-managed. In digital-supported art applications, children need applications to use individually and produce their products individually. Degennaro & Mak (2002-2003) and Gregory (2009) obtained findings supporting this conclusion in their studies and emphasized that many teachers today either rarely use digital learning resources or hesitate to use them. In this context, it would be helpful for teachers to learn the applications/tools determined within the scope of the research, which children can also apply and use in their classes. According to the findings obtained from the study prepared by Taşkesen (2020) to reveal the opinions and suggestions of the students receiving visual art education about the use of mobile technological tools for workshop lessons, it was emphasized that the applications/tools such as Photoshop, pixel art, PicsArt, etc. used in the lessons are effective in helping students access information faster and increase their motivation.

Early childhood teachers said they used digital art applications primarily for digital mandalas (Doodle) and making the pictures 3-dimensional. However, in digitally supported art activities, some applications can be used for purposes such as color, line pattern, artist/artwork, and museums. However, teachers need more awareness of this issue to allow the size of the digital art activities implemented. As in concrete/sensory art activities, emphasizing digital art to cover all areas of art will increase its effectiveness. In this context, its prevalence can be increased by organizing training for teachers on digital art applications and how to use these applications in which areas.

This study includes some applications/tools that are free of charge. However, the fact that teachers today follow the ever-changing and developing digital world in an up-to-date manner and become entrepreneurs constitutes the basis of today's digital literacy. Many things cannot be expected from a digital application/tool; it is recommended to include various digital applications/tools at different intervals without being bound to a digital application/tool because it has limitations.

Findings from teachers implied that they need training in digital art and digital art applications/tools. Educators play a vital role in guiding children to use technology creatively. Therefore, to fully bring the benefits of digitally supported art education to children, educators need to have a qualified education on integrating technology into art by the level of education to use technology effectively. As personal computers have started to be actively used in our lives, art educators have also adopted digital technologies and started to use them in art education, although the transition process has been slow (Gude, 2007; Leonard & Leonard, 2006; Lu, 2005). When the reasons for art teachers' reluctance to use technology in teaching are examined, software difficulties, increased stress, increased teaching loads, time constraints, lack of hardware, and lack of teacher training (Black, 2002; Browning, 2006; Delacruz, 2004; Gregory, 2009). The institutions to which teachers are affiliated can organize digital training for teachers. Teachers should keep digital/technological developments up to date, as it should be considered that digital art will be updated rapidly. In this context, there are easily accessible video explanations on using the digital applications proposed in the study. Teachers can learn how to apply these videos by obtaining them free of charge individually without the need for a particular training organization.

Considering all the results, in today's world where practices show incredible diversity, this study is limited to the data obtained from 23 teachers in the study group and reached by semi-structured interview technique from the practices/tools determined by the researchers. An observational study could not be conducted in the teachers' classrooms. In future studies, teachers' practices related to digital art in their classrooms can be observed, inferences about the implementation process can be obtained, and a contribution to the literature can be provided.

REFERENCES

Avcı, E. (2015). integration of digital technologies into fine arts education in the context of digital art. *Journal of International Social Research*, 8(41).

Black, J. (2002). Topsy-turvy teacher-student relationships: An examination of digital multimedia teaching and learning. *Dissertation Abstracts International*, 63, 6.

Browning, K. (2006). Digital applications in elementary visual arts: A case study in Ontario and Newfoundland schools. *Canadian Review of Art Education*, 33(1), 25–41.

Browning, K. (2008). Kathy Browning's digital photographyprofiled. In F. Blaikie (Ed.), *Canadian art/ works: A resource for primary, junior, intermediate, and senior teachers* (pp. 38-40; 127-131).Victoria BC: Canadian Society for Education Through Art.

Caeli, K., Ray, L., & Mill, J. (2003). 'Clear as mud'. Toward greater clarity generic qualitative research. *International Journal of Qualitative Methods*, 2(2), 1–13. 10.1177/160940690300200201

Canbek, G., & Sağıroğlu, Ş. (2007). Computer and internet safety of children and young people. *Polytechnic Journal, 10*(1).

Degennaro, A., & Mak, B. (2002-2003). A diffusion model for computer art in education. *Journal of Educational Technology Systems*, 31(1), 5–18. 10.2190/B69J-FDFR-UKBY-4LEL

Delacruz, E. (2004). Teachers' working conditions and the unmet promise of technology. *Studies in Art Education*, 46(1), 6–19. 10.1080/00393541.2004.11650065

Dilmaç, S. (2019). The Effect of Web-Based Asynchronous Learning Environment on Academic Achievement and Attitudes of Secondary School Students in Visual Arts Course. *Journal of Ağrı İbrahim Çeçen University Institute of Social Sciences*, 5(2), 159–184.

Edwards, B. (1997). Drawing on the Right Side of the Brain. In *CHI'97 Extended Abstracts on Human Factors in Computing Systems* (pp. 188-189). 10.1145/1120212.1120336

Gregory, D. (2009). Boxes with fire: Wisely integrating learning technologies into the art classroom. *Art Education*, 62(3), 47–54. 10.1080/00043125.2009.11519020

Gude, O. (2007). Principles of possibility: Considerations for a 21st-century art & culture curriculum. *Art Education*, 60(1), 6–17. 10.1080/00043125.2007.11651621

Kümbetoğlu, B. (2005). *Qualitative Method and Research in Sociology and Anthropology*. Bağlam Publishing.

Nisenholt, M. (2007). Picturing paradox. Profiling artist Kathy Browning's art: Images on icebergs and art educator including digital photography student exemplars. *Canadian Art Teacher, 6*(1).

Patton, M. Q. (2014). *Qualitative research and evaluation methods* (Bütün, M., & Demir, S. B., Trans.). Pegem Akademi.

Taşkesen, S. (2020). Students on the Use of Mobile Technology in Art Education Opinions and Motivations. *Ekev Academy Journal*, (84), 585–600.

Ulutaş, İ., & Demiriz, S. (2019). The importance of visual art education in preschool and visual art education programs features. In Ulutaş, İ. (Ed.), *Visual Art Education in Early Childhood Education*. Hedef Cs.

Wentzel, K. R., & Watkins, D. E. (2002). Peer relationsips and collaborative learning as contexts for academic enablers. *School Psychology Review*, 31(3), 366–377. 10.1080/02796015.2002.12086161

Winner, E., & Hetland, L. (2008). Art for our sake school arts classes matter more than ever-but not for the reasons you think. *Arts Education Policy Review*, 109(5), 29–32. 10.3200/AEPR.109.5.29-32

Yıldırım, A., & Şimşek, H. (2006). Qualitative research methods in social sciences (5th edition). Seçkin Publishing.

Chapter 2
Crafting Seeding Imagery for Artmaking Generative AI Tools

Shalin Hai-Jew
https://orcid.org/0000-0002-8863-0175
Hutchinson Community College, USA

ABSTRACT

There is an important value in human-machine collaborations using artmaking generative AI tools: that is, the preservation of the human hand (the human mental-emotional-embodied manual contribution) in the artwork. One way to ensure the original look-and-feel involves using multimodal prompts—both text and visual—with a twist. The visual may be one that is human-generated—either born-analog (and then digitized) or born-digital (such as imagery created on tablets or laptops, on digital drawing systems)—in a way that is unrelated or only peripherally related to the text prompt. This chapter explores how to craft seeding imagery for use in artmaking generative AI tools for innovations in color, color blends, textures, layouts, various perspectives, style blends, and others. This work describes some early ways to introduce human-touch novelty in seeding imagery from analog and digital approaches.

INTRODUCTION

The preservation of a human sensibility in the visuals created by the artmaking generative AI (A-GAI) tools of today is an important value. One way to maintain this is to control the text prompt and to curate the outputs by deciding whether something is worth keeping and / or worth keeping into various forms of post-production. Another approach may be to go with multimodal prompts to the A-GAI tools, that is, creating various forms of "seeding" imagery (whether born-analog or born-digital), to direct the tools to create more unique imagery. Seeding imagery refers to those used as a basis or reference for the A-GAI image outputs; the input visual is used to grow a new derived or semi-derived image. There are various controls in the technical tools that affect how much influence the seeding image has. "Born-analog" seeding images are those based on physical materials originally, including pigments, papers, and other material works, which are then captured digitally (by scanner, by smartphone camera, by DSLR, and by other devices). "Born-digital" seeding images are those created using software on tablets, laptops, mobile phones, and other devices, which do not require digitization for the A-GAI tools to use. The external images may enable "combinatorial complexity" along with the prompting text, image tag modifiers,

DOI: 10.4018/979-8-3693-2927-6.ch002

processing pipelines, invited serendipity, and other factors (Hai-Jew, July 8, 2023). Multi-dimensional prompts enable the creation of some pseudo-novel visuals from A-GAI tools, to avoid unwelcome repeating patterns and hackneyed visuals. Using both text and image prompts (as a multimodal command) to "condition the model" can help users get closer to the visual they want (Qiao, Liu, & Chilton, June 2022, p. 15).

This work explores some ways to create seeding visuals for use in the Deep Dream Generator (DDG) (https://deepdreamgenerator.com/), which was originated at Google in 2015 (v. 1) and has gone through several version updates in 2021 (v. 2) and late 2023 (v. 3). A number of models are included in this tool, and they have different energy point costs to run. (Extra energy points may be purchased.) The energy points replenish at different rates depending on the role-level of the users.

The latest version of the DDG enables a smooth iterating workflow to test various outputs from the respective models and a "proof sheet" of output images as a comparison. (Figure 1)

Figure 1. A proofsheet view of synthetic images output by various models in the Deep Dream Generator

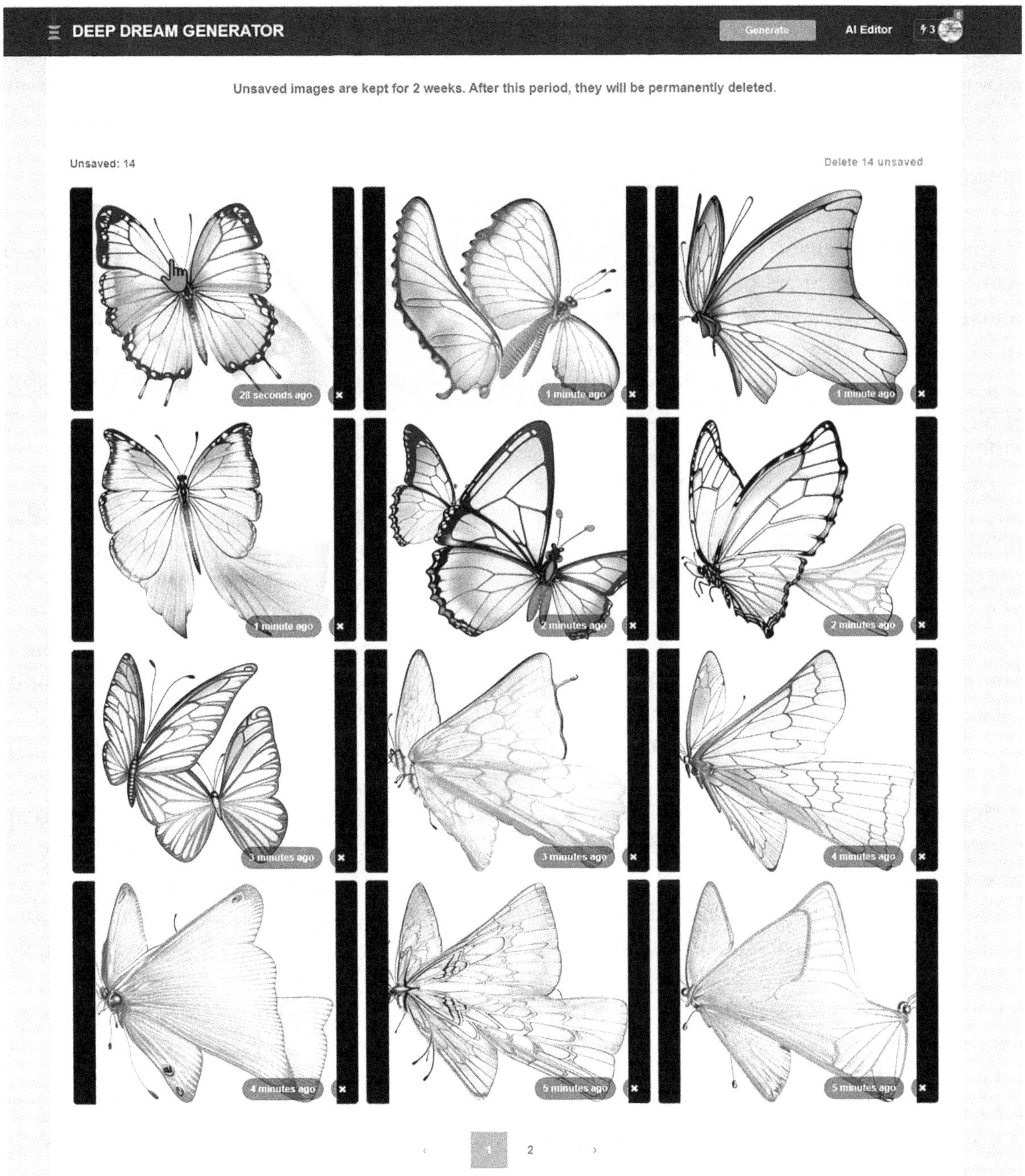

The platform not only generates visuals from various prompts, modifiers, seeding images, and models, but there is a social component which enables mutual engagement among the users of the platform. Users may publish their works on the platform, upvote others' co-creations, comment on others' works publicly or privately, and so on. This technology tool has been labeled a "famous project" (Yuan, Chen, & Wang, Mar. 2022, p. 1), with Alexander Mordvintsev's DeepDream architecture focusing on patterns in visual data. A number of different computational models are integrated within this tool, enabling a fast pipeline to experiment. This A-GAI tool is currently run by Aifnet Ltd. Some of the insights of this work may apply to the particular web-facing artmaking generative AI tool, but some may be generalized to others.

REVIEW OF THE LITERATURE

The popularization of artmaking generative artificial intelligence tools (A-GAI) has been lauded by many as enabling a broad public to share visual ideas and make visual-supported social commentary without necessarily having the necessary art skills. These tools enable users to use text and / or imagery as prompts to the technology to evoke a visual. They may also go through various iterations (or inceptions) to version different visuals over time. This capability enables a democratization of visual expression, without the need for programming knowledge (Maerten & Soydaner, 2023) or even much in the way of art knowledge.

This is not to say that the reception of generative AI has been necessarily positive. There have been concerns about generative AI taking artists' jobs, infringing on intellectual property (Ghosh & Fossas, 2022, p. 1; Franceschelli & Musolesi, 2022, p. e17-4), and changing up the sense of human aesthetic taste, among others. One research team observed:

> A work of art created by AI has its own beauty and composition and may be very divergent from human aesthetics and aesthetic methods, but the machine does not destroy the aesthetic ability of human nature, but only transforms the inherent mode of thinking of human intelligence and offers another possibility beyond aesthetic standards. (Chen, Shidujaman, Jin, & Ahmed, 2020, p. 25)

Human-machine generated art is bound to result in novel creations. Machine learning-based applications enable human to harness "access to extensive data" for "associations previously unexploited by human artists" (Luo, 2019/2020, p. 12).

Researchers have gone to social media to better understand people's reported preferences for images to train computers to understand what is liked by people (Chatterjee, 2022, p. 04). Some generative AI platforms capture information about people's publishing select images, likes and upvotes of other's works, commenting, and other data, to understand what is visually appealing to people (vs. just to machines) and to deliver more of the desired visuals to people.

For all the early resistance, the artworks of generative AI have been sufficiently appealing and perhaps lucrative to have made headway into the formal contemporary art scene, which has accepted machine-made art pieces (Franceschelli & Musolesi, 2022, p. e17-1). They have been featured in exhibitions and shows; they have attracted serious money (in the six figures and even higher).

Some observe that "it is difficult for limited human biological intelligence to combat the development of non-biological intelligence" (Chen, Shidujaman, Jin, & Ahmed, 2020, p. 22). Still, these concerns are coupled with a sense of hopefulness that such models can provide "a positive, new modality in art" (Ghosh & Fossas, 2022, p. 1) and serve as "a prosthetic extension to the human imagination" (Leach, 2019, p. 298). Some predict: "AI will play a significant role in a quintessential creative activity, the appreciation and production of visual art" (Chatterjee, 2022, p. 01). Another work describes the A-GAI acting as an auxiliary and "behind-the-scenes worker" (Chen, Shidujaman, Jin, & Ahmed, 2020, p. 14), with the human creator at the forefront. The setup of A-GAI technologies suggests a symbiotic relationship between humans and machines to co-create and co-design, with the benefits of working "smarter and better" (Mahmud, Hong, & Fong, 2023, p. 1).

The vision is nothing less than the interweaving of humans and machines in shared endeavors, with some risks of moral hazards (such as people taking credit for the work of machines, selling "forgeries" as originals and other frauds, and others).

Machine Creativity

Philosophical questions have been raised as well. One central one has been whether computational systems may be creative, in this age of the Fourth Industrial Revolution (4IR). New thinking is in order: "...by using what humans believe about machines to subvert our preconceived notions, we are making both humans and machines more creative" (Luo, 2019/2020, p. 15)

One research team asks: "Are we finally reaching an age where machines are learning, thinking, and deciding on their own? Or is creativity merely engineered according to what society currently values" (Gruner & Csikszentmihalyi, 2019, p. 448). To enable more flexibility, the co-researchers redefine creativity as an ability to change how things are done to adapt to a changing external environment. Their definition includes both "a human enterprise and a salient capacity of artificial intelligence" (Gruner & Csikszentmihalyi, 2019, p. 450). They take two general approaches: an individualist one in which the person is paramount, or a sociocultural one in which "innovators that revolutionize entire fields and transcend time" are judged by the gatekeepers in particular domains (Gruner & Csikszentmihalyi, 2019, p. 451). It is the latter part of the model—the social one—that is more inclusive of generative AI, which itself is entangled with humanity.

The posited Creativity 4.0 model involves "the individual, or groups of individuals, program AI to perform tasks and process information in specific ways. The field still influences the individual but does not directly affect the AI. Given that the collective field has no direct influence over the algorithms, but continues to impact decisions made by individuals, we suggest that the field influences AI indirectly through the individual. However, depending on the learning algorithm, AI can draw directly from information it encounters in the domain. As AI improves its predictive capacities and draws on more information from the domain, it begins to make new combination s that are perhaps increasingly independent from the original information provided by individual programmers" (Gruner & Csikszentmihalyi, 2019, p. 451). Both people and computers are thought to engage in computational mind wandering in an age of "post-enlightened cognition" which does not only consider human intelligence the only main intelligence in the world (Bruder, 2018, p. 154).

From a computer science angle, art novelty is defined as deviation from defined style norms in a statistical sense. This means creating art "with increased levels of arousal potential in a constrained way without activating the aversion system and falling into the negative hedonic range" (Elgammal, Liu, Elhoseiny, & Mazzone, 2017, p. 4). This suggests that people have a range within which they accept visual works but react aversively beyond this range. It is safer to riff off the known. Another work describes a statistical definition of creativity as "the generation of out-of-distribution novelty" (Cherti, Kégl, & Kazakçı, Nov. 2017, p. 1), in a definition that enables systematized computational analysis of novelty. This definition of artful creativity emphasizes the need to create models "that can generate objects from future (hold-out) classes, unknown at training time" in an algorithmic way (Cherti, Kégl, & Kazakçı,

Nov. 2017, p. 1). Neural images are part of a "search for new visual languages," based on "unusual combinations of realistic visual cues…with weird and intriguing variations" (Hertzmann, 2019, p. 1). Visual interestingness "is contextual, and fades as it loses novelty…" (Hertzmann, 2019, p. 3).

Generative AI artmaking does not only involve creations on a 2d plane, but there are works in the interactive art space (Chen, Shidujaman, Jin, & Ahmed, 2020), vector art, digital character design, and others. Many generative AI tools have built-in neural style transfer capabilities, to apply a style to an image from a text prompt or an image prompt. The style may come from a particular image, or it may come from a body of work by an artist. There are styles that may be drawn from a collection of artworks that typify a particular art movement. (Digital image editing software also has this capability.) Neural style transfer involves taking content from one (seeding) image and style from another image (Al-Khazraji, Abbas, & Jamil, 2022, p. 134).

Machine "Consciousness"

Another philosophical approach involves the sci-fi notion of technical Singularity, when machines will surpass the intelligence of humanity, attain sentience and agency, and become a potential threat to humanity. (This concept is credited to novelist Vernor Vinge in his novel *Marooned in Realtime* from 1986.) That concept is seen as perhaps practically realize-able, through a mix of technical savvy and engineering. One research work proposes a "machine consciousness architecture" or "cognitive architecture" that may create machine consciousness based on computational "cognitive processes" and "conscious behavior" (Merchán & Molina, 2020, p. 350). Machine consciousness may be validated "with practical tests" (Merchán & Molina, 2020, p. 360).

The underlying processing approach of DeepDream is also thought to be getting closer to human thinking:

> DeepDream seems able to draw some parallels with our ability to recognize patterns. Humans are also functioning with a priori forms in their minds, with archetypes that use them, in order to conceive and understand—in forms known to them—the world, DeepDream is approaching human cognition 'but it doesn't do so in a particularly human way.' (Auerbach, as cited in Gkotzos, Oct. 30, 2015, n.p.)

This parallel discussion of machine advances into sentience and thinking, with the advent of A-GAI technologies, is a theme in academic research literature. Computational neurons are fast advancing on the capabilities of the biological ones.

Generation of Visual Imagery by Trained Models on Computing Machines

Current generations of artmaking generative AIs are based on large language models (LLMs), trained on unlabeled big data using artificial neural networks (ANNs) and mapped to text. Deep learning neural networks (DNNs) are tools "where high-level behavior is not explicitly programed but emerges from the complex interactions of thousands or millions of simple computational elements" (Wyse, 2019, n.p.). These neural networks enable modeling of contents based on subtle patterns found in the training data, used for machine-based reinforcement learning. The models are fine-tuned or adapted to particular downstream uses once the model has been trained. The respective A-GAIs perform differently based not only on the underlying training but the algorithms built into the respective platforms, the graphical user interface (GUI), and other aspects. There are various strengths and weaknesses to each technology and various tradeoffs. Various generative models have different creative ranges and can respond to even ambiguous inputs (Poole, Jain, Barron, & Mildenhall, 2022).

The training imagesets are known and defined for some but not others (Jiang, Brown, Cheng, Khan, Gupta, Workman, D., ... & Gebru, T., Aug. 2023), with some calling for more transparency to protect the copyright of artists and photographers and other content creators. Some makers of A-GAI suggest that they only use images transiently and retain extracted parameter weights data, but the learning of particular art styles requires learning "from the whole work as it is" potentially requiring the storage of "protected works in their expressive form, which is what is protected by copyright, and not by means of features or small chunks if not of their underlined ideas" (Franceschelli & Musolesi, 2022, p. e17-4). [The transferred artist art styles capture some stylistic elements, but they do not capture the spirit or animation of an artist hand, imbued with the artist's biography and temperament and life.]

Some generative models engage in "introspection," including the ability to "self-evaluate the difference between its generated samples and the given training data" to avoid hallucinating original feeder images from the image training set and to better model styles and textures (Lazarow, Jin, & Tu, 2017, p. 2774).

One critique of A-GAI tools is that there is "an uncanny sameness and...a certain blurriness" with the generative AI images, which emerge from "a kind of statistical unconscious" (Schröter, 2023, p. 112). Images from a different A-GAI "oscillate between a hyperreal...and unnerving clarity on the one hand and an incomprehensible blur on the other" (Schröter, 2023, p. 119). Some visuals are based on a "pre-generated semantic layout" (Li, Zhang, Zhang, Huang, He, Lyu, & Gao, 2019, p. 12174), which does not enable offsets or decentering (which may work better in some visual contexts). Some also seem to cut corners, instead of drawing hands, feet, and limbs (which are problematic for current-generation A-GAIs), such as going for simplicity over complexity, and such as using recognizable color palettes again and again.

The text-to-image (TTI) function enables a computation backwards mapping from text to image characteristics, in a computational "hermeneutics" (interpretation of texts) and transcoding to a visual. Text-to-image synthesis requires "handling ambiguous and incomplete information in natural language descriptions and learning across vision and language modalities" (Li, Zhang, Zhang, Huang, He, Lyu, & Gao, 2019, p. 12174). Similar tools are trained on image/text pairings in a diffuse sense.

The academic literature shows various challenges that these tools faced and suggest ways that they were addressed, such as the emergence of "checkerboard artifacts" in models using layers based on how the stacking of visual was done (Odena, Dumoulin, & Olah, 2016, p. 2). There were similar challenges with color gradients. There are sets of current-day challenges that are being worked as well with this class of tools. There are technologies that can fairly effectively predict what should go into a particular area of an image and fill it with appropriate pixels through "inpainting" (Yeh, Chen, Yian Lim, Schwing, Hasegawa-Johnson, & M. N., 2017, p. 5485). This means digital and digitized images may be amended, and occlusions may be replaced with what is behind the occlusion.

In the computer science space, there is wide experimentation for other ways to achieve generative AI through other means. One work suggests that trained classification neural networks may be used as image generators to create "human-meaningful images" at less computational cost (Wang & Torr, 2022, n.p.) Work done in machine vision to help people differentiate between different visual textures that may seem similar otherwise may enable the generation of images "subject to certain perceptual constraints" (Gatys, Ecker, & Bethge, 2017, p. 8).

About the Deep Dream Generator

This slideshow provides some observations of how to think about seeding images, particularly in terms of how the DDG handles them, with its "algorithmic pareidolia" ("Deep Dream," Wikipedia, Dec. 20, 2023) and tendency towards "over-processing" by enhancing visual patterns. This A-GAI takes the scatter of colors and lines and pixels from seeding imagery and makes shapes. DDG tends to fill the whole digital canvas. A model's over-response to "perturbations" (or disturbances) may be considered a "bug" in some technologies but a "feature" in another context. "DeepDream-style perturbations" (Baluja & Fischer, 2017, n.p) are a feature even as critics consider a DeepMind algorithm as suffering "from pathological obsession with miniscule detail, also known as apophenia" (Bruder, 2018, p. 136).

One researcher explains:

> DeepDream, a convolutional deep neural network algorithm, caused quite a stir after it was let loose in 2015. It's (sic) online interface, the Deep Dream Generator, invites users to turn their run-of-the-mill photographs into beautiful, dream-like hallucinations and in turn provides Google with an abundance of free, unlabelled training data. Instead of analysing images for defining features that help identify particular animals, however, Deep Dream performs the obverse: it takes miniscule details as evidence for the presence of creatures it has been trained to recognize. Effectively, the algorithm, projects its cognitive bias onto pictures—a technique that Google, by reference to Christopher Nolan's (2010) dream-heavy science fiction movie, calls "inceptionism" (Bruder, 2018, p. 137)

DeepDream enables "inceptionism," which synthesizes imagery to "provoke a particular response of a trained neural network" (Luo, Sandler, Lin, Zhmoginov, & Howard, 2020, p. 3).

Underlying the DDG is the DeepDream approach. One research team writes:

> Another very interesting GDL ("generative deep learning") architecture is Google's DeepDream (Mordvintsev et al., 2015). The designers of DeepDream trained a convolutional neural network for image classification, and then they used the network as a generative model working in reverse: the image is not obtained as an output, but through modifications of an image provided in input, where the modifications are done according to the patterns learned from the network. In particular, the input image is modified in such a way that the 'excitement' of a selected layer is maximized; this entails the emergence of the patterns that the specific layer has learned to recognize, which might just be simple ornament-like patterns, but also more sophisticated features. (Franceschelli & Musolesi, 2022, p. e17-3)

DDG harnesses Deep Convolutional Neural Networks and Inception "to build the dream through layer-by-layer implementation" (Al-Khazraji, Abbas, & Jamil, A systematic review…, 2023, p. 192). There are different focuses on the different layers of the activated feature maps. The DDG works on the principle of "activation maximization (Mordvintsev et al., 2015, s cited in Gatys, Ecker, & Bethge, 2017, p. 10). One work explains:

> Deep Dream synthesizes or manipulates images to maximize the activation of specific feature maps. Since these features encode semantic properties, such as objects or parts of objects or scenes, the synthesized images look like hallucinations of these semantic entities. (Gatys, Ecker, & Bethge, 2017, p. 10)

The processing of DeepDream is not only applied to imagery but also to "natural language processing (NLP), images, videos, and audio" (Al-Khazraji, Abbas, & Jamil, A systematic review…, 2023, p. 192). In terms of processing, low-level features apply to issues like layout, and high-level ones focus on textures and visual details. DDG modifies images "with motifs" (Al-Khazraji, L. Abbas, & Jamil, The effect of changing…, 2023, p. 34).

Some years after the release of the DDG tool, one researcher observed that it had lost its entrancement:

> The DeepDream imagery was briefly fascinating, but, within a year or two, it lost its novelty and appeal. The DeepDream images eventually seemed very repetitive, with the same mutant doggies and eyeballs appearing over and over again. This may be, in part, because the DeepDream tools provided relatively little opportunity for artistic control or artistic expression" (Hertzmann, 2019, pp. 10 - 11)

In the ensuing years, the platform has certainly evolved to enable greater controls by users and to integrate a larger variety of models through which images can be made. It has continued to evolve new features and levers of human control.

People are slated to play a critical role in some artmaking generative AIs (A-GAI), such as the DDG:

> DeepDream Generator fits into this framework as it needs the human operator to select a style, i.e., provide a direction, i.e., like to a certain layer. In DeepDream Generator's website, the opening screen states: 'human-AI collaboration'. The word collaboration leads us to think of the interdependencies between the human and the technological, of the inability of one to function without the other…The layers of imagination that AI produces can guide the user's imagination. Yet, there is an important role for the human—to bring in new layers (new pictures, new runs) and reveal the meaning (or the political context) of the links between the layers. (Wellner, 2019, p. 66)

The human is not shunted aside with the advent of A-GAI and other AI tools.

CRAFTING SEEDING IMAGERY FOR ARTMAKING GENERATIVE AI TOOLS

For a visual to "work," it has to achieve a number of things. It has to be generally meaningful between the human (and machine) maker of that image and the human receiver of that image (based on information theory). It has to be aesthetically pleasing within and across cultures. It has to be eye-popping and garner attention. A work has to align with conventions of that image type but still go beyond the conventional. Ideally, the visuals would be so original that they would not be possible without the seeding image, the human inputs, and the A-GAI. If it is a conceptual creation, the concept has to "work," and the execution of the visual expression also has to work. If a work is abstract, it has to still be aesthetically pleasing. If a work is figurative, its form has to make visual sense.

The *pareidolia* feature of the Deep Dream Generator enables a purposeful sloppiness in the making of seeding imagery. A typical session of making seeding imagery involves working at a cheap card table with various media and tools around: alcohol markers, paint markers, Sharpies, gel pens, colored pencils, paintbrushes, palette knives, isopropyl alcohol, acrylic paints, watercolors, glitter, glue, tape, hairspray (as a fixative), scissors, and various paper types (synthetic and non-synthetic). There is plastic wrap from the kitchen. There are cans of compressed air for blowing paint. The materials are a hodge-podge, and the works that are made only have to be different from each other. The intermixing and interplay enable a wide range of outcomes. If there is any planning, it is only a light sense of the surface area of particular colors, the placement of colors on the 2d plane, the uses of fine lines, and the more visceral parts of an image. The materials are mundane and range from craft-shop goods to higher end markers and paints and papers. The GAI and the prompt fills out the gaps and may result in works that are engaging.

The Deep Dream Generator is perfectly capable of outputting communicative visuals without an underlying seeding image. Figures 2 and 3 show works created in the DDG that convey visual information with simple prompts (and no underlying seeding imagery as prompts). The prompt for "Breadwinner" involved "a stack of bread piled to the rafters." The visual conveys visual wit and visual coherence. (Figure 2)

Figure 2. "Breadwinner": visual wit in Aivision model in the Deep Dream Generator

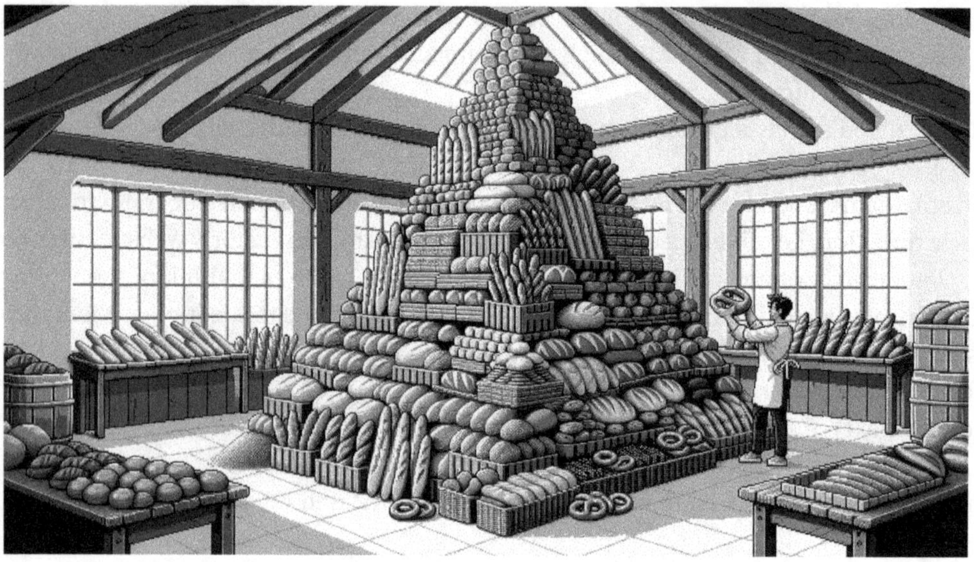

The prompt for "Fashionable Dance Party" was "fashionable dance party at a cool venue." The generative AI model selected the scene, the colors, and everything depicted. (Figure 3) A few modifiers were used in each to emphasize structure. The generative AI interpreted the rest.

Figure 3. "Fashionable Dance Party" in AIVision model in the Deep Dream Generator

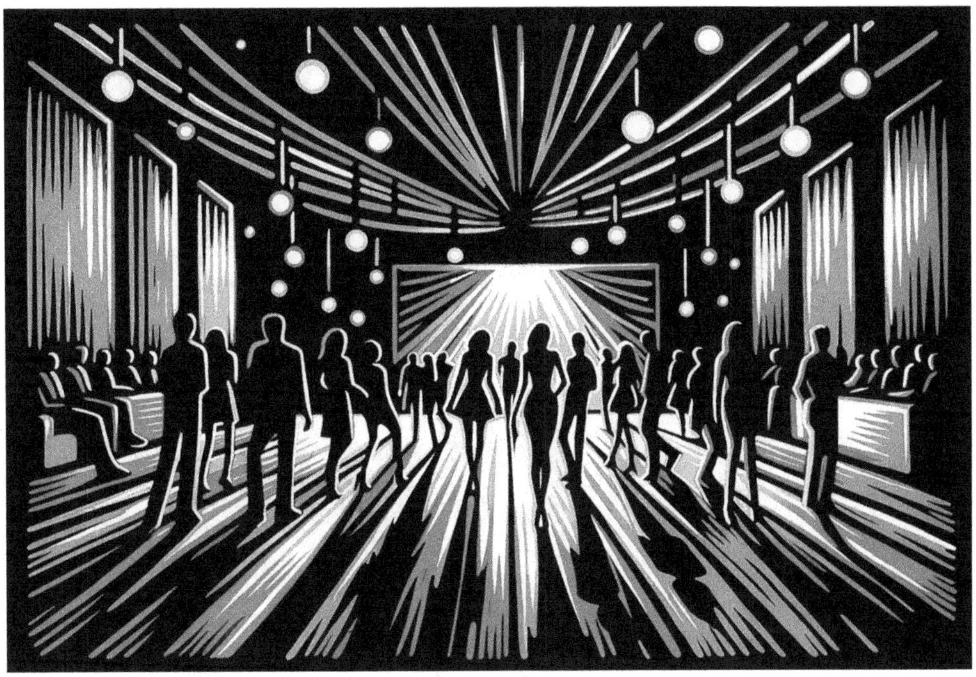

In terms of how many users use the DDG, many evoke various characters, humanoid mostly, but also some animals and robots, among others. The human characters have nearly perfectly symmetrical facial features and are evoked with "goddess" and "god" as seeding text terms. The female characters are often buxom and in full makeup (including digital eyeliner and mascara). There are often applied styles. Common terms seem to be "epic," "insane," "breathtaking," and others of the same ilk. There is a drawing to fantasies and myths. The similar usage is hard to break up without new visual topics in the text prompt box…and perhaps new seeding images as an under structure to change up color palettes, color combinations and blends, global color mixes, line work, and compositing layouts.

A Sampler of Seeding Images

Any 2d visual may be used as a seeding image, to provide a combined textual and visual multimodal prompt to an A-GAI tool. (Figure 4) Note that language itself is ambiguous and polysemous, even within longer and more detailed prompts, and some A-GAI tools thrive in that interpretive space while others flounder.

In most cases in the author's experience, the GAI offers some obvious usage of the seeding image in the output image. There is some degree of predictability in the readout. There is some visual translation, some mapping, from the seed to the iterated output. In some rarer cases, such as the usage of subtle color, the translation may be more latent or concealed.

Figure 4. A mish-mash of seeding images (analog and digital)

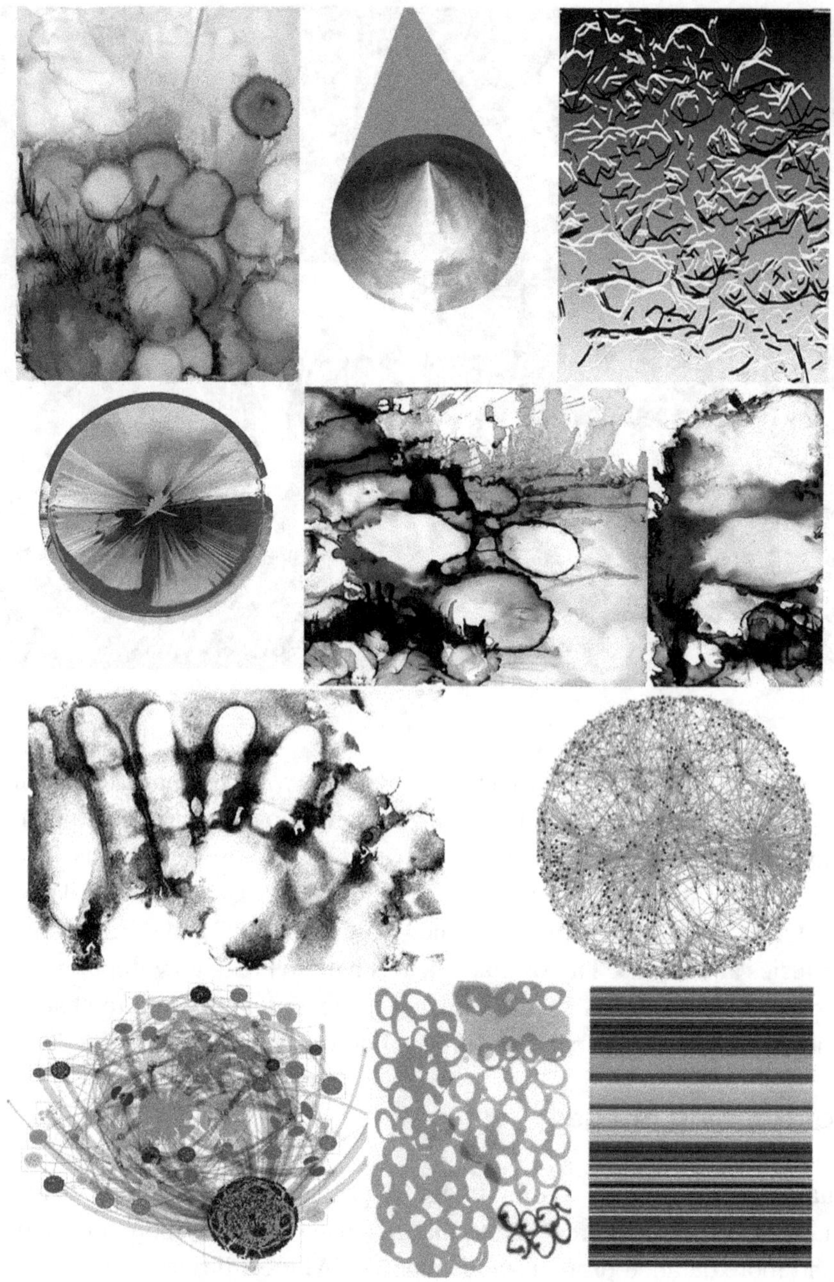

A Mish-Mash of Seeding Images

Users harness different strategies to try for different outputs. Some offer heavy verbiage while others take a less-is-more approach. There can be long sequences of processing on the platform, with a seeding prompt and then versioning the image through different iterations, different models, and different modifier tags, and so on. Similarly, images may be processed through long sequences in digital image editing software programs. To see some of the visuals created with the seeding imagery, go to https://deepdreamgenerator.com/u/sjjalinn/.

Figure 5 shows a screenshot of the top-level of the account as of late 2023.

Figure 5. Top-level screenshot of the Sjjalinn account on the Deep Dream Generator

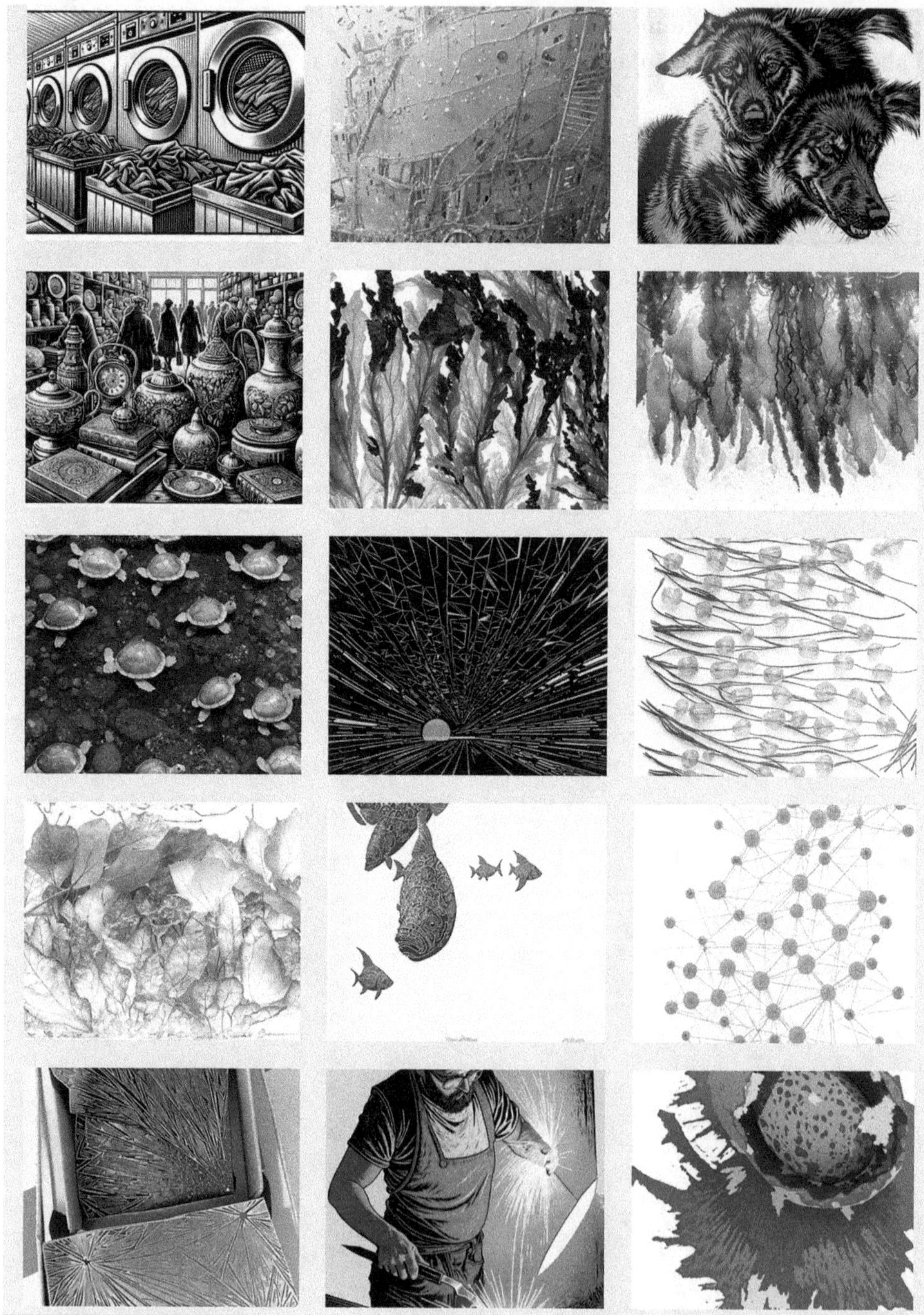

Seeding images may inform different types of visuals. For example, color in text (in a verbal sense) may be freighted with cultural meanings and implications. By contrast, color in a seeding image feels just like something on the light spectrum, something more inherently neutral, something non-meaning-bearing, a-semantic, pre-cultural in its sensibility. Or this line of reasoning may just be a mental justification for using seeding imagery.

A general flowchart (Figure 6) shows how seeding imagery is used in an artmaking generative AI.

Figure 6. Seeding Imagery Used with Artmaking Generative AI

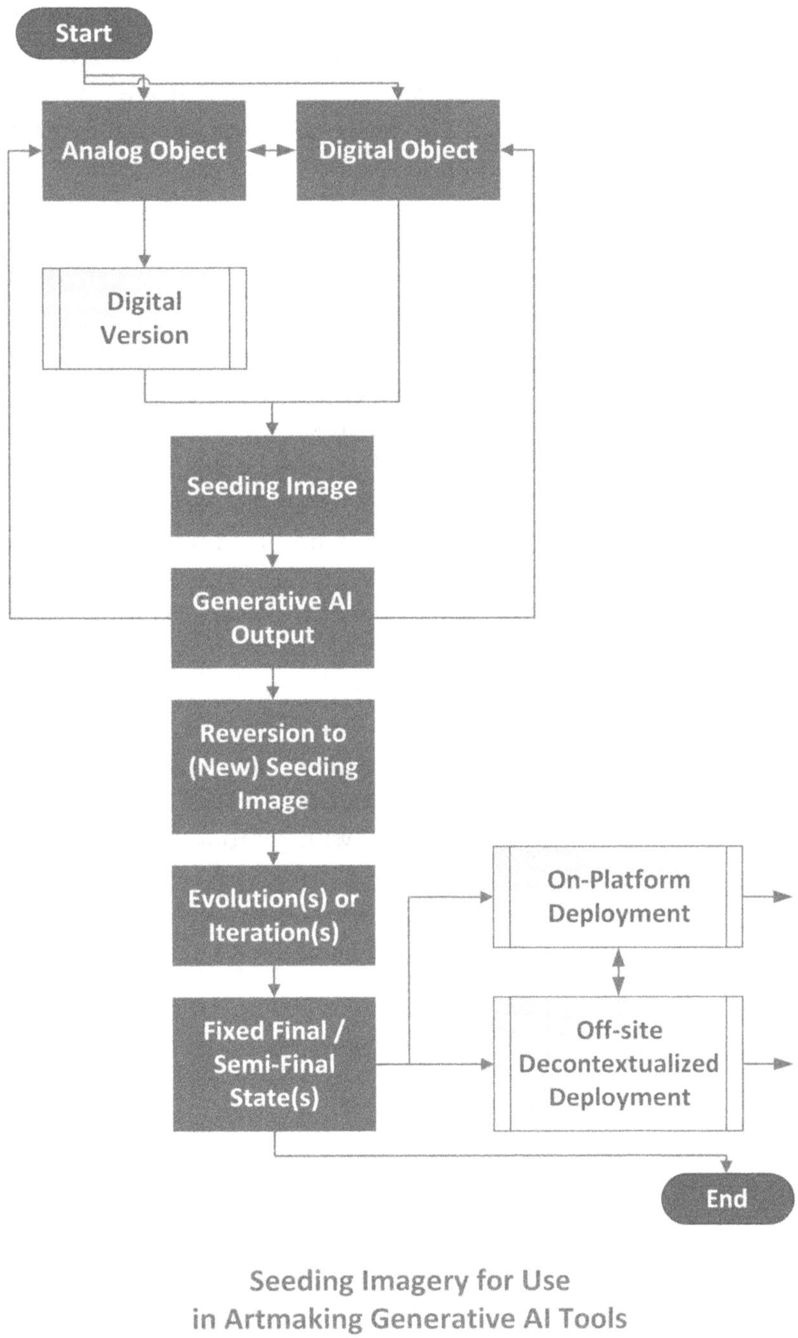

Getting visuals on paper enables a "distributed cognition," where the person transfers thought into something material that can capture some aspect of the original inspiration in fixed form. In terms of analog art materials, there are essentially various forms of pigment (inks, paints, chalk, hard and soft pastels, crayons, color pencils, felt tip markers) applied through various tools (pens, paint brushes, stamps, palette knives) onto various surfaces (paper whether from wood or synthetics, 3d objects). There are a variety of techniques for application, such as dripping, spattering, dabbing; various art techniques (reference imagery; wet on wet, wet or dry, dry on wet; rewetting alcohol inks; layering; and others), uses of blown air, uses of typewriters, uses of printing presses, and other approaches. In common art practice, various stickers and other materials may be applied on surfaces. There are crafting approaches, such as collage and other effects. Art materials range from low-cost to high-end, but over time, the materials are non-negligible in costs. Then, the analog works translate differently through digital photography, flatbed scanning, and other digital capture methods. Transcoding across material-to-digital and digital-to-digital results in various visual gains and losses with each transcoding.

Digital canvases offer many opportunities for drawing (with pen and tablets), coloring (including with high screen reflectance and digital colors), painting, artificial light effects, distortions, neural style applications, digital tracing, image filters, cropping, hue and saturation adjustments, values changes (dark and light), and other editing functions. There are experiments in color and form. There are experiments with toned paper, mixed inks, and paints. Across the models, there are no two outputs alike based on human manual outputs. On a larger scale, perhaps, there may be more similarities identified.

Having external sources of seeding imagery can diversify outputs on the A-GAI platform, as compared to evolving an image made by the A-GAI alone. With an unoriginal seeding image, the follow-on iterations can read as very plasticine and derivative as well. Certainly, it is possible to mute or accentuate aspects of a seeding image with modifiers and other controls on the platform.

Having physical art materials around serves as a "forcing function" to keep creativity top-of-mind. Their aging out (alcohol markers drying out and leaking, liquid inks and paints drying, powder pigment turning into spilled dust, inks darkening or lightening or discoloring, and others) is a reminder of the passive of the time and the need to capture and fix progress. There is pressure to put the art materials to some valuable use. Where digital offers an elusive sheen of immortality, physical pigments and papers show time. This is so even as one re-wets alcohol marker with isopropyl alcohol soaks and other endeavors.

For all the real-world inputs, though, generative AI in its present form does seem to offer an alternate universe, a parallel space, where physics does not apply. One way to see this is in a seeded series of visuals from different models that depict shadow play in non-physical ways.

Figure 7. Inferred shadows (by a GAI tool)

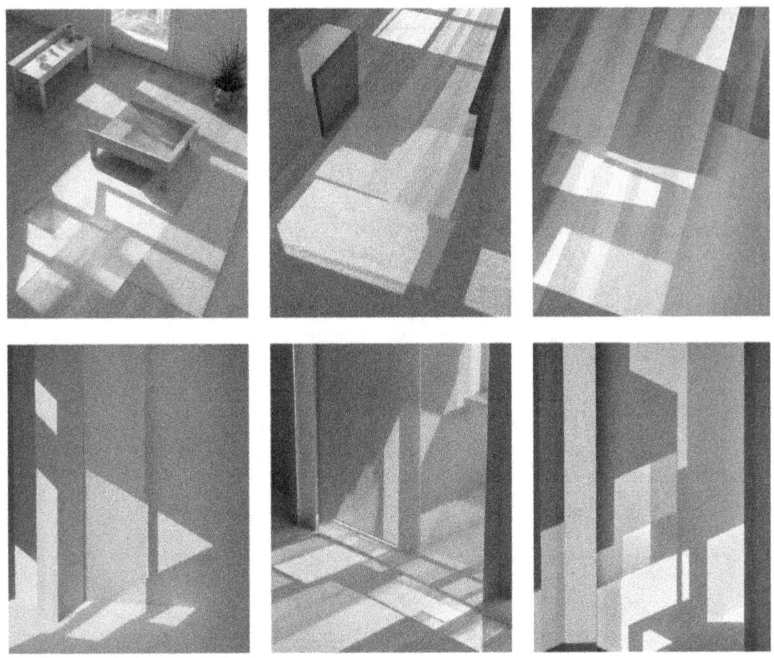

Inferred Shadows (by a GAI tool)

DISCUSSION

What is actual human-machine teaming in terms of application in the artmaking generative AI (A-GAI) space? There is a way to separate these out, based on multiple years of experience in space. The human hand, eye and brain are interconnected. For the early years of learning art, though, just coordinating the various elements can be challenging, and works that are manual are often clumsy and distortive and messy. Perhaps the magic of A-GAI is more powerful for non-professional "common artists" in these early days than in others when the mystique is less powerful.

Table 1 separates out some of the human vs. machine contributions in the use case that this work describes.

Table 1. Human-machine collaborations and respective contributions to the melds

Human Contributions to the Collaboration	Artmaking Generative AI (A-GAI) Contributions to the Collaboration
Human conceptualization Meaning-making Human subjectivity Human intersubjectivities Social context Human culture Human sociality Intercommunications with others Audience targeting Artful learning Aesthetics Value-added Visual coherence Image curation Multimodal and cross-modal inspirations Pre-production Post-production Digital image layering Ranges of color palettes, color blends, gradients Ranges of line work Ranges of shapes Ranges of topics Human pacing of work, of publication Design sensibility Found visuals or found art (advertisements, diagrams, data visualizations, stock imagery, templates, maps, photos, composites, text, and others) Serendipity courting And others	Visual coherence Shape and form Scene setting, context setting Digital character design Areas of visual interest Art style transfer Aspect ratio Directions of canvases Implausible Light-bending Non-physics-sensibility And others

What inspires visuals that may be created in an A-GAI? Inspiration may come from words: a phrase, song lyrics, a poem, a story, dialogue, a turn of phrase, a name, a news article, a riddle, or other words. The spark of an idea may come from imagery, a scene, an object, a relationship, a public personality, a film, a situation, an art method (whether analog or digital or both), a symbol, an icon, lettering or font, and others. Inspiration may strike when working on other issues. It may arise when iterating (inceptioning) through various visual outputs, in or out of sequence. Users may think directly in an imagistic way (visual thinking) or conceptually (language-based thinking). There are a variety of ways to ideate. For those who may be stumped (common artist's "block"), they can always auto-generate prompts on the platform and tweak those directions for output imagery.

As to what may inspire seeding imagery, that inspiration may come from other images, videos, phrasing, art materials, serendipity and accidents, and other references, and also combinations of the prior. Having some other inspiration for the seed may lighten the cognitive load in the making.

One of the motivations to take seeding images into an A-GAI is a "hacker mentality," to make the technology do things it wasn't intended for. This is not for malicious purposes but more for experimentation and curiosity and creation/innovation.

As to what may be created, there are a wide range of possibilities. One favorite involves implausible visuals. One work involves the bending of light in ways that are not true to the world, for example. Even so, the human mind sense-makes from what is seen through the retina, the optic nerve signals, and what hits the brain.

A Constructive Learner Mindset

To play in this space, it helps to have a learner mindset, with images that are high-dimensional and semi-structured, and with polysemous interpretations of the meanings of the visuals. There are dead-ends and blind alleys in terms of achieving certain desired outcomes. For learning, it is important to have fun and to forgive the self (even for those who may be somewhat perfectionistic). It helps to take as many tries as one wants. It helps to see a blank surface or digital canvas as an opportunity. To immerse in this space requires the willingness to engage mentally, to think through the work as one is working. It helps to be persistent, to iterate again and again, until one arrives at a usable image, and then to iterate beyond that, too, for learning's sake. Often, each inception involves small tweaks, with small changes. As to the images that make it to publication, the image has to offer something of visual interest, something original, even if it is only in an aspect of the visual: the atmospherics, the layout(s), the texture(s), the shape(s), and other aspects. This experimentation involves a kind of "brute force" (trial and error) learning, which can be tedious without the learner's curiosity at play. It helps to think of seeding images as drafts, as disposable works, as nothing serious. As a case in point, with watercolor paper and multi-media paper (vs. synthetic paper made from plastic), the author used both sides of the paper to create seeding images and then shredded the paper works for recycling. There is some degree of wastage in new learning in this space. To stay loose and limber, it helps to not have to commit to any visual during the making of the seeding images and then to experiment on the A-GAI once the work has been uploaded in digital form. It also helps to be comfortable with messiness and so-called "ugly" in the in-between and liminal states. It is freeing to be open to outcomes that are messy and even unaesthetic. The idea is to push for a range of visual expressiveness.

Seeding Image Affordances

Seeding images should not just be something pro forma, without true capability to change what made be created by the artmaking generative AI. There is a balance, too, to not intrude on the prerogative of artmaking generative AI. What can seeding images provide on DDG, based on this one experiential case?

On the DDG (and potentially other A-GAIs), seeding images may…

- Introduce new visual effects from mixed media works on various physical media (papers, wood, foil, plastics, and other surfaces)
    - Offer collages
- Enable minimalism and sparsity (instead of filling the whole canvas with visual content)
    - Define white spaces, negative spaces
    - Enable single-line drawings (which cannot be done by text prompts alone at this time)
- Enable the creation of unusual or different or variant textures and patterns
- Enable visual complexity or visual simplicity
- Introduce much broader color palettes (including neon colors and metallics from physical paints)
    - Offer toned paper with overlays of pigment from various liquid and dry mediums

- Introduce serendipity and chance factors
- Include seeding photos, diagrams, data graphs, data visualizations, art doodles, paintings, and other "found" and "made" seeding visuals
- Include underpainting for more textured color and texture and line
- Include special effects from different color blend modes
- Include complexity from neural filters (AI in Photoshop), filter gallery effects, and digital image editing effects (offset effects, imagery tracing, and others)
- Include generative AI images from other platforms (like Craiyon, MidJourney, Adobe Firefly, and others)
- Enable deep control of the underlying image by having the generative AI (GAI) offer only a low percentage of overlay or change
- Enable the introduction of grids (gridlines); enable the use of pixel-scaled visuals as feedstock; enable the uses of "frames" with closed shapes (circles, squares, rectangles, triangles, polygons) that may serve as small area pullouts or scenes by the GAI
- Bring in 3d illusions

Seeding images enable the introduction of more complex dimensionality in the AI-output images. These do require rich experimentation over time.

As with other forms of artmaking, much of the work involves training the eyes to see accurately and also differently. DDG enables the learning of art concepts, with some degree of pseudo-accuracy, based on textual concepts. This work shows various levels of attention to details in the seeding imagery, but more careful work may result in very different visual outcomes, perhaps even more effective visuals. The ease of experimentation encourages creative play. Sometimes, as a user is clicking through options, it may be only a second or two later that she realizes, "Oh, that might be interesting!" The combinatorial complexity enabled by the software can be potent.

> If many forms of art are about expression, culture, collective memory (history), and pleasure, the clarity of the visual as a communication medium is important. This is so whether the visual is figurative or abstract. Including the original seeding imagery is an option on many A-GAI platforms, but this author does not prefer to include seeding images in the public online catalog since they can be distractive from the original and may break the illusions in the finalized refined image (Hai-Jew, July 8, 2023). Also, seeing the seeding image may make it too easy to dismiss the finalized image: "Oh, it only came from that!" Perhaps there is a psychological dynamic going on where there is more satisfaction with visuals that are more representative of the individual (and less of the machine). Indeed, user pages on DDG convey something of personal brands expressed in the world. It is both the world that people imagine but also the one that they want to immerse themselves in. Some images are more palatable than others.

As a side note, it is probably not possible to reverse engineer to an original seeding image at present given the high dimensionality of images (Hai-Jew, July 8, 2023).

Images created by generative AIs are not only used on the generating platform, but they have uses in many other contexts: websites, news stories, slideshows, videos, video games, digital learning objects, books, and other applications. Given that images created by generative AIs cannot be copyrighted, there seem to be few legal restrictions against their use except if the visual somehow takes after a real-world work. In many cases, depending on the requirements of the generative AI platform, the visuals may or may not be labeled as AI-generated contents. In most cases, their context will provide an informational surround, a meaningful context. The context may affect the reception of people to the digital visual and its consumption and / or usage.

As to what resulting output images may "work" or "pass muster," that does depend on the particular use case. If the depiction is a photorealistic one, is it accurate to the object and context? If it is about conveying an emotional message, eliciting an emotional response, is the image compelling? If the image is depicting a scene for a particular story, does it meet the depiction needs of characters and backdrops? And so on. The seeding image used to machine-generate the refined visual will not even be anything directly apparent in the eyes of the consumers of the final image.

Further, the A-GAI does not enable much in the way of control, at least not compared to the pixel-level and mathematical equation-level controls in various digital image editing tools. There are occasions when the A-GAI is totally bypassed; rather, a reference image is collected, edited, traced, and a style applied… to achieve the desirable visual. There are other work sequences (work pipelines) that may make much more sense and enable much more control. The magic of digital imagery happens in a variety of ways.

Caveat: Seeding images may be used again and again, in theory. They may be re-edited and applied to new output images. The challenge is that from a zoomed-out view, the original seeding image patterns may be seen as a pattern. For example, if an original seeding visual was used to depict, say, "a stack of papers" and then used again for "a dangerous alleyway," the two images will have sufficient similarities that they are recognizable as originating from a similar seed, even if different models and descriptive modifiers were used for the respective works. This may be a byproduct of the particular A-GAI platform, but this is an issue of which to be aware.

Another important caveat is that even though the Deep Dream Generator has a "Try it" button to emulate the text and visual prompts used to seed the image by the artmaking generative AI, each image looks to be a one-off and difficult to emulate closely. Some bits of style may transfer, but the core originality of an output image is hard to reproduce, to recreate. This is even when the original seeding image is available for re-use (or even if the seeding image hasn't been deleted from the page with the published final image). After some experiences with the DDG, one learns to appreciate the sparkling image when it emerges and not to delete willy-nilly. [A respected and prolific user of the site posted a note to the other "dreamers" on the Deep Dream Generator site asking them not to use the "Try it" button without crediting the original thinker by their public handle. She took exception to the use of "Try it" and then editing out her name from the "derived" future work. A long chain of threaded comments, some several paragraphs long, followed. One noted the commonality of remix culture. Another noted how much heavy lifting is done by the generative AI, not the human. Another reported on a person who was absconding with the prompts to a third-party site. Quite a few seemed to buy into the incantatory power of written prompts. All writing comes with a cost in human effort, time, investment, and thinking. That said, people signed away their rights releases to their ideas when they joined the platform. They are knowingly sharing on a social platform. It is perhaps onerous to have all future derived works carry the name of an individual who built their work on the micro-contributions of those whose works were used to train the LLMs. For many, the experiments of "Try it" end up on the proverbial cutting room floor. Regardless, this is a fractious topic. People do feel ownership over what they "create" with the aid of the generative AI. They are investing a part of their creative selves into the effort. Intriguingly, the seeding images made by the author feel somewhat throwaway, even those that have been refined digitally in post-production, to effect certain visual outcomes. Note that none of the principals were mentioned here. Sometimes, topics are easier to engage without people named, which can personalize the issue in ways that are undesirable. It is unclear if the originator of the original post would even want her name on some of the derived works depending on their quality. That issue did not come up in the open and public social discussion thread.

FUTURE RESEARCH DIRECTIONS

The use of seeding imagery in generative AI tools is part of wider user practice. However, it is not a common element in terms of extant research. In this work, various materials and digital approaches were described, but there are numerous other approaches that may be taken and other work sequences. Future research may benefit from other insights along different lines. It is too easy to fall into repeating recurring images and practicing hackneyed ideas. Additional research in this area of creating seeding visuals may help fulfill the extraordinary promise in the A-GAI space.

Another approach may involve a research angle. Since A-GAI technologies have been used by researchers as the basis for generating new visuals, from which synthetic visual data is extracted, this angle of using such imagery for research may be valuable.

The dynamics of artful interactions between the users in the Deep Dream Generator platform would also be promising to study. What are the remote social dynamics between the users of this technology? What encourages users to intercommunicate and about what topics? What are the characteristics of the short-term users of the site, the mid-term users of the site, and the long-term users of the site? What aesthetics are desirable among particular users in different regions, and why? There are many approaches that may be taken. What feeds the mystique of artmaking generative AI? What are ways to expand such mystique across different populations and to extend their interest over time? How do professional artists use such tools, and how do their senses of creativity expand and evolve? What are more sophisticated ways to use A-GAIs, and why?

There is personal satisfaction in making seeding images, independent of A-GAI technologies. The work is relaxed, loose, almost stream-of-consciousness. It reads of dabbling. It reads of limbering up for some actual work (in actual full paintings, in the generative AI). There are ways to recoup value, even with rinsing water from brushes. Why is there power in doodling and experimenting? (Perhaps the visual play evokes childhood?) As a side note: If artists are losing freelance jobs to generative AI (Ghosh & Fossas, 2022), perhaps enabling their work in creating seeding imagery may be a protection for their livelihoods although the work may be much less challenging than creating more finalized works. Having feeder image stock for seeding A-GAI tools can be value added. Such images are not as refined as stock images. Their draftiness and roughness are their strengths. *Ceteris paribus.* Such a shift would require more strategic and tactical designs for particular outputs. It would require some knowledge by users of how a particular seed might affect the output image from the A-GAI tools.

In the immersion in the artmaking generative AI space, many of the works are about imposing human vision and imagination on the A-GAI tool and acquiring outputs that reflect that. There are other rarer approaches where the machine imagination is given free reign. There is promise in that approach as well, which may prove valuable, artistically, and research-wise, and in other ways.

CONCLUSION

A-GAIs are in their early phases. An A-GAI tool shows "naivete of the world, its wonky physics, the extra limbs, the mixed species of animals, and the imaginarium" (Hai-Jew, July 8, 2023). For many years, they could not draw grids. They could not wrangle numbers or letters or characters. The tools are evolving, however, and they are now more and more capable. Based on feedback from users and other details, the makers of A-GAIs are reworking their technologies. There is much yet to come. People will build up their knowledge of such systems and offer original works well into the future (perhaps even if they do not improve their actual drawing and painting skills in analog materials and in digital canvases). GAI tools can auto-generate images that "embody artistic intentions" (Pan, 2021, p. 52). Seeding images—used as prompts—enable the sense of human touch in human-computer co-created art. They enable the inclusion of both analog (material) and digital (virtual) seeds into the work stream in the making of folk art. They enable fresh visuals beyond what generative AI tools may create alone, and these visuals enable new seeing. They enable the building out of a "long tail" of visual works that explore variance; they enable the expression of fresh talent. The uses of seeding images in A-GAI may mitigate some of the current over-reliance on paragraphs of text, dozens of modifying tags, and language-based verbiage alone. For those who include the seeding image with their refined final image, they will enable others to emulate the visual style of the refined image via the A-GAI platform (those who remove the seeding images take away from the power of the A-GAI tool to reproduce the look-and-feel more fully).

There is a value in human touch in art, even if it shows struggle and imperfection, especially if it shows struggle and imperfection. So much of human life is lived in human-made and machine-made artifice and the imagined and imaginary. So much is lived in the lulling comforts and informative spaces of aesthetics and design. The GAI tools that have come to the fore will further amplify the abilities of people to express with pixel-perfect allure for themselves and each other. They will continue to provide entertainment and surprises and laughter at what the machine generates from the seeding text and visuals.

There will be space for those artists who choose to eschew computational means. There are those who will define what art spaces are theirs and theirs alone, and that is right and good, too. Regardless, generative AI tools are contributing to the look-and-feel of this time period in human history. In real time, people's eyes are adjusting to the changes.

DEDICATION

Thanks to the various organizations and companies that have created and evolved the generative AI tools and then made much of it available for general public use, for free, no less. It is so heartening to see the advances in tool capabilities, such as the models that enable accurate spelling and inclusion of text in the output visuals.

REFERENCES

Al-Khazraji, L. R., Abbas, A. R., & Jamil, A. S. (2022). Employing neural style transfer for generating deep dream images. *ARO (Koya)*, 10(2), 134–141. 10.14500/aro.11051

Al-Khazraji, L. R., Abbas, A. R., & Jamil, A. S. (2023). The effect of changing targeted layers of the Deep Dream technique using VGG-16 Model. *International Journal of Online & Biomedical Engineering*, 19(3), 34–47. 10.3991/ijoe.v19i03.37235

Al-Khazraji, L. R., Abbas, A. R., & Jamil, A. S. (2023). A systematic review of Deep Dream. *Iraqi Journal of Computers, Communications. Control and Systems Engineering*, 23(2), 192–209.

Baluja, S., & Fischer, I. (2017). Adversarial transformation networks: Learning to generate adversarial examples. *arXiv preprint arXiv:1703.09387.*

Bruder, J. (2018). Where the sun never shines: Emerging paradigms of post-enlightened cognition. *Digital Culture & Society*, 4(1), 133–154. 10.14361/dcs-2018-0109

Chatterjee, A. (2022). Art in an age of artificial intelligence. *Frontiers in Psychology, 13*, 1 - 9.

Chen, W., Shidujaman, M., Jin, J., & Ahmed, S. U. (2020). A methodological approach to create interactive art in artificial intelligence. *HCI International 2020–Late Breaking Papers: Cognition, Learning and Games: 22nd HCI International Conference, HCII 2020, Copenhagen, Denmark, July 19–24, 2020Proceedings*, 22, 13–31.

Cherti, M., Kégl, B., & Kazakçı, A. (2017, November). Out-of-class novelty generation: an experimental foundation. In *2017 IEEE 29th International Conference on Tools with Artificial Intelligence (ICTAI)* (pp. 1312-1319). IEEE.

Elgammal, A., Liu, B., Elhoseiny, M., & Mazzone, M. (2017). Can: Creative adversarial networks, generating" art" by learning about styles and deviating from style norms. *arXiv preprint arXiv:1706.07068.*

Franceschelli, G., & Musolesi, M. (2022). Copyright in generative deep learning. *Data & Policy*, 4, e17–e1. 10.1017/dap.2022.10

Gatys, L. A., Ecker, A. S., & Bethge, M. (2017). Texture and art with deep neural networks. *Current Opinion in Neurobiology*, 46, 178–186. 10.1016/j.conb.2017.08.01928926765

Ghosh, A., & Fossas, G. (2022). Can there be art without an artist? *arXiv preprint arXiv:2209.07667.*

Gkotzos, K. (2015, Oct. 30). *Google's DeepDream: Algorithms on LSD.* Media Studies, University of Amsterdam.

Gruner, D. T., & Csikszentmihalyi, M. (2019). Engineering creativity in an age of artificial intelligence. *The Palgrave Handbook of Social Creativity Research*, 447-462.

Hai-Jew, S. (2023, July 8). *Creating seeding visuals to prompt art-making generative AIs.* Slideshow. SlideShare. Retrieved Dec. 10, 2023, from https://www.slideshare.net/ShalinHaiJew/creating-seeding-visuals-to-prompt-artmaking-generative-ais

Hertzmann, A. (2019). Aesthetics of neural network art. *arXiv preprint arXiv:1903.05696.*

Jiang, H. H., Brown, L., Cheng, J., Khan, M., Gupta, A., Workman, D., & Gebru, T. (2023, August). AI art and its impact on artists. In *Proceedings of the 2023 AAAI/ACM Conference on AI, Ethics, and Society* (pp. 363-374). 10.1145/3600211.3604681

Lazarow, J., Jin, L., & Tu, Z. (2017). Introspective neural networks for generative modeling. In *Proceedings of the IEEE International Conference on Computer Vision* (pp. 2774-2783). IEEE.

Leach, N. (2019). Do robots dream of digital sheep. *Proceedings of ACADIA 19: Ubiquity and Autonomy.* 10.52842/conf.acadia.2019.298

Li, W., Zhang, P., Zhang, L., Huang, Q., He, X., Lyu, S., & Gao, J. (2019). Object-driven text-to-image synthesis via adversarial training. In *Proceedings of the IEEE/CVF Conference on Computer Vision and Pattern Recognition* (pp. 12174-12182). IEEE.

Luo, L., Sandler, M., Lin, Z., Zhmoginov, A., & Howard, A. (2020). Large-scale generative data-free distillation. *arXiv preprint arXiv:2012.05578.*

Luo, R. (2019/2020). Artistic intelligence. *Kritikos. Proceedings of Art Machines:International Symposium on Computational Media Art,* 12 - 19.

Maerten, A. S., & Soydaner, D. (2023). From paintbrush to pixel: A review of deep neural networks in AI-generated art. *arXiv preprint arXiv:2302.10913.*

Mahmud, B., Hong, G., & Fong, B. (2023). A Study of Human–AI Symbiosis for Creative Work: Recent Developments and Future Directions in Deep Learning. *ACM Transactions on Multimedia Computing Communications and Applications*, 20(2), 1–21. 10.1145/3542698

Merchán, E. C. G., & Molina, M. (2020). A machine consciousness architecture based on deep learning and gaussian processes. *Hybrid Artificial Intelligent Systems: 15th International Conference, HAIS 2020, Gijón, Spain, November 11-13, 2020Proceedings*, 15, 350–361.

Odena, A., Dumoulin, V., & Olah, C. (2016). Deconvolution and checkerboard artifacts. *Distill*, 1(10), e3. 10.23915/distill.00003

Pan, P. (2021). "Deepfakes" and the end of the photographic age. *Aporia*, 21, 52–64.

Poole, B., Jain, A., Barron, J. T., & Mildenhall, B. (2022). Dreamfusion: Text-to-3d using 2d diffusion. *arXiv preprint arXiv:2209.14988.*

Qiao, H., Liu, V., & Chilton, L. (2022, June). Initial images: using image prompts to improve subject representation in multimodal AI generated art. In *Proceedings of the 14th Conference on Creativity and Cognition* (pp. 15-28). 10.1145/3527927.3532792

Schröter, J. (2023). The AI Image, the Dream, and the Statistical Unconscious. *Image*, 37(1), 112.

Wang, G., & Torr, P. H. (2022). Traditional classification neural networks are good generators: They are competitive with DDPMs and GANs. *arXiv preprint arXiv:2211.14794.*

Wellner, G. (2019). Digital subjectivity: From a network metaphor to a layer-plateau model. *Digital Subjectivity: From a Network Metaphor to a Layer-Plateau Model*, 55-66.

Wyse, L. (2019). Mechanisms of artistic creativity in deep learning neural networks. *arXiv preprint arXiv:1907.00321.*

Yeh, R. A., Chen, C., Yian Lim, T., Schwing, A. G., Hasegawa-Johnson, M., & Do, M. N. (2017). Semantic image inpainting with deep generative models. In *Proceedings of the IEEE Conference on Computer Vision and Pattern Recognition* (pp. 5485-5493). 10.1109/CVPR.2017.728

Yuan, T., Chen, X., & Wang, S. (2022, Mar.). *Gorgeous pixel artwork generation with VQGAN-CLIP*. Preprint. 1 - 9.

ADDITIONAL READING

Hai-Jew, S. (2024). *Generative AI in Teaching and Learning*. IGI Global.

KEY TERMS AND DEFINITIONS

Analog: Physical or material.

Artmaking Generative AI: A technology that can take text and visual inputs to prompt a visual output; based on large language models (LLMs), also known as text-to-image (TTI) tools.

Digital: Electronic technology (based on numeric digits)

Seeding Imagery: A base (or reference) image from which an artmaking generative AI may create a derived and original new image.

Section 2
Computational Exploration of Art and Culture

Chapter 3
Athos Bulcão's Tile Distribution Logic Using Common Digital Art

Marília Lyra Bergamo
https://orcid.org/0000-0001-9105-7886
University of Newcastle, Australia

ABSTRACT

Athos Bulcão is a renowned Brazilian artist recognized for his outstanding surface work with tiles on murals of Brasília's buildings, the 1960s-designed modern capital of Brazil, and other localities. The beauty of his work can be expressed by how it has become part of the city landscape and people's everyday encounters. It is also very contemporaneous regarding how he used logic to organize his tiles, using rotation and pattern distribution, allowing chance and error while architectural surfaces are assembled. Explaining logic and making it into tile distribution is difficult to explain to students; using paper prototypes helps, but Common Digital Art coding takes it a step further in the complexity of tiling art. This chapter proposes a method for students to learn those skills and also to learn to develop their logic if they intend to create authorial tiling works in murals.

INTRODUCTION

Brasília is the capital of Brazil, an idealization project that had started more than 100 years before the first design draft. José Bonifácio de Andrada Silva suggested changing the capital to the country's interior and the city's name in 1823 to protect the capital from possible attacks by foreign forces. Surrounded by the prophecy of a Catholic saint called Dom Bosco that a promised land would emerge between the 15th and 20th parallels, precisely where Brasília was built, the city is, after all, a livid monument of modernism.

The project emerged during the 1050s in the government of the iconic president, Jucelino Kubitchek. The entire scheme was monumental, and the architect responsible for it was the renowned Oscar Niemeyer. The entire city was projected from scratch to become a garden city, and after more than 60 years of existence, a lot has changed. Gardens have grown more prominent, but many of their original designs coexist with the locals that sometimes cross those modern monuments without even knowing how it all had come to live.

DOI: doi

In this everyday scenario, in the middle of the city park, a rest stop had an astonishing surface artwork by the artist Athos Bulcão, a friend of Oscar Niemeyer who became an official member of the Brasília construction team. A joggler can easily relax from his daily exercise, leaning on the wall without paying attention to the logical complexity of the composition formed by a series of black and white tiles where her body rests (Ribeiro & Perpétuo, 2008, p. 142).

Athos Bulcão tiles have interesting logic; each surface possesses its own intrinsic rules of distribution that were planned by the artist and mapped as groups of possible arrangements. In one of the archive's official pictures of Brasília's construction (Ribeiro & Perpétuo, 2008, p. 6), it is possible to see him holding an umbrella and explaining how to display his tiles to the constructors. He could not have supervised each of the works, and it is clear that he embraced chance due to accepting human error and the enormous space that some compositions occupy. Now, his work can be perceived as living and organic compositions, resulting in vivid structures of color where repetition seems absent, and logic has extensive but limited possible alternatives.

Those artworks' proximity to people's everyday lives can motivate local students to experiment with Athos Bulcão artwork. However, explaining the logic and making it into tile distribution is difficult; using paper prototypes helps, but Common Digital Art coding takes it a step further in the complexity of tiling art. Teaching students to develop their logic is even harder if they intend to create authorial tiling works in murals using digital technology. This chapter will describe how this process of paper prototyping, logic understanding, coding recreation and computer-assisted manufactured machines can help students overcome these difficulties.

Although this chapter will use Athos Bulcão's artwork in tile composition, the skills that will be demonstrated are from a broader understanding of using logic as material to compose dynamic and visual structures. Having an artist's work in the background exemplifies the processes adopted here. Because this chapter uses concrete real work as an example, examining historical sites and guiding diagrams to deconstruct them into coding is feasible. Still, navigating the observable legacy of Athos Bulcão artworks is a visualizing approach to reconstructing the thinking of modern architecture, design and art.

Finally, this chapter illustrates and explains how prototyping, digital coding, and manufactured crafting solve the process of experimentation and teaching such a complex form of art development in a classroom. Please access the online resources in references to view or reuse the codings used in this chapter directly.

BACKGROUND

In Brasília, a person will not find street names and the entire city was planned to be navigated logically. The city project is based on the design of an aircraft, with one wing turned to the north and another turned to the south. An entire avenue called *Eixão* crosses both wings with a distance of fourteen kilometers between one point and the other. The aircraft faces east, and in its nose, it welcomes the buildings representing the powers of a democracy: judiciary, legislative and executive. Inside this logic, moving around ample avenues, are the monumental architectonic sites of Oscar Niemeyer, and inside the residential areas, buildings are sustained by pilotis. While some distance is better for seeing the architectonic sites, most Athos Bulcão artwork can be seen by close eyes within the buildings or between straight lines at the pilotis.

While Brasilia was under construction, Athos Bulcão was developing his language in tiles distribution. A diverse artist, his interests were broad. In an inventory of his creations, it is possible to see works from different media, complex use of colors, abstract and expressive drawings, and many different techniques (Ribeiro & Perpétuo, 2018). His tile panels are the ones where language has achieved extreme complexity. To achieve this level of expressiveness, the artist had to be multidisciplinary, and the inventory produced a specific view where its historical context could be understood. It also reveals the technical challenges regarding producing such tile artworks and their monumental sizes. Unfortunately, the document is only available in Portuguese. However, the measurements, location and historical time information are easily accessible in the online document.

Figure 1 shows an image of the concrete relief made for the National Theater of Brasília. According to the authors of the inventory, the relief panes are molded in five-piece patterns multiples of 30 centimeters. There is a total of 3,391 pieces fixed on the south and north facades of the building. The concrete pieces are fixed on two walls of concrete slopes located on the gables or facades from the sides of the theater. The facades of the National Theater are monumental artworks due to the vast space they occupy and because the sun's movement during the day makes the shadows dance within the structure, creating a movement where the relief can be seen. The action of time also brings some marks that will make it possible to navigate this composition without losing sight of where the beginning and the end are. Nothing in Athos Bulcão's work for the National Theater in Brasilia can be perceived as linear. It differs from Athos Bulcão's latter works, which were more intimate and complex.

Figure 1. Relief in white painted concrete, National Theater

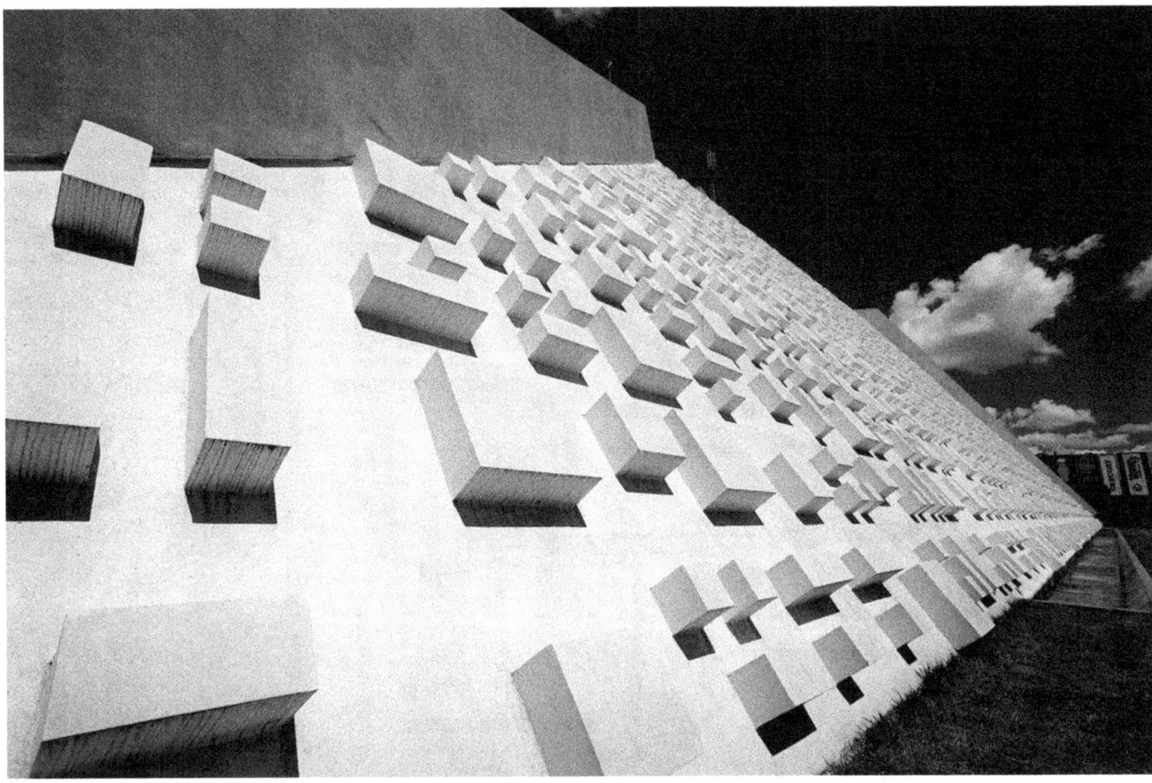

Note. Athos Bulcão, 1966. White-painted concrete relief, National Theatre Claudio Santoro, Brasilia-DF, Brazil. Photo: Athos Bulcão Foundation Collection / Patrick Grosner.

In a different project, a tile panel to the TV Tower in Brasília, Figure 2, the language still in development already show complexity. Athos Bulcão uses only two types of tiles in different positions to create the composition, and there is no area in highlighting where a figure could be perceived against the background. The entire pieces reflect movement, from the arrows created with the triangles that make the perception of directions to follow to the lines broken from horizontal to vertical without long line formations.

Figure 2. Tile panel, TV Tower in Brasília

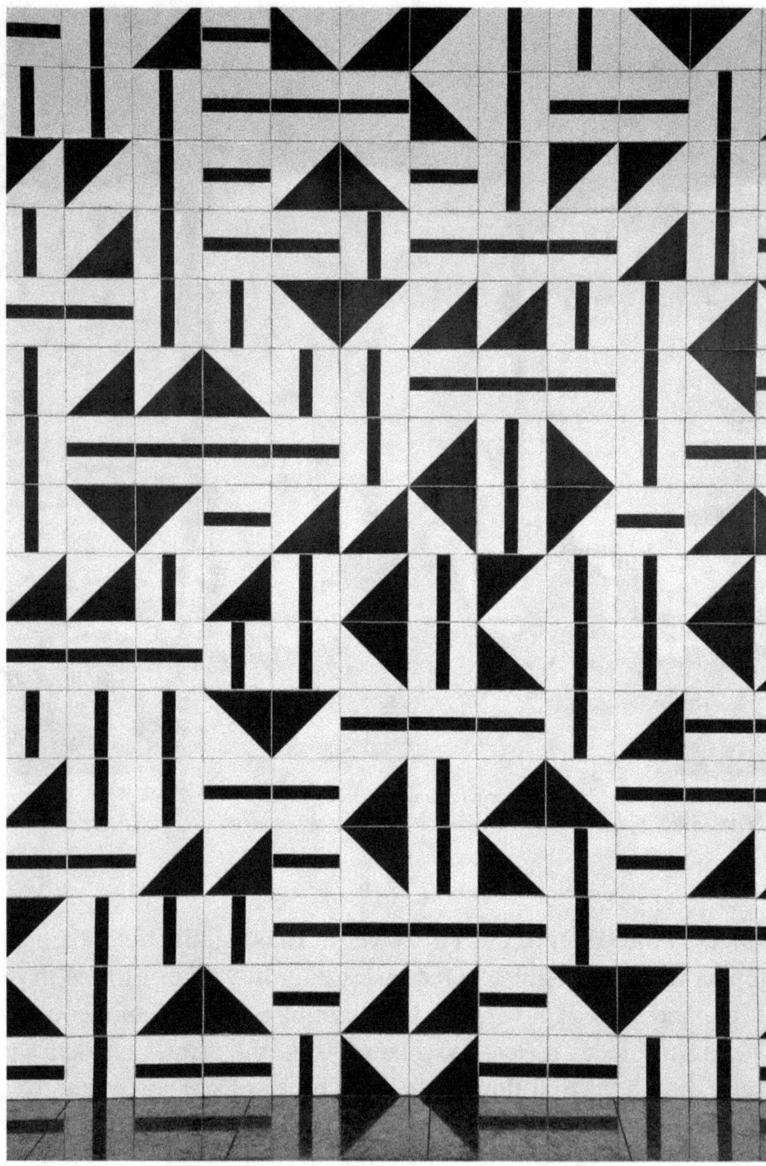

Note. Athos Bulcão, 1966. Tile panel, TV Tower, Brasilia-DF, Brazil. Photo: Athos Bulcão Foundation Collection / Edgar César.

In Figure 3, the language has become complex, and the form inside the tile itself is formed before the arrangements. Using a complex drawing in one tiling and an empty one, Athos Bulcão created a surface where the visual movement happens within the tile and the distribution. The artist uses only rotation, blank areas, and white lines are perceived between the organization. With the tiles with a form inside, sometimes a semicircle emerges within the visual distribution. Due to the great contrast between black and white, the entire panel vibrates, not allowing the eyes to rest. This idea is contradictory, considering the piece is a resting point within a city park. Also, the artwork is very intimate, within the proportion of humans, compared to the monumental work presented in Figure 1. However, it is extensively dispersed; there are many similar resting points within the 420 hectares of the city park, all with Athos Bulcão's tile panels, drinking water distribution and concrete benches connected to the panels.

Figure 3. Tile panel, rest stop, city park

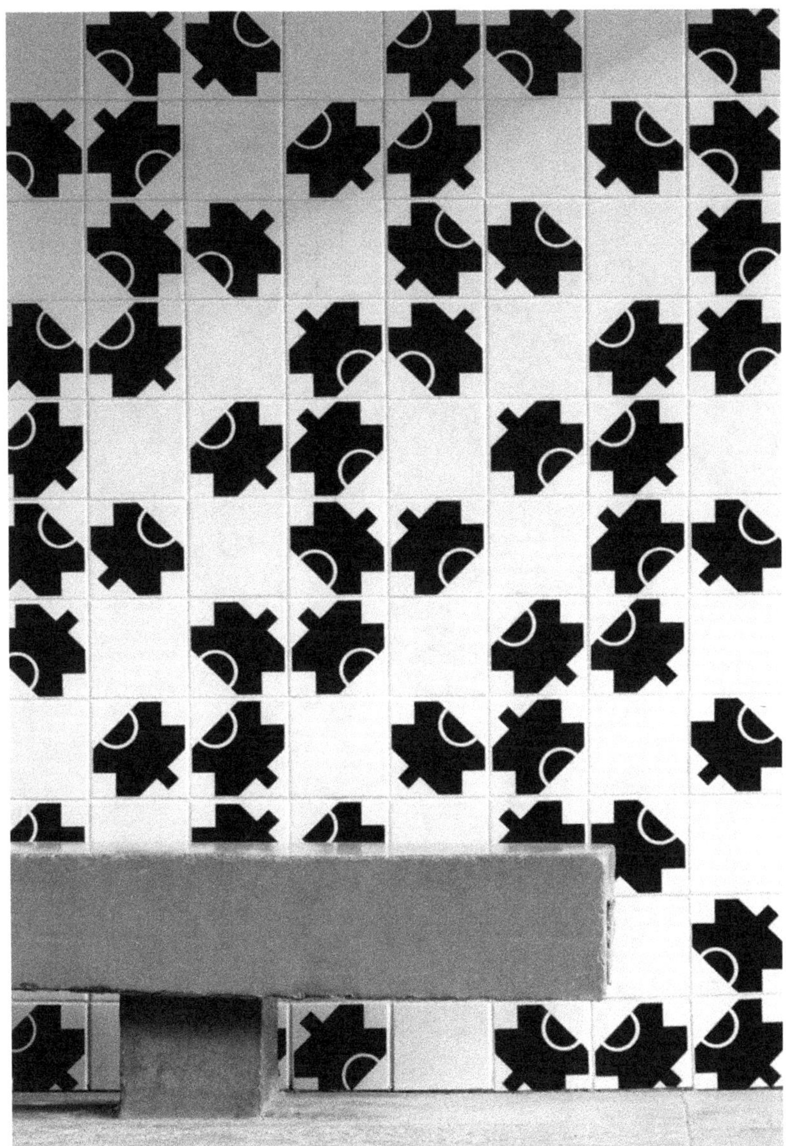

Note. Athos Bulcão, 1985. Tile panel, City Park, Brasilia-DF, Brazil. Photo: Athos Bulcão Foundation Collection / Patrick Grosner.

Figure 4 presents the 1998 tile panel created for the Institute of Arts at the University of Brasilia. The campus is a tribute to modernism and a traditional site of labor disputes within the government of rights. It was also critical during Brazil's military dictatorial period between 1964 and 1985. The tile developed by Athos Bulcão in this project is complex; it has many levels of perceived abstract movement created by the different forms of arcs, circles and triangles. There is also a perceived color pallet of greens and blues. Very different from the project of the TV tower, this one seems to demonstrate an interest in experimenting with the tile, to create a tile that itself was a painting, and also to be randomly rotated and distributed within the building walls. The perception of movement is highly dynamic, and the entire piece seems alive, reflecting the day's sun and shadows.

Figure 4. Institute of Arts at the University of Brasilia

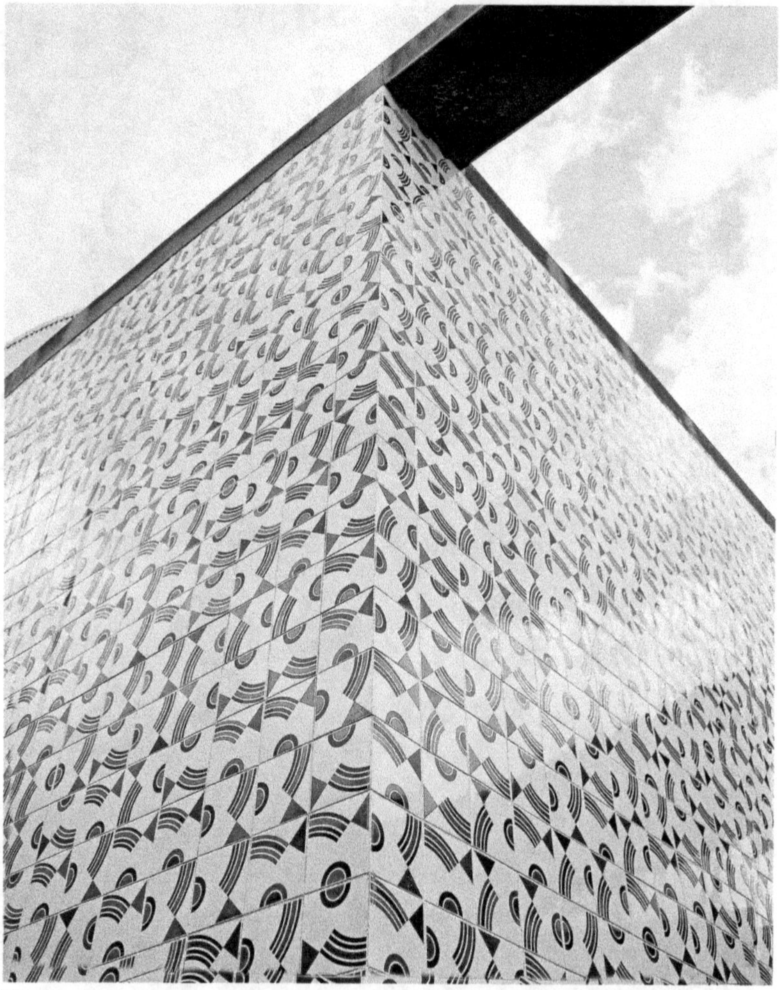

Note. Athos Bulcão, 1998. Tile panel, Institute of Arts at the University of Brasília, Brasilia-DF, Brazil. Photo: Athos Bulcão Foundation Collection / Tuca Reinés.

The artworks presented in this section are a selection in order of the difficulty level of reproduction as abstract logic. For a better understanding of Athos Bulcão's history and art, it is advisable to access the documentation provided by the exhibition by (Centro Cultural do Banco do Brasil, 2024), which was documented both in Portuguese and English. The exhibition was developed by a highly competent curatorial team and navigated many cities within Brazil.

LOGIC DIAGRAMS

This chapter section shows how Athos Bulcão's work is based on abstract forms and logic. He made some diagrams (Centro Cultural do Banco do Brasil, 2024) where his logic was demonstrated and planned; in one example (p. 141), two thinner arches are placed inside a thicker one; the thinner ones have an opening. The composition is distributed across four tiles, but instead of maintaining the original composition, Athos Bulcão makes a distance with irregular angles and redistributes the content again into four tiles. This act creates an irregular effect on the structure, which is then repositioned by rotating the pieces on the mural. This design was created in 1983 and is a *Sambódromo*, Rio de Janeiro project. The original drawing of *Sambódromo* is 92 x 158 cm and made by Naquin over tracing paper. In another example (p. 129), Athos Bulcão creates a massive map of random tile placements for the builders to follow. The original design was developed for the TV Tower, Brasília tiled panel. The drawing made in 1966 was also Nanquin and over tracing paper, 46 x 180 cm. Even with such a detailed map, there is always the possibility of misreading one tile for another. Thus, chance was accumulated through the various tile distribution assembling processes. It is even more apparent in the design of *Estação de Transbordo da Lapa* in the city of Salvador in 1982 (p. 131); in this composition, color is added to the drawing using color pencil and Naquin over tracing paper, the piece is 74 x 132 cm. The addition of color creates another level of complexity, but also dynamic on the entire perception of the piece. In this section of the chapter, logic Diagrams based on the original designs of Athos Bulcão *Sambódromo*, the TV tower, and *Estação de Transbordo da Lapa* will be analyzed. Those diagrams are composition schemes of abstract drawings and maps of the distribution of tiles.

The logic diagram in Figure 5 is a schematic drawing of tiles to *Sambódromo* in Rio de Janeiro, made in 1983. From right to left, button top, students should be encouraged to draw those elements in squared papers. Drawing stimulates the mind to think abstractly while you still use concrete perceptions within the paper and the pencil. Squared papers are helpful because the students can visually perceive the proportion of abstract forms and, as such, are free to understand the drawing in front of them continually.

Figure 5. Logic drawing diagram, to be used to learn how to create the tiles using squared paper

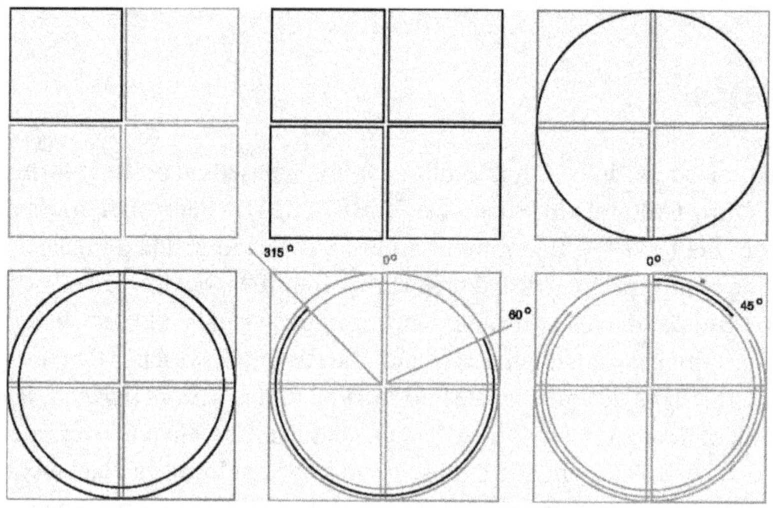

Note. This image replicates the drawing process of abstract figures used by Athos Bulcão. In this reconstruction, the students should start drawing a square, followed by three more proportional ones. The next step is to draw a circle within the limits of the squares, then draw a reduced circle within the first one. Finally, a first arc should be placed within both circles, starting at more or less 30 degrees on the second square to 315 degrees (a quarter of the first square). The last drawing is an arc from 0 to 45 degrees in the first square—an illustration by Marília Bergamo.

Once students have tested the drawing on Figure 5, it is essential to separate the tiles; the process may consist of drawing them again, but they are now separated (Figure 6). This process, although repetitive, is informative because it motivates the students to think about the same drawing using a different logic. Figure 6 demonstrates how a student can do the second approach of drawing.

Figure 6. Logic drawing diagram with separated tiles

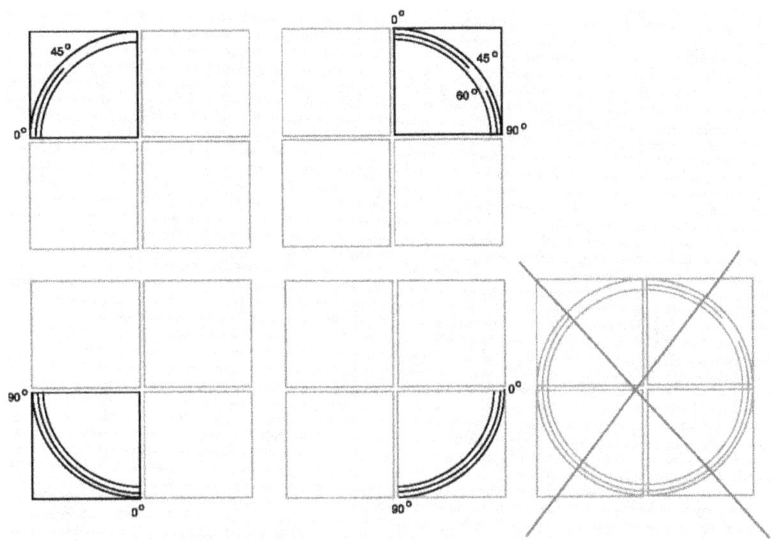

Note. This image represents the same drawing process, but each tile is separate. In this reconstruction, the students should start drawing a square; within this square, create three arcs. The graph considers 0 degrees on the bottom left, so one arc should be the width of the square from 0 to 90 degrees, a second smaller one again from 0 to 90 degrees and a third one within both arcs from 0 to 45 degrees. The student would follow the process to the fourth tile following a logical drawing. Finally, one last image shows tiles should not be grouped as a circle—an illustration by Marília Bergamo.

Athos Bulcão's original drawing has the exact circle group placement with a cross, like Figure 6, indicating that the disposition of the tiles should never be like a circle; any other position is ok. At this moment of learning, avoiding this form of grouping depends only on the student's perception; later in this chapter, it will be essential to demonstrate that coding this rule is fundamental to creating a dynamic rule for this specific design.

In Figure 7, it is possible to see the reproduction of Athos Bulcão's original distribution map. In this case, the distribution map does not need to be long but is wide enough to establish the number of available possibilities.

Figure 7. Distribution map of tiles

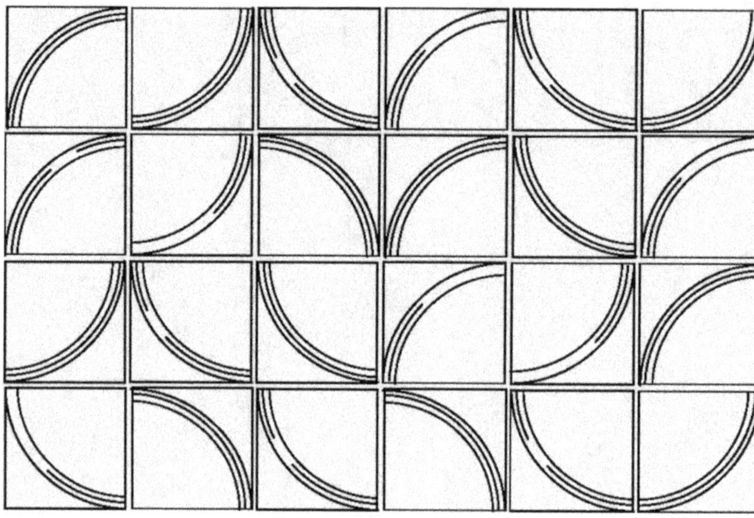

Note. This image shows that students can replicate the same pattern in different rotations and as many times as possible, just having to avoid the circle configuration described in Figure 2.—an illustration by Marília Bergamo.

While the diagrams illustrated in Figures 5 and 6 are exercises to think about the possible forms of drawing inside the tile, Figure 7 presents the challenge of distributing a form thought space. The same level of thinking can be achieved using a simple shape; in Figure 8, a logic diagram of only two designs represents Athos Bulcão's solution to cover the surface of the hall of the TV tower of Brasilia.

Figure 8. Distribution map of simpler shapes

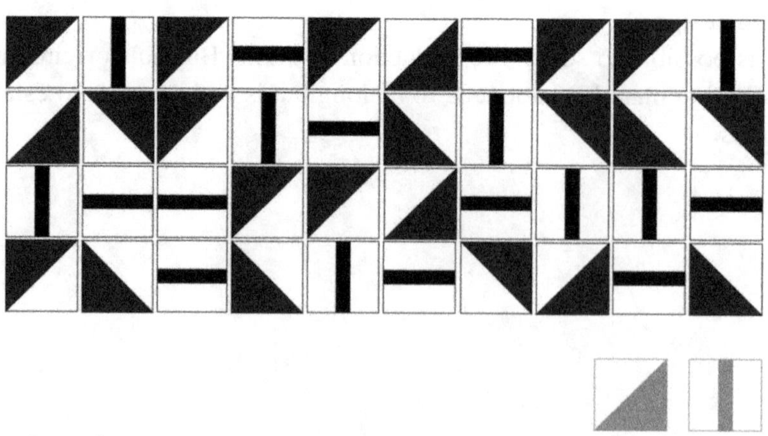

Note. This image shows only two shapes to create a compelling distribution map using rotation—an illustration by Marília Bergamo.

The last diagram presented in this section in Figure 9 could be replicated only by coloring the surface of a squared paper following a limit of six possibilities. Here, logic is built only with colors; the form is created when colors are placed together within the distribution. In this case, blank areas are also possible alternatives influencing the space. As wide as the composition follows, possible alternatives also grow. The most interesting point here is that students would find forms while drawing and may think about what other abstract forms can emerge from extending, adding or removing color from a specific square. This exercise works with reduced color pallets and fewer square fill forms. Otherwise, observing patterns would become too complex. In Athos Bulcão's work for *Estação de Transbordo da Lapa*, the coloured pattern he created is a large surface, and it is challenging to find repetitive patterns, but similarities can emerge in the form of arrows and blank spaces.

Figure 9. The distribution map of colors follows only six alternatives

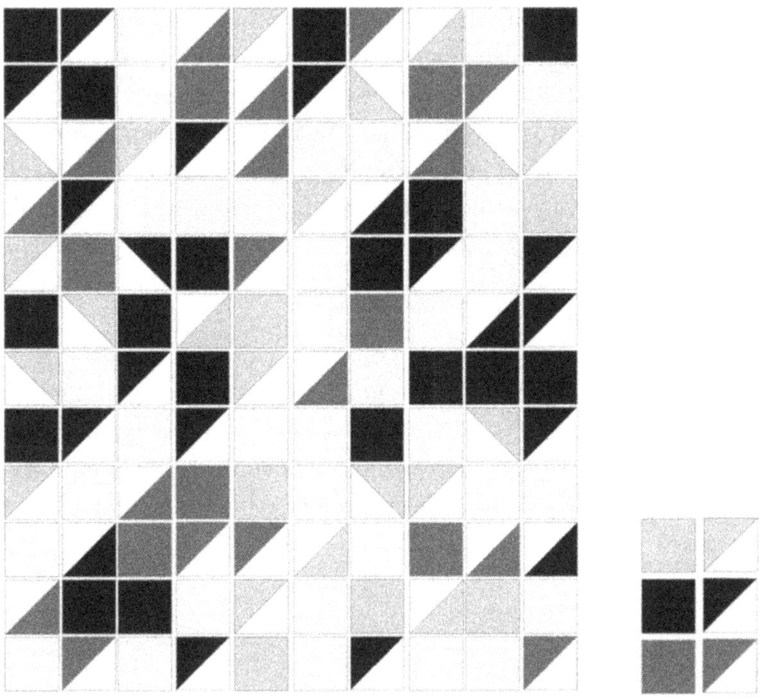

Note. This illustration shows a possible configuration of coloring using limited options in color and forms of painting. There are only two ways of painting. First, paint part of the square as if it were a triangle; rotation is available. A complete painting of the square is also possible, as well as leaving it blank—an illustration by Marília Bergamo.

LOGIC PROTOTYPE

This section introduces Common Digital Art logic within this chapter to resolve the context of education through prototyping. Logic can take different forms: tactile, experimental, and abstract thinking. Paper prototyping is tactile thinking and demonstrates how a theoretical subject, such as artistic logic, can be made more tangible to students.

Using papers with a limited color pallet as modules, those can be manually organized to create different arrangements. Determined color palettes are part of the fundamentals of creative thinking because the limitation of color helps focus on the relation between the ones available in the composition. Another possibility is abstract drawings over the square paper, which work if it is also made as modules. The modular paper prototype is the most suitable tool to give the Common Digital Art logic a concrete reality in which students can manipulate the pieces with their hands before moving to more abstract thinking.

Paper is accessible and can be purchased in colors or different textures and forms. It can also be easily painted and transformed into patterns. This material's flexibility makes it a very appropriate solution to engage students in converting touchable pieces into logic. Using hands and playing with composing to experiment with materials has always been part of creative processes. As a result, students should be encouraged to play with it first and then take notes of the most promising configurations.

Prototyping With Triangles

Figure 10 demonstrates how to explore different triangle sizes and positions using triangles to find configurations within the tile area. In this case, yellow will work as an expansive light compared to black and dark blue. Forms created by blue and black will be detached from the proximity of yellow and white. The visual movement is a constant vibration between what is the figure and what is the background due to those color light effects.

Figure 10. Paper prototype using color paper shaped of triangles

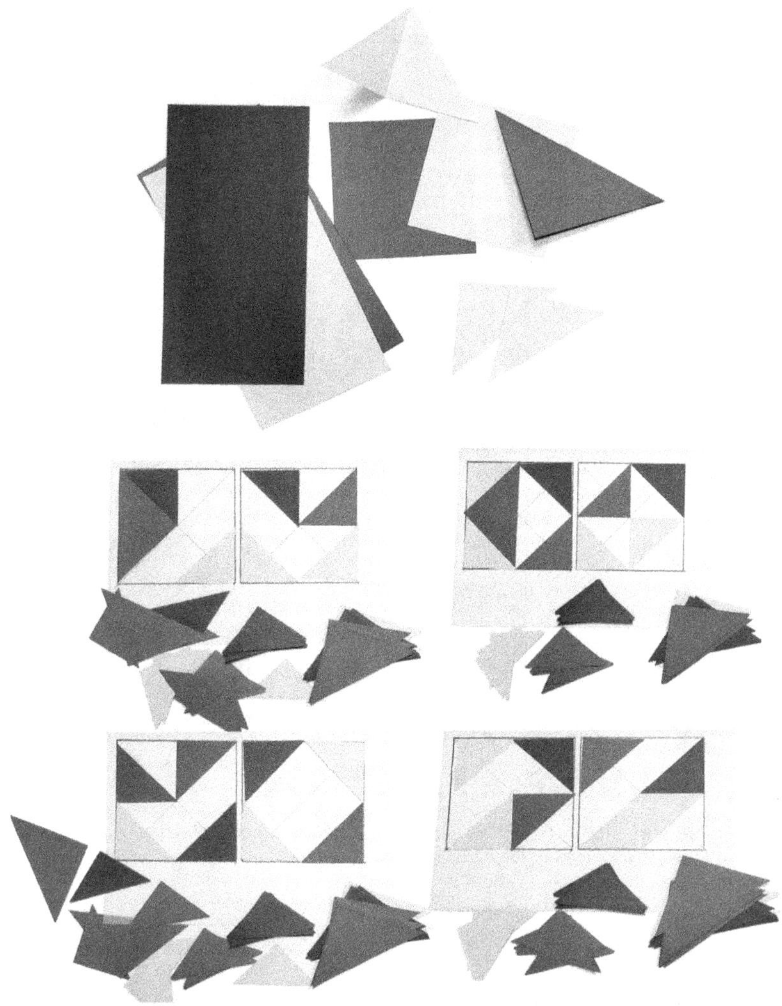

Note. This image presents a series of black, yellow and blue papers of 12,5 x 25 centimeters. The paper was folded into squares, then sequentially folded into triangles to be cut. Two squares of 12,5 x 12,5 were drawn on tracing paper, and the space within the squares was split into two crossing diagonals. The image also presents four prospects with the number of possibilities available within this set —photo by Marília Bergamo.

Prototyping With Triangles and Rectangles

Figure 11 shows a more straightforward experiment with paper prototyping. In this case, a light blue paper was cut into triangles of 4 x 4 x 5,5 cm and rectangles of 1 x 4 cm. Those two simple forms can be distributed through a grid of 5 x 7 squares, 4 x 4 cm each over tracing paper. The organization can be random or built over a criterion the student defines. Again, taking notes is fundamental; if the conditions are not random, it will be necessary if the student intends to transform it into logic.

Figure 11. Paper prototype with triangles and rectangles

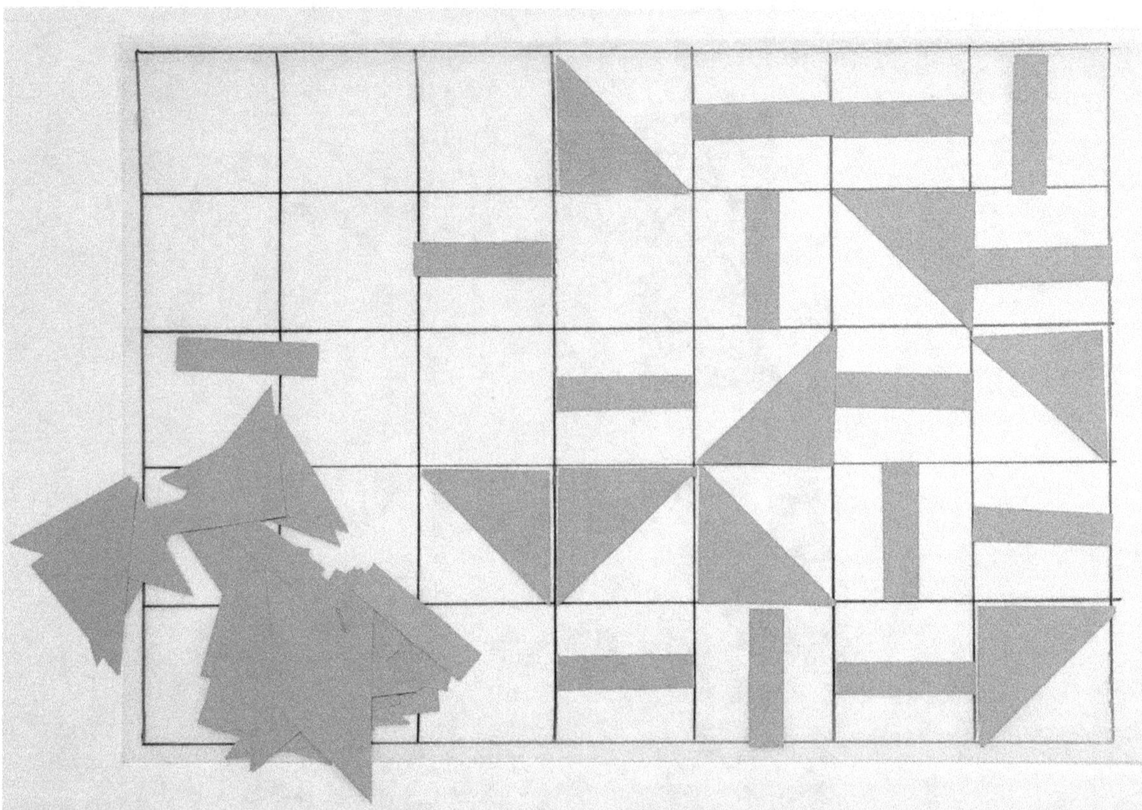

Note. This image presents a series of light blue papers cut into triangles and rectangles. On tracing paper, a series of 4x4cm squares create frames to experiment with the rotation of the forms in the blue paper—a photo by Marília Bergamo.

Prototyping With Drawing Tiles

Figure 12 shows the potential to create a prototype with drawings, which relies on the artists to make a drawing that could be transferred to a module. Previously, within the section about Athos Bulcão's artwork, it was highlighted that at some moments, it is possible to observe that the artist had developed his particular technique where inside the tile itself, he started to include the logic that previously would be configurated through larger spaces. It is the case from the TV Tower to the City Park projects in Brasília. The latter is a simple form configuration into space, the former a configuration of forms within one tile, and organized with blanc spaces. Relying on the artist's choice rather than the transferable logic to the computer is the case of prototyping with drawing tiles.

Figure 12. Paper prototype with drawings

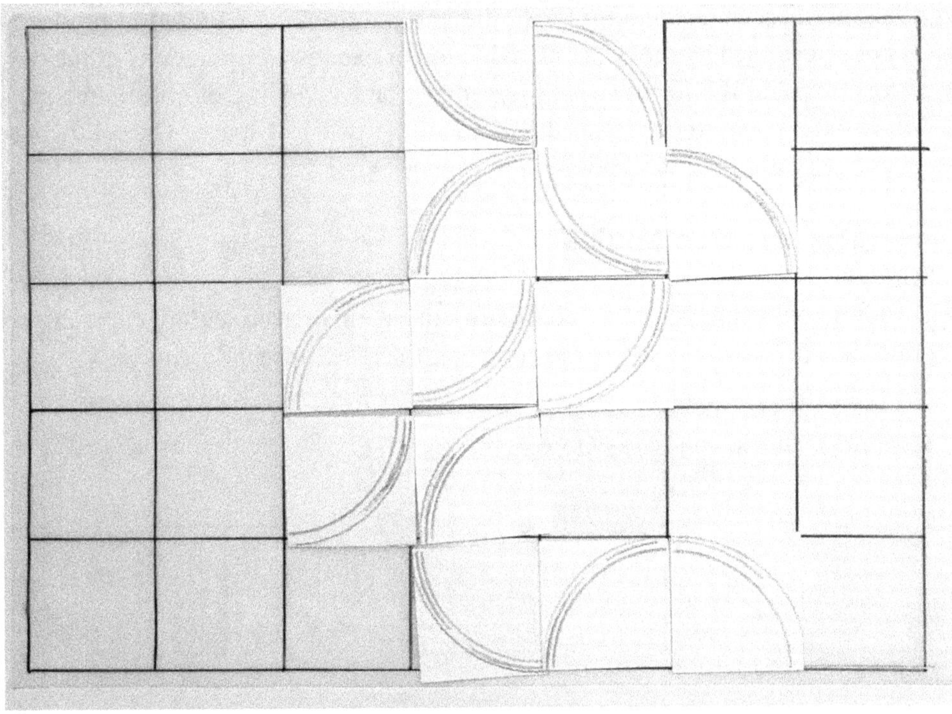

Note. The image shows some drawings within a square paper organized within the grid. On tracing paper, the same series of 4x4 squares created to prototype with triangles and rectangles is used to configure possible arrangements—a photo by Marília Bergamo.

CODING WITH P5.JS

Common Digital Art logic is paramount in this section to encourage creativity through abstract thinking, and here, it takes the form of coding. The coding solutions presented here cannot be considered definitive, and students should explore abstract thinking differently. Finding a personal solution to the problem is where the advance of authoring coding can occur. Usually, this is a moment where students require more guidance and attention to become confident that their logic is not incorrect. They may achieve a result slower than other people's logic, but the most crucial point is that they find a solution. It must resolve the aesthetical challenge of transforming an abstract composition of paper into a language the computer can replicate.

This chapter will present Common Digital Art logic in the format of P5.js coding, a well-documented language with the advantage of being facilitated using an online editor that allows solutions to be shared between collaborative teams and makes it easy for a tutor to offer feedback and help. There are many documented tutorials on mastering P5.Js, which is different from the goal of this chapter. The intention here is to introduce specific coding contexts necessary to transform a paper prototype into an abstract logic. It is essential to encourage students to have their free account so that no work is lost. P5.js is prepared for use in digital art, facilitating the development of abstract forms using 2D and 3D primitive functions that help art, design, and architecture students manipulate these forms into abstract logic without previous knowledge of a more advanced understanding of coding.

Finally, it is crucial to understand that with the abstract thinking required to produce any coding, the solution is not determined by the concrete reduction or expansion limitations of the paper, allowing recursivity of forms within the forms, which is a robust understanding of constraints presented at the time when Athos Bulcão had to deal with the limits of the physical space. The following section will demonstrate recursivity after the incorporation of chance.

Coding Triangles and Rectangles

Figure 13 shows how using P5.js can configure images in an abstract language. 2D primitives are functions within the P5.js that will allow the computer to create primary forms.

Figure 13. Mapping forms within cartesian space

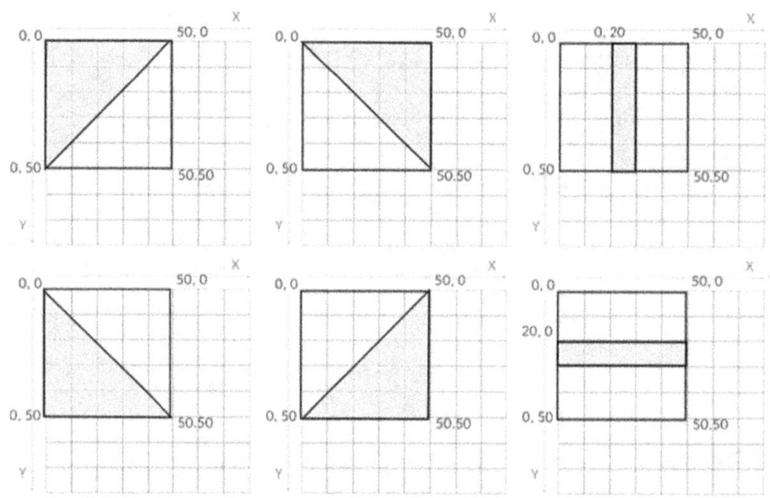

Note. This image will present rectangles and triangles disposed within the Cartesian space. In P5.js, the left/up corner of the canvas is the 0,0 point of the map. Anything from left to right, top to down, will increase in value—an illustration by Marília Bergamo.

In the case of Figure 13, to implement this code, the 2D primitive functions *rect()* and *triangle()* are necessary. The rectangle function uses the following configuration *rect(x, y, width, height)*. Observing that the canvas is the Cartesian space, to draw a rectangle, it is necessary to describe where the corner right will begin and the width and height of it. Figure 13 shows that the tile is a rectangle and will receive the following values *rect(0, 0, 50, 50)*.

To produce a triangle in P5.js, the function used is called *triangle(x1, y1, x2, y2, x3, y3)*. The information differs from the rectangle, and only the vertices within the Cartesian space are necessary. In Figure 13, four different forms of triangles can be created: *triangle(0,0,0,50,50,0)*, *triangle(0,0,50,0,50,50)*, *triangle(0,0,0,50,50,50)* and *triangle(0,50,50,50,50,0)*. Another option for drawing is the second rectangle, which can be perceived as a thick line within the tile. This second rectangle can be vertical *rect(20,0,10,50)* or horizontal *rect(0,20,50,10)*. Because both rectangles and triangles are 2D primitives, P5.js will allow them to have color on them, *fill()*, and *stroke()*. Those functions will receive values of

RGBA, allowing things to have a specific color or even transparency. This chapter's [code example 01] shows how to create all the forms; the results will show one primitive form over another. The code was built to demonstrate that P5.js will draw things in sequence, from the first to the last instructions, one over another.

`[code example 01 - P5.js Web Editor | Coding Examples Athos Bulcão Experiments, 2024]`

In [code example 01] the drawing functions can be placed in *Setup()* or *Draw()* and would work properly. However, due to the goals of this section, placing the code in *Setup()* will create a static image, and students will not need to worry about the concept of the loop in time regarding the animation power of P5.js. However, a more organized structure is recommended to guarantee the normalization of coding. To achieve this organization, the tile should be drawn in an authorial function such as *drawMe()*. Here, authoral means that this author created it and does not exist on the P5.js reference. The [code example 02] illustrates this authorial function and adds a different value to each tile to place them side by side in the Cartesian space. This solution is only temporary because repetition is the best way to display tiles on a screen, which will be soon explained in this section.

`[code example 02 - P5.js Web Editor | Coding Examples Athos Bulcão Experiments, 2024]`

Coding Triangles and Adding Transformations

Figure 14 presents one chosen layout within the many available possibilities within the experiment of the paper prototype. In this layout, a triangle is placed using the following coordinates: *(0,0)*, *(50,0)* and *(0,50)*.

Figure 14. Adding transformation in P5.js

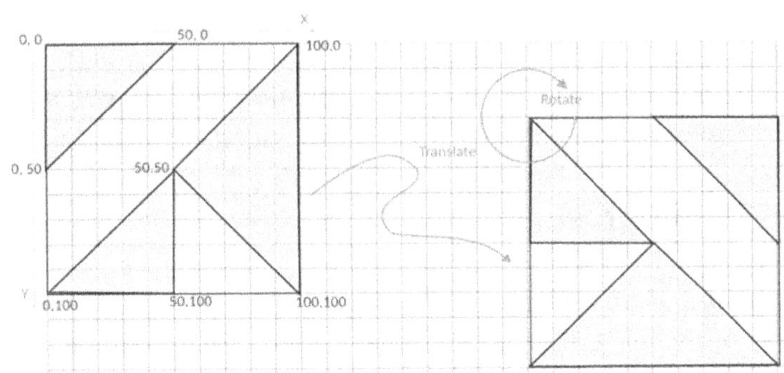

Note. This image highlights the triangles' point and the coding properties that will be necessary for translation and rotation—an illustration by Marília Bergamo.

In the sample presented here, a stroke is not necessary. The [code example 03] creates the tile described in Figure 14.

`[code example 03 - P5.js Web Editor | Coding Examples Athos Bulcão Experiments, 2024]`

In Figure 14, there is a highlight of two critical actions that can be done with the tiles: *translate()* and *rotate()*. Translation means the piece can be carried to any place within the canvas, while rotation can be used to rotate the tile. Regarding those transformations, it is essential to explain that P5.js works with the concepts of *push()* and *pop()*. This concept means that when *push()* is called, it is like a tracing paper was added to the canvas, and any change with it can be transferred to the canvas once the function *pop()* is called without interfering with any further drawings within the coding; please refer to Processing Handbook (Reas, 2014, p.134) to understand this concept better. [code example 04] exhibits how the functions can translate the tile from one point to another without changing the drawing information, as done in [code example 03].

`[code example 04 - P5.js Web Editor | Coding Examples Athos Bulcão Experiments, 2024]`

To learn about the rotation action in Figure 13, this section presents the [code example 05]. In P5.js, rotation can be coded both in degrees or radians. However, this author's teaching experience showed that degrees had worked better with design, architecture, and art students. To conclude, P5.js uses radians as the default setting, and changing the values from degrees is necessary while coding, which is done using the function *radians()*.

`[code example 05 - P5.js Web Editor | Coding Examples Athos Bulcão Experiments, 2024]`

Finally, it is necessary to create a loop to organize the tiles as a repetitive process, and a loop is a sequence of actions that has to be done until a determined event finishes the repetition. In the case of [code example 06] presented by this chapter, the screen size will determine when the pieces should stop. The loop used is *for()*, which will include the following parameters: start at *0* in *the x* position until it is the *size or less* of the *screen size*, and keep adding *100 pixels* to *x* each repetition. [coding example 06] is the solution to Figure 14, and for it to work, the function *drawMe()* had to be modified from previous examples in this chapter. *drawMe()* has to receive the values created while the loop is in progress within the *Setup()* function.

`[code example 06 - P5.js Web Editor | Coding Examples Athos Bulcão Experiments, 2024]`

At this point of the chapter, *the code described the repetition of tiles without rotation*; it will be done in detail in the next section when the concept of chance is added to the code.

Coding Drawings Using Arcs

The last coding example of this section is learning how to draw arcs. Arcs are created as specific functions in P5.js. As explored in rotation, arcs will use radians or degrees. Arcs can be described in many details in P5.js; however, we will use the following configuration: *arc(x, y, w, h, start, stop)*. Where *x,y* is the center, like the dry point of a compass, *w* and *h* are the width and height of the curve, which can create circles or ellipses and *start* and *stop* refers to the degree where the arc starts and stops.

In Figure 15, the drawing will happen with arcs, but the logic is more descriptive than the previous examples in this section. The arcs in the first tile have the center on the points $x = 50$ and $y = 50$, but the arcs that cover the tile from one side to the other have different sizes and exact start and end points. Meanwhile, the minor arc has different sizes and start and stop points.

Figure 15. Drawing arc with P5.js

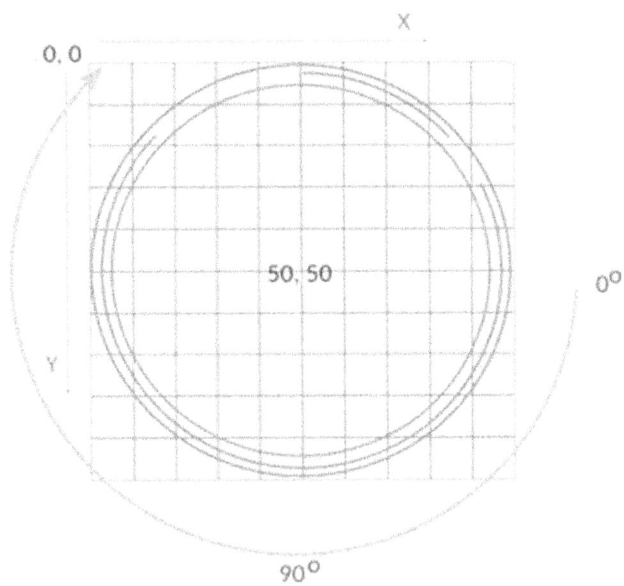

Note. x.—an illustration by Marília Bergamo.

The [code example 07] produces the image in Figure 15, and *different colors* are defined for the same arcs in different tiles to make the cuts of the tiles more visible within the coding, `[code example 07 - P5.js Web Editor | Coding Examples Athos Bulcão Experiments, 2024]`

INCORPORATING CHANCE AND RECURSIVITY

Athos Bulcão used maps of distribution and accepted human error interpretation as part of his artistic process. With coding, we can use randomness and noise as elements of chance. Random can be less chaotic with constraints on color palettes and forms, while noise will create a smooth distribution pattern. While implementing this is relatively easy once the logic is achieved, the challenge is to convince students to let go of some control over their creative process. Usually, art, design, and architecture students are very attached to their creations, and controlling each step of the process is a common characteristic of these fields. However, both random and noise use within those described conditions allow the compositions to become vivid and organic, which, in the case of Athos Bulcão's artistic tile murals, becomes the most expressive characteristic of his work. Another critical point of Athos Bulcão's artwork is the massive spaces he used, permitting the chance to occur more often. Due to this unique characteristic, chances had even more probability of happening. In the case of Common Digital Art logic made with coding, it is resolved through time, with animation or extending the canvas to produce larger images.

Basic Chance With Options

Usually, random is the first function to learn to incorporate chance. In this example of Figure 16, the code will be straightforward, focusing on learning the function *random()*. When called, this function will return a number between an interval of values. The function can be written *random(number)* or *random(initial, final number)*. In the first mode, when only one value is presented, the interval will be between 0 and the number defined. Figure 16 shows a coding experiment based on Athos Bulcão's design for the TV Tower in Brasília. Because the code has a chance incorporated into it, Figure 16 is improbable to happen again.

Figure 16. Athos Bulcão's Brasília TV Tower experimental logic

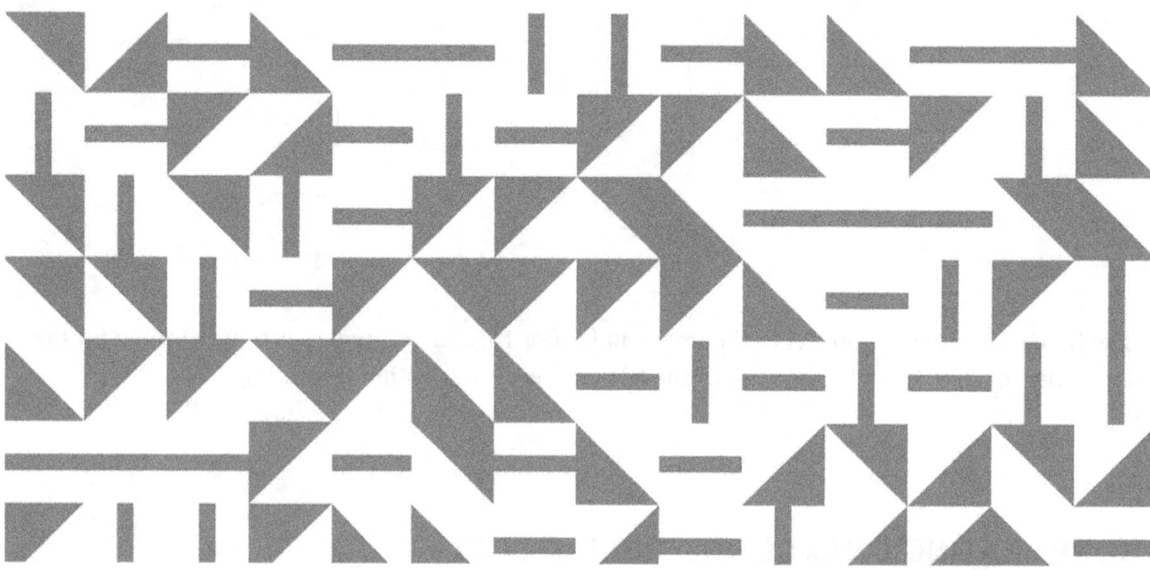

Note. Please access Experiment with Athos Bulcão _ Brasília TV Tower—MariliaBergamo—OpenProcessing (2024) to access the online coding.—image generated by Marília Bergamo.

The following code is responsible for generating Figure 16. In the code, the function *drawMe()* is modified to incorporate a variable called *myChance*. This variable will receive a value of any integer number between 0 and 8, which means 0,1,2,3,4,5,6, and 7, excluding 8. This value will be used by a function Switch/Case that receives the value and sets an action according to the result. Because there are four drawings of triangles and only two of rectangles, the code duplicates the rectangles to increase the chance of occurrence.
`[code example 08 - P5.js Web Editor | Coding Examples Athos Bulcão Experiments, 2024]`

At this point of the chapter, exploration can be made only by changing the recursive functions *for()* to set *x y* positions and *drawMe()* from *Setup()* to *Draw()*. The [code example 08, animated] shows that this chance creates an animation. A slower framerate of four frames per second had been set in the coding so changes could be better seen.

[code example 08, animated - P5.js Web Editor | Coding Examples Athos Bulcão Experiments, 2024]

Chance Distribution With Conditions

Figure 17 presents an experiment with the tile artwork *Sambódromo*. The coding to generate this image is very similar to the [code example 08] previously presented regarding using random. However, [code example 09] adds a *condition* that Athos Bulcão has reinforced in his original drafts: to avoid full circles.

Figure 17. Athos Bulcão Sambódromo experimental logic

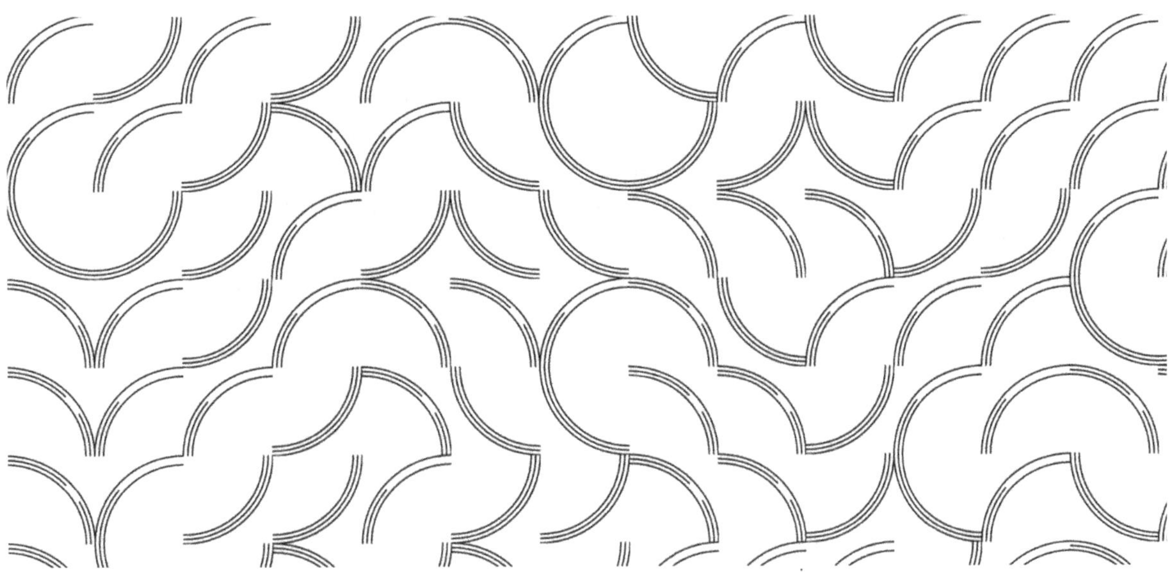

Note. Please access Experiment with Athos Bulcão _ Sambódromo —MariliaBergamo—OpenProcessing (2024) to access the online coding.—image generated by Marília Bergamo.

There is more than one way of thinking abstractly about this specific condition, and the solution presented in [code example 09] is one option. In this particular example, by avoiding a sequential tile, like 2 after 1, or 3 after 2, and so on, it is possible to save the last value the code had chosen by chance, and if it is not in the sequence, it is okay to use this new value. Otherwise, it will repeat the previous choice made.
[code example 09 - P5.js Web Editor | Coding Examples Athos Bulcão Experiments, 2024]

Chance With Rotation

The [code example 10] introduces a series of concepts yet to be discussed in this section to demonstrate rotation with chance. The approach here illustrates how a change in the form of a random function can be approached from diverse forms of abstract thinking. The code starts creating an inventory of four numbers that will define the color of triangles. The logic defines two authorial functions, *getMyColor(n)* and *myRotation()*. The former function will return a color value based on the number it has received and is called when filling the color before drawing a triangle. The inventory of colors is shuffled before they are assigned to each triangle. The latter will create another level of chance that will define the tile's rotation before it is drawn.

`[code example 10 - P5.js Web Editor | Coding Examples Athos Bulcão Experiments, 2024]`

As previously presented, the rotation will alter the original position of the drawing structure; for this reason, the last function, *myRotation()*, will define a distinct translation applied to each different degree of rotation. Using this solution helped to determine the exact position on the Cartesian space of the final structure based on the four positions possible by tiles *0*, *90*, *180* and *360* degrees.

Chance With Noise in Colors

Noise is a different form of chance, usually creating patterns that change slowly from one to the other. In the [code example 11], the same solution discussed with the rotation of the tiles takes an entirely different approach, one not found within the artwork examples used in this chapter. Athos Bulcão used analogue colors in his artworks, but they are scarce within the tile murals. Here, the notion of analogue color, colors close to each other in the color circle, is used within the noise while still using a defined color pallet. It chooses colors to create a slow transition between the first and last tiles; the code also uses a bigger scale image to demonstrate the result.

`[code example 11 - P5.js Web Editor | Coding Examples Athos Bulcão Experiments, 2024]`

Figure 18 shows the result of the code; it is possible to see that the tiles are placed in each column before going to the other because this is the transition followed by the colors.

Figure 18. Slow color transition using noise

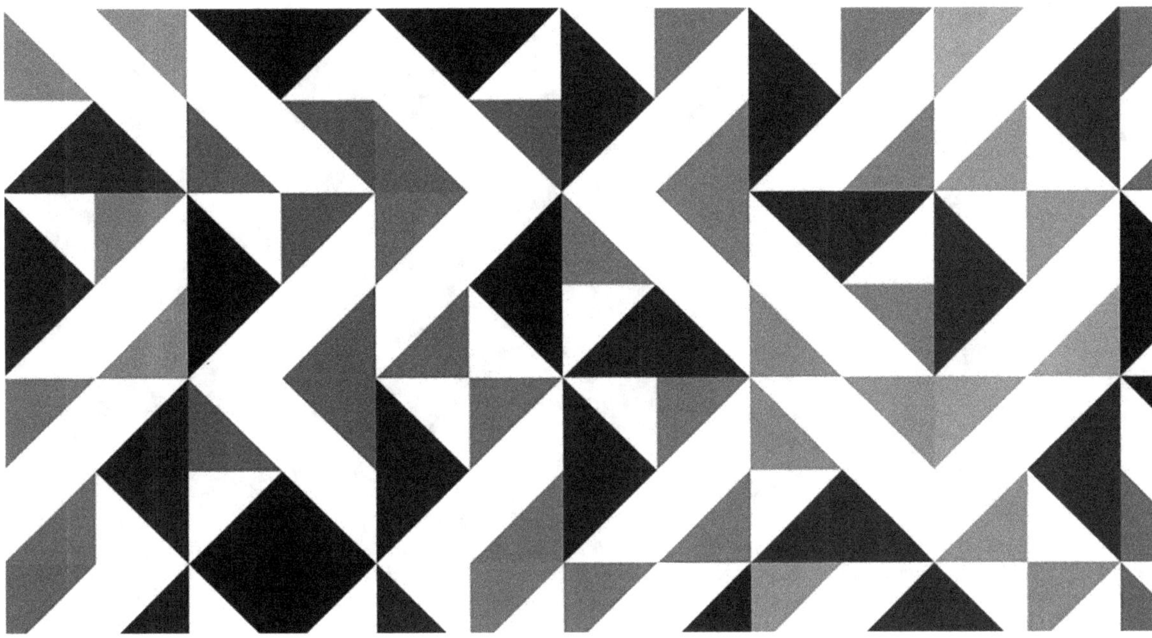

Note. The image is one of the possible results of the coding—image generated by Marília Bergamo.

Adding More Levels of Chance and Recursivity

The last coding of this section [code example 12] adds more levels of chance, including random actions in different parts of the [code example 10]. The solution implemented creates another authorial function named *mylastTriangle()* inside *DrawMe()*. This function *mylastTriangle()* creates a random choice with three different outcomes. If the first happens, a fourth triangle will be drawn in the coordinates *(0, 50, 25, 75, 0, 100)*; if the second possibility happens, the fourth triangle will be drawn in the coordinates *(50, 50, 100, 100, 50, 100)*, the last possibility will draw the fourth triangle in the coordinates *(50, 0, 100, 0, 75, 25)*. The color of the last triangle is also determined by the shuffle of the inventory colors explained in [code example 10].

A second level of chance introduces recursivity. Recursivity is a conceptual idea that, in this chapter, will be represented as the same chance of tile pattern happening in a similar mode with slight differences. Using the function *DrawMe()* inside itself will produce recursivity. [code example 12] does this by adding to the *DrawMe() within* a rotation of 45 degrees to the drawing and reducing the scale by 35%. In a determinate moment, it becomes impossible for the eye to see such a tiny pattern repetition. However, introducing the concept in this chapter aims to reveal that Common Digital Art adds a different order of complexity to a representation of modernism, one not even imaginable during the 1960s when Athos Bulcão created Brasília's tile murals. Recursivity in [code example 12] is a contemporaneous reinterpretation of modern artwork logic.

`[code example 12 - P5.js Web Editor | Coding Examples Athos Bulcão Experiments, 2024]`

Figure 19. Digital coding interpretation of Athos Bulcão's tiles with recursivity

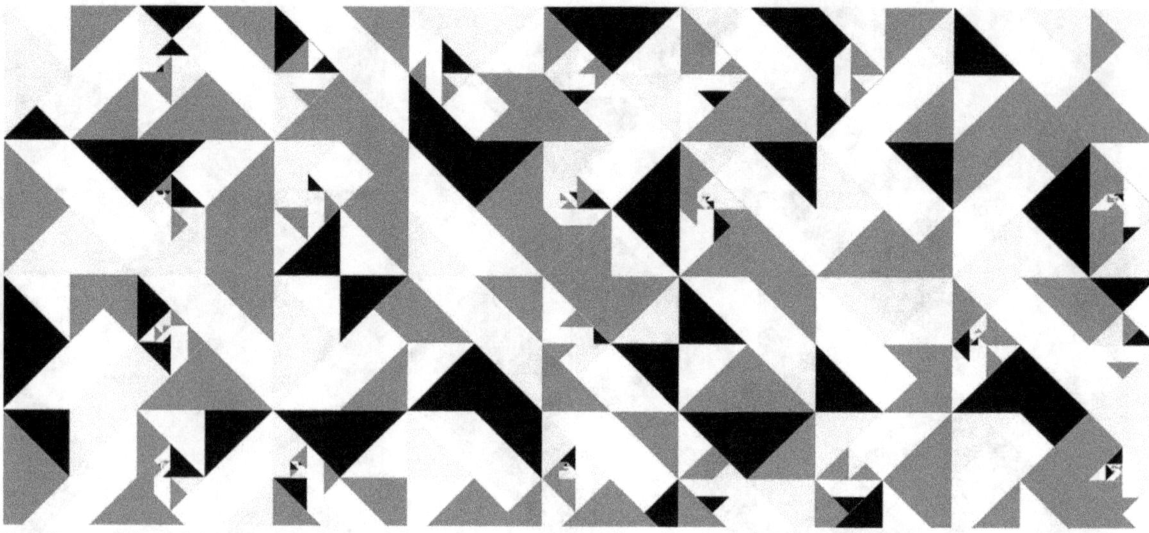

Note. Because the code incorporates chance and recursivity, it is unlikely that anyone will encounter the same image using the same code. However, a pattern emerges from it, and the piece resembles the original design of Estação de Transbordo da Lapa from Athos Bulcão. Please access Experiment with Athos Bulcão _ Estação de Transbordo da Lapa—MariliaBergamo—OpenProcessing (2024) to access the online coding.—image generated by Marília Bergamo.

BRINGING THE PROJECT BACK TO THE PHYSICAL WORLD

This section will explore techniques that allow Common Digital Art logic to be transferable to physical. Those techniques described by (Iwamoto, 2009) and (Jonathon Anderson, 2021) as Digital fabrication take advances in 3D printing and CNC processes. The goal is to take advantage of the flexibility of the calculation power of computers to generate forms and use those filling, cutting, carving and engraving machines to transform them into something touchable.

There are many digital tools to use in the generation of the form. Here, it will be described using TinkerCad (2024), and the choice of the platform follows the same logic as P5.js because of its online environment and the easy access to creating a classroom where a tutor can help students during the development process. TinkerCad allows the use of a language called Codeblocks, which will be used here to demonstrate how the Common Digital Art logic can be transferred to the platform. TinkerCad can be a first step towards more complex and powerful Cad software or even professional animation and 3D modeling software. Codeblocks use the same block of codes usually applicable in the latter years of school programs. A natural transferable knowledge from Codeblocks coding to more sophisticated languages opens the potential for complex digital fabrications in art, architecture and design.

To use Common Digital Art logic in TinkerCad, a student may need to get used to cutting from primitive forms to generate the desired structure once the parameters available in the TinkerCad primitives differ from coding in P5.js. Triangles are good examples because TinkerCad's polygonal primitive of 3 sides will create only isosceles triangles. However, it has the advantage that once a form is created with

Codeblocks, it can be exported as a shape to the student's library—figure 20 below exemplifies this principle. The advantage of exporting a form to the library is that it will consume less processing power while being used in other designs. Also, the student starts developing their library of possible primary forms to be further explored, like the paper prototype modules previously discussed in this chapter.

Figure 20. Cutting principle in TinkerCad

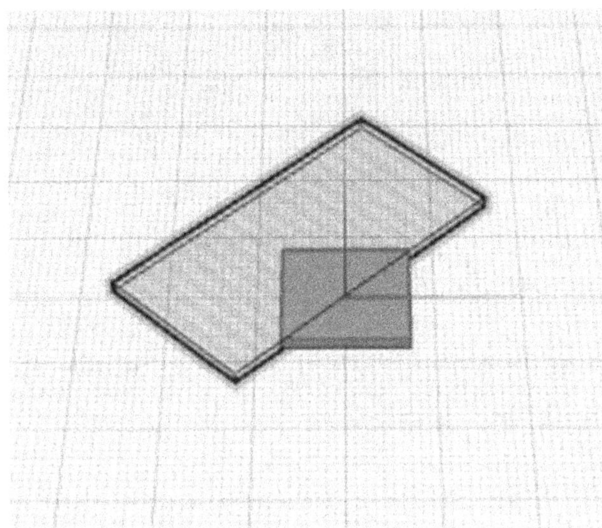

Note. This image represents the cutting principle used in TinkerCad. The original cube in blue has the measures of 20 x 20 x 1. A second cube set as a 'hole' with the measurements of 40 x 20 x 1 is placed in the same position but receives a rotation of 45 degrees and a dislocation of -5 on axis X and 9 on axis Y. The final action is to add both figures as a group before exporting to shape—image generated by Marília Bergamo.

Finally, describing the principle of an object in TinkerCad Codeblocks will be relevant. An object is a series of actions that can replace the necessity of shape exporting. The same principles in Figure 20 can be used within the Create New Object function. The Create New Object principle will be explored in this chapter to avoid the possibility of exporting the shape not being done during the attempt to replicate the processes presented here.

3D interpretation of *Sambódromo* Tiles

Figure 21 presents a process of generating tiles using TinkerCad Codeblocks in the coding, which will create the possible tiles using many Create New Object functions. Many objects must be created, one in a sequence with the other. The process always follows the logic of creating a solid form and cutting from it the desired one. In this interpretation, the space corresponds to the space between arcs, and a third thin arc is placed within this space to create the alternative tile designs of the original artwork. The Create New Object function can isolate tiles and export them into shapes to explore this tile organization further. With complex drawings such as those, saving shapes is recommended for deeper exploration of random possibilities.

Figure 21. Tiles of Sambódromo in TinkerCad

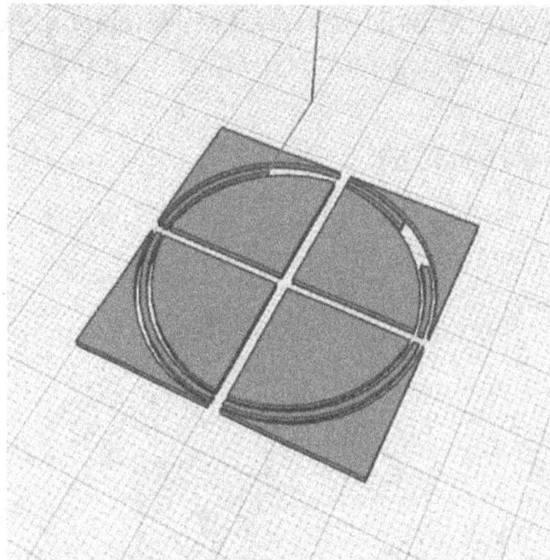

Note. This is the final image of the Codeblock execution, where four tiles are placed together to represent an interpretation of the four possible tiles of the original artwork Sambódramo of Athos Bulcão. Please access Athos Bulcão 3D Experiment - Sambódromo - TinkerCad, 2024 to view the process online—image generated by Marília Bergamo.

3D interpretation of Brasília's TV Tower Tiles

Figure 22 shows the power of using random repetitions within Codeblocks in TinkerCad. In the below image, a simple shape based on cube primitive was created to be the rectangles, and a shape created by the process of cutting previously described created the triangle, both using the Create New Object function. Then again, the Create New Object function finishes adding instances of the first two objects in random rotations through a 5 x 5 triangles or rectangles grid.

Figure 22. Random configuration of tiles using TinkerCad

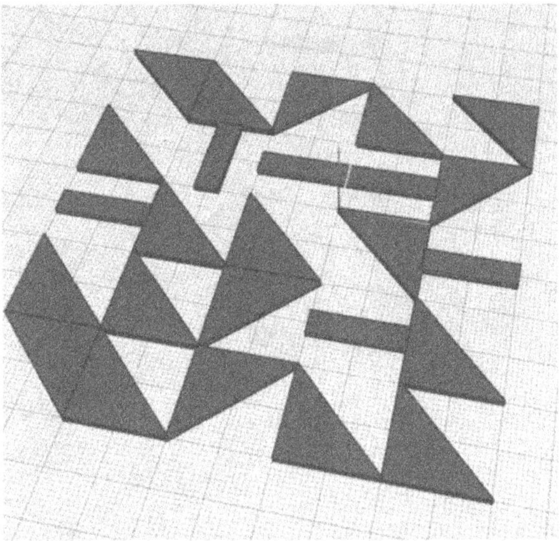

Note. Image of the Codeblocks execution: due to the random process, it is unlikely that the exact image will be formed precisely the one presented. Please access Athos Bulcão 3D Experiment - TV Tower Brasília - TinkerCad, 2024 to view the process online—image generated by Marília Bergamo.

3D Interpretation of *Estação Transbordo da Lapa*

A more complex process is necessary to generate Figure 23, where a different Create New Object function generates three different forms of triangles, which further receive a random rotation through a 5 x 5 grid. Depending on the computation power of the graphic board, the computer may need more time to run this process. Although this is not as complex as the recursivity power described in this chapter, the effect on a tridimensional structure has deeper explorations that can be conducted manually, such as changing the final scale of the 3D files to generate different sizes that can be instructed within each other.

Figure 23. Complex 3D drawing and random configuration

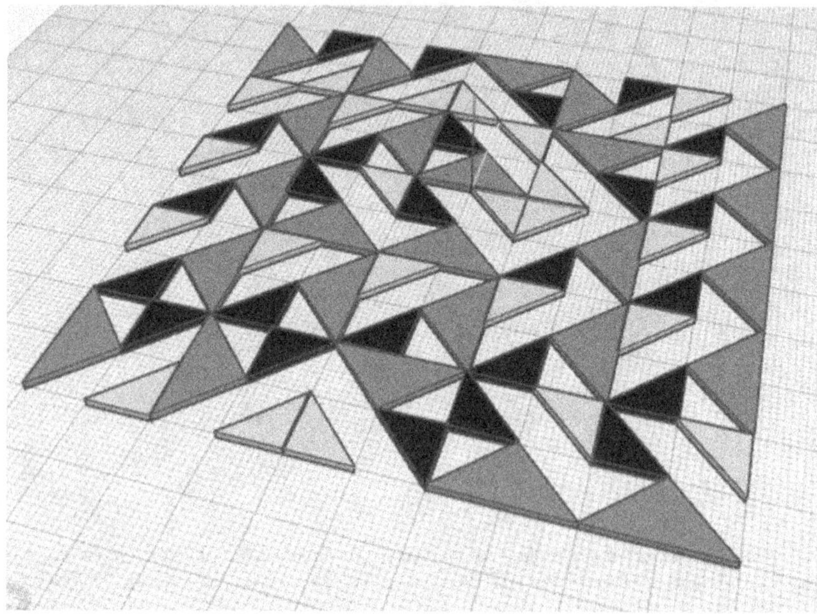

Note. Image of the Codeblocks execution: due to the random process, it is unlikely that the exact image will be formed precisely the one presented. Please access Athos Bulcão 3D Experiment - Estação Transbordo da Lapa - TinkerCad, 2024 to view the process online—image generated by Marília Bergamo.

FUTURE RESEARCH DIRECTIONS

The 50s were the pinnacle of modernism in Brazil, and it expressed minimalist forms of concrete where the lines and curves become part of the landscape. Modern thinking is far from the complex world of more than 70 years of cultural differences. It is not only about simpler forms or abstract ideologies. Today's world is perceived as multiplicities and diversities, and more than anything, by a fractal view of repetitive patterns. As such, the interpretations discussed in this chapter can end with a brief discussion of how these methods are absorbed today.

The dialogue between experimentation with tiles and art, design, and architecture education comes as a response to this complex world. Through this interchange, new materials, technologies and media become part of the evolution of the city landscapes. The contemporaneous cities of today have different models of tiles, some even tridimensional over facades of new buildings. *The recursive capacity of computational logic has expanded to fabric, design and architectural modules. In this scenario, the search for more authorial logic may be the biggest motivation for writing this chapter to engage students in producing it.* Logic abstraction is fundamentally human, distinguishing this process from other recent models of automation creativity. It also challenges the present solutions, pushing them to further emergences of form.

As a result, the concepts here can benefit further from 2D dimension logic to more extensive 3D experimentations. The tile does not need to be flat; layers can be added to it. Furthermore, while the process is not automated, it invites creatives to interfere in those layers, generating diversity instead of convergence.

In Brasilia, the reappropriation of the cultural history of Athos Bulcao is growing as a phenomenon in social media such as instagram (fundathos, 2024). Due to its potential logic, many contemporaneous interpretations are emerging in fashion and design products and local businesses' tiling companies. The same reappropriation can grow within Common Digital Art products. For this reason, this chapter intends to introduce methods to the process to future Creative Coding students, hoping to produce an emergent authorial tiling culture.

CONCLUSION

In conclusion, this chapter is an exploration not limited to one artist's language. The method of transforming artistic thinking in logic has its historical background with artists such as Vera Molnar and other experimental computer artists of the 1960s such as Manfred Mohr, Georg Nees, Frieder Nake and A Michael Noll. The difference here is that this chapter tried to transform the modern thinking of Athos Bulcão, previously from computation as art, to show students that translations are possible and sometimes a valuable tool to continue approaching traditional thinking to contemporary technologies. It is rethinking the world within its past and emerging cultural developments.

ACKNOWLEDGMENT

I thank the institution Fundação Athos Bulcão for its support in providing the necessary information and official images presented in this chapter. The University of Newcastle for allowing the time and space to produce this writing and practical work, and finally, Dominic Lindus for consultancy time.

REFERENCES

Anderson, J. L. (2021). *Digital Fabrication in Interior Design: Body, Object, Enclosure*. Taylor & Francis. 10.4324/9781003025931

Athos Bulcão 3D Experiment - Estação Transbordo da Lapa - TinkerCad. (n.d.). Retrieved February 23, 2024, https://www.tinkercad.com/codeblocks/gn8I6cQ6VEg-athos-bulcao-3d-experiment?sharecode=b0J_9YtAulSy7xUmPpGJtCizGeM5IAlullLlEDfqBBo

Athos Bulcão 3D Experiment - Sambódromo - TinkerCad. (n.d.). Retrieved February 24, 2024, from https://www.tinkercad.com/codeblocks/l1a65wx51EC-athos-bulcao-3d-experiment-sambodramo?sharecode=prK4QCH76bvQuQYr5Om_hi0-0Cuy_HS4zzs1UtdMJqM

Centro Cultural do Banco do Brasil. (n.d.). *100 anos de Athos Bulcão*. CCBB Brasília, Brasília, Distrito Federal, Brazil. Exhibition catalog Retrieved February 14, 2024, from https://ccbb.com.br/wp-content/uploads/2021/07/100AnosdeAthosBulcao.pdf

Experiment with Athos Bulcão _ Brasília TV Tower— MariliaBergamo—OpenProcessing. (n.d.). Retrieved February 20, 2024, from https://openprocessing.org/sketch/2181226/

Experiment with Athos Bulcão—Estação de Transbordo da Lapa- MariliaBergam—OpenProcessing. (n.d.). Retrieved February 20, 2024, from https://openprocessing.org/sketch/1238424/

Experiment with Athos Bulcão—Sambódromo—MariliaBergamo—OpenProcessing. (n.d.). Retrieved February 20, 2024, from https://openprocessing.org/sketch/2181225/

Fundathos—Fundação Athos Bulcão. (n.d.). Retrieved February 14, 2024, from https://www.fundathos.org.br/

Home | p5.js. (n.d.). Retrieved February 17, 2024, from https://p5js.org/

Iwamoto, L. (2009). *Digital fabrications : architectural and material techniques*. Princeton Architectural Press.

Reas, C. (2014). *Processing: A Programming Handbook for Visual Designers and Artists 2ed* (2nd ed.). MIT Press.

Ribeiro, S. B., Perpétuo, T. P., & Instituto do Patrimônio Histórico e Artístico Nacional. (Eds.). (2018). *Inventário da obra de Athos Bulcão em Brasília*. Iphan DF. Retrieved February 14, 2024, from http://portal.iphan.gov.br/uploads/publicacao/athosbulcatilde_menor.pdf

Tinkercad | From mind to design in minutes. (n.d.). Tinkercad. Retrieved February 24, 2024, from https://www.tinkercad.com/

ADDITIONAL READING

Artut, S. (2023). *Geometric Patterns with Creative Coding: Coding for the Arts* (1st ed.). Apress L. P. 10.1007/978-1-4842-9389-8

Franco, F. (2022). Interview with Vera Molnar: Interview Recorded in Paris, 19 April and 29 May 2017. In *The Algorithmic Dimension* (pp. 83–100). Springer International Publishing. 10.1007/978-3-319-61167-9_4

Shiffman, D. (2012). *The nature of code* (S. Fry, Ed.; Version 1.0.). D. Shiffman.

Zhang, Y., & Funk, M. (2021). *Coding Art: The Four Steps to Creative Programming with the Processing Language* (1st ed.). Apress L. P. 10.1007/978-1-4842-6264-1

KEY TERMS AND DEFINITIONS

Assembling Processes: Consist of the act of putting things to work together as an assemblage.

Complex Drawing: Includes the understanding that the drawing is not only made by one agent but the interaction of many.

Complexity: In this chapter reflects complex sciences studies, where complex phenomena such as the relation of parts, their autonomies, and the evolutive process generate emerging results.

Computer-Assisted Manufactured Machines: Are mechanical devices that can communicate with computers. Acopled with motors, they can perform cuts and instructions within materials according to the instructions received by a program.

Digital Coding: Is considered when logic can be transcribed into a language and a compiler can execute such a program.

Digital Fabrication: Is a process of using computer-assisted manufactured machines and algorithms to create material products and structures.

Digital Technology: Is based on introducing algorithms and programs that a computer can interpret to execute a determined function.

Paper Prototyping: Is a traditional technique used in Experience Design (UX). It involves starting to design an interactive solution using paper and notes to test its viability, usually introducing user tests and iterative processes.

Chapter 4
The Concept of Digital Art and Refik Anadol

Ferda Çelik
İstanbul Aydın University, Turkey

Rıza Aktürk
İstanbul Aydın University, Turkey

Gökçen Firdevs Yücel Caymaz
İstanbul Aydın University, Turkey

Hilal Türkdoğdu
İstanbul Aydın University, Turkey

ABSTRACT

Humanity is moving forward in a process of evolution where technology and art intersect. In the modern era, the spread of computers and the internet has enabled works of art to reach a wider audience and has brought innovations in the way art is created and exhibited. Digital art has emerged as a product of this transformation and has become a developing discipline using the aesthetic and creative potentials of computers and the internet. With the spread of the internet, fundamental changes have been experienced in the media and communication order, and digital media and encodings have created new forms of communication. Refik Anadol, one of the leading names of digital art in Turkey, has built bridges between the physical and digital worlds through the use of data and artificial intelligence, and has taken art to a new dimension. Dec. Anadol's works have transformed the perception of space and presented alternative realities to the audience. These works change and expand the way art is perceived by making the audience active participants.

1. INTRODUCTION

One of the most remarkable phases of human history is the interaction of technology with art and the transformations brought about by this process. Starting with the industrial revolution, this transformation marks a period in which technological discoveries came to the fore in the 19th century. In this

DOI: doi

period, inventions such as the steamship, train, automobile, telephone, telegraph, camera and airplane pioneered the advancement of science and technology. These advancements opened new doors in the fields of information and communication, marking an important turning point in human history.

From past to present, artistic production can be handled in three stages: “traditional method”, “mechanical reproduction” and “digital method”. The uniqueness and originality of works produced with traditional methods came to an end with mechanical reproduction methods. With the Industrial Revolution and the development of mechanization, followed by technical developments and the invention of photography in the 1830s, reproduction has brought the works produced by traditional methods to a wider audience. Image production and the production of virtual works through computer and digital means have become widespread with the digital method (Özel Sağlamtimur, 2010).

Public space is a fundamental component of democratic society and public life. Often outdoors and (most importantly) accessible to the public, especially passersby who do not wish to encounter a work of art, the civic, political and artistic components of public space all influence how contemporary artists create public art projects and how audiences interact with them (Dell'Aria, 2021: 16).

ublic spaces are vital organisms that live, evolve, transform, and circulate over time as a part of everyday life. Therefore, it is inevitable that public space's definers and mass are affected by digitalization.

Public art is art outside museums and galleries and must fit into at least one of the following categories:

accessible or visible to the public: public
relating to or affecting the community or individuals: public interest
maintained for or used by the community or individuals: public space
publicly paid: publicly funded

This definition is useful for its extensibility and flexibility, and for recognizing public art as a separate category that deals with physical, thematic and financial accessibility. The digital revolution, which affects the world, inherently is starting to affect the urban tissue and therefore the social ground and context in which public life develops. Digital art only made its official entry into the art world in the late 1990s, when museums and galleries began to become increasingly involved in digital art. By the beginning of the 21st century, an increasing number of exhibition spaces devoted exclusively to new media art had developed around the world (Paul, 2023: 12).

The 20th and 21st centuries stand out as a period in which digital technologies developed rapidly and art redefined itself. The global spread of computers and the internet has enabled artworks to reach wider audiences and to be recreated in digital media. In this process, digital art has become the center of attention of both academic research and the art world. Digital art is defined as a field that develops by utilizing the aesthetic and creative potentials of computer and internet technologies.

The emergence of the Internet has led to the construction of a digital world, and new media has transformed the traditional understanding of media, bringing radical changes to the communication order. This transformation has been made possible through the use of digital coding and algorithms. Digital art is at the center of these new media technologies and is shaped by the use of the computer as a creative tool. Theorists such as Lev Manovich, Christiane Paul and Bruce Wands have defined digital art as new media art and created the ontological and epistemological framework of this field.

Paul (2008) states that digital art works were first called computer art, then multimedia art and finally new media art.

Digital art has its origins in avant-garde art movements such as Cubism, Futurism and Dadaism. These movements paved the way for the integration of technology with art and transformed traditional art forms. Thanks to the rapid development of digital art and its proximity to science and technology, it has emerged as an interdisciplinary field. In this field, multidisciplinary studies are carried out with the contributions of professionals from different fields of expertise.

The creative process of digital art is often based on collaboration between an artist and a team of programmers, engineers, scientists and designers. Digital art is a body of work that breaks down the boundaries between disciplines such as art, science, technology and design and originates from a variety of fields, including research and development laboratories and academia (Paul, 2023, 12).

The most striking examples of this transformation are Anadol's use of data and artificial intelligence technologies to create works that transcend the boundaries between physical and digital realities. These works demonstrate the development of art as a technological field of research and exploration, rather than merely a form of aesthetic expression. In this process, digital art redefines the interaction between art and science by integrating technical knowledge and skill with aesthetic value and expressive power.

Definition, Scope and Characteristics of Digital Art

Digital art is a combination of digital media and art and is broadly defined as art produced in a computer environment. In this process, the computer plays an active role in different positions in an evolution that extends from an auxiliary tool in the traditional sense to a creative position. In digital art, which is also called new media art, where new media technologies are in a central position, artistic expressions and productions gain a different dimensional function, while the position of the artist is naturally affected by this change. The technical environment that shapes the relationship between the producer and the viewer stands out as a dominant element in the creation processes of digital art.

In the current period, numbers, signs, virtual formations and expressions are diversifying in digital artworks; works such as animations and software are evaluated in the category of digital art. While digital art generally exists as a collection of ones and zeros in the digital storage environment, it is up to the decision of the artist whether the digital artwork that is created tends towards a more realistic form or not. As computers become more powerful and software becomes more advanced, the variety of forms that data can take is relatively increasing (Wands, 2006, 14).

The forms a digital artwork can take include installation; film, video and animation; internet art, networked art and software art; and virtual reality and musical environments (Paul, 2023, 19). Digital art was first introduced as new media art by authors such as Lev Manovich, Christiane Paul and Bruce Wands. While Manovich explored the media's capacities in representation, automation, transformation and adaptation, Paul reviewed new media art practices in the context of digital art and presented ontological categories. In his book 'The Art of the Digital Age', Wands considers digital art as a subset of contemporary art (Winegard 2019,74).

Avant-garde art, one of the main sources of digital art, made significant contributions to the development of artistic trends such as Cubism, Futurism and Dadaism. Although it did not have a direct impact on the emergence of interactive art, the search for innovation by avant-garde artists paved the way for the merger of technology with art (Shen & Fang, 2021 2; Toy 2017, 111). Traditional art forms have been transformed in many fields such as music, sculpture, painting, photography, printing and video through computer technologies; new forms such as internet art, pixel art, software art, digital exhibitions and virtual reality have also taken place in artistic works.

The rapid development of digital art has caused changes among artists, their works and audiences due to its proximity to sciences such as mathematics and physics (Çokokumuş 2012, 51). In addition to the advancement of new technologies in the digital field, it has become a branch of art that allows people from different fields of expertise, computer programmers, engineers, architects, sound technicians and professionals from various disciplines to come together and work as a team (Özel Sağlamtimur 2010, 220). In digital art, which came into existence with the crossing of the paths of traditional art and computer technology, experiencing has turned into both a mental and physical act and has begun to involve all the senses. Digital art basically questions the interaction of human beings with their environment, information, technology, aesthetics and, as a result, their self-consciousness. Digital art, which requires imagination and creativity, is a computer-aided art form. For this reason, the computer also needs various tools to produce digital art. In the production of digital art, in addition to technology, basic art elements such as point, line, light, form, texture and color are used as in other fields of art.

Refik Anadol said that the existence of the human being is accompanied by the existence of technology in the period of its existence; he said that the inventions in the period in which cultures lived made life easier and that these inventions were a result of existing needs and continued as follows: "The relationship between human beings and technology has always been very contrasting, the best ideas that develop us, unite us and make us think, and the worst ideas that separate us and destroy us have emerged, we have always been aware of this, but artificial intelligence has brought a new dimension to human informatics capacity for the first time. For the first time we have the chance to think with the concept of "consciousness", the computer is not a very new idea, but with the acceleration of the technology we have and the information we have, called data, becoming machine-readable, a great era has begun" (Anadol, 2019, vogue.com.tr).

The driving force of this change, in which mass and collective works stand out in today's understanding of art, is the advances in communication technologies and the new understanding of communication of the age. Thanks to digital art, the work of art has evolved from a unique creation process to a collaborative process with the prominence of expertise.

The distinctive features of digital art are as follows;

It uses new media technologies and is computer-based.
It has a structure that focuses on the aesthetic values of virtual objects.
It creates multi-sensory perception, i.e. synesthesia, with the support of the technical and virtual environment.
It has an understanding focused on interaction with the viewer through virtual environments.
It allows the artwork to be easily reproduced, copied and stored.
Collective works created with the participation of people with different areas of expertise stand out.

Today's understanding of art transforms the viewer into an interactive participant rather than a passive spectator, allowing them to get closer to the process of the artwork and perceive it more easily. In the age of digital communication, the tendency to delegate the objective production of art to machines aims to create a virtual sense of here and now centered on interaction with the viewer. Digital art contributes to the development of a new understanding of art based on interaction and experience by creating an experience of perception and emotion that is not the center of the subject and is thought in a state of becoming through innovations in communication technologies.

Works presented in public also demonstrate the importance of moving away from the artworks and their locations to examine their wider physical context. Many forms of encountering and responding to artworks in public space do not require bodily presence with a solid object; the artwork can be abstract or mediated experience, and this offers new kinds of engagement and meaning. While embodiment and physical interaction are often emphasized, uses that lack bodily interaction or respond to the inaccessibility of an artwork are also important (Lossau, and Stevens, 2015, 10).

Moving image artworks in public spaces produce moments that can renew and intensify our experience of public space. These artworks also offer an opportunity to understand how moving images function in public space, how they mobilize audiences and how they reconfigure the space of the screen outside the critique of spectacle. Moving image-based public art particularly enriches the in-between spaces on the street, creating meaningful shared experiences in public spaces (Dell'Aria, 2021, 6).

The basic idea behind the exhibitions is to create a dialog between artists, the city and the public. Hall and Robertson (2001) elaborate on the claims of public art under seven headings: developing civic identity, developing a sense of place, developing a sense of community, meeting social needs, combating social exclusion, educational value and promoting social change.

The relationship between interactive public art, users, and the environment, according to (Edmonds, Turner and Candy, 2004'ten aktaran Saleh vd., 2022), can be static, dynamic-passive, dynamic-interactive, or dynamic interactive (varying).

Static: The art object remains unmodified. The artwork itself does not respond to its surroundings.

Dynamic-Passive: The art piece contains an inbuilt mechanism that allows it to change or be altered by an external factor such as temperature, sound, or light.

Dynamic-Interactive: All of the characteristics of the dynamic passive category apply, with the addition that the human 'viewer' actively influences the changes in the art object.

Dynamic-Interactive (Varying): Both 2 and 3 above apply, with the addition of a modifying agent that modifies the original specification of the art object. The agent could be a person or a computer program.

Digital Art Forms and Themes

Digital Art has brought about the need for a positioning in terms of Art History with its structure that permeates many fields. In addition to being accepted as one of the contemporary art types within the fields of art, it is subjected to various classifications (Tellan, 2019, 651) (Visual 1). In making these classifications, the environment and tools in the formation process of the artwork are taken into account (Paul, 2008,8). In addition, the forms and themes that fall within the scope of digital art are other issues that should be mentioned in this regard (Özel Sağlamtimur, 2010, 220-228).

Forms in Digital Art

There are applications that include three-dimensional sculptures designed in a digital environment using sculpture, prototyping, digital laser technologies and color-material applications. While these applications are sometimes exhibited with reflectors, sometimes they can be physically realized by using materials such as clay, metal waste and stone, remaining faithful to the model designed (İba, 2020, 157; Turhab, 2006, 3). Installation art is a type of art form that can include computer, video, sound, performance and similar components (Taştan, 2018, 49). Such artworks can be created in the digital environment, or they can be exhibited outdoors or indoors. Film, video and animation, animation essentially aims to give movement to static images drawn on paper, photographed or designed in computer environment (Kaba, 1994, 1-4). Software art is a field that is used in many digital application areas and is based on codes. When we focus on software in digital art, it is observed that the action performed through codes carries a creative, aesthetic and artistic meaning (Wants, 2006, 164).

Themes in Digital Art

Artificial intelligence, a type of intelligence that learns and evolves on its own using data, includes software used in the creation processes of digital art (Artut, 2019, 772; Yakar, 2020, 375). Abstraction is the process of transferring the physical elements, space, colors and sound to the digital environment with techniques such as coding, installation, software and scanning (Akten, 2008, 49). Cyberspace is another name for virtual space that can be experienced, and this refers to the internet, a digitally supported space (Yücel, 2017, 510).

Virtual reality aims to create a new environment using technological possibilities and to enable the audience to interact with this environment through the senses (Başar, 2020, 623). In this context, interacting with the artwork itself can be evaluated in line with this goal. Augmented reality is a concept that is sometimes confused with virtual reality and is a form of reality that is integrated into non-print applications and can be experienced in cinema, music, print, radio, television, internet and mobile networks (Bozat & Dedelioğlu, 2018, 932).

Contextual design refers to the planning of the elements required to achieve the intended effect in a work of art. In other words, contextual design involves creating a structure or domain (Akten, 2008, 55). Interactivity refers to the fact that a work of art in an artistic context can change according to the audience's reactions. The participation of the audience plays an effective role in determining the form of the artwork (Akten, 2008, 57). Binary coding is a name given to the commands used for the computer to perform the desired task (Brookshear & Brylow, 2016: 222). In this context, artworks are created through computers using digital codes, algorithms and mathematical symbols.

Encoding and Algorithm

He pointed out that there is an order in nature, that all phenomena have a certain rhythm. Algorithms have been in perfect harmony with computers. Computers have made an algorithm subject-specific through codes. Algorithms provide a simple method for solving a particular problem, and these methods are translated into codes in the computer environment, creating a software language. The term coding is often referred to as the computerized software language of algorithms. Coding, which is widely used in applications and websites, contains operations that must be performed according to certain conditions and order. Coding is considered as a sequence of instructions for assemblies including computers, electronic circuits and mechanical systems. According to another definition, coding includes software encryption that decides how the computer will act in the digital environment and contributes to its hardware. It also refers to all the arithmetic operations created with specific numbers, words and symbols. To write code, it is necessary to create an algorithm, which means the sequential coding of operations that must be applied in a certain order to write a program on the computer. An algorithm is a step-by-step path from a problem to a solution and is a structure of thought with a starting point and an end point.

Digital Animation and Video

In the 21st century, artists who work with time-based tools are highly technologized and have professional production tools that are compatible with all kinds of computers and can easily present their works via the internet and reach international distribution channels. Many artists embrace the idea that video art, as well as technology-based art forms, began with an invention (Wands, 2006, p. 143).

The development of software database and game art has been shaped by computer experimentation and experimental work. However, these artists initially resorted to traditional methods in an attempt to transform them into installations. Today, it is seen that they integrate space by using projection mapping on the computer. As virtual reality technologies become more widespread, it will be possible to provide this experience to a wider audience with just glasses.

Yapay Zekanın Sanat Ortamında Kullanılması

Throughout history, the interconnected development of technology and art have stood out as the main elements that distinguish humans from other beings. In this context, the role of technology in the formation process of an object has affected the production of art and caused it to move away from nature. Artists have tended to produce works that are difficult to realize in the computer environment with other objects or different techniques. With the participation of computers, the concept of reality has changed significantly, and in art production, content, location and virtual beings have come to the fore by challenging reality. When we look at the history of digital art, which emerged in the late 20th century, we see that experimental works were at the forefront in the beginning. The development of digital art almost coincided with the emergence of computers, and this art form started a new phase in art by taking its place among contemporary artworks. In the beginning, the use of computers was common in the field of science, but after the 1970s, they began to be used effectively in the field of art.

Digital art has influenced the art movements of the 21st century, evaluated today's understanding of art in different dimensions, and created a new form of expression by using computer software and hardware. The stage of digitalization has formed the basic lines of the perception of light, electricity, energy, simulation, manipulation, virtual reality, time and place in different dimensions. With the perceptual difference created by digitalization on human beings and the features of reinterpreting life in an imaginary universe of its own creation, digital art is considered as a type of art that does not belong. Artists have always taken care to adopt the advanced technologies and materials of their time and to use them in their works to realize their imagined creations. Digital technologies, which followed the electronic technology that emerged in the early 20th century, and all the systems and structures that developed with digitalization, offered new and rich areas of experience for artists.

The effort to transform the opportunities offered by technology into art has become one of the main goals of a person who thinks, questions and aims to reveal the best. In this context, he has shown what achievements can be achieved when imagination and science serve a common purpose. If the purpose of science is to reach scientific information and data, the task of art is to find different ways of expressing oneself. When we focus on today's technologies, it has been seen that when technical knowledge and skill are combined with the aesthetic value of art and the power of expression, the process experienced by the artist and the scientist proceeds in parallel with each other.

Original works produced through artificial intelligence have added different dimensions to art production when created by a computer. The fact that the work can be easily reproduced, copied, or made several different versions of the work has allowed it to be in new approaches with other disciplines. This digital culture created has also given the opportunity for the work to reach a wider audience and for the proliferation of individual art and information sharing spaces. The use of artificial intelligence in the art environment has also changed the audience's perspective on art and technology.

Digital Art and Refik Anadol in Turkey

The relationship between artificial intelligence and art in Turkey is in a developing process. The Ouchhh team is one of the young artists who have attracted attention with their digital installation works. This team, founded by Ferdi Alıcı and September Duranoğlu, has brought a new perspective to the field by launching Turkey's first award-winning new media agency. Ouchhh combines art, science and technology with a multidisciplinary approach by producing interactive new media platforms, kinetic sculptures, sound Deconstructions and data-driven art installations with artificial intelligence using data as paint and algorithm as brush. Their works have won many national and international awards, including Felis, Kristal Elma, Red Dot Award, IDA (International Design Awards, LA) and ADC (Art Directors Club New York) (Manimold, 2019). The art directors club of the art Dectors club of the art directors club of the art directors club of the art directors club of the art directors club of the art directors club of the art directors club of the art directors club of the art directors club of the art directors club of the art directors club of the art directors club of the art directors club

Refik Anadol is an internationally renowned media artist, director and pioneer of machine intelligence aesthetics. The main theme in Anadol's groundbreaking visualizations of the unseen world is data. Anadol's works address the challenges and possibilities imposed on humanity by ubiquitous computing and what it means to be human in the age of artificial intelligence. Anadol investigates how the perception and experience of time and space have radically changed with the dominance of machines in our daily lives. It goes beyond both integrating media into established forms and transforms the logic of new media technology into art and design. Anadol's space-specific three-dimensional data sculptures and paintings, live audio/visual performances and immersive installations take on various virtual and physical forms. Things that were once invisible to the human eye become visible, giving the viewer a new perspective and story about their own stories (URL7).

Technological innovations have changed the way the art field can express ideas and concepts in the most accurate way with various visual forms, and contemporary culture has been designed in a digital environment to offer visual presentation. Thanks to this digitalization, it is expected that the works of art will continue to exist in the future. Refik Anadol, one of the unorthodox new generation artists in accordance with the needs of technology, aesthetics and dynamic space concepts, is a media artist and director who has become a name for combining art with unorthodox forms, specializes in space-specific public art, explores the intersection of physical and digital realities.

The works of the artist, who uses data and artificial intelligence to intertwine different architectural structures and spaces in his works and to make invisible elements visible, reveal the power and immensity of art. In addition, the artist emphasizes that new aesthetic, technology and space perceptions should be reconsidered as contemporary cultural themes develop in his works.

Shaping his works according to data and machine intelligence, Anadol combines media art with architecture to question the future of post-architecture, as well as inviting viewers to imagine an alternative reality and offering them the opportunity to redefine the traditional functions of interior and exterior architecture (URL7).

Figure 1. Refik Anadol & Alper Derinboğaz (Aktif Strüktürler v1.1: Akustik Formasyon / İstiklâl Caddesi, 2011)

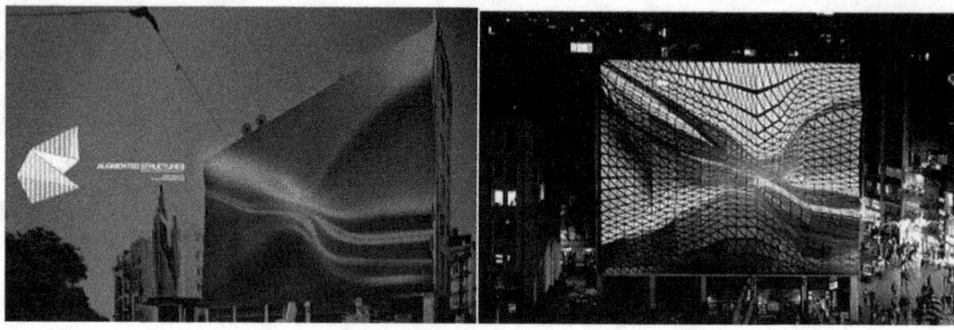

Anadol's works show that every space and facade has the potential to be used as a canvas of a media artist. Refik Anadol's "Active Structures Acoustic Formations" project, whose works have been exhibited in numerous galleries, biennials and digital editing platforms, which has made his name in the art world, was implemented on Istiklal Street in 2011 (Anadol, refikanadol.com, 2013).

Figure 2. Refik Anadol & Alper Derinboğaz (Augmented Structures v1.1: Akustik Formasyon / İstiklâl Caddesi, 2011)

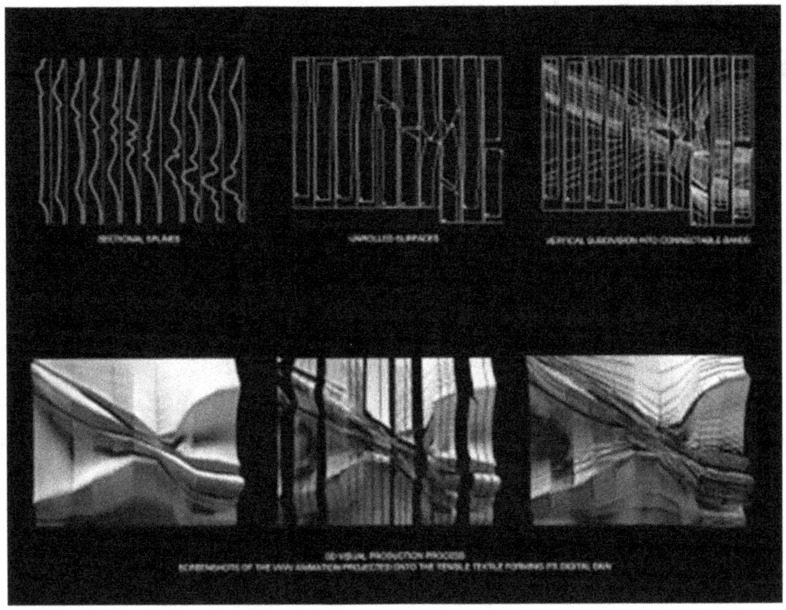

Anadol's works show that every space and facade has the potential to be used as a canvas of a media artist. Refik Anadol's "Active Structures Acoustic Formations" project, whose works have been exhibited in numerous galleries, biennials and digital editing platforms, which has made his name in the art world, was implemented on Istiklal Street in 2011 (Anadol, refikanadol.com, 2013).

Combining these visuals with the third dimension has turned the project into a media installation. The main purpose of the research is to integrate different disciplines by creating new generation designs with different themes, enrich perception and create a multi-layered experience. This project, which covers architecture and urban fabric, is designed as a media installation that shows the relationship between image, sound and architecture, as well as the main goal is to involve city residents in art, attract public attention and create awareness of the area Dec. This installation is an urban experience beyond being a work of art. Istiklal Avenue will definitely take place in the collective memory of its visitors (URL6).

Figure 3. Refik Anadol, Melting Memories, 2018

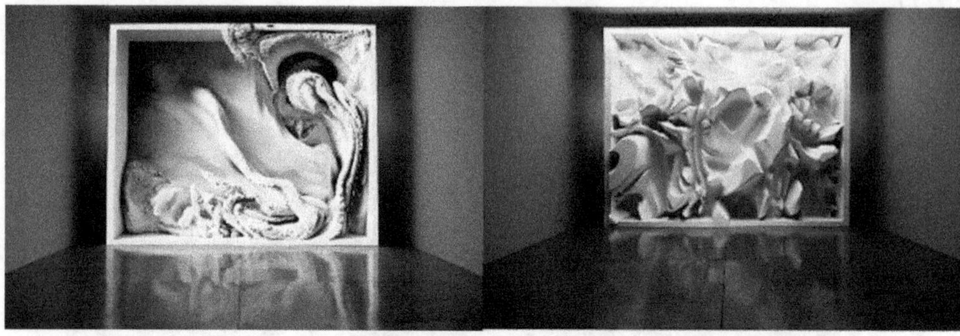

Refik Anadol has combined light projection and artificial intelligence algorithms to transfer how the brain stores memories from a visual perspective with this work he has done with the "Melting Memories" project.

Figure 4. Refik Anadol'un Makine Hatıraları: Uzay Sergisi, 2021, İstanbul

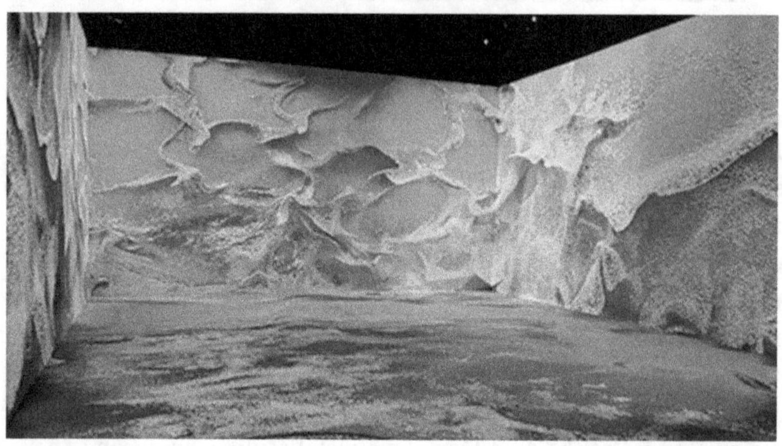

The 3D design exhibited on a special LED media wall has been animated using projection lights at Istanbul Pilevneri Gallery. Anadol used the experiments conducted at the Neuroscape Institute at the University of California, San Francisco to obtain these data, and the data obtained from the EEG measuring brain wave activity revealed valid evidence of the neural mechanisms of cognitive control. By combining these data sets with artificial intelligence algorithms, he has created a unique study by creating a multidimensional visual structure.

Refik Anadol's work "Machine Memories: Space", which will be exhibited at the Pilevneli Gallery in Istanbul in 2021, was created by using space data thanks to a collaboration with NASA JPL. In this work, these data have been transformed into an artistic process using machine learning algorithms. Anadol has brought an innovative perspective to design by researching the universe, topography, machines, human senses, memory and memories through digital art.

Figure 5. Refik Anadol'un Makine Hatıraları: Uzay Sergisi

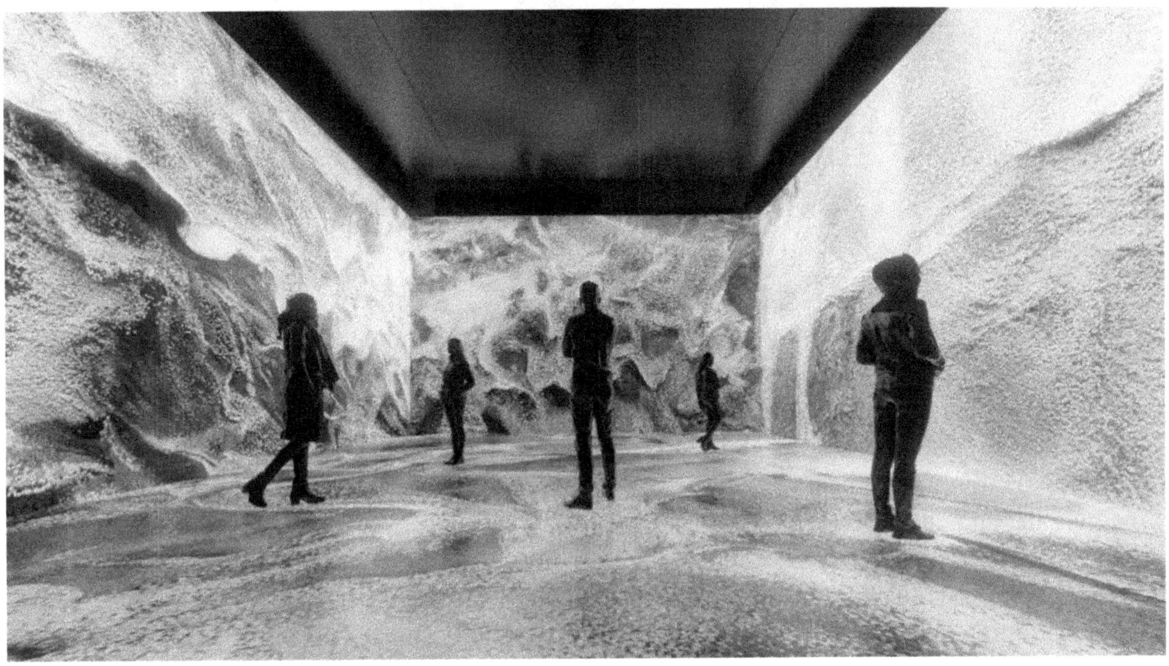

The two main concepts that stand out in Anadol's works are memories and dreams. While memories are based on the concrete data obtained, dreams are shaped by the reinterpretation of these data using digital tools. The section of Refik Anadol's work entitled "Dream" includes the dimensioning of the obtained data by bringing it into a concrete form. In the creation of this section, it was inspired by the first part of the work, which is called "Memory". In the work, the properties of water, earth and sky such as color, shape, sound and light are decomposed by changing. In this decomposition process, elements such as pigment, texture, movement and rhythm are used to create a surreal atmosphere and a real space experience. The experience is realized by dimensioning the color, light and formal changes by gaining a fluid quality. By creating a surreal and changeable space with digital visualizations, Anadol ensures that the audience integrates with the work and conveys the "Machine Dream".

Figure 6. Refik Anadol, Su, Toprak ve Gökyüzü, 2021, İstanbul

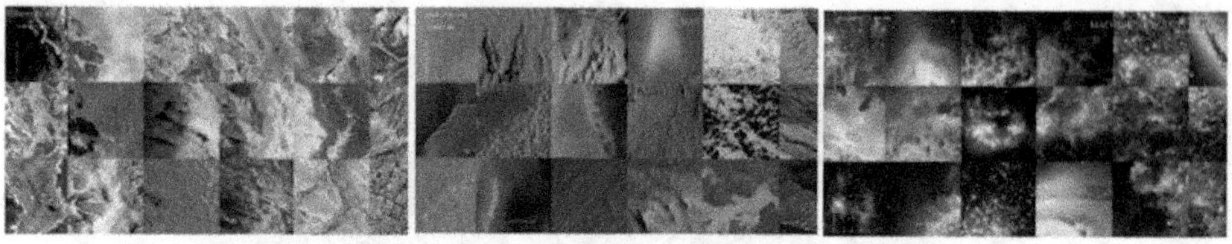

CONCLUSION

As a result, Refik Anadol's works and the historical development of digital art comprehensively summarize the effects of technology on art. The data and artificial intelligence used in Anadol's works show that art is not only an aesthetic, but also a technological research field by bringing new dimensions to the creation process of art. Using data and algorithms, Anadol creates interactive and dynamic works that exceed the traditional understanding of art. These works change and expand the way art is perceived by making the audience active participants.

This integration between art and technology has been especially emphasized by Deceptors and theorists of digital art. Names such as Lev Manovich, Christiane Paul and Bruce Wands have played a leading role in positioning digital art as new media art. Among the main features of digital art are the use of new media technologies, focusing on the aesthetic values of virtual objects, the creation of multi-sensory perceptions and a focused understanding of interaction with the audience.

With the development of technology, coding and algorithms have become the basic elements of art, and new forms such as digital animation and video art have emerged. Artificial intelligence has opened new doors in art production, allowing artists to develop their works in different dimensions and perspectives. This has enabled art to turn from being just a visual form of expression into a technological field of research and discovery.

The development of digital art in Turkey, together with names such as Refik Anadol and the Ouchhh team, shows the impact of technology on art. By using data and artificial intelligence, these artists are transforming traditional art forms and reaching a wide audience. Anadol's works expand the boundaries of art and represent a new understanding of art, especially by exploring the intersection of digital and physical realities.

In the light of these developments, digital art remains a field that is constantly developing with the combination of technology and art. In this process, artists and audiences continue to discover new ways of how art is perceived, produced and shared. It provides a concrete example of how powerful and impressive digital art, science and technology can be when combined with aesthetics and expressive power. This is an important indicator of how art and technology feed and enrich each other, indicating that this integration will deepen even more in the future and reveal new art movements. In addition, public art works that cross the boundaries of physical space by leaving indoor spaces and Octave into the public space enable the user to interact with the public space and increase their sensitivity to the environment.

REFERENCES

Adar, M. (2021). *Dijital Sanat Formlarına Yönelik Bir İnceleme* (Yayımlanmamış Yüksek lisans tezi), Kocaeli Üniversitesi, Sosyal Bilimler Enstitüsü: Kocaeli.

Anadol, R. (2013). http://refikanadol.com/about

Anadol, R. (2018). *Melting Memories*. https://refikanadol.com/works/melting-memories/

Dell'Aria, A. (2021). *The Moving Image as Public Art: Sidewalk Spectators and Modes of Enchantment*. Springer Nature. 10.1007/978-3-030-65904-2

Hall, T., & Robertson, I. (2001). *Public art and urban regeneration: advocacy, claims and critical debates*. Academic Press.

Kaba, F. (1994). *Çizgi Film*. Anadolu Sanat.

Kutlay. (2014). *Algoritma Nedir? Çeşitleri Nelerdir?*https://www.kodlamamerkezi.com/algoritma/algoritma-nedir algoritma-cesitleri/

Lossau, J., & Stevens, Q. (Eds.). (2015). The uses of art in public space. Routledge, Taylor & Francis Group.

Oğuzhan, Ö. (2020). Dijital Sanat ve Yeniden Üretim ve Refik Anadol. Dijital İletişim Kuram ve Araştırmaları, 1-9, Ankara: Nobel Akademik Yayıncılık.

Özel Sağlamtimur, Z. (2010). Dijital Sanat. *Anadolu Üniversitesi Sosyal Bilimler Dergisi*, 10(3), 213–238.

Paul, C. (2008). *Digital Art*. Thames and Hudson.

Paul, C. (2016). *A Companion to Digital Art*. Wiley-Blackwell. 10.1002/9781118475249

Paul, C. (2023). *Digital art*. Thames & Hudson.

Taştan, R. T. (2018). *Türkiye'de Çağdaş Sanatta Yerleştirme (Enstalasyon) ve Kültür* (Yayımlanmamış Sanatta yeterlilik tezi), Gazi Üniversitesi, Güzel Sanatlar Enstitüsü: Ankara.

Tellan, T. (2019). *Sanatın Dönüşümünde Dijital Süreçler ve Yeni Medya Sanatı*, Üsküdar Üniversitesi İletişim Fakültesi 6. Uluslararası İletişim Günleri Dijital Dönüşüm Sempozyumu'nda sunulmuş bildiri, Üsküdar Üniversitesi, İstanbul, s. 651.

Wands, B. (2006). Dijital Çağın Sanatı. Çev. Osman Akınhay. İstanbul: Akbank Kültür ve Sanat Dizisi.

Section 3
Conducive Physical Spaces for Making

Chapter 5
Setting Up a Home "Making Space" After Professional and Academic-Based Ones Built for Everyday Learning, Creativity, and Innovation

Shalin Hai-Jew
https://orcid.org/0000-0002-8863-0175
Hutchinson Community College, USA

ABSTRACT

Common artists, crafters, artisans, and DIY (do-it-yourself) makers need spaces to explore their inspirations and creativity and to advance their making skills. They need a place to set up their equipment. They need a physical location to store their supplies and reference materials and incomplete works. They may need a virtual space to create, too, to harness the power of computation. They need a market for their goods. They need a community, in the real and the virtual, for emotional support, ideas, and camaraderie. There is little known in the way of how these at-home making spaces may be set up for the best outcomes, broadest ranges of possibilities, and ultimate creativity, but it is thought that some insights from professional maker spaces and the academic literature may inform on this challenge. This exploratory work offers some initial ideas from the literature review and applied action research in an auto-ethnographic case.

INTRODUCTION

Making is a phenomenon with roots going back centuries, with influences from manufacturing. Technical innovations along the way have energized this approach. One research team suggests that making goes back to "the founding of America" as a beginning point, and then the industrial revolution and the advent of mass-scale manufacturing sparked greater interest (Bull, Rutter, Garofalo, & Littman, 2022, pp. 8-9). Another researcher suggests that making has been in formation for many generations, with the "embryonic period (1870s-1990s), transition period (2000s-2010s) and outbreak period (after 2011)" in

DOI: 10.4018/979-8-3693-2927-6.ch005

one conceptualization (Yu, 2016, p. 1). The maker movement, as part of progressive education, was "a revolution in waiting for a century" (Blikstein, 2018, p. 437). The technological advances (Tan, Yang, & Yu, 2016, p. 93), heightened affordability of digital fabrication, and the focus on empowerment of learners (even children), contributed to this maker education's popularization. Makerspaces and labs emerged with the idea that the experiential learning there resulted in "an adaptable and transferrable skillset" (Tomko, Newstetter, Alemán, Nagel, & Linsey, 2020, p. 371).

In one adaptation of a makerspace course during the pandemic, an instructor "emphasized the notion that the home was, and continues to be, the original makerspace for humans. As such, students were encouraged to extend their capacity for creativity and curiosity from their homes and into the virtual classroom space. Adaptability was both a core value and a coping mechanism for students and instructor to navigate a semester under the duress of uncertainty and fear" (Melo, March, & Hirsh, Sept. 2021, n.p.) An at-home making space is defined here as a home-based studio or workshop or workspace that combines both material and digital means of ideating, designing, prototyping, making, and refining, and that provides space for social collaboration. It is a space for hobbyist explorations as well as for career advances and side gigs. [Some variations on domestic making spaces may include an external site such as a studio or one-bedroom apartment or some other variation.]

This work offers a review of the literature on various types of professional and academic making / fabrication / hacker spaces / tech shops and takes a page from those to inform on what may be effective for a home "making space," whether in a contiguous area or a distributed one. A famous quote reads: "Amateurs talk strategy; professionals talk logistics." This quote is commonly attributed to General Norman Schwarzkopf, an American military leader. Strategy is a plan of actions that lead to a destination. Logistics is the process of moving resources from their origin to their destination (the how). Various researchers have observed that there is limited research about makerspaces (Sagbauer & Ebner, 2021).

Further, some major definitions have not been explicated, nor methods: "In the fledgling world of makerspaces, what counts as 'expert' making is not clearly defined, nor is how a spatial set up can encourage accomplished making" (Keune, Gomoll, & Peppler, 2015, n.p.). Still, some ground has been covered, and that will be presented here.

Note: The term "making space" is used as a general and generic sort of small-scale production space to be inclusive of the various types of Makerspaces, fabrication labs, hacker spaces, and others.

REVIEW OF THE LITERATURE

For several decades now, makerspaces have been set up at academic institutions, libraries, community centers, and other locations, as a way to advance human learning and small-scale creating and manufacturing. The formalization of the "maker movement" is thought to have started with "Make: magazine" in 2005. That the maker movement did not originate from academic settings (Wilczynski & Adrezin, Nov. 2016, p. 1). The first Maker Faire occurred in 2006 in California.

Making is "a class of activities focused on designing, building, modifying, and / or repurposing material objects, for playing or useful ends…" (Martin, 2015, p. 31, Katterfeldt, 2013, pp. 139 – 141, as cited in Iwata, Pitkänen, Laru, & Mäkitalo, June 2020, p. 87). The research literature lists various activities in makerspaces. In terms of material work, they mention rock polishing, home economics, cooking, gardening, theatre arts, fashion design, sculpting, woodworking, robotics, 3d printing, auto shop, ceramics, board game design, metal work, laser cutting, fiber arts, and others. In digital design, they mention audio design, digital game design, web design, e-textile design, programming, coding, and others. Makerspace workshops include those focused on "electronics, DIY crafting, graphic design, sewing/wearables, and Arduino robotics" (Benton, Dempsey, Mullins, & Shelley, 2013, p. 25).

Common equipment in general makerspaces includes the following: "3D printers; laser cutters and engravers; vinyl cutters; sewing machines and embroidery machines; CNC mills, lathes, and routers; manual knee mills and lathes; band saws, table saws, and routers; hand tools such as drills, saws, routers, and grinders; projection equipment; mobile whiteboards, couches, and work surfaces" and others (Levy, Morocz, Forest, Nagel, Newstetter, Talley, ... & Linsey, June 2016, n.p.)

Makerspaces are a throwback to some older types of education. One research team observes:

> In many countries, traditional workshops for craft have either never existed or been removed from schools for various reasons (e.g. modernization, financial savings, a lack of appreciation or safety concerns). As a result, there is an insufficient culture of design and technology as a curricular subject. (Jaatinen, & Lindfors, 2019, n.p.)

What is old is new again in a sense.

Some practices are clearly from more traditional vocational courses; others are newer from the making space. Makerspaces have roots based in machine shops, project spaces, and social or community space (Andrews, & Roberts, Aug. 2017, p. 1).

Traditionally, some activities are seen as more masculine and others more feminine. For example, in the latter category might include "weaving, sewing, knitting, humanitarian/service projects" (Ahn, & Noh, 2018, p. 5). If there is a signature technology often tied to making spaces, it may be 3d printing. Models made with wood and clay may serve as visual aids, but they are not often functional prototypes where 3d printed objects may be (Kantaros, Diegel, Piromalis, Tsaramirsis, Khadidos, Khadidos, ... & Jan, 2022, p. 2712). 3d enables printing in hyper-precision in ways that other materials are not.

Makers are defined in various ways but are "thought to be focused on using tools and materials to turn their ideas into real products through self-design and production, as well as cooperating and sharing their experiences with others in the process" (Tan, Yang, & Yu, 2016, p. 89). A maker "is a person or a organization that designs, assembles and develops products based on imagination and creativity" (Ahn, & Noh, 2018, p. 6). Makers participate in "production culture" (Ahn, & Noh, 2018, p. 6). One makerspace in an academic library was described as "a hotbed of passion projects" (Radniecki, Klenke, & Purpur, 2016, p. 41). Makers then have to bring the passion and the ideas and the effort.

Maker spaces are described as "an experience-led community space where people gather to make things together with the assistance of both digital and traditional making tools" (Wang, Dunn, & Coulton, 2015, p. 1). Users of makerspaces are expected to be open to collaboration with others (Kang, Kim, & Yoon, 2017, p. 253). The social dimensions of a Maker education include "interaction, sharing, openness, empathy" with others (Kang, Kim, & Yoon, 2017, p. 255). They are "places where *making* happens in *community*" (Litts, 2015, n.p.) One study engages makerspaces as "both a community space and a space for communities" (Wang, Dunn, & Coulton, 2015, p. 1).

Some common synonyms for makerspaces are "design studios" and "invention studios" (Andrews, & Roberts, Aug. 2017, p. 1). Makerspaces, hackerspaces, and fabrication labs are three types of spaces that "developed independently but have appeared to converge towards a similar structure and use" as community workshops where "members share access to tools in order to produce physical goods" (Van Holm & Joseph, 2014, n.p.).

A common framework for such spaces involves "learning by doing" and "learning by making," with activities including "cooking, sewing, welding, robotics, painting, printing, and building" (Peppler & Bender, 2013, as cited in Hsu, Baldwin, & Ching, 2017, p. 589). Makerspaces are "a location with tools (electronic and hand) for fast prototyping" (Nadelson, Villanueva, Bouwma-Gearhart, Soto, Lenhart, Youmans, & Choi, Jan. 2020, n.p.) For many makerspaces, there are ties to entrepreneurship and markets; these are "places to develop professionally and launch new ventures" (Hui, & Gerber, Feb. 2017, p. 2023). The makerspaces are connected to the larger entrepreneurial systems of the community that rewards new thinking and doing (Benton, Dempsey, Mullins, & Shelley, 2013). Entrepreneurship features include the following: "desire to accomplish, self-regulation, risk-taking, creativity, (and) self-efficacy" (Kang, Kim, & Yoon, 2017, p. 256).

The advent of making and making education started out with plenty of hype and high expectations (Halverson, & Sheridan, 2014, p. 497). It is unclear as to whether these endeavors have unleashed mass creativity and innovation. In terms of new products, some works mention smart watches, 3d printers, virtual world headsets, thermostats, and other materials. While some may visualize smart clothing and 3d-printed forms and gadgets, one makerspace project was a "two ton interactive metal sculpture" (Hoople, Mejia, Hoffoss, & Devadoss, 2020, p. 1184). Finally, while makerspaces are thought to enable the emergence of "the next great idea," but "like investing in start-ups, the vast majority can/will be duds, with some moderate or great successes" (Wu, Burg, & Burg, 2020, p. 8). [In some ways, the focus on social sharing among users of makerspaces might suggest that they are sharing at a low-level instead of anything with monetary value or unique IP. It is not in student interests to give away IP.]

The maker movement is seen as emerging globally around the world. It is considered by some to be the third industrial revolution, which may be a hyped term (Beavers, Cady, Jiang, & McCoy, 2019, p. 215). It has attracted users based on a variety of values and practices. The movement has been conceptualized as "a reaction against consumer culture, a pathway to increasing innovation and economic growth, a mindset encouraging personal engagement with technology, a community of hobbyists who build whimsical contraptions, a philosophical creed that defines the critical aspects of our humanity, and a way to empower individuals to solve technical problems that traditionally reside in the domain of experts" (Weiner, Lande, & Jordan, 2018, p. 834). The movement has been about ensuring that making is available to the broad masses in an egalitarian and democratic way. The reasoning goes: "…when the library provides maker experiences throughout the day for little or no money, anyone can have a chance" (Mann, 2018, p. 84) to think up an idea and materialize it and release it into the real world.

The maker spirit is typified by "being sharing, open, and tolerant" (Wu & Ma, 2022, p. 629). There is a liberatory thread to makerspaces, with the "democratization of tools and skills needed for innovation" as a core goal (Masters, Foster, Groen-McCall, McNair, & Riley, 2019, p. 1). The Maker movement is defined as involving "innovative forms of production and do-it-yourself work" (Schön, Ebner, & Kumar, 2014, p. 14). A Maker Movement Manifesto spells out nine principles involving making, sharing, giving, learning, tooling up, playing, participating, supporting, and engaging change (Hatch, 2013, as cited in Schön, Ebner, & Kumar, 2014, n.p.) As another influence, DIY culture focuses on "activism and action" and is "politically charged" (Willett, 2016, p. 316). Another take: "maker culture is inevitably open to criticism on the grounds of being an unrealistic ideological movement" (Curry, 2017, p. 212). Indeed, there is some research that claims around makerspaces are not supported by data: Claims of ties to economic development or that makerspaces are "socially inclusive" and enable "environmentally sustainable practices" seem to lack empirical support (Vinodrai, Nader, & Zavarella, 2021, p. 205).

Maker spaces are spaces for "digital fabrication" (Kantaros, Diegel, Piromalis, Tsaramirsis, Khadidos, Khadidos, ... & Jan, 2022, p. 2715); virtual maker spaces are spaces for creativity and innovation using virtual or digital or online tools. "Virtual making" involves making in online environments (Lock, Redmond, Orwin, Powell, Becker, Hollohan, & Johnson, 2020). Makers require a social media presence to share what they make and to attract relevant attention (Hui, & Gerber, Feb. 2017, p. 2023). The requisite social distancing during the SARS-CoV-2 / COVID-19 pandemic (2020 – 2023) required many who ran academic makerspaces to shift to virtual services, limiting the number of participants in a physical workspace, remote access to digital fabrication machines, cancelling in-person events otherwise, and others. Why the pandemic was such a challenge was because the heart of makerspaces and fabrication labs involve "working with physical materials in collaboration with others" (Kinnula, Milara, Norouzi, Sharma, & Iivari, 2021, n.p.) Others describe "Zoom fatigue" in adapting to the pandemic by adhering to various biosafety protocols. They describe the challenge of teaching an online class on makerspaces "without hands-on instruction, in-person collaboration, and without physically visiting a makerspace" (Crawford et al., 2020, as cited in Melo, March, & Hirsh, Sept. 2021, n.p.) Melo, et al. (2021) describe the challenges of not being able to offer over-the-shoulder real-time critiques as learners were making. Indeed, "guided working" is an important part of the learning in makerspaces (Friessnig, Karre, Schnöll, & Ramsauer, Nov. 2016, p. 56). In light of the pandemic: "University makerspace staff and resources were directed to support efforts related to research, design, manufacturing, and testing solutions" (McGuffin-Cawley, & Wilczynski, 2021, p. 41). Some suggest that permanent changes would occur in makerspaces post-pandemic (McGuffin-Cawley, & Wilczynski, 2021, p. 47).

The analog and digital are combined in "hybrid" makerspaces.

> The dichotomy of digital and non-digital artefacts is re-solved in a hybrid learning space by seamlessly bridging different types of artifacts, making digital data touchable and graspable, enhancing physical objects with digital information and digitizing physical objects. (Kohls, July 2022, p. 1)

Computer-controlled tools enable new users to "produce objects with a relatively high level of finish" or refinement (Martin, 2015, p. 32). There is high fidelity between the material and the digital, and the digital is available for broad sharing (Martin, 2015, p. 32).

Academic makerspaces are where "traditional machine shop equipment has been combined with digital design and manufacturing tools to establish creative communities" (Wilczynski, June 2015, p. 26.138.2). A core pedagogical construct underlying makerspaces in higher education is constructivism (Brahimi, Khalifa, & Benaouda, 2019, p. 67), which posits that learners actively construct and co-construct the mental constructs of their learning. Maker activities harness "hands-on inquiry learning" (Houston, 2013, n.p.). Some academic makerspaces are standalone while others are part of a network of specialized makerspaces around the campus. A community college system has built a network of makerspaces (Pepper-Kittredge, & Bird, 2020). Another work describes how to program education and learning for making (in an out-of-school network) to meet target learner needs (Santo, Peppler, Ching, & Hoadley, 2015, p. 1).

Mobile makerspaces are "maker locations that can move" from their original premises (Moorefield-Lang, When makerspaces…, 2015, p. 463). Some travel a day at a time, a week at a time, and some all year-round (Moorefield-Lang, When makerspaces…, 2015). They may offer classes and trainings, and making experiences. Some are housed in bookmobiles.

Even though makerspaces have been integrated into pre-K12 through higher education, formal learning spaces, the origins of makerspaces are informal and nonformal; in many cases, campus-based making spaces are "unstructured student-centric environments for design, invention, and prototyping" (definition) (Forest, Farzaneh, Weinmann, & Lindemann, June 2016, n.p.). In higher education, they are "informal sites for creative production in art, science and engineering" (Jaatinen, & Lindfors, 2019, n.p.). Academic makerspaces focus on STEM (science, technology, engineering and mathematics) and STEAM (science, technology, engineering, art, and mathematics). One definition of an academic makerspace reads: "a physical space where people with an interest in Science, Technology, Engineering, Art and Math (STEAM) can meet up, work on projects, and learn through 'Doing-it-Yourself' or "Doing-it-Together'" (Rees, Olson, Schweik, & Brewer, June 2015, p. 26-1751.1). Academic makerspaces are "informal sites for creative production in art, science, and engineering where people of all ages blend digital and physical technologies to explore ideas, learn technical skills, and create new products" (Sheridan, Halverson, Litts, Brahms, Jacobs-Priebe, & Owens, 2014, p. 505). Some academic and community makerspaces stem from "town-gown" efforts, involving both the institution of higher education and the community. Many are built in libraries, continuing a long tradition of libraries being "a home for innovative technology" (Maceli, 2019, p. 781). (Figure 1)

Figure 1. A "Makerspace" or "Fabrication Lab" in a Library (as drawn by the Deep Dream Generator with the AIVision Model)

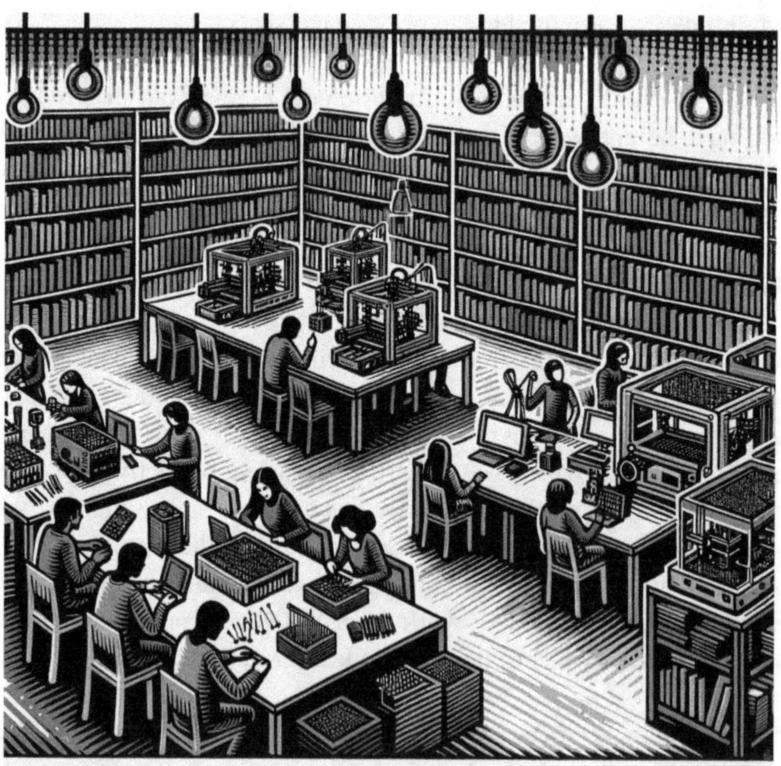

There are between 1,600 (Makerspace Directory, 2024) and over 2,000 (BardAI query) makerspaces in the world today, not including informal ones. By the early 2020s, there were thousands of makerspaces around the world (Hoople, Mejia, Hoffoss, & Devadoss, 2020). Such spaces include "makerspaces, hackerspaces, and fab labs" (fabrication laboratories), which are community spaces "where members share access to tools in order to produce physical goods" (Van Holm, 2014, n.p.). Fabrication labs mostly focusing on 3d design and printing, hackerspaces on "programming, open hardware / software, electronics, sensors, robotics," and makerspaces on "creative cultural and social engagement, using various digital and other tools" (Geser, Hollauf, Hornung-Prähauser, Schön, & Vloet, 2019, p. 62). While these three types of spaces have different points of origin, they have converged on some shared practices. (Van Holm, 2014, n.p.)

A systematic review of the literature found numerous gaps in makerspace research, especially in relation makerspaces in PreK-12 school libraries in the U.S. (Mersand, 2021, p. 174). A systematic review of library makerspaces research found a prevalence of descriptive research, which is seen as less rigorous than empirical approaches (Kim, Jung, & Choi, 2022, p. 1). Another work described the application of phenomenologically based interviewing (PBI) used to learn about makerspaces such as examining the types of learning occurring and the socially informed aspects of participation and roles, among others (Tomko, Aleman, Newstetter, Linsey, & Nagel, 2021, p. 113). Another study involved the developing of assessment tools to measure the learning in library makerspaces (Cun, Abramovich, & Smith, 2019, p. 39). Some studies have mapped parts of the research literature to understand research directions in the study of makerspaces and their use to support the development of "21st century skills" (Konstantinou, Parmaxi, & Zaphiris, 2021, p. 223) and computational thinking (Iwata, Pitkänen, Laru, & Mäkitalo, June 2020). Another work maps the research on makerspaces for a higher level view of the field (Pallaris, Zaphiris, & Parmaxi, 2022).

One study took the approach that it is important to collect as much data as possible to learn about makerspaces, including card reader data, photo ID scanner data, sign-in applications, gate counters, and user surveys (Cooke, & Charnas, 2021, p. 2). There is value in examining grant applications, grant reports, publications, and other gray literature. One study involved a content analysis from an analysis of user agreements, acceptable use policies (AUPs), liability waivers, and other makerspace documentation. This study also included pop literature including "blogs, magazines, zines, etc." (Moorefield-Lang, User agreements…, 2015, p. 358).

Didactic designs in makerspaces are designed to support "digital competence, programming and computational thinking" for the future (Kjällander, Åkerfeldt, Mannila, & Parnes, 2018, p. 18). There is a need for more methodological diversity in the studies around the labs of the makerspace movement (Rosenbaum, & Hartmann, 2017).

The academic literature around making is relatively rich in terms of academia but offers less in terms of professional or industrial making spaces and nothing on home "making" spaces.

One work considers "makerspaces, incubators, and co-learning environments as types of Creative Knowledge Environments" (Salman, 2023, p. 73), given the centrality of creativity. The designed environment of makerspaces are to stimulate creativity and social sharing. Several works used classifications to summarize the makerspaces, given how different makerspaces are designed differently. One study found four main categories of makerspaces: "external makerspaces, school makerspaces, open makerspaces located in schools, and temporary (Pop-up) makerspaces" (Sagbauer & Ebner, 2021, p. 65). An older classification system of makerspaces is based on "scope, accessibility, user-base, footprint, and management staffing" as indices for a framework (Wilczynski, June 2017, n.p.). Such a classification may also be used as a planning tool based on the type of makerspace others want to create (Wilczynski, June 2017). Indeed, makerspaces in higher education range from maker trolleys or "portable carts to entire buildings" (Wilczynski & Hoover, 2017, n.p.). Spaces can be scheduled out in different ways for different uses based on scheduling (Mann, 2018).

Some makerspaces are created for particular populations, such as a constructionist learning lab space for incarcerated youth (Stager, June 2013, p. 487). Humanitarian makerspaces are set up in crisis-afflicted communities to support "migrants, refugees, and asylum seekers" (Corsini, & Moultrie, 2020, p. 374), the displaced and the dispossessed. Some makerspaces are designed to create assistive technologies, in part to promote the capabilities of adults with intellectual and developmental disabilities, In such spaces, users help build assistive technologies in coordination with those with needs, in some cases (Boccardi, Szucs, Ebuenyi, & Mhatre, 2022, p. 1). One makerspace has a pro-environmental and sustainability bent (Mylonas, Hofstaetter, Friedl, & Giannakos, June 2021, p. 1), to train (lifelong) learners to help solve some of the hard problems of the world (Whitmer, 2016). Makerspaces may pique learner interests in extant hard problems of the world such as those related to "energy, disease, fresh water and food, climate change" and others (Hira, Joslyn, & Hynes, Oct. 2014, n.p.). Another making space encourages "eco-making" to design around environmental issues and speed-based design sprints (Roeder, Klemichen, & Stark, 2020, n.p.). Makerspaces may be used to "address interdisciplinary socio-scientific problems" (Choi, Bouwma-Gearhart, Lenhart, Villanueva, & Nadelson, 2021, p. 1).

Affordances of making spaces

One research team worked out what some of the capabilities of makerspaces are. They write:

(1) The capability to skillfully make and do
(2) The capability to assume and perform a valued maker identity
(3) The capability to establish and maintain maker community
(4) The capability to sustain livelihood
(5) The capability to modify one's place in the world
(6) The capability to participate in material culture (O'Donovan & Smith, 2020, p. 70)

How makerspaces are set up may focus on different objectives. Many literacies come with making, such as those surrounding coding, programming, language, visuals, information, and others. There are focuses on a set of various "knowledge, skills, and dispositions" (Andrews, 2017, p. 1).

Different Instantiations of Makerspaces Around the World

The broad spread of making spaces around the world has meant different build-outs of this concept (Wang, Lim, Lavonen, & Clark-Wilson, 2019, p. 1), and differing acceptance and rejection of values linked to the movement (Irie, Hsu, & Ching, 2019). In China, for example, mass innovation spaces have been built out to enable alternate imaginaries to fuel population creativity. Theirs involves a "mix of socialism and technological determinism and a fusion of social conservatism and economic progressivism" (Fu, Li, & Xie, 2022, p. 1). There is encouraging of entrepreneurship. Different areas choose to innovate in their own ways. Another research team observes the centrality of creativity for problem solving (Choi, Lam, Chen, de Sousa, Liu, & Ni, 2022, p. 179). They also observe that socializing and making are separated out instead of integrated to meet the needs of Chinese makers (Choi, Lam, Chen, de Sousa, Liu, & Ni, 2022, p. 188). Making in China is integrated with entrepreneurship. Makerspaces do evoke a "start-up mentality" to try to help users achieve innovative insights (Meyer, 2019, p. 2) and to help makers take their products to market. Makerspaces are seen as aiding national economic development (Aiyeblehin, Onyam, & Akpom, 2018). Similarly, "makification" is built partly off the idea that DIY will turn to "Made in America" (Obama, 2014, as cited in Cohen, Jones, Smith, & Calandra, 2017, p. 217). It is debatable whether top-down policies may actually inspire creativity and innovations, however (Li, Li, & Qiu, 2023, p. 1).

Those who run makerspaces can affect the population of users who use their services by various features (locations), policies (rules, procedures), outreach (who is recruited to use the space), cost policies (charging fees for usage), and other actions. Directors of makerspaces need to engage in active work to encourage and recruit students from all backgrounds to participate in makerspaces (Dukart, Orser, & Guengerich, June 2020, n.p.), The making of mobile "curricular spectacle" draws in learners of various types and backgrounds (Jordan, Knochel, Meisel, Reiger, & Sinha, 2021, p. 52).

An intriguing study suggests that the materials available for usage in a makerspace "…can promote co-constructive learning, for example by distributing workflows across artifacts, and that the study of material artifacts might inform the design of makerspaces based on educational theory" (Keune, Gomoll, & Peppler, 2015, n.p.). The available materials in a makerspace "inadvertently limits who uses the space, how learning happens, or how materials in a space will interact and intra-act over time" (Keune & Peppler, 2019, p. 280). It is important also to consider the logistics around workstations, technologies, programs and workshops, too, as affecting usage (Keune, & Peppler, 2019). How the handiwork of the respective makerspace users is displayed may "legitimize the experiences and expertise" of the users, such as that of "a woman in engineering" (Keune, Peppler, & Wohlwend, 2019, p. 371). Recognition and affirmations are important to motivate learners in their learning and persistence.

One work proposes the harnessing of the Internet of Things (IoT) into makerspaces. IoT refers to the linking of digital objects (sensors, devices, computers) to enable the exchange of data over the Internet (Banerjee, Ferron, Bailey, Imam, & Jariwala, 2020, n.p.) A sensor network in a makerspace may enable the collection of data from various machines and devices. It may enable the collection of use data. There may perhaps be an imbalance in terms of costs to retrofitting "the space and equipment with interconnected sensors and interlocks communicating in sync with a central network" (Banerjee, Ferron, Bailey, Imam, & Jariwala, 2020, n.p.).

PreK-12 and Making

The pipeline for developing world class learners in STEM ("science, technology, engineering, and mathematics") and STEAM (the prior list with the addition of "art") begins in early childhood. One study suggests that STEAM "holds more relevance to learning and experiences in the early childhood years, and perhaps across the lifespan" based on a review of the literature (Johnston, Kervin, & Wyeth, 2022, p. 1). That insight may be relevant for the building of teaching and learning in makerspaces for early childhood learners. Early childhood makerspaces are used for "positive technological development" (Bers, Strawhacker, & Vizner, 2018, p. 75).

Those who would lead, work, and teach in makerspaces require various competencies. These include "technical skills, creative mindset, sense of agency, communication skills, contextual reflection, (and) self-expression" based on applied strategies in makerspaces, including "scaffolding learning, encouraging failure, fostering collaboration, building relationships, (and) assessing performance" (Turakhia, Ludgin, Mueller, & Desportes, Apr. 2023, n.p.) Teachers need to understand the learning opportunities in order to structure the learning activities (Turakhia, Ludgin, Mueller, & Desportes, Apr. 2023). Part of the change in teacher role may mean that they are decentered from their central role in the classroom.

Primary school teachers need to be exposed to theoretical grounding and hands-on learning in order to adapt to teaching in makerspaces (Stevenson, Bower, Falloon, Forbes, & Hatzigianni, 2019).

There may be some discomfort between the informal elements of makerspaces and the formal and even classist elements in accredited learning where some of the makerspaces have been set (Campos, Soster, & Blikstein, 2019, p. 96). Accredited learning in K-12 may be regimented and focused around standardized testing and high-risk learning performance. Making focuses on the concept of innovating from below, a type of bottom-up experimental creating. DIY and design are about remix and learning from others. The phenomenon of "invention through emulation" is common human practice (Bull, Rutter, Garofalo, & Littman, 2022, p. 9). A formal teacher identity may contrast with that of a tinkerer (Campos, Soster, & Blikstein, 2019). Examining tensions and "contradictory discourses" is an effective starting point to better understand maker programs in schools and to work to adjust the tone of these spaces for more effective learning (Campos, Soster, & Blikstein, 2019).

An important goal is equitable access and inclusivity in practice at the high school level of makerspaces (Martin, Dixon, & Betser, 2018, p. 36). Library makerspaces for youth need to enable users to "geek out" with friends and others (Koh, & Abbas, 2015, p. 114). Users of makerspaces also need access to food, which is important to creativity (Sullivan, 2010, p. 142).

A making space for young learners involves a proper design to inspire students to "own their learning and deepen their thinking by exploring the world with all their senses" (Kurti, Kurti, & Fleming, 2014, p. 1). To this end, it makes sense not to over plan the space (Kurti, Kurti, & Fleming, 2014, p. 10). The practices in the space need to affirm some core concepts, including that failures are "growth opportunities" (Harron, & Hughes, 2018, p. 266). Researchers caution that due diligence is required before moving in the direction of makerspaces given the costs of space, staffing, and resources (Kirio, 2022, p. ii), as well as potential opportunity costs. There are practical challenges such as constant equipment maintenance and repair (Oswald, & Zhao, 2021). A lack of specialized staff to train users on technologies result in superficial or "passive use" of the technology tools (Vinodrai, Nader, & Zavarella, 2021, p. 215). At minimum, it is important to first define the purpose of the makerspace and then designing from there for the library context (Nagle, 2021). There may be insufficient information as to the value of makerspaces for teaching and learning (Kirio, 2022). In an academic setting, the standing up of a makerspace requires 2-3 years (NMC Horizon Report, 2015, as cited in Wong, & Partridge, 2016, p. 143). Placing makerspaces under the auspices of the library may mean a source of funding for makerspaces though (Burke, 2015). Depending on the build-out of the makerspace, such spaces are "reasonably cheap to try out and experiment with" (Moorefield-Lang, Makers in the library…, 2014, p. 590). One work about a higher education makerspace described the building out of a "pilot facility" to test out how a makerspace may fit with the institution (Nichols, Melo, & Dewland, 2017, p. 363).

Another researcher emphasizes professional development for those who would stand up makerspaces for learning (Oliver, 2016, p. 160). Formal teacher training does not include "informal teaching and spaces, which can include the integration of science, mathematics, engineering, and technology (STEM) content areas and experiences" (Douglass, 2023, p. 538). It is important for the teacher to take on the learner role to better teach in makerspaces (Douglass, 2023, p. 546). A graduate course for new teachers helps them learn to lead justice-oriented teaching and learning in makerspaces to make it as "equitable and consequential" as possible (Heredia, & Tan, 2021, p. 173 and 177). It helps for teachers to have some experiences as makers themselves (Petrich, Wilkinson, & Bevan, 2013, as cited in Godhe, Lilja, & Selwyn, 2019, p. 320).

Librarians-in-training would benefit from learning how to support makerspaces as part of their education. Makerspace library services do not necessarily "come standard" and involve complexities that are not included in librarian trainings given the teaching and learning approaches and technologies, among others (Moorefield-Lang, Change in the making…, 2015, p. 108).

Another emphasizes the need for users to personally own the learning and engage independent thinking (Kurti, Kurti, & Fleming, 2014, p. 20). One work suggests that the technological literacies in makerspaces focus more on generalist technologies than "exploration and fabrication technologies" (EFTs) (Blikstein, Kabayadondo, Martin, & Fields, 2017, p. 149). Effective leadership around makerspaces requires balance: One researcher suggests that the machine shop, the project space, and the community space, should be set up in balance (Culpepper, Nov. 2016, p. 12). The designed curriculum should be both "enjoyable for students" and "support academic objectives" (Julian, & Parrott, 2017, p. 15). Spaces have to be designed in user-centered ways to encourage their use, with spaces conveying "coherence, complexity, legibility, and mystery dimensions" to draw learners from across various majors and to be more inclusive (Hynes, & Hynes, 2018, p. 881). "User-centric" makerspaces are designed to meet user needs (Santos, Barber III, Harris, & Haymore, 2021).Learners have to be motivated to spend time in makerspaces and to take on work and learning projects (Hilton, Forest, & Linsey, 2020). Another motivator may be the inspiring of "wonder" to connect to their curiosity and sense of "playful exploration" (Kurti, Kurti, & Fleming, 2014, p. 10).

Virtual making may expand teaching and learning possibilities. One study did identify some "inhibitors" to virtual making that were "pragmatic rather than theoretical" (Lock, Redmond, Orwin, Powell, Becker, Hollohan, & Johnson, 2020, p. 964). Virtuality enables socially connected making through "connected virtual makerspaces" (Khadri Ahmed, 2023, n.p.). Setting up making spaces is not only about buildings and workstations and technologies; it is about "building a great community that embraces the maker movement and advocates for learning by making or doing" (Wang, Wang, Wilson, & Ahmed, 2016, p. 13).

Some making spaces used for youth learning require the use of maker portfolios to document student work and to encourage their learning reflection. A common practice involves sharing their work via digital portfolios (Keune, & Peppler, 2017). Constructivism as a core underlying educational theory, which includes "making" and "sharing" (Cohen, Jones, Smith, & Calandra, 2017, p. 220). In other work, in makerspaces positioning learners to civic action, learners had to understand how to move people:

> To mobilize audiences into meaningful publics oriented toward collective action, young people needed to see themselves as civic actors who could contribute to broader public conversations and whose opinions, perspectives, and experiences mattered. (Stornaiuolo, & Nichols, 2018, p. 1)

Part of this work involves having a voice in the world by cultivating receptive audiences and publics.

How do youth form maker identities? Do these maker identities lead to future interests in engineering? One study explores the identities emerging from the experiences of using makerspaces, with the importance of a "failure-positive mindset, grit, and self-motivation" as part of making culture (Weiner, Lande, & Jordan, 2018, p. 833). There is a sense that the core design focus of makerspaces is "identity-building through design and technology" (Fasso, & Knight, 2020, p. 289). As a platform, makerspaces enable users to "nurture their tacit knowledge" (Lam, Cruz, Kellam, & Coley, Jan. 2019, n.p.)

Ideally, makerspaces would spark a "will to learn" in people (Pernia-Espinoza, Sanz-Garcia, Peciña-Marqueta, Martinez-de-Pison-Ascacibar, Urraca-Valle, & Antoñanzas-Torres, 2018, p. 2702), which is needed in a world saturated with information.

One work explores possible futures of makerspaces as basic components of K-12 education (Khadri Ahmed, 2023). These were seen as the next versions of educational technology in K-12 schools (Strycker, 2015, p. 28).

Higher Education and Making

Maker learning is thought to promote "design thinking" that aligns with STEM and STEAM learning and work (Lindstrom, Thompson, & Schmidt-Crawford, 2017, p. 89). Problem solving using digital technology is part of being a digital citizen; it is a core digital competency (LeBlanc, Freiman, & Furlong, 2018). Makerspaces enable the acquiring of the knowledge and skills "crucial for work, conviviality, and citizenship" that changes over time (Blikstein, & Krannich, June 2013, p. 613), so the spaces themselves have to evolve. Academic makerspaces are created around three purposes: " i) to make 'makers,' ii) to democratize technology, and iii) to create the opportunity for students to learn by doing" (Wu, Burg, & Burg, 2020, p. 2). These may be general access makerspaces or discipline-specific ones in higher education (Wu, Burg, & Burg, 2020, p. 4). Another way to label general access makerspaces is discipline-agnostic makerspaces (Musick Peery, & Chivers, 2018, p. 1). The primary focus on of academic makerspaces in higher education are "coursework projects," followed by "collaborative and personal projects" (Wong, & Partridge, 2016, p. 153).

DIY making originates out of a radical and countercultural pedagogy, which perhaps challenges established orders. Making activities involve "freedom and minimal restrictions" in a time when formal education is highly defined and standardized (Cohen, Jones, Smith, & Calandra, 2017, p. 222). Learning by making is part of the "institutional periphery" (Fordyce, Heemsbergen, Mignone, & Nansen, 2015, p. 203), in higher education as well as PreK-12. And yet, they affordances of makerspaces are seen as sufficiently relevant that they have been adopted in various curricula.

Makerspaces enable low-, mid- and high-complexity learning (Oswald, & Zhao, 2021, pp. 6-7). The idea is to go beyond surface learning to deeper knowledge and insights. For example, there is the study of physical phenomena such as "balance, forces and motion, light electricity and magnetism, resonance, symmetry, and others" (Bevan et al., 2015, p. 99, as cited in Hsu, Baldwin, & Ching, 2017, p. 590). While some of the making may be "by numbers," there may be underlying lessons about electronics, physics, digital literacy, coding, and other phenomena.

Safety training and practices are important to keep STEM labs (as compared to makerspaces) as safe as possible for staff and learners (Love, 2022). Researchers write:

> Integrated STEM labs can pose increased hazards in comparison to makerspaces, including physical, chemical, biological, and other hazards (e.g., chemistry experiments, biological dissections, construction and materials processing. (Love, Roy, Gill, & Harrell, 2022, p. 113)

The equipment and technologies in various makerspaces are not without risk. A lack of engineering knowledge may also lead to potential safety risks (Kohls, July 2022). For some invention studios, students may propose an idea, and the work may be done by others with more direct expertise (Forest, Moore, Jariwala, Fasse, Linsey, Newstetter,... & Quintero, 2014, p. 1), belying the direct hands-on aspects of making.

The design-creation-innovation sequence and the hypothesize-test-build-assess sequence in the making of objects and artifacts can expose learners to different ways of learning. Makerspace learning supplements engineering education, for example, with "a different way of learning" (Morocz, Levy, Forest, Nagel, Newstetter, Talley, & Linsey, June 2015, p. 26.1631.1). As "low-risk, high-reward" spaces, makerspaces are thought to help bring more diverse learners into engineering, including "mechanical, biomedical mechanical, civil, software, chemical, and computer (Boudreau, & Anis, 2019, pp. 1 and 5). Makerspaces are thought to benefit learning by engineering students in the following ways (as observed by faculty):

1. Improving students' communication, collaboration, and teamwork skills;
2. Developing problem-solving and investigation skills;
3. Nurturing entrepreneurial, leadership, and management skills;
4. Increasing students' self-confidence;
5. Providing opportunities for hands-on and technical experience;
6. Demonstrating manufacturing/prototyping methods and the challenges/limitations involved (Taheri, Robbins, & Maalej, 2020, p. 13)

Further, critical thinking is an important part of making (Taheri, Robbins, & Maalej, 2020, p. 7). The work involves "hands-on minds-on learning experiences" (Trust, Maloy, & Edwards, 2018, p. 19). Manufacturing laboratories enable a deeper understanding of digital manufacturing and related technologies (Alía, Ocaña, Caja, Maresca, Moreno-Díaz, & Narbón, 2019, p. 938). They enable a sense of the importance of speed to market for various industries. Makerspaces are designed to contribute to "venture creation" (Oswald, & Zhao, 2021, p. 1).

For makerspaces to be well-used on a campus, faculty allies are critical because they may integrate the makerspace into in-class learning (Carnasciali, Gillespie, & Hossain, Oct. 2021). One work highlights the adoption of maker practices into a university's undergraduate curriculum (Wallace, Trkay, Chivers, & Peery, 2017), requiring collaborations with subject faculty. Makerspaces in academia are focused on engineering and technology education (Tan, Yang, & Yu, 2016). For thriving future careers in engineering, students would benefit from the competences of "teamwork, problem-solving, communication and life-long learning" and transferable technical skills (Youmans, Villanueva, Nadelson, Bouwma-Gearhart, Lenz, & Lanci, 2020, p. 3). Given the competitiveness of the world's job markets, learners in engineering would benefit from interdisciplinary knowledge and the hands-on work which builds on theoretical knowledge (Bengü, & Keçeci, 2021; Galaleldin, Bouchard, Anis, & Lague, 2016).

Instructors who use makerspaces have shared some challenges they've faced. In one case, there were risks of projects that "were poorly constructed, lacked effort, and fell apart quickly" and others that required excessive "teacher input" or did not convey the desired concepts (Carbonell, Boklage, Clayton, & Borrego, June 2020, n.p.). Many students used the most recent concept introduced by the professor as the basis for their projects instead of offering something novel. Another study found that engineering faculty members found that they engaged in "curricular and instructional innovations" while using makerspaes for teaching (Lenhart, Bouwma-Gearhart, Villanueva, Youmans, & Nadelson, 2020, n.p.). There are pedagogical improvements from makerspaces (Colegrove, 2017). Didactic models from mechanical engineering are being created for use in makerspaces (Perez, Arroyo, Reyes, Rossino, Rocha, & Ayerdi, 2023).

Users of makerspaces need to transform into "active learners" who engage in "learning-by-making" (Stager, June 2013, p. 490).

To be effective, makerspaces have to be integrated into the formal assigned learning. Researchers write:

> Contrary to popular perceptions, the power of makerspaces is not the space itself or the expensive tools that can be part of those spaces. The promise of making is its orientation toward empowering students to bring their interests, curiosity, and creativity to bear in content-area learning. (Salisbury & Nichols, 2020, p. 52)

The respective makers have to find the learning meaningful (Gladson, 2023). They have to experience a sense of self-efficacy in the work.

One study found "a positive correlation between levels of participation in university maker spaces during freshman year and two engineering design self-concepts…" of heightened motivation and lessened anxiety about "performing engineering design tasks" (Morocz, Levy, Forest, Nagel, Newstetter, Talley, & Linsey, June 2016, n.p.).

In higher education, makerspaces apply to STEM and non-STEM courses as a central learning focus. However, they also bridge "the humanities and the sciences" (Jaatinen, & Lindfors, 2019, n.p.). One study examined the phenomenon of non-STEM student engagement in makerspaces, with student participants hailing from education and geography. A core tenet of the learning involves the importance of solving authentic problems in their makerspace work to be effective (Pendergast, 2020). Instructors would do well to understand that there is a "potentially wide range of experience and skills among students working on maker projects" (Pendergast, 2020,p. 142). Some learners described a techno-phobia response, so work to mitigate those fears is important. This study found a broad range of ways that the respective makers, even with different roles, showed engagement and reflection. A particular type of reflection was found to be important: "in-action reflection" or thinking while doing (Pendergast, 2020,p. 163). Academic makerspaces are also used to support design classes in higher education (Wilczynski & Adrezin, Nov. 2016, p. 3), literacy classrooms (Nichols, 2020), and others.

Some institutions of higher education enable outside innovator teams to work with those on-campus to co-develop innovations (White & Burg, 2019). Informed by the memes of garage innovations and Silicon Valley startups, some courses are set up to serve as academic incubators to support the work of young entrepreneurs, to fast track their designs and ideas (Delphenich, & Broz, 2015). These spaces help connect universities and industry, in a shared innovation economy. The takeaway skills may enable makers to better compete in the global economy (Pines, Sullivan, & Nogales, June 2015, p. 26.295.1). While many may think that makerspaces are about making designs and objects, they are also about "turning creative ideas into social innovations" (Geser, Hollauf, Hornung-Prähauser, Schön, & Vloet, 2019, p. 60) and turning out individuals with entrepreneurial education and a sense of self-efficacy and creativity in that space (Unterfrauner, Voigt, & Hofer, 2021).

Some makerspaces in higher education claim intellectual property (IP) rights to what the users design and create in makerspaces while others release rights to inventions to the user-creators (Forest, Farzaneh, Weinmann, & Lindemann, June 2016). Students who are not working under a grant and are not using significant makerspace resources do not have to sign over rights (Forest, Moore, Jariwala, Fasse, Linsey, Newstetter,... & Quintero, 2014, p. 14). For some makerspaces, those decisions seem to be made in a case-by-case basis.

If makerspaces are about innovative thinking, that also applies to their creation and management. For example, one group transitioned to a student-managed maker space and found that resulted in "more innovative and entrepreneurial initiatives" vs. "traditional course-based projects" (Sullivan, Pines, Sassenfeld, & Nogales, 2016, p. 1). Another study found "no negative impact on student satisfaction or grades" with the student-led makerspace in higher education and the added benefit of savings on staff costs (Mylon, Wood, & Dolmansley, July 2019, p. 253).

Various works explore best practices for creating and leading makerspaces, including how to plan and conduct active-learning workshops in academic makerspaces (McCue, Huculak, & Johnson, 2020); redefine necessary 21st century skills (Rayna, & Striukova, 2021); 21st century soft skills and others (Andrews, 2017, p. 2); design teaching for "future learning spaces" (Eyal & Gil, 2020, p. 1061); use hybrid formal and informal teaching patterns including "convergent groups; teaching in an interactive orchestrated learning space; presentation fair; and Think-Join-Share" patterns (Eyal & Gil, 2020, p. 1061); and share what is learned about makerspaces, especially in the early days of these spaces (Fehringer, Kaar, & Stary, Sept. 2019, p. 1). There is a risk of being a STEM makerspace being a "waste of space" if improperly designed (Benjes-Small, Bellamy, Resor-Whicker, & Vassady, 2017).

Ensuring Diversities of Users

Those who run makerspaces need to understand how informal spaces may have different "inclusion and invitation to experiences" (Douglass, 2023, p. 538). There is an observed risk of makerspaces lapsing into "hegemonic, marginalizing norms" that define "making" in exclusivist and non-inclusive ways (Andrews, & Boklage, 2023, p. 1). To head off this possibility, it is important to engage purposeful work in the area of diversity, equity, and inclusion (DEI). One study involves evaluating the various social identities mentioned in research works around makerspaces [such as "gender identity, racial/ethnic identity, socioeconomic status, 'diverse learners,' disability status, first-generation immigrants, sexual orientation, first-generation college students, indigenous peoples, multilingual status, (and) age"] (Andrews, & Boklage, 2023, p. 11). One goal of makerspaces is to enable boundary crossing, such as "between adults and youths, insiders and outsiders" (Keune, Gomoll, & Peppler, 2015, n.p.). There are concerted efforts to be inclusive of diverse participation, including the homeless and other dispossessed, racial minorities, women, veterans, those with diverse gender identities, those with variant sexual orientation, and all (Riley, McNair, & Masters, 2017). There is benefit from a cross-fertilization of ideas from a diversity of peoples, with "divergent mindsets" (Cohen, Jones, Smith, & Calandra, 2017, p. 229) and a density of ideas to enable mixing to make new connections (Farritor, 2017). One study found that "engaging in makerspaces was found to promote agency and engineering identity for Black male undergraduates," but those located in predominantly white institutions were found to "reflect the heteronormative culture of engineering" resulting in a sense of barriers (Greene, Kellam, & Coley, 2019, p. 2).

Makerspaces show tensions between social inclusion and exclusion. One research team explains it this way:

> The makerspace habitus is characterized by the cultivation of a mindset of innovation and creativity shepherded through supportive interactional forms. Yet, the cultures and the contexts of the spaces themselves produce a tension of accessibility and exclusivity—cultivating privileged statuses and identities for some students who accumulate capital more readily than others or who enter the space with capital that others do not hold, (Alemán, Tomko, Linsey, & Nagel, 2022, p. 356)

The observed gender imbalances in the uses of makerspaces have been concerning and resulted in calls for more balanced representation among users through more appealing spaces, increasing comfort learning about technologies, and events to bridge to the makerspace (Lewis, 2015, p. 1). Having more diverse users of all backgrounds at makerspaces is thought to enable diversifying perspectives and production skills (Ahn, & Noh, 2018). One work proposes "multipronged" approaches to encouraging women's participation in makerspaces, including expanding definitions of making to legitimize the arts and crafts as part of design" (Tomko, Alemán, Newstetter, Nagel, & Linsey, 2021, p. 700).It is important to "change the narrative of who makers are, what making is, and who belongs in makerspaces to reduce barriers and create inclusive making communities" (Tomko, Alemán, Newstetter, Nagel, & Linsey, 2021, p. 700). The researchers even suggest the need to "attend to early childhood experiences" to better understand where the barriers and supports are for their participation in educational makerspaces and ultimately engineering and other fields (Tomko, Alemán, Newstetter, Nagel, & Linsey, 2021, p. 700).

There are a range of applications and digital tools to make ambient learning spaces more functional and welcoming (Herczeg, Winkler, & Ohlei, 2019, p. 5116). Users of makerspaces must experience "positive experiences" based on the space and the support and other factors; students' "different personal characteristics" need to be recognized and affirmed in "a safe place that encourages various kinds of solutions based on learning tasks" (Jaatinen, & Lindfors, 2019, n.p.)

There are efforts to ensure makerspaces are accessible, based on a universal design and intersectionality approach. One seminal work proposes the principles of SCAFFOLD, which include the following: "Simplicity, Collaboration, Accessibility, Flexibility, Fail-safe, Object-oriented, Linkability, (and) Diversity" (Seo, & Richard, 2021, p. 804). Another work suggests three components to designing makerspaces to be more welcoming to those with disabilities, including "a tour, design activity, and brainstorming session" to achieve the work (Steele, Blaser, & Cakmak, 2018, p. 114). Such reviews may suggest reconfiguring the space with wider entries and exits, offering various equipment, and enabling white boards to be set at adjustable heights (Steele, Blaser, & Cakmak, 2018, p. 117).

One researcher suggests flexible responses to user needs in makerspaces. For example, makers do not have privacy as they work in the makerspace, but some makerspaces enable students to perhaps bring boxes of maker tools home to continue the learning and work (Kohls, July 2022, p. 9). Some learners prefer to work for various lengths of time, including, extended periods, without interruption (Kohls, July 2022).

SETTING UP A HOME "MAKING SPACE" AFTER PROFESSIONAL- AND ACADEMIC-BASED ONES BUILT FOR EVERYDAY LEARNING, CREATIVITY, AND INNOVATION

The research on professional- and academic- makerspaces has some limited value for the making of an at-home making space. In terms of overlap between the professional and the academic to the domestic home, there is only a sliver of overlap. Certainly, if the home "maker" has professional and academic ambitions, perhaps more of the research may be directly relevant. The level of sophistication of each maker may vary depending on the target knowledge set and skill: Novice, advanced beginner, competence, proficiency, or expert? At every level of expertise, the DIY ethos of being self-sufficient and capable, humble, open-to-learning, and social, may benefit the work.

From the research, an initial list of askable questions was created. There are some practical questions to ask about what is desired from the at-home making space:

OBJECTIVES

Defined Objectives of the Home Making Space

- What knowledge, skills, and attitudes / abilities (KSAs) does / do the makers want to acquire and maintain from the at-home making space? What do they want to learn, and how?
- What about entrepreneurial production? Small-scale manufacturing? Ghost studios without storefronts? Sales activities? Marketing activities?
- What about publicity? Marketing? Social media?
- What sorts of problem solving will need to be achievable in the space?

CREATIONS, DELIVERABLES

Typical Projects and Deliverables

- What types of projects will they take on? And for what deliverables? Will the deliverables be for commerce and market?
- What information will be needed for these projects? What technologies? What equipment? What materials?

BUDGETING, RESOURCING

Budgets and Resources

- How much of a budget is there to work with? What are the anticipated monetary intakes?
- What may be phased for an early build? What may be phased for a later build?

SPATIALITY: PLACE

Available Physical Spaces

- What space is there to work with? Is it an extant and built-out space, or will it be built from scratch?
- What are the various options for the physical space layout? What configurations are possible?

- What is needed for spatial security? Air ventilation? Electronics? Lighting? Ceiling features? Wall features? Floor features? Door features?
- What sorts of storage is needed? Drying spaces?
- What is the space design to enable multiple simultaneous users?

Integration With the Home

- How does the home-based making space integrate with the rest of the home? (a refurbished garage? An attic space? An extra room? A basement space?) Or is it a stand-alone structure?

VIRTUAL SPATIALITY

Available Virtual Spaces

- What are virtual communities that the users may be part of for new learning and mutual supports?
- What virtual spaces are available for marketing the work?
- How do the home "makers" connect with the larger community? How do they convey their sense of "ownership" over their own work? And how does the larger community know to connect to the home "makers"?

(PHYSICAL AND VIRTUAL) RESOURCES AND EQUIPMENT

Analog Resources and Equipment

- What media equipment will be used in the space?
- What material supplies will be needed? What will the replenishment cycles be?
- What sorts of lighting are needed in the space?
- What are the refresh cycles for analog resources and equipment?

Digital Resources

- What wireless connectivity will be needed?
- What sorts of wireless and wired connectivity?
- What computers?
- What equipment for digitizing (scanners, digital cameras, and others) is needed?

- What online and virtual making sites and technologies will be used?
- What web-facing stores will be used? What archival systems to store digital imagery and showcase works (in digital form)?
- If there are ambitions for inventorship, what are some "accelerator" elements? Bridging to the inventing community?
- What are the refresh cycles for digital resources?

Analog and Digital Meshing

- How will analog and digital mesh in the space?

SAFETY

Safety Equipment

- What safety features will be available? Fume hoods? Air handling units?
- Safety equipment?
- Safety clothing? Safety wearables?

SECURITY

Secure Space

- Controlled access
- Spatial awareness
- Sensors for threats (such as smoke, monoxide detection)

ACCESSIBILITY

Accessibility

- What sorts of accessibility accommodations are there?
    - In physical space

- In virtual space
- Others

INSPIRATION

Inspirational Contents

- What subscriptions to paid content?
- What about to music? To film? And others?
- What about to imagesets? Videosets? Animations? Others?

PRINCIPLES AND VALUES

Principles and Values

- Are there principles and values that may further inform the development of the home making space? Particular aesthetics? The *fengshui* of the space(s)?

ENVIRONMENTAL FRIENDLINESS

Environmentally Friendly Buildouts

- How can the space be built out and used in environmentally friendly ways?

WORK PROCESSES

Walk-Throughs and Workstations

- How will users use the space? What are different walk-throughs? What are different work stations? How flexible will the space be for different uses?
- What are ways to optimize the space design?

PUBLICITY SPACE

Publicity Staging

- If the home making space is a backdrop for video-making and photo-taking, what lighting is needed? What backdrops? What staging areas?

MOBILE VERSIONS

Mobile Versions

- Is there need for a mobile version of a home making lab? What would it look like?
- What sorts of ruggedized equipment is needed?
- What sorts of "pop-up" making space or studio may be set up? With how much effort for the setup and the takedown?
- How would it pack up and out? (A go-bag with a stool and tripod?)

PROGRAMMING, LEARNING

Programming

- How will users of home making spaces program their own learning? How will they self-lead and self-discipline?

The above list of questions may suggest an expensive outlay. Maybe a more appropriate one is the spirit that "any dedicated educator can create a makerspace, regardless of budget, as long as there is vision and willingness to try" (Julian, & Parrott, 2017, p. 18). A space does not have to be stood up at once, but it may be funded and built out over time.

This work is augmented with some visuals created in the Deep Dream Generator tool. Some of the images were seeded with alcohol ink paintings for different color looks-and-feels. (Figures 2 – 7)

Figure 2. A Makerspace Work Station that Resonates as a Professional Space (as envisioned by the Deep Dream Generator, using the AIVision model)

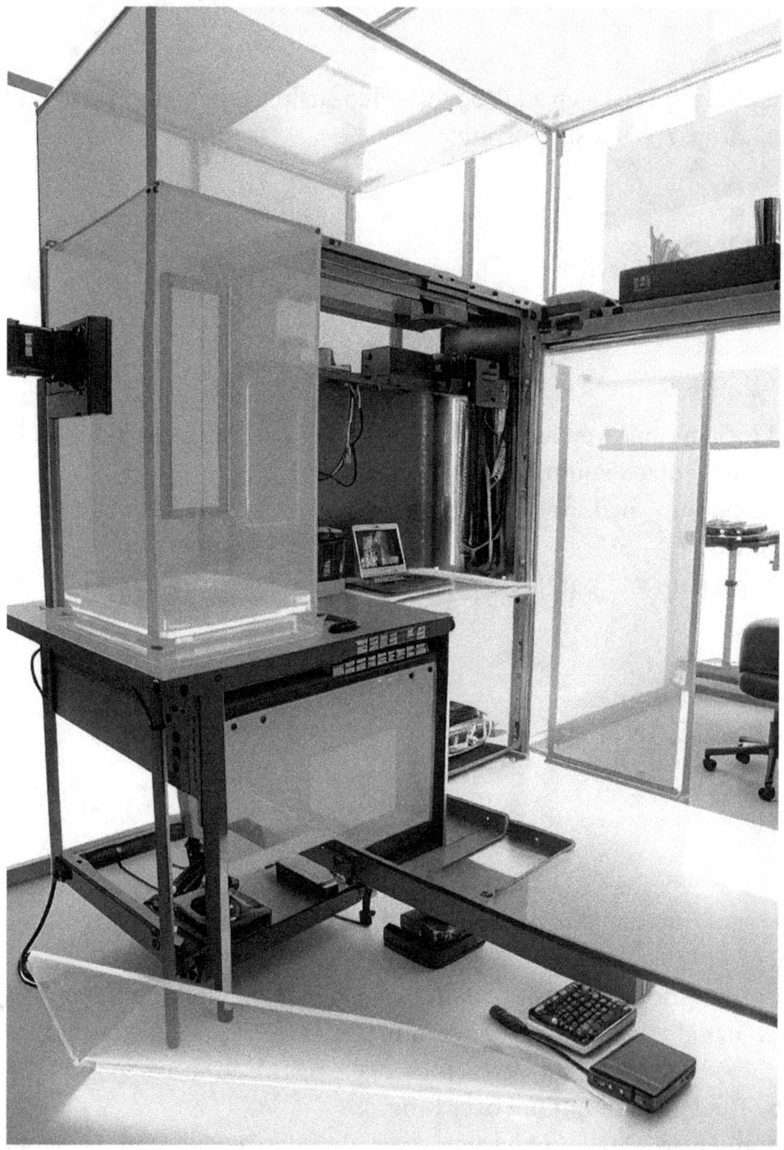

Figure 3. Desktop 3d Making as Depicted by Deep Dream Generator

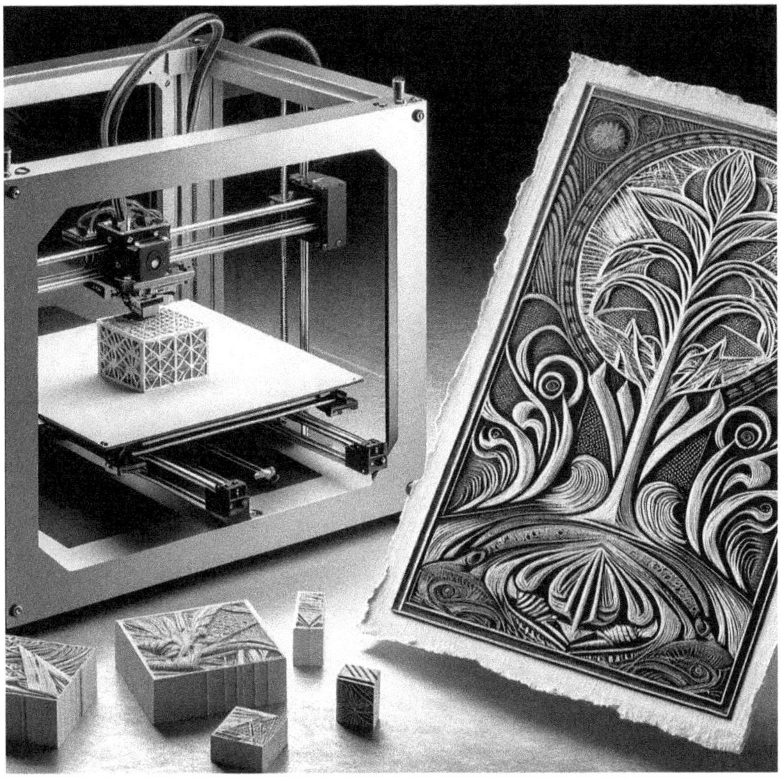

Figure 4. Supplies for a Making Space (as envisioned by the Deep Dream Generator, using the Photonic model)

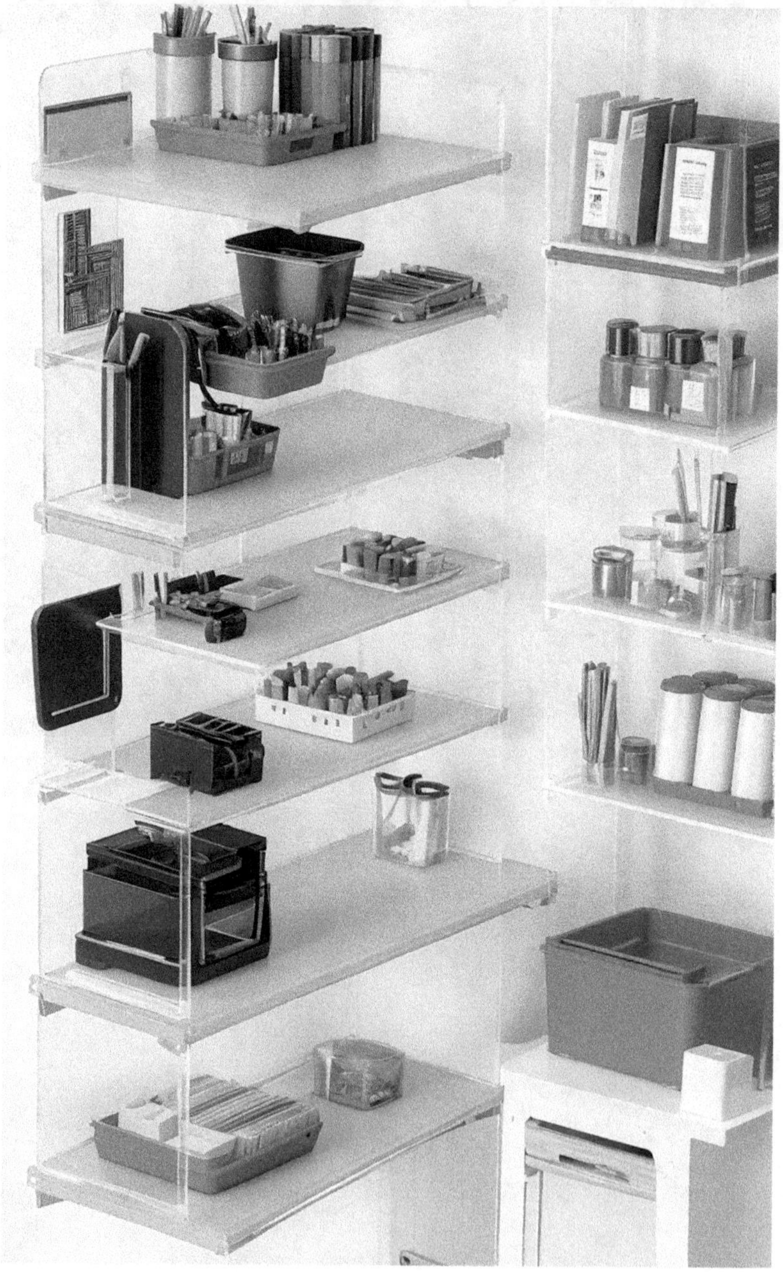

Figure 5. A Display of Made Objects (as drawn by the Deep Dream Generator with the AIVision Model)

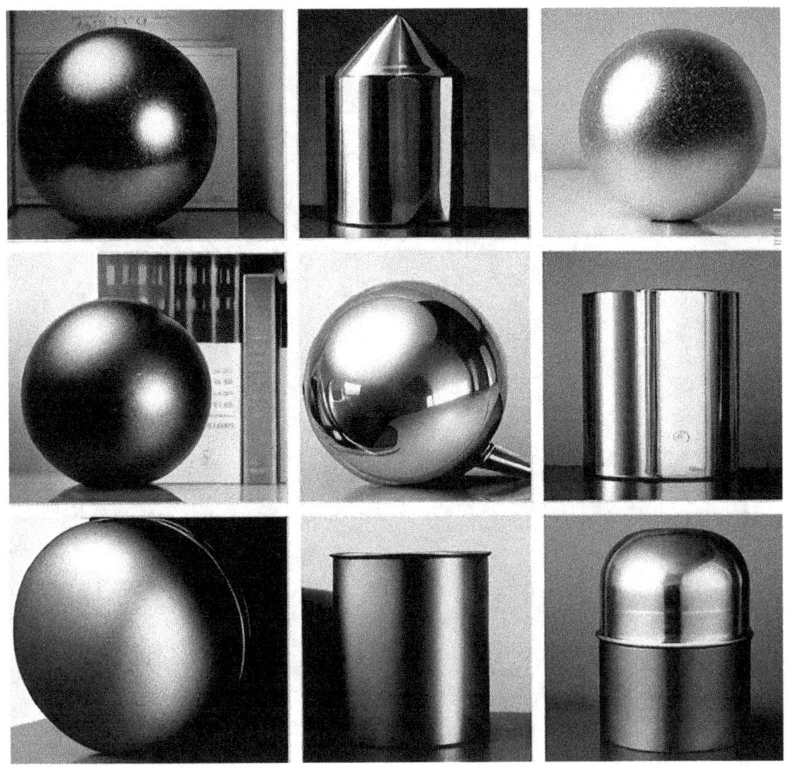

Figure 6. A Makerspace Work Station that resonates as a Home Space(as envisioned by the Deep Dream Generator, using the AIVision model)

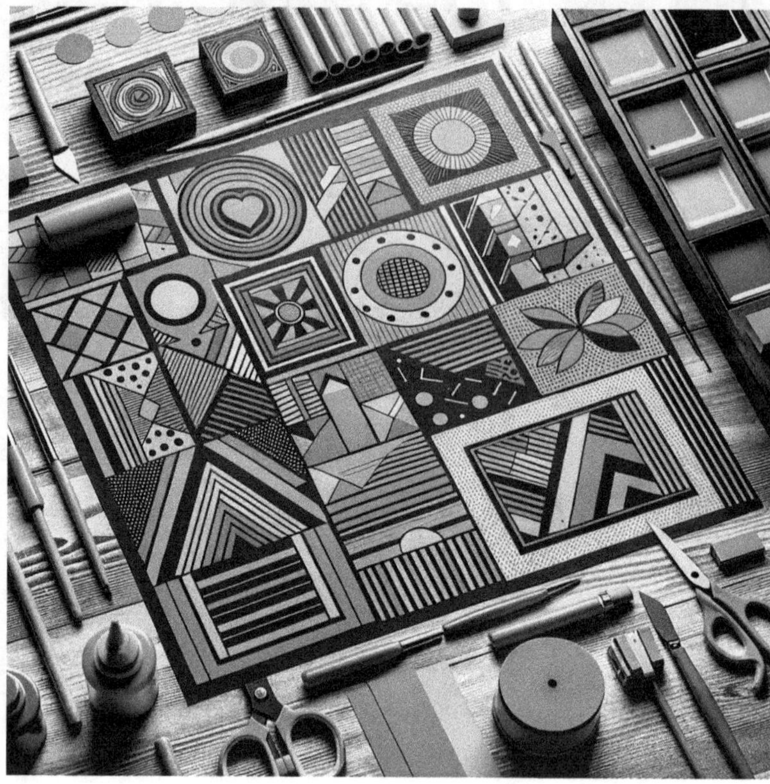

Figure 7. A Kitchen Making Space as Depicted by Deep Dream Generator

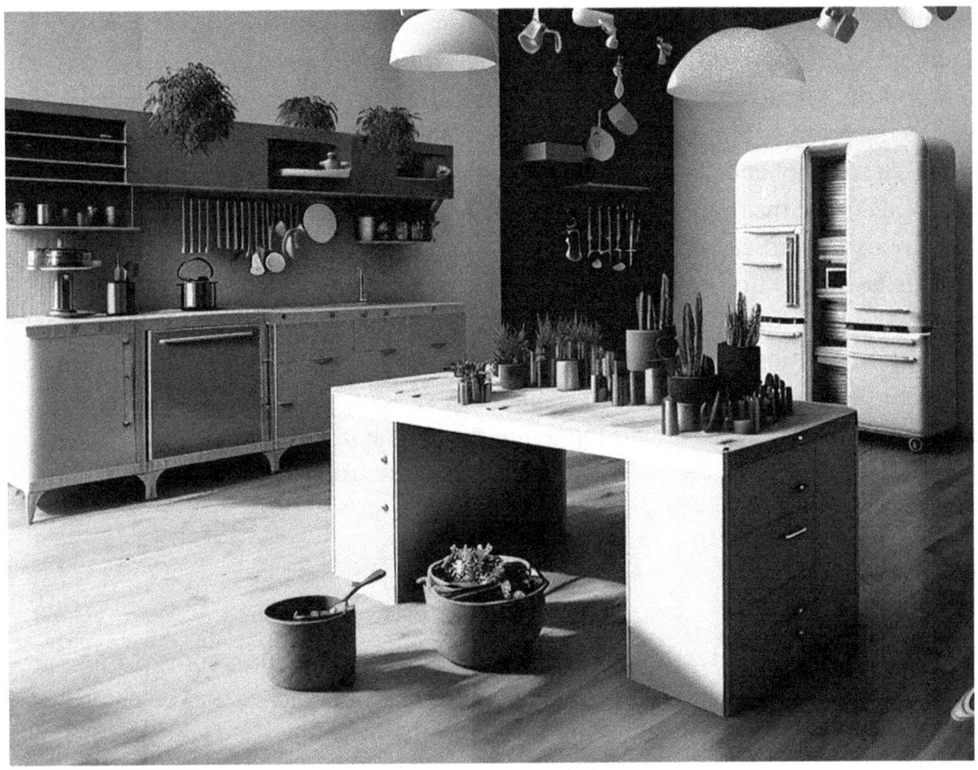

Makerspaces are said to align with the ideals of heterotopias (a term coined by Foucault from 1966), which are physical places "with different norms, regulations, forms, or orders to daily life" (Wu & Ma, 2022, p. 631). These spaces enable new thinking in their lack of uniformity, and they enable change. Technologies play a core role in making spaces, but technologies are not necessarily only a positive factor. One technology "can expand capabilities for some users under certain circumstances, whilst diminishing capabilities for others situated differently" (O'Donovan & Smith, 2020, p. 63). Ideally, users would master technologies sufficiently and position correctly to use technologies in optimized ways.

People may find profound meaning in their work lives. The author moved from a house to a one-bedroom apartment in late 2023 for a new job. The move itself was challenging, given logistics. The new apartment, which was from the WWII era, was reminiscent of when the author first moved out of her parents' home when she had just turned 15 and found herself among adults in a low-cost rooming house. Given the cost of professional movers, she downsized and donated her furniture and other possessions to local charities instead of retaining any of it. The cost of the moving would have been about the same as replacing all the old furniture with new. She had already dissolved a personal professional library a few years earlier. In the move, the materials that were retained were art supplies, a paper shredder, a laptop, a digital sketchpad, and the like, beyond the necessary documentation and clothing. Without realizing it, she had created a portable making kit with her. Having a making workspace in a time is a way to affirm that aspect of personal identity.

DIY empowers but requires that the individual actually know the field in depth. During this transition, she made an offer to buy an older home that had been "remodeled," but a home inspection found problems with the structure, termites; inappropriate grading of land around the house; a lack of gutters for rain handling; a clawfoot tub in the attic, plumbing equipment in the crawl space; and other problems. There was wood right up against the dirt. The author did not go through with the purchase because of the failed home inspection, but she did come away with the observation that the home was an example of failed DIY. To remodel and flip a property is not as easy as it may look on television. There is much cultural romance around making, of buying a wreck and fixing it, but skillsets are challenging to acquire and may take years of hard-earned experience.

Just prior to the publication of this work, the author did purchase a new home in a small town where she had already resided for six months. While the new home had a basement with a well-lit window well with plenty of lighting, she ended up tuning the crowded kitchen space into a making space. At arms reach were the paints and inks, the scanner, the various papers, and other materialia. She had a new lamp set up above the table. This is the temporary home making space. Indeed, a more permanent making space may be set up in the basement or garage or bedroom ultimately.

DISCUSSION

The popularization of AI and especially generative AI has sparked mass conversations around whether people will need to continue their labor. The idea is that all human labor will be delegated to machines. People will have to find meaning in other aspects of their lives than labor. There is talk of universal basic incomes, so that people will not need to provide for themselves in terms of basic needs. That vision is not likely to come to be for various reasons, though. There are not sufficient materials to make all the machines needed, and there are various types of labor that computing and robotics may not substitute. Regardless, people find enjoyment in making. And making spaces and workshops of various types will always have a place in some people's homes.

This work informs on various dimensionalities that may be considered for when people set up and evolve these spaces. Specifically, there is both a virtual and a physical angle to this space. There are both digital and physical technologies and equipment and resources, and the melding between such elements. Human safety of the maker is a concern, and the security of the space is also relevant. Given the need for maneuverability and convenience, for both the maker and for guests, the home making space needs to be accessible, physically and virtually. The focus on creativity means the need for inspiration, in whatever modalities those are required. The space should align with the makers' principles and values, whether these are spiritual, religious, environmental, artful, or others. A home making space needs to be aligned to the work processes and walk-throughs of the maker, so that whatever is being made is done in a convenient way. Given the need for publicity for most endeavors, the home making space needs to have a space for virtual sociality and social media connectivity. Those who find working virtually and via mobile tools do well to have a mobile aspect to the home making labs. And finally, to keep the maker relevant and engaged, the maker has to continue learning…so a part of the making space has to be amenable to learning programming.

FUTURE RESEARCH DIRECTIONS

One obvious future research question involves how people develop and evolve their home making spaces. Given the unique interests and needs of people, perhaps there are more unique making spaces in the home. Perhaps a future study may include how they built out these spaces and what their lessons learned were from this experience.

Or a more formal study may capture data about home making spaces to identify common patterns. Perhaps that can be research on home making spaces that are physical ones…mobile ones…or virtual ones… and other variations by modality and mixed modalities. Another approach may involve how home-based makers acquire learning effectively in a variety of crafting and skills spaces. A major challenge has been how to operationalize making in a way that the promise of such spaces may be actualized and captured (Penney, Watkins, Levy, Linsey, Nagel, Newstetter,, ... & Smith, June 2016). Recent studies suggest that "scaffolding and structure over an extended period of time is required for makerspaces to be effective learning environments" (Bull, Rutter, Garofalo, & Littman, 2022, p. 10). How to operationalize home "making" spaces to promote effective learning and creativity and innovation is an important question.

Home "makers" also likely emerge from various backgrounds. Some may be children, or young adults just starting out, or those in retirement. Perhaps there may be a study on the respective need patterns from each of the population groups to better understand the different types of making spaces.

CONCLUSION

A simple definition of making spaces is that they are learning environments, set up in different ways to meet user needs (Sheridan, Halverson, Litts, Brahms, Jacobs-Priebe, & Owens, 2014). How to meet the learning and making needs of home-based makers is the core aspect of this chapter. This work involved conducting a review of the literature around spaces designed for making in both professional and academic contexts. This work was also informed by years of working adjacent to an academic making space at an institution of higher education. From this analysis, a set of questions were created to aid in the design of a home "making" space to be as inclusive as possible of the learning from the more formal contexts.

REFERENCES

Ahn, I. J., & Noh, Y. (2018). A study and survey of the perception towards makerspaces of the public library. *International Journal of Knowledge Content Development & Technology*, 8(2), 5–22.

Aiyeblehin, J. A., Onyam, I. D., & Akpom, C. C. (2018). Creating makerspaces in Nigerian public libraries as a strategy for attaining national integration and development. *International Journal of Knowledge Content Development & Technology*, 8(4).

Alemán, M. W., Tomko, M. E., Linsey, J. S., & Nagel, R. L. (2022). How do you play that makerspace game? An ethnographic exploration of the habitus of engineering makerspaces. *Research in Engineering Design*, 33(4), 351–366. 10.1007/s00163-022-00393-035974995

Alía, C., Ocaña, R., Caja, J., Maresca, P., Moreno-Díaz, C., & Narbón, J. J. (2019). Use of open manufacturing laboratories (Fab Labs) as a new trend in engineering education. *Procedia Manufacturing*, 41, 938–943. 10.1016/j.promfg.2019.10.018

Andrews, C. (2017). Learning and teaching in library makerspaces: A literature review on making literacies. *International Symposium on Academic Makerspaces (ISAM).*

Andrews, D., & Roberts, D. (2017, August). Academic makerspaces: Contexts for research on interdisciplinary collaborative communication. In *Proceedings of the 35th ACM International Conference on the Design of Communication* (pp. 1-7). 10.1145/3121113.3121230

Andrews, M. E., & Boklage, A. (2023). Supporting inclusivity in STEM makerspaces through critical theory: A systematic review. *Journal of Engineering Education*, jee.20546. 10.1002/jee.20546

Banerjee, R., Ferron, L. M., Bailey, D., Imam, R., & Jariwala, A. S. (2020). IoT in Makerspaces-Review of usage and future potential. *Proceedings of the 4th International Symposium on Academic Makerspaces.*

Beavers, K., Cady, J. E., Jiang, A., & McCoy, L. (2019). Establishing a maker culture beyond the makerspace. *Library Hi Tech*, 37(2), 215–228. 10.1108/LHT-07-2018-0088

Bengü, E., & Keçeci, E. F. (2021). Makerspace: Innovation in mechanical engineering education. *Yükseköğretim ve Bilim Dergisi*, 11(1), 207–213.

Benjes-Small, C., Bellamy, L. M., Resor-Whicker, J., & Vassady, L. (2017). *Makerspace or waste of space: Charting a course for successful academic library makerspaces*. Academic Press.

Benton, C., Dempsey, T., Mullins, L., & Shelley, K. (2013). *Makerspaces: Supporting an entrepreneurial system.* 2013 Co-Learning Plan Series, University Outreach and Engagement, Michigan State University.

Bers, M. U., Strawhacker, A., & Vizner, M. (2018). The design of early childhood makerspaces to support positive technological development: Two case studies. *Library Hi Tech*, 36(1), 75–96. 10.1108/LHT-06-2017-0112

Blikstein, P. (2018). Maker movement in education: History and prospects. *Handbook of technology education, 419*, 437.

Blikstein, P., Kabayadondo, Z., Martin, A., & Fields, D. (2017). An assessment instrument of technological literacies in makerspaces and FabLabs. *Journal of Engineering Education*, 106(1), 149–175. 10.1002/jee.20156

Blikstein, P., & Krannich, D. (2013, June). The makers' movement and FabLabs in education: experiences, technologies, and research. In *Proceedings of the 12th International Conference on Interaction Design and Children* (pp. 613-616). 10.1145/2485760.2485884

Boccardi, A., Szucs, K. A., Ebuenyi, I. D., & Mhatre, A. (2022). Assistive Technology Makerspaces Promote Capability of Adults with Intellectual and Developmental Disabilities. *Societies, 12*(6), 155, 1 - 19.

Boudreau, J. B., & Anis, H. (2019). The role of makerspaces in inclusivity in engineering. *Proceedings of the Canadian Engineering Education Association (CEEA)*. 10.24908/pceea.vi0.13749

Brahimi, T., Khalifa, S., & Benaouda, B. (2019). Integrating makerspaces in higher education: Constructionism approach to learning. In *Research & Innovation Forum 2019: Technology, Innovation, Education, and their Social Impact 1* (pp. 65–73). Springer International Publishing. 10.1007/978-3-030-30809-4_7

Bull, G., Rutter, J., Garofalo, J., & Littman, M. (2022). *Maker education: A historical perspective*. Academic Press.

Burke, J. (2015). *Making sense: Can Makerspaces work in academic libraries?* Academic Press.

Campos, F., Soster, T., & Blikstein, P. (2019). Sorry, I was in teacher mode today: Pivotal tensions and contradictory discourses in real-world implementations of school makerspaces. *Proceedings of FabLearn*, 2019, 96–103. 10.1145/3311890.3311903

Carbonell, R. M., Boklage, A., Clayton, P., & Borrego, M. J. (2020, June). Making Improvements: Pedagogical Iterations of Designing a Class Project in a Maker Space. In *2020 ASEE Virtual Annual Conference Content Access*. 10.18260/1-2--34942

Carnasciali, M. I., Gillespie, S. M., & Hossain, A. M. (2021, October). Integrating Makerspaces into the Curriculum-Faculty Development Efforts. In *2021 IEEE Frontiers in Education Conference (FIE)* (pp. 1-7). IEEE. 10.1109/FIE49875.2021.9637230

Choi, Y., Lam, B., Chen, X., de Sousa, S., Liu, L., & Ni, M. (2022). Co-Design visions of public makerspaces in China. *International Journal of Design Creativity and Innovation*, 10(3), 179–192. 10.1080/21650349.2022.2048696

Choi, Y. H., Bouwma-Gearhart, J., Lenhart, C. A., Villanueva, I., & Nadelson, L. S. (2021). Student development at the boundaries: Makerspaces as affordances for engineering students' development. *Sustainability (Basel)*, 13(6), 3058. 10.3390/su13063058

Cohen, J., Jones, W. M., Smith, S., & Calandra, B. (2017). Makification: Towards a framework for leveraging the maker movement in formal education. *Journal of Educational Multimedia and Hypermedia*, 26(3), 217–229.

Colegrove, P. T. (2017). Makerspaces in libraries: technology as catalyst for better learning, better teaching. *Ingeniería solidaria, 13*(21), 19-26.

Cooke, M. N., & Charnas, I. C. (2021). *The value of data, metrics, and impact for higher education Makerspaces. IJAMM, 1.*

Corsini, L., & Moultrie, J. (2020). Humanitarian makerspaces in crisis-affected communities. *Artificial Intelligence for Engineering Design, Analysis and Manufacturing*, 34(3), 374–386. 10.1017/S0890060420000098

Culpepper, M. L. (2016, November). Types of academic Makerspaces, their import to the education mission, and the characteristics of their culture and community. In *Proceedings of the 1st International Symposium on Academic Makerspaces* (pp. 10-13). Academic Press.

Cun, A., Abramovich, S., & Smith, J. M. (2019). An assessment matrix for library makerspaces. *Library & Information Science Research*, 41(1), 39–47. 10.1016/j.lisr.2019.02.008

Curry, R. (2017). Makerspaces: A beneficial new service for academic libraries? *Library Review*, 66(4/5), 201–212. 10.1108/LR-09-2016-0081

Delphenich, P., & Broz, D. (2015). Garage innovation+ higher education= the academic incubator. *Planning for Higher Education*, 43(4), 10.

Douglass, H. (2023). Makerspaces and making data: Learning from pre-service teachers' STEM experiences in a community Makerspace. *Education Sciences*, 13(6), 538. 10.3390/educsci13060538

Dukart, K., Orser, D. J., & Guengerich, B. (2020, June). Maker Spaces for the Multitudes-Strategies to Expand Access and Use of a College Maker Space. *2020 ASEE Virtual Annual Conference Content Access*. 10.18260/1-2--34938

Eyal, L., & Gil, E. (2020). Design patterns for teaching in academic settings in future learning spaces. *British Journal of Educational Technology*, 51(4), 1061–1077. 10.1111/bjet.12923

Farritor, S. (2017). University-based makerspaces: A source of innovation. *Technology and Innovation*, 19(1), 389–395. 10.21300/19.1.2017.389

Fasso, W., & Knight, B. A. (2020). Identity development in school makerspaces: Intentional design. *International Journal of Technology and Design Education*, 30(2), 275–294. 10.1007/s10798-019-09501-z

Fehringer, H., Kaar, C., & Stary, C. (2019, September). Makerspaces in Academic Education: An Exploratory Analysis and Design Framework. In *2019 18th International Conference on Information Technology Based Higher Education and Training (ITHET)* (pp. 1-10). IEEE.

Fordyce, R., Heemsbergen, L., Mignone, P., & Nansen, B. (2015). 3D printing and university makerspaces: Surveying countercultural communities in institutional settings. *Digital Culture & Education*, 7.

Forest, C., Farzaneh, H. H., Weinmann, J., & Lindemann, U. (2016, June). Quantitative survey and analysis of five maker spaces at large, research-oriented universities. *2016 ASEE Annual Conference & Exposition*. 10.18260/p.26023

Forest, C. R., Moore, R. A., Jariwala, A. S., Fasse, B. B., Linsey, J., Newstetter, W., & Quintero, C. (2014). The invention studio: A university Maker space and culture. *Advances in Engineering Education*, 4(2), n2.

Friessnig, M. H., Karre, H., Schnöll, H. P., & Ramsauer, C. (2016, November). Development of an educational program using capabilities of (academic) Makerspaces. *Proceedings of the 1st International Symposium on Academic Makerspaces.*

Fu, P., Li, L., & Xie, X. (2022). Reconstructing makerspaces in China: Mass innovation space and the transformative creative industries. *Humanities & Social Sciences Communications*, 9(1), 1–8. 10.1057/s41599-022-01383-2

Galaleldin, M., Bouchard, F., Anis, H., & Lague, C. (2016). The impact of makerspaces on engineering education. *Proceedings of the Canadian Engineering Education Association (CEEA).*

Geser, G., Hollauf, E. M., Hornung-Prähauser, V., Schön, S., & Vloet, F. (2019). Makerspaces as social innovation and entrepreneurship learning environments: The DOIT learning program. *Discourse and Communication for Sustainable Education*, 10(2), 60–71. 10.2478/dcse-2019-0018

Gladson, J. T. (2023). *Student Engagement in Makerspaces: Connecting Research in Student Engagement and Making in Education* (Doctoral dissertation, The University of North Carolina at Greensboro).

Godhe, A. L., Lilja, P., & Selwyn, N. (2019). Making sense of making: Critical issues in the integration of Maker education into schools. *Technology, Pedagogy and Education*, 28(3), 317–328. 10.1080/1475939X.2019.1610040

Greene, M., Kellam, N., & Coley, B. (2019). Black men in the making: Engaging in maker spaces promotes agency and identity for black males in engineering. *2019 CoNECD-The Collaborative Network for Engineering and Computing Diversity.*

Halverson, E. R., & Sheridan, K. (2014). The maker movement in education. *Harvard Educational Review*, 84(4), 495–504. 10.17763/haer.84.4.34j1g68140382063

Harron, J. R., & Hughes, J. E. (2018). Spacemakers: A leadership perspective on curriculum and the purpose of K–12 educational makerspaces. *Journal of Research on Technology in Education*, 50(3), 253–270. 10.1080/15391523.2018.1461038

Herczeg, M., Winkler, T., & Ohlei, A. (2019). Ambient learning spaces for school education. In *ICERI2019 Proceedings* (pp. 5116-5125). IATED. 10.21125/iceri.2019.1240

Heredia, S. C., & Tan, E. (2021). Teaching & learning in Makerspaces: Equipping teachers to become justice-oriented maker-educators. *The Journal of Educational Research*, 114(2), 171–182. 10.1080/00220671.2020.1860871

Hilton, E. C., Forest, C. R., & Linsey, J. S. (2020). *Slaying dragons: An empirical look at the impact of academic makerspaces*. Academic Press.

Hira, A., Joslyn, C. H., & Hynes, M. M. (2014, October). Classroom makerspaces: Identifying the opportunities and challenges. In *2014 IEEE Frontiers in Education Conference (FIE) Proceedings* (pp. 1-5). IEEE.

Hoople, G., Mejia, J., Hoffoss, D., & Devadoss, S. (2020). Makerspaces on the Continuum: Examining undergraduate student learning in formal and informal settings. *IJEE International Journal of Engineering Education, 36*(4).

Houston, C. (2013). Makerspaces@ your school library: Consider the possibilities! *IASL Annual Conference Proceedings*, 1 – 5.

Hsu, Y. C., Baldwin, S., & Ching, Y. H. (2017). Learning through making and maker education. *TechTrends*, 61(6), 589–594. 10.1007/s11528-017-0172-6

Hui, J. S., & Gerber, E. M. (2017, February). Developing Makerspaces as sites of entrepreneurship. In *Proceedings of the 2017 ACM Conference on Computer Supported Cooperative Work and Social Computing* (pp. 2023-2038). ACM.

Hynes, M. M., & Hynes, W. J. (2018). If you build it, will they come? Student preferences for Makerspace environments in higher education. *International Journal of Technology and Design Education*, 28(3), 867–883. 10.1007/s10798-017-9412-5

Irie, N. R., Hsu, Y. C., & Ching, Y. H. (2019). Makerspaces in diverse places: A comparative analysis of distinctive national discourses surrounding the maker movement and education in four countries. *TechTrends*, 63(4), 397–407. 10.1007/s11528-018-0355-9

Iwata, M., Pitkänen, K., Laru, J., & Mäkitalo, K. (2020, June). Exploring potentials and challenges to develop twenty-first century skills and computational thinking in K-12 maker education. *Frontiers in Education*, 5, 87. 10.3389/feduc.2020.00087

Jaatinen, J., & Lindfors, E. (2019). Makerspaces for pedagogical innovation processes: How Finnish comprehensive schools create space for Makers. *Journal of Design and Technology Education*, 24(2), n2.

Johnston, K., Kervin, L., & Wyeth, P. (2022). STEM, STEAM and makerspaces in early childhood: A scoping review. *Sustainability (Basel)*, 14(20), 13533. 10.3390/su142013533

Jordan, A., Knochel, A. D., Meisel, N., Reiger, K., & Sinha, S. (2021). Making on the move: Mobility, makerspaces, and art education. *International Journal of Art & Design Education*, 40(1), 52–65. 10.1111/jade.12333

Julian, K. D., & Parrott, D. J. (2017). Makerspaces in the Library: Science in a Student's Hands. *Journal of Learning Spaces*, 6(2).

Kang, I., Kim, Y. S., & Yoon, H. J. (2017). Fostering entrepreneurship by maker education: A case study in an (sic) higher education. *Journal of the Korea Convergence Society*, 8(7), 253–264.

Kantaros, A., Diegel, O., Piromalis, D., Tsaramirsis, G., Khadidos, A. O., Khadidos, A. O., Khan, F. Q., & Jan, S. (2022). 3D printing: Making an innovative technology widely accessible through makerspaces and outsourced services. *Materials Today: Proceedings*, 49, 2712–2723. 10.1016/j.matpr.2021.09.074

Keune, A., Gomoll, A., & Peppler, K. (2015). Flexibility to learn: Material artifacts in makerspaces. In *Fifth Annual FabLearn Conference: Equity and Diversity in Making*. Palo Alto, CA: Stanford University.

Keune, A., & Peppler, K. (2017). Maker portfolios as learning and community building tools inside and outside makerspaces. In *Making a Difference* (pp. 545–548). Prioritizing Equity and Access in CSCL.

Keune, A., & Peppler, K. (2019). Materials-to-develop-with: The making of a Makerspace. *British Journal of Educational Technology*, 50(1), 280–293. 10.1111/bjet.12702

Keune, A., Peppler, K. A., & Wohlwend, K. E. (2019). Recognition in makerspaces: Supporting opportunities for women to "make" a STEM career. *Computers in Human Behavior*, 99, 368–380. 10.1016/j.chb.2019.05.013

Khadri Ahmed, H. O. (2023). Exploring possible futures of makerspaces as an important basic component of K-12 education. *Pedagogies*, 18(3), 450–472. 10.1080/1554480X.2022.2065997

Kim, S. H., Jung, Y. J., & Choi, G. W. (2022). A systematic review of library makerspaces research. *Library & Information Science Research*, 44(4), 101202. 10.1016/j.lisr.2022.101202

Kinnula, M., Milara, I. S., Norouzi, B., Sharma, S., & Iivari, N. (2021). The show must go on! Strategies for making and makerspaces during pandemic. *International Journal of Child-Computer Interaction*, 29, 100303. 10.1016/j.ijcci.2021.10030336570421

Kirio, C. H. (2022). *School Librarian and Teacher Collaboration in Virtual Makerspace Instructional Design* (Doctoral dissertation, University of Hawai'i at Manoa).

Kjällander, S., Åkerfeldt, A., Mannila, L., & Parnes, P. (2018). Makerspaces across settings: Didactic design for programming in formal and informal teacher education in the Nordic countries. *Journal of Digital Learning in Teacher Education*, 34(1), 18–30. 10.1080/21532974.2017.1387831

Koh, K., & Abbas, J. (2015). Competencies for information professionals in learning labs and makerspaces. *Journal of Education for Library and Information Science*, 56(2), 114–129.

Kohls, C. (2022, July). Maker Spaces for hybrid education. In *Proceedings of the 27th European Conference on Pattern Languages of Programs* (pp. 1-9). Academic Press.

Konstantinou, D., Parmaxi, A., & Zaphiris, P. (2021). Mapping research directions on makerspaces in education. *Educational Media International*, 58(3), 223–247. 10.1080/09523987.2021.1976826

Kurti, R. S., Kurti, D., & Fleming, L. (2014). The environment and tools of great educational makerspaces. Part 2 of Making an educational Makerspace. *Teacher Librarian*, 42(1), 8.

Kurti, R. S., Kurti, D., & Fleming, L. (2014). Practical implementation of an educational makerspace: Part 3 of making an educational makerspace. *Teacher Librarian*, 42(2), 20.

Kurti, R. S., Kurti, D. L., & Fleming, L. (2014). The philosophy of educational makerspaces part 1 of making an educational makerspace. *Teacher Librarian*, 41(5), 8.

Lam, C., Cruz, S., Kellam, N., & Coley, B. (2019, January). Making space for the women: exploring female engineering student narratives of engagement in makerspaces. *2019 ASEE Annual Conference & Exposition*. 10.18260/1-2--33078

LeBlanc, M., Freiman, V., & Furlong, C. (2018). STEAMing soft-skills in makerspaces: What are the mathematical connections. In *Actes de l'International Symposium MACAS* (pp. 87-97). Academic Press.

Lenhart, C. S., Bouwma-Gearhart, J., Villanueva, I., Youmans, K., & Nadelson, L. S. (2020). *Engineering faculty members' perceptions of university makerspaces: Potential affordances for curriculum, instructional practices, and student learning. International Journal of Engineering Education, 36(4).*

Levy, B., Morocz, R. J., Forest, C., Nagel, R. L., Newstetter, W. C., Talley, K. G., & Linsey, J. S. (2016, June). MAKER: How to make a university maker space. *2016 ASEE Annual Conference & Exposition*. 10.18260/p.25623

Lewis, J. (2015). *Barriers to women's involvement in hackspaces and makerspaces*. The University of Sheffield.

Li, Y., Li, Y., & Qiu, S. (2023). Analysis on the effectiveness and mechanisms of public policies to promote innovation of high-tech startups in Makerspaces. *Sustainability (Basel)*, 15(9), 7027. 10.3390/su15097027

Lindstrom, D., Thompson, A. D., & Schmidt-Crawford, D. A. (2017). The maker movement: Democratizing STEM education and empowering learners to shape their world. *Journal of Digital Learning in Teacher Education*, 33(3), 89–90. 10.1080/21532974.2017.1316153

Litts, B. K. (2015). *Making Learning: Makerspaces as Learning Environments* (Doctoral dissertation, The University of Wisconsin-Madison).

Lock, J., Redmond, P., Orwin, L., Powell, A., Becker, S., Hollohan, P., & Johnson, C. (2020). Bridging distance: Practical and pedagogical implications of virtual Makerspaces. *Journal of Computer Assisted Learning*, 36(6), 957–968. 10.1111/jcal.12452

Love, T. S. (2022). Examining the influence that professional development has on educators' perceptions of integrated STEM safety in makerspaces. *Journal of Science Education and Technology*, 31(3), 289–302. 10.1007/s10956-022-09955-2

Love, T. S., Roy, K. R., Gill, M., & Harrell, M. (2022). Examining the influence that safety training format has on educators' perceptions of safer practices in Makerspaces and integrated STEM labs. *Journal of Safety Research*, 82, 112–123. 10.1016/j.jsr.2022.05.00336031238

Maceli, M. G. (2019). Making the future makers: Makerspace curriculum in library and information science graduate programs and continuing education. *Library Hi Tech*, 37(4), 781–793. 10.1108/LHT-01-2019-0005

Makerspace Directory. (2024). Retrieved Jan. 22, 2024, from https://makerspaces.make.co/

Mann, L. (2018). Making a place for makerspaces in information literacy. *Reference and User Services Quarterly*, 58(2), 82–86. 10.5860/rusq.58.2.6927

Martin, L. (2015). The promise of the maker movement for education. *Journal of Pre-College Engineering Education Research (J-PEER), 5*(1), 4.

Martin, L., Dixon, C., & Betser, S. (2018). Iterative design toward equity: Youth repertoires of practice in a high school maker space. *Equity & Excellence in Education*, 51(1), 36–47. 10.1080/10665684.2018.1436997

Masters, A. S., Foster, E. K., Groen-McCall, C., McNair, L. D., & Riley, D. M. (2019). Exploring liberatory makerspaces: Preliminary results and future directions. *Advances in Engineering Education*, 7(3), 1–8.

McCue, R. A., Huculak, J. M., & Johnson, D. K. (2020). *Best practices for creating and leading active-learning workshops in academic makerspaces*. IJAMM.

McGuffin-Cawley, J. D., & Wilczynski, V. (2021). University Makerspaces and Manufacturing Collaboration: Lessons from the Pandemic. *The Bridge*, 51(1), 41–47.

Melo, M. M., March, L., & Hirsh, K. (2021, September). Examining the impacts of the covid-19 pandemic on library makerspaces and LIS makerspace curricula. *Proceedings of the Association for Library and Information Science Education Annual Conference*.

Mersand, S. (2021). The state of Makerspace research: A review of the literature. *TechTrends*, 65(2), 174–186. 10.1007/s11528-020-00566-5

Meyer, B. (2019). Makerspaces in Higher Education: An overview. *eLearn, 2019*(5).

Moorefield-Lang, H. (2014). Makers in the library: Case studies of 3D printers and maker spaces in library settings. *Library Hi Tech*, 32(4), 583–593. 10.1108/LHT-06-2014-0056

Moorefield-Lang, H. (2015). Change in the making: Makerspaces and the ever-changing landscape of libraries. *TechTrends*, 59(3), 107–112. 10.1007/s11528-015-0860-z

Moorefield-Lang, H. M. (2015). User agreements and makerspaces: A content analysis. *New Library World*, 116(7/8), 358–368. 10.1108/NLW-12-2014-0144

Moorefield-Lang, H. M. (2015). When Makerspaces go mobile: Case studies of transportable maker locations. *Library Hi Tech*, 33(4), 462–471. 10.1108/LHT-06-2015-0061

Morocz, R. J., Levy, B., Forest, C., Nagel, R. L., Newstetter, W. C., Talley, K. G., & Linsey, J. S. (2016, June). Relating student participation in university maker spaces to their engineering design self-efficacy. In *2016 ASEE Annual Conference & Exposition*. 10.18260/p.26070

Morocz, R. J., Levy, B. D., Forest, C. R., Nagel, R. L., Newstetter, W. C., Talley, K. G., & Linsey, J. S. (2015, June). University maker spaces: Discovery, optimization and measurement of impacts. *2015 ASEE Annual Conference & Exposition*. 10.18260/p.24967

Musick Peery, K., & Chivers, M. (2018). *Intentionally cultivating diverse community for radically open access makerspaces*. Academic Press.

Mylon, P., Wood, G., & Dolmansley, T. (2019, July). Using student-led manufacturing in Makerspaces to support transition into engineering higher education. In *HEAD'19.5th International Conference on Higher Education Advances* (pp. 253-260). Editorial Universitat Politècnica de València. 10.4995/HEAD19.2019.9502

Mylonas, G., Hofstaetter, J., Friedl, A., & Giannakos, M. (2021, June). Designing effective playful experiences for sustainability awareness in schools and makerspaces. In *FabLearn Europe/MakeEd 2021-an international conference on computing, design and making in education* (pp. 1-9). 10.1145/3466725.3466755

Nadelson, L. S., Villanueva, I., Bouwma-Gearhart, J., Soto, E., Lenhart, C., Youmans, K., & Choi, Y. H. (2020, January). Student perceptions of and learning in makerspaces embedded in their undergraduate engineering preparation programs. In *Zone 1 Conference of the American Society for Engineering Education* (Vol. 30699). Academic Press.

Nagle, S. B. (2021). Maker services in academic libraries: A review of case studies. *New Review of Academic Librarianship*, 27(2), 184–200. 10.1080/13614533.2020.1749093

Nichols, J., Melo, M. M., & Dewland, J. (2017). Unifying space and service for makers, entrepreneurs, and digital scholars. *Portal (Baltimore, Md.)*, 17(2), 363–374. 10.1353/pla.2017.0022

Nichols, T. P. (2020). Innovation from below: Infrastructure, design, and equity in literacy classroom makerspaces. *Research in the Teaching of English*, 55(1), 56–81. 10.58680/rte202030901

O'Donovan, C., & Smith, A. (2020). Technology and human capabilities in UK makerspaces. *Journal of Human Development and Capabilities*, 21(1), 63–83. 10.1080/19452829.2019.1704706

Oliver, K. M. (2016). Professional development considerations for makerspace leaders, part one: Addressing "what?" and "why?". *TechTrends*, 60(2), 160–166. 10.1007/s11528-016-0028-5

Oswald, K., & Zhao, X. (2021). Collaborative learning in makerspaces: A grounded theory of the role of collaborative learning in makerspaces. *SAGE Open*, 11(2). 10.1177/21582440211020732

Pallaris, G., Zaphiris, P., & Parmaxi, A. (2022). Mapping the landscape of Makerspaces in higher education: An inventory of research findings. *Interactive Technology and Smart Education.*

Pendergast, S. C. (2020). *Makerspaces in Higher education: Student Engagement* (Doctoral dissertation, University of Calgary).

Penney, M. F., Watkins, J. D., Levy, B., Linsey, J. S., Nagel, R. L., Newstetter, W. C., & Smith, S. F. (2016, June). 'Making' an impact: An ethnographic approach to university Maker Spaces. *2016 ASEE Annual Conference & Exposition.*10.18260/p.26226

Pepper-Kittredge, C., & Bird, D. (2020). *Growing a network of makerspaces in California Community Colleges: Moving towards implementation and adoption.* Academic Press.

Perez, M., Arroyo, Z., Reyes, S., Rossino, R., Rocha, A., & Ayerdi, V. (2023). *Using Makerspaces to develop didactic models for mechanical engineering*. IJAMM.

Pernia-Espinoza, A., Sanz-Garcia, A., Peciña-Marqueta, S., Martinez-de-Pison-Ascacibar, F. J., Urraca-Valle, R., & Antoñanzas-Torres, J. (2018). A review of makerspaces for stem degrees and the UR-Maker experience. *EDULEARN18 Proceedings*, 2702-2711.

Pines, E., Sullivan, P. A., & Nogales, L. (2015, June). Broadening participation through engagement in the maker space movement. In *2015 ASEE Annual Conference & Exposition* (pp. 26-295). 10.18260/p.23634

Radniecki, T., Klenke, C., & Purpur, E. (2016). Makerspaces in academic libraries: Opportunities for teaching and learning. In *ICERI2016 Proceedings* (pp. 41-48). IATED.

Rayna, T., & Striukova, L. (2021). Fostering skills for the 21st century: The role of Fab labs and makerspaces. *Technological Forecasting and Social Change*, 164, 120391. 10.1016/j.techfore.2020.120391

Rees, P., Olson, C., Schweik, C. M., & Brewer, S. D. (2015, June). Work in progress: Exploring the role of makerspaces and flipped learning in a Town-Gown effort to engage K12 students in STEAM. *2015 ASEE Annual Conference & Exposition.* 10.18260/p.25087

Riley, D. M., McNair, L. D., & Masters, S. (2017). MAKER: An ethnography of maker and hacker spaces achieving diverse participation. In *2017 ASEE Annual Conference & Exposition*. ASEE. 10.18260/1-2--27724

Roeder, I., Klemichen, A., & Stark, R. (2020). *Be (com) ing an eco-maker–a pre-structured self-learning concept for environmentally-friendly product creation in Makerspaces*. Academic Press.

Rosenbaum, L. F., & Hartmann, B. (2017). Where be dragons? Charting the known (and not so known) areas of research on academic makerspaces. *Proceedings of ISAM*.

Sagbauer, N. N., & Ebner, M. (2021). Developing a Taxonomy Concerning Physical Existing Makerspaces in and Used by Schools. *Int. J. Eng. Pedagog.*, 11(2), 57–68. 10.3991/ijep.v11i2.17021

Salisbury, K., & Nichols, T. P. (2020). School makerspaces: Beyond the hype. *Phi Delta Kappan*, 101(8), 49–53. 10.1177/0031721720923792

Salman, H. (2023). University-based incubators, makerspaces and co-learning spaces as Creative Knowledge Environments: The case of a university-based CKE in Karachi, Pakistan. *Journal of Research and Innovation in Higher Education*, 4(1), 73–97.

Santo, R., Peppler, K., Ching, D., & Hoadley, C. (2015). Maybe a maker space? Organizational learning about maker education within a regional out-of-school network. *Makerspace Expansive Learning Fablearn Submission, C*, 1-9.

Santos, A. F., Barber, D.III, Harris, M., & Haymore, J. (2021). What can universities learn from organizational creative space design research? A Look at Maker Spaces. *Journal of Higher Education Theory and Practice*, 21(6).

Schön, S., Ebner, M., & Kumar, S. (2014). The Maker Movement. Implications of new digital gadgets, fabrication tools and spaces for creative learning and teaching. *eLearning Papers, 39*, 14-25.

Seo, J., & Richard, G. T. (2021). SCAFFOLDing all abilities into makerspaces: A design framework for universal, accessible and intersectionally inclusive making and learning. *Information and Learning Science*, 122(11/12), 795–815. 10.1108/ILS-10-2020-0230

Sheridan, K., Halverson, E. R., Litts, B., Brahms, L., Jacobs-Priebe, L., & Owens, T. (2014). Learning in the making: A comparative case study of three makerspaces. *Harvard Educational Review*, 84(4), 505–531. 10.17763/haer.84.4.brr34733723j648u

Stager, G. S. (2013, June). Papert's prison fab lab: implications for the maker movement and education design. In *Proceedings of the 12th international conference on interaction design and children* (pp. 487-490). 10.1145/2485760.2485811

Steele, K., Blaser, B., & Cakmak, M. (2018). Accessible making: Designing makerspaces for accessibility. *International Journal of Designs for Learning*, 9(1), 114–121. 10.14434/ijdl.v9i1.22648

Stevenson, M., Bower, M., Falloon, G., Forbes, A., & Hatzigianni, M. (2019). By design: Professional learning ecologies to develop primary school teachers' Makerspaces pedagogical capabilities. *British Journal of Educational Technology*, 50(3), 1260–1274. 10.1111/bjet.12743

Stornaiuolo, A., & Nichols, T. P. (2018). Making publics: Mobilizing audiences in high school maker-spaces. *Teachers College Record*, 120(8), 1–38. 10.1177/016146811812000804

Strycker, J. (2015). Makerspaces: The next iteration for educational technology in K-12 schools. *Educational Technology*, 28–32.

Sullivan, P., Pines, E., Sassenfeld, R., & Nogales, L. (2016). Transiting to a student-managed maker space. In *VentureWell.Proceedings of Open, the Annual Conference* (p. 1). National Collegiate Inventors & Innovators Alliance.

Sullivan, R. M. (2010). Common knowledge: Learning spaces in academic libraries. *College & Undergraduate Libraries*, 17(2-3), 130–148. 10.1080/10691316.2010.481608

Taheri, P., Robbins, P., & Maalej, S. (2019). Makerspaces in first-year engineering education. *Education Sciences*, 10(1), 8. 10.3390/educsci10010008

Tan, M., Yang, Y., & Yu, P. (2016). The influence of the maker movement on engineering and technology education. *World Transactions on Engineering and Technology Education*, 14(1), 89–94.

Tomko, M., Aleman, M., Newstetter, W., Linsey, J., & Nagel, R. (2021). A methodological roadmap for phenomenologically based interviewing in engineering education: Identifying types of learning in Makerspaces. *Studies in Engineering Education*, 2(1), 100. 10.21061/see.32

Tomko, M., Alemán, M. W., Newstetter, W., Nagel, R. L., & Linsey, J. (2021). Participation pathways for women into university makerspaces. *Journal of Engineering Education*, 110(3), 700–717. 10.1002/jee.20402

Tomko, M., Newstetter, W., Alemán, M. W., Nagel, R. L., & Linsey, J. (2020). Academic Makerspaces as a "design journey": Developing a learning model for how women students tap into their "toolbox of design". *Artificial Intelligence for Engineering Design, Analysis and Manufacturing*, 34(3), 363–373. 10.1017/S089006042000030X

Trust, T., Maloy, R. W., & Edwards, S. (2018). Learning through making: Emerging and expanding designs for college classes. *TechTrends*, 62(1), 19–28. 10.1007/s11528-017-0214-0

Turakhia, D. G., Ludgin, D., Mueller, S., & Desportes, K. (2023, April). What Can We Learn From Educators About Teaching in Makerspaces? In *Extended Abstracts of the 2023 CHI Conference on Human Factors in Computing Systems* (pp. 1-7). 10.1145/3544549.3585687

Unterfrauner, E., Voigt, C., & Hofer, M. (2021). The effect of maker and entrepreneurial education on self-efficacy and creativity. *Entrepreneurship Education*, 4(4), 403–424. 10.1007/s41959-021-00060-w

Van Holm, E. J. (2014). *What are makerspaces, hackerspaces, and fab labs?* Hackerspaces, and Fab Labs.

Van Holm, E. J., & Joseph, E. (2014). What are Makerspaces, Hackerspaces, and Fab Labs? SSRN *Electronic Journal.* Preprint.

Vinodrai, T., Nader, B., & Zavarella, C. (2021). Manufacturing space for inclusive innovation? A study of makerspaces in southern Ontario. *Local Economy*, 36(3), 205–223. 10.1177/0269094221101353234650320

Wallace, M. K., Trkay, G., Chivers, M., & Peery, K. M. (2017). *Making Maker literacies: integrating academic library makerspaces into the undergraduate curriculum*. Academic Press.

Wang, D., Dunn, N., & Coulton, P. (2015). Grassroots maker spaces: a recipe for innovation? *Proceedings of the 11th European Academy of Design Conference*.

Wang, F., Wang, W., Wilson, S., & Ahmed, N. (2016). The state of library Makerspaces. *International Journal of Librarianship*, 1(1), 2–16. 10.23974/ijol.2016.vol1.1.12

Weiner, S., Lande, M., & Jordan, S. (2018). The engineer of 2020, in the making: Understanding how young adults develop maker identities and the implications for education reform. *International Journal of Engineering Education*, 34(2), 833–842.

White, N., & Burg, K. (2019). From university to invention to entrepreneurship. *Technology and Innovation*, 20(4), 377–383. 10.21300/20.4.2019.377

Whitmer, S. (2016). Makerspaces that set the stage for lifelong learning. In *VentureWell.Proceedings of Open, the Annual Conference* (p. 1). National Collegiate Inventors & Innovators Alliance.

Wilczynski, V. (2015, June). Academic maker spaces and engineering design. *2015 ASEE Annual Conference & Exposition*.

Wilczynski, V. (2017, June). A classification system for higher education Makerspaces. *2017 ASEE Annual Conference & Exposition*. 10.18260/1-2--27448

Wilczynski, V., & Adrezin, R. (2016, November). Higher education makerspaces and engineering education. In *ASME International Mechanical Engineering Congress and Exposition* (Vol. 50571, p. V005T06A013). American Society of Mechanical Engineers.

Wilczynski, V., & Hoover, A. (2017). Classifying Academic Makerspaces: Applied at ISAM 2017. *Proceedings of the International Symposium on Academic Makerspaces*.

Willett, R. (2016). Making, makers, and makerspaces: A discourse analysis of professional journal articles and blog posts about makerspaces in public libraries. *The Library Quarterly*, 86(3), 313–329. 10.1086/686676

Wong, A., & Partridge, H. (2016). Making as learning: Makerspaces in universities. *Australian Academic and Research Libraries*, 47(3), 143–159. 10.1080/00048623.2016.1228163

Wu, K. J., Burg, T. C., & Burg, K. J. (2020). Reshaping the higher education Makerspace and harnessing current disruptive events. *Technology and Innovation*, 21(4), 1–10. 10.21300/21.4.2020.6

Wu, Y., & Ma, Z. (2022). The power of Makerspaces: Heterotopia and innovation. *Sustainability (Basel)*, 15(1), 629. 10.3390/su15010629

Youmans, K., Villanueva, I., Nadelson, L., Bouwma-Gearhart, J., Lenz, A., & Lanci, S. (2020). *Engineering students perceived value of Makerspaces in relation to future career preparation*. Academic Press.

Yu, S. (2016). *Makerspaces as learning spaces: An historical overview and literature review*. Academic Press.

ADDITIONAL READING

Hai-Jew, S. (2024). *Generative AI in Teaching and Learning*. IGI Global.

KEY TERMS AND DEFINITIONS

Home Making Space: A home-based studio that combines both material and digital means of ideating, designing, prototyping, making, and refining; it also provides space for social collaboration.

Maker: Individuals who are creative and innovative and engage in making activities of various types using either physical or digital materials or both.

Maker Space: A community space where people may gather to innovate and create physical and digital objects.

Virtual Making: The uses of digital and online tools for creation of objects (or deliverables).

Seciton 4
Boundaries in the Digital Art and Crafting Spaces

Chapter 6
Making Original 2D Visual Deepfakes With a Generative AI Tool

Shalin Hai-Jew
https://orcid.org/0000-0002-8863-0175
Hutchinson Community College, USA

ABSTRACT

In the research and popular literature, there are many concerns about the deepfakes that may be generated using generative AI and other tools to mislead people and to compromise them in various ways through deception. This work explores the nature of deepfakes, generative AI, and manual and computational and combined means to identify (and neutralize) potential deepfakes, as described in the academic literature. Deepfakes may have positive effects as well to enhance human creativity and to expand the toolkit for digital making. This work also explores how to create a credible (non-malicious) 2D visual deepfake using a popular generative AI tool to understand some affordances and constraints for this particular "use case". For this basic work, the idea is only to trick the eyes, not the more in-depth detection methods based on computation.

INTRODUCTION

Deepfakes (or "deep fakes") refer to content "generated by an artificial intelligence, that is authentic in the eyes of a human being" (Mirsky & Lee, 2021, p. 1). "Deepfake" is a portmanteau word that refers to "deep learning" and "fakes," so there is an implied artificial neural network (ANN) machine learning angle. Neural networks are computational systems that are somewhat emulative of how the human brain works. A neural network is made up of "one or more layers of neurons or units. A neuron/unit is associated with a set of weights for its connections, a bias term, and an activation function. Each unit computes a linear combination of its inputs and weights and then outputs the result of the activation function (typically a non-linear function) on this combination. Neural networks that have arbitrarily many layers can approximate any function to any degree of precision. Layers between the input layer and

DOI: doi

output layers are called hidden layers and a neural network with more than one hidden layer is called a deep neural network" (Bauer & Bindschaedler, 2021, p. 2)

In terms of an origin story, deepfakes were "first created by a Reddit user named Deepfake" (Bauer & Bindschaedler, 2021, p. 17). Deepfakes refer to…

> …synthetic media where a person in an image or video is swapped with another person's likeness. AI-generated deepfakes have emerged as a complex and pervasive challenge in today's digital landscape, enabling the creation of remarkably convincing yet falsified multimedia content. (Singh & Dhiman, 2023, n.p.)

The deepfake phenomenon "initially gained public awareness in late 2017 within online hobbyist communities" (Whittaker, Kietzmann, Kietzmann, & Dabirian, 2020, p. 91). As the tools improved, people were more able to create convincing synthetic media. The deepfakes are created to mislead, provoke, trigger, and spark others' erroneous ideas and mistaken actions.

Some point to the risks of the "deep fakification" of the Internet, with a correlating diminishment of trust in anything digital (even as so much of people's lives are lived virtually and on social media) (Tolosana, Rathgeb, Vera-Rodriguez, Busch, Verdoliva, Lyu,... & Tiits, 2022). Common narratives involve the risks of deepfakes, with "crucial security, ethical, and human factors involved in the production and use of deepfakes" (Caporusso, 2021, p. 241). Some researchers see a core challenge with deepfakes, with a challenging core:

> At the core of deepfakes is deception, which involves intentionally, knowingly, and / or purposefully misleading another person. (Hancock & Bailenson, 2021, p. 149)

This work offers a light attempt at making a few deepfakes using the Deep Dream Generator as a basis for a thought experiment. What are ways to try to make a generated 2d visual more "real"? What are optimal ways to create that sense of illusion? Beyond self-amusement, what can be done with the generated deepfakes?

REVIEW OF THE LITERATURE

Generative AI (GAI_ has applications in "art, entertainment, design, and scientific research" (Ramdurai & Adhithya, 2023, p. 1). It is used for synthetic creative content generation, data augmentation, simulation, modeling, scenario creation for planning, design support, scientific discovery, filling data gaps, and others (Ramdurai & Adhithya, 2023, p. 2).

GAI is "a catch-all name for a massive ecosystem of loosely related technologies" (Takale, Mahalle, & Sule, Jan. – April 2024, p. 20). GAI is used in "image synthesis, text generation, music composition and creative design," among others (Takale, Mahalle, & Sule, Jan. – April 2024, p. 20).

In the academic literature, there are works both describing how deepfakes are generated through generative AI (GAI) and also ways that these are detected, in a continuing so-called arms race between the computer scientists creating the respective tools. There are many efforts to "limit the production of unethical and illegal deepfakes" with a variety of techniques and technologies (Gong, Goh, Kumar, Ye, & Chi, 2020).

Skilled attackers have been honing their strategies and tactics based on their knowledge of how media forensics tools work in order to launch their own counter-forensics efforts to "evade detectors" (Cozzolino & Verdoliva, 2022, p. 64). Creators of GAIs work hard to ensure their visuals "credibly pass muster" (Mirsky & Lee, 2021, p. 31). A universal detector does not exist yet to identify deepfakes across a range of type and models. It is very much "a cat and mouse game" with advances made between generators and detectors simultaneously (Gragnaniello, Marra, & Verdoliva, 2022, p. 191). Some users of GAIs will introduce "perturbations" to throw off classifiers; they may remove digital fingerprints (Gragnaniello, Marra, & Verdoliva, 2022). Images may also be transformed through pre- and post-production, which may change up the frequencies of various measures (used to identify digital forgeries) (Cocchi, Baraldi, Poppi, Cornia, Baraldi, & Cucchiara, Sept. 2023, p. 345). "AI synthetic face detection is not a trivial task" (Gragnaniello, Marra, & Verdoliva, 2022, p. 208), and nor is detecting deepfakes of other types (Zobaed, Rabby, Hossain, Hossain, Hasan, Karim, & Md Hasib, 2021).

The speed of change affects how long any discovery of a deepfake "tell" lasts; once a discovery is made, patches are made by the other side, and the deepfake becomes "more difficult to discover the next time. Each discovery improves the deep fakes, thus, each new method of discovery only works once" (Dack, 2019, p. 3). Some of the media forensics approaches may be applied to the identification of some deepfakes.

What Is a Deepfake? What Are Generative AI Tools?

A contemporary definition of deepfakes are that they are "AI-generated media content" (Jia, Lyu, Zhao, Chen, Yan, Ju,... & Lyu, 2024, n.p.) or artificial intelligence generated content (AIGC) (Cao, Li, Liu, Yan, Dai, Yu, & Sun, 2023, p. 1). Some include an exploitive aspect: Deepfakes are "a kind of forged image or video that is developed to spread misinformation and facilitate vulnerabilities to privacy hacking and truth masking with advanced technologies, including deep learning and artificial intelligence with trained algorithms" (Kandasamy, Hubálovský, & Trojovský, 2022, p. 1).

Some imbue the term with particular types of outputs and technologies, such as "face-swapping technologies that enable quick creation of fake images or videos which appear incredibly realistic" (Meskys, Kalpokiene, Jurcys, & Liaudanskas, 2020, p. 24); these types are also known as "puppet-master deep fakes in which one person's facial expressions and head movements are mapped onto another person" (Agarwal, Farid, El-Gaaly, & Lim, Dec. 2020, p. 6). Deepfakes are "digital fabrications in which realistic likenesses of things are synthetically generated or entirely altered to say or do something that never occurred" (Shoaib, Wang, Ahvanooey, & Zhao, Nov. 2023, p. 1). Deepfakes are "hyperrealistic videos that use artificial intelligence (AI) to show someone saying and doing things that never happened" (Sharma, 2023, p. 272).

Researchers suggest humanity is approaching a "post-epistemic" world in which truth cannot be validated and fiction cannot be invalidated, leaving people with truths and fictions differentiated or discerned (Horvitz, Nov. 2022, p. 653). that interactive and compositional deepfakes are emerging:

> Interactive deepfakes have the capacity to impersonate people with realistic interactive behaviors… compositional deepfakes leverage synthetic content in larger disinformation *plans* that integrate sets of deepfakes over time with observed, expected, and engineered world events to create persuasive *synthetic histories*. Synthetic histories can be constructed manually but may one day be guided by *adversarial generative explanation* (AGE) technologies" (Horvitz, Nov. 2022, p. 653)

Indeed, such technologies have been used in financial scamming frauds as reported in mainstream media already. Ways to defend against integrative and compositional deepfakes including savvy journalism, media literacy, authenticity "protocols" like "real-time *authenticity challenges,"* content provenance (or origin), watermarking and fingerprinting, detection, regulation and self-regulation, red-teaming testing, and continuous monitoring (Horvitz, Nov. 2022, pp. 659-660). Digital contents that are real, with an established provenance, are referred to as "authentic" and "pristine" vs. "fake" or "faux."

Various technologies have been used to create digital fakes over the years, including general digital image or digital video or digital audio or digital animation or digital multimedia editing tools. Some are dedicated tools and applications for the making of particular types of deepfakes. The most recent iterations of tools in this space are generative artificial intelligence (GAI) tools, which enable text-to-image/video/audio/animation/multimedia as output. Generative AI refers to "computational techniques that are capable of generating seemingly new, meaningful content such as text, images, or audio from training data" (Feuerriegel, Hartmann, Janiesch, & Zschech, 2024, p. 111). A common form of GAI is built from large language models (LLMs) that are trained to learn from big data (of uni-modal or multi-modal digital contents). These deep generative models capture parameters from neural networks, and the learned parameters are used to create new samples from the underlying distributions. Large vision-language models are created by processing text and image data simultaneously (Manduchi, et al., 2024, p. 4). Such models are complex and expensive to train and make:

> Efforts to scale deep generative models (DGMs) for tasks like language modeling and text-to-image synthesis often involve training large models with billions of parameters, which demands significant computational resources. This leads to practical issues such as high energy costs…and expensive inference, limiting access for many users. (Manduchi, et al., 2024, p. 5)

The concept is that the more data that is used, the more powerful such models can be and perhaps the more subtle and even clairvoyant in each. There are smaller language models that may be made for more limited usages, such as for unique art. Such tools generate or make or produce some digital output, often with informational value. GAIs "produce new, previously unseen information dependent on the data on which they were trained" (García-Peñalvo & Vázquez-Ingelmo, 2023, p. 7), with a focus on novel "human-like material" generated (García-Peñalvo & Vázquez-Ingelmo, 2023, p. 8). To wit, GAI is "not some form of arcane magic but the procedure of training a model with input data" (García-Peñalvo & Vázquez-Ingelmo, 2023, p. 14).

One common model of generative AI tools involves Generative Adversarial Networks (GANs), described as pitting counterfeiters against police (Goodfellow, as cited in Hancock & Bailenson, 2021, p. 149). In other words, there are generators (counterfeiters) and discriminators (police) that are pitted against each other:

> A generator attempts to fabricate new data (fake) that is indistinguishable from real data, while a discriminator tries to distinguish between real and fabricated data. (Bengesi, El-Sayed, Sarker, Houkpati, Irungu, & Oladunni, 2023, n.p.)

Deepfakes are enabled by GANs, "a branch of machine learning that applies neural net simulation to massive data sets, to make a fake"; GANs use a "synthesis engine" to create visuals which are then graded in order to make them more real-looking (Yagnik, Kurani, & Joshi, 2020, p. 382). There is a creator-critic dynamic. GANs are also used for various types of transcoding between and across different modalities from image-to-image, voice to text, image editing, speech synthesis, 3d video generation, graph generation, and others (Zhang, Zhang, Zheng, Qiao, Li, Zhang,... & Hong, 2023).

Generative foundation models (GFMs) refer to "machine learning systems that are: 1) 'generative'—they generate text, images, or other sequences of information based on some input prompt, and 2) 'foundation models' – neural network models trained on a large dataset comprising diverse origins and content, and can be adapted to a wide range of tasks" (Huang & Siddarth, 2023, p. 1). Prior deepfakes often required digital editing expertise and was "time and effort consuming" (Juefei-Xu, Wang, Huang, Guo, Ma, & Liu, 2022, p. 1678). Contemporaneous tools enable a much lower cost-of-entry. Essentially, human users may input textual prompts, which are then broken down by the GAI and mapped to "structural similarities that it identified in the data it was trained on" (Ferrari & McKelvey, 2023, p. 356). They may input visual "seeding images" along with the textual prompts as well. Many such applications offer AI-generated prompts to help users seed ideas or evolve them until they are satisfied with the outputs.

"Artificial intelligence," as an inclusive umbrella term, refers to computer systems that performatively emulate human intelligence and capabilities, such as creativity, among others. Neural rendering is "based on machine learning techniques such as generative adversarial networks and is used to infer human face features and their animation from large amounts of (video) training data" (Seymour, Riemer, Yuan, & Dennis, 2021, p. 4859). There are four types of facial manipulation "i) entire face synthesis, ii) identity swap (DeepFakes), iii) attribute manipulation, and iv) expression swap" (Tolosana, Vera-Rodriguez, Fierrez, Morales, & Ortega-Garcia, 2020, p. 131). There is the making of entire "non-existent face images," replacing the face of one person with another, "face editing or face retouching," and "face reenactment" or changing the facial expression of a person (Tolosana, Vera-Rodriguez, Fierrez, Morales, & Ortega-Garcia, 2020, p. 133) respectively. Said another way, facial reenactment refers to the "transferring (of) the facial expressions between people" (Pashine, Mandiya, Gupta, & Sheikh, 2021, n.p.)

Generative AI is a capability based on various technological and data collection advances:

> ...the continuous growth in computing power has used deep neural networks, transformers and other innovative models like generative adversarial networks and variational autoencoders. All these models can effectively capture the complexity of data, making them adept at modeling high-dimensional probability distributions of language or images from specific or general domains. (Gozalo-Brizuela & Garrido-Merchán, 2023, p. 1)

Generative AI models are "equipped with vast data and intricate designs" (Gozalo-Brizuela & Garrido-Merchán, 2023, p. 1). This technology offers "unprecedented capabilities in content creation, problem-solving, and decision-making" (Gozalo-Brizuela & Garrido-Merchán, 2023, p. 1).

There is a divergence between public and expert understandings of the computational terms. One research team explains:

> While a model that produces any output can be technically seen as generative, the Artificial Intelligent research community often reserves the term for complex models that generate high-quality, human-like material... While the broader public often interprets 'Generative AI' as AI-driven creation of tangible content, the AI research community mainly discusses generative implementations with an emphasis on the models in use, without explicitly categorizing their work under the term 'Generative AI.' (García-Peñalvo & Vázquez-Ingelmo, 2023, p. 7)

Generative AIs are built on GANs, GPTs (Generative Pre-trained Transformers), autoencoders, diffusion models, and transformers, to create outputs like "text generation and music composition, image creation, video production, code generation, and even scientific work" (Bengesi, El-Sayed, Sarker, Houkpati, Irungu, & Oladunni, 2023, n.p.). Diffusion models or diffusion probabilistic models refer to "a family of generated models that are Markov chains trained with variational inference," used to create a variety of samples (Zhang, Zhang, Zhang, & Kweon, 2023, n.p.)

Observed Potential Harms of Deepfakes

Deepfakes are proliferating apace in the wild, whether those who consume the content know it or not. One study reports:

> The AI firm Deeptrace found 15,000 deepfake videos online in September 2019, a near doubling over nine months. A staggering 96% were pornographic and 99% of those mapped faces from female celebrities onto porn stars. (Paul, 2021, p. 19)

The broad sharing of non-consensual deepfake pornography serves to "enforce gendered disparities within visual information" (Wagner & Blewer, 2019, p. 32). They "pose a threat particularly to women, ranging from celebrities to journalists" (Agarwal, Farid, El-Gaaly, & Lim, Dec. 2020, p. 1).

People are highly influenced by visual signals. The plasticity of the human mind enables deepfakes to "modify our memories and even implant false memories, and they can also modify a person's attitudes toward the target of the deepfake" (Hancock & Bailenson, 2021, p. 150). People may be affected by false memories; they may have interpersonal relationships affected by deepfakes (Hancock & Bailenson, 2021, p. 150).

Generative AI poses risks to the concept and practice of "good society" by offering ways to disrupt politics and culture (Sætra, 2023, p. 1). The risks emerge at various levels of scale: micro-level ones (such as of preferring robot companionship to actual human companionship) to meso ones such as further pushing aside marginalized peoples to macro ones such as threats to political systems (Sætra, 2023). At the individual level, the person may experience "character defamation" based on deepfake falsehoods (Yadav & Salmani, May 2019, p. 852). This is a scenario in which people have lost their privacy to technology and experience predation by those who use AI to manipulate them (Dhoni & Kumar, 2023). A person may be the victim of document and signature forgery and suffer monetary and other losses (Katarya & Lal, Oct. 2020). Deepfake technologies bring "serious consequences in the private life of every involved person" (Giudice, Guarnera, & Battiato, 2021, p. 1) because of the deployable risks. National security issues have also come to the forefront with the advent of deepfakes (Rahman, Islam, Moon, Tasnim, Siddique, Shahiduzzaman, & Ahmed, 2022). The criminal justice system and the courts may also be at risk, given that video is often used as evidence. If videos have been tampered with, the miscarriage of justice may be deeply serious. Researchers observe: "…evidentiary materials—including documents, videos, audio recordings, and more—that are AI-generated are becoming increasingly difficult to distinguish from those that are non-AI generated" (Grossman, Grimm, Brown, & Xu, 2023, p. 3).

There are also risks by foreign governments, trolls, conspiracy theorists, "hyper-partisan media," trolls, politicians, and others using deepfakes for their own ends (Masood, Nawaz, Malik, Javed, Irtaza, & Malik, 2023, p. 4). AI has "acquired human-level mastery" in a number of domains (Frey & Osborne,

2023, p. 1), putting into question whether humans may maintain their status in 1) creative, 2) inherently social, and 3) unstructured work" (p. 2).

Some publicly viewable deepfakes include "deep fake porn, political campaigns, deep fakes for commercial uses and creative deep fakes" (Meskys, Kalpokiene, Jurcys, & Liaudanskas, 2020, p. 24). Others anticipate "synthetic advertising" as a subset of "manipulated advertising" (Campbell, Plangger, Sands, & Kietzmann, 2022, p. 22). A different study suggests that the "…journalism industry is going to face a huge consumer trust issue thanks to deepfakes" (Yagnik, Kurani, & Joshi, 2020, p. 384).

Deepfakes may "turbo-charge" disinformation, with the capability of causing societal level changes (Dack, 2019). There can be serious damage from the manipulating of public opinion, promoting of distortion, "manipulation of elections, undermining journalism, inflicting reputational damage," spreading misinformation, and destabilizing society (Veerasamy & Pieterse, Mar. 2022, p. 347). One study involved the making of digital replicas of people, including "a figure that people trust to report the truth about world events" in the form of a TV news anchor (Bohacek & Farid, 2024, p. 1).

At the time of the work, the researchers did find some limits: "We did run into some limitations. Large camera or head motions, for example, made it difficult to maintain temporal coherence, and unusual words in the script occasionally led to visually obvious errors in the shape of the mouth" (Bohacek & Farid, 2024, p. 2). With the wide availability of public videos of public figures, though, like journalists, more contemporaneous tools can make more believable fakes.

Those who make deepfakes do so for some of the following objectives: "misconstruction of truth, spread of fake news, mislead(ing), creation of shock or alarm, discredit(ing) high profile individuals, entertainment, fraud, manipulation of events like elections, intimidation or blackmail, (and/or) damage to stability or relations" (Veerasamy & Pieterse, Mar. 2022, pp. 343 - 344).

There is serious effort needed to identify misinformation:

> By scrutinizing manipulation traces such as signal manipulation, semantic inconsistencies, logical incoherence, and psychological strategies, our objective is to tackle AI-generated misinformation and provide a conceptual design of systematic explainable solution. (Xu, Fan, & Kankanhalli, Oct. 2023, p. 9291)

The researchers elaborate further:

> Authentic content should be easily comprehensible to humans. Conversely, content that is unrecognizable or misleading is often the result of a potential AI generation. (Xu, Fan, & Kankanhalli, Oct. 2023, p. 9295)

They assess the credibility of the shared information against known facts in a knowledge base. They also evaluate the "logical coherence," "contextual reasonability," and "overall one-sidedness of the information based on subjective expression and breadth of coverage" (Xu, Fan, & Kankanhalli, Oct. 2023, p. 9296). The due diligence is necessary but costly in effort.

Deepfakes may be at the nexus of various deceptions. Deepfakes may be "realistic and convincing" (Veerasamy & Pieterse, Mar. 2022, p. 340) to dupe vast swaths of the human population.

> Deepfakes provide a means to generate fake digital content in order to impersonate a person. With the use of audio, images and videos, artificial intelligence is used to depict the speech and actions of people. (Veerasamy & Pieterse, Mar. 2022, p. 340)

While early generation deceptions have been of poor quality, more recent generations of such works have become more compelling and convincing. Such deceptions may have expanding and cascading impacts.

Willingness to See the Fakeness or Not?

Another area of deepfake usage includes advertisements "generated or edited through the artificial and automatic production and modification of data" including through deepfake technologies (Campbell, Plangger, Sands, & Kietzmann, 2022, p. 22), which stand to affect how ads are conceptualized and developed and deployed. The advent of such sophisticated ads requires heightened awareness and sophistication of the general public:

> With ever more sophisticated manipulation of ads, consumers are faced with what the authors term an *advertising calculus* in deciding how they will react to them. Advertising calculus refers to the evaluation of trade-offs between an ad's benefits (e.g., personalization) and its costs (e.g., privacy). (Campbell, Plangger, Sands, & Kietzmann, 2022, p. 12)

People have to decide what tradeoffs they want to engage, between sophisticated but also inauthentic advertisements. One researcher observes: "How might the phenomenology of video spectatorship shift given a default suspicion of deepfakery?" (Fletcher, 2018, p. 469) A more relevant question may be, How apathetic will a general public be in the face of deepfakes that convey messages that they want to hear?

Another study suggests the importance of perceivers' beliefs as "an important factor for the impact of deepfake images, whether in beneficial or potentially harmful applications" (Eiserbeck, Maier, Baum, & Abdel Rahman, 2023, n.p.) This study found "neurocognitive evidence that we are differentially vulnerable to presumed deepfakes displaying positive or negative facial expressions" (Eiserbeck, Maier, Baum, & Abdel Rahman, 2023, n.p.) Specifically, positive contents (like smiling faces) were more "vulnerable to being labeled as fake, whereas fake negative content may still retain its effectiveness even after being exposed" (Eiserbeck, Maier, Baum, & Abdel Rahman, 2023, n.p.) Human cognitive biases are also highly influential in what people believe, whether the source is fake or not.

One study explores the potentials of deepfake geography or the manipulation of geospatial data, the falsification of maps, of satellite data, using generative AI. The convergence of AI and GIS science comes with risks: "Our proactive study warns of the emergence and proliferation of deep fakes in geography just as 'lies' in maps" (Zhao, Zhang, Xu, Sun, & Deng, 2021, p. 338). This work identifies various "tells" of manipulated GIS data. This includes methods for how to detect deepfake satellite images (Zhao, Zhang, Xu, Sun, & Deng, 2021, p. 341).

A World Shifting on Its Axis

Deepfakes may presage a "post-fact" world (Fletcher, 2018, p. 456), an "era of deepfakes" where deepfakes are "a form of fake news" (Karnouskos, 2020, p. 138). Creative AI "might undermine the distinction between fact and fiction" (De Vries, 2020, p. 2110). The "underlying reality of the post-fact era" is that "humans have never really cared about facts" and are perhaps not necessarily rational (Fletcher, 2018, p. 466). Another work reads: "Given the ease with which false information may be created and spread, it has become increasingly difficult to know the truth and trust the information, which may result in harmful consequences" (Masood, Nawaz, Malik, Javed, Irtaza, & Malik, 2023, p. 1). Another work reads: "In this AI era, we are living in a world where we cannot believe our eyes anymore" (Wang, Juefei-Xu, Guo, Huang, Ma, Liu, & Wang, 2020, p. 7). The lack of human discernment is a major factor: "Generated data has become difficult, if not impossible, to be distinguished from real data" (Yu, Skripniuk, Chen, Davis, & Fritz, 2020, p. 1). There are cultural effects predicted from the creative AI tools enabled to make deepfakes (Hanif & Dave, 2022), and "hyperproduction" of digital contents is seen to cycle through and result in more homogenization (Ferrari & McKelvey, 2023, p. 338). Some suggest that the over-abundance of generative AI works may leave humanity desensitized to human-made imagery, how they are created, what they mean, and what their potentials may be for human expression and intercommunications. Perhaps such works may change up human preferences, bending those towards even more artifice, than the real.

The ability to create floods of digital contents with little effort poses the risks of releasing "low-quality data" into the public sphere, "eroding self-determination and democracy," "homogenizing content" and lessening the diversity of available contents, "misaligning incentives for humans to contribute to the open digital ecosystem," "driving further economic concentration" to well-funded technology companies, lessening the value of human labor, "accelerating unpredictable risks from highly capable AI systems," causing economic implications, and outpacing human production in terms of outputs to the digital commons (Huang & Siddarth, 2023, pp. 2-5). These technologies may be used to promote "political manipulation" and "spread of misinformation" (Beerbaum, 2023, p. 1).

One researcher suggests "that if GAN images and photographs become indistinguishable, then photographs will come to occupy a role in society similar to that of paintings today, in that they will lose their epistemic authority but continue to be valued aesthetically" (Pan, 2021, p. 52). The human-machine collaborations around generated images do "embody artistic intentions" (Pan, 2021, p. 52). The works capture original visions.

> A GAN consists of a competing pair of algorithms, a 'generator' and a 'discriminator'. The generator is tasked with turning random numbers called 'seeds' into images that resemble those from the training set. The discriminator then rece3ives a mix of images created by the generator and images from the training set and attempts to determine the origin of each image. Both algorithms receive the discriminator's results and use them to improve through trial and error: the generator learns to operate more closely to when it succeeded in deceiving the discriminator, while the discriminator learns from its mistakes. Over time, the generator learns to turn any seed number into an image that the discriminator would guess is part of the training set. (Pan, 2021, p. 56)

Where photos were seen as visual representations of reality without artful value, initially, GAN images enable "a skilled image creator to fulfill their artistic intentions through the skilful (sic) use of the process" (Pan, 2021, p. 62). This aspect means that GAIs are game changers in terms of human expression and artful creativity.

In particular domains, there may be various sorts of malicious usage of deepfakes at scale, such as in business (Houde, Liao, Martino, Muller, Piorkowski, Richards, ... & Zhang, 2020). Researchers suggest the importance of "thorough, responsible evaluations of generative AI models before widespread adoption into domains where decisions with substantial life-altering consequences are routinely made" (Tortora, 2024, p. 01).

Observed Potential Benefits of Deepfakes

Deepfake technology "is neutral and can be used both benignly and maliciously" (Juefei-Xu, Wang, Huang, Guo, Ma, & Liu, 2022, p. 1679). Given their broadening uptake by the general population, people are working on how to "leverage this intelligence for good" (Paul, 2021, p. 48). These technologies and deepfakes may even be neutral in how people use them. There are deepfakes "for the good" (Caporusso, 2021, p. 235). They advance human capabilities and expressiveness. There are positive uses in areas such as "entertainment, to humanitarian efforts and education" (Danry, Leong, Pataranutaporn, Tandon, Liu, Shilkrot, ... & Sra, Apr. 2022, p. 1). [The tools of this "new machine age" are not seen as fully positive in education. The "common assumption" is that learner creations can show their "mastery of knowledge and skills" (Southgate, n.d., p. 41). If contents from generative AI are submitted in lieu of actual learner original work, that can foil the learning process. Similarly, there are risks of deepfakes in academic publishing, "during manuscript submission and the publication process, as well as on academic social network sites" (da Silva, 2023, p. 71).]

Real people may be brought back to life (digitally) to comfort the living. Virtual humans may be seen as a positive (Rahman, Islam, Moon, Tasnim, Siddique, Shahiduzzaman, & Ahmed, 2022). Virtual humans may be used for social commenting, satire, digital characters, and other applications. Face-swap impersonation will "open up a range of new fields of application that are not associated with the often malicious and harmful uses of deep fakes in the public space" such as uses in healthcare, financial decision-making, employment, and other uses (Seymour, Riemer, Yuan, & Dennis, 2021, p. 4866).

Regardless of intentions of the makers and the various uses, many people prefer to know if a digital object is generated by human, by machine, or by both together. Various methods have been launched to detect deepfakes, such as through manual observations, computational means, media forensics, and "programmed machine learning algorithms" (Jia, Lyu, Zhao, Chen, Yan, Ju,... & Lyu, 2024). There are efforts to have makers of deepfake technologies embed some code to validate the makers and provenance of the digital content.

Deepfakes are used by corporations (such as for AI influencers and models, providing service to customers), law enforcement (such as the uses of underage AIs to help catch pedophiles), and a range of other practical and positive uses.

Ethics of Using Generative AI Tools

The creations of generative AI are seen to possibly "degrade the 'digital commons'" (Huang & Siddarth, 2023, p. 1). The training data used includes copyrighted works without compensation to the original creatives. Generative foundation models "do not have processes in place to return value captured to data producers and stakeholders" (Huang & Siddarth, 2023, p. 1).

Given the widespread uses of generative AI tools in the world, it is important to strive to ensure ethicality and safety in their use (Takale, Mahalle, & Sule, Jan. – April 2024, p. 20). One point of contention has been whether GAI's supply chain contravenes copyright and who would be responsible at each stage. Researchers write about foundational understandings:

> The hornbook statement of United States copyright doctrine is that original works of authorship are protected by copyright when they are fixed in a tangible medium of expression. A defendant directly infringes when they engage in conduct implicating one of several enumerated exclusive rights (reproducing, publicly distributing, etc.), with a work of their own that is substantially similar to a copyrighted work because it was copied from that work. (Lee, Cooper, & Grimmelmann, 2023, p. 55)

Infringing conduct is "legal when it is protected by one of several defenses, including the DMCA Section 512 safe harbors, fair use, or an express or implied license" (Lee, Cooper, & Grimmelmann, 2023, p. 56). Whether works by generative AIs may be copyright-able vary globally, in part, based on how much of a person's creative investment has gone into the work. If a work is created wholly by automation, that work is not eligible for copyright because a machine created that work, not a human creator. There are various complexities in arguing copyright law, so there is not necessarily a clear foregone conclusion. Also, whether generative AI infringes copyright does not have a yes-or-no binary answer (Lee, Cooper, & Grimmelmann, 2023).

Methods for Identifying Deepfakes: Manual and Computational and Combined

Researchers suggest a multidimensional approach to addressing deepfakes. One work proposed four main ways: "1) legislation and regulation, 2) corporate policies and voluntary action, 3) education and training, and 4) anti-deepfake technology" (Yagnik, Kurani, & Joshi, 2020, p. 385). In terms of legal considerations related to large GAI, these include the following: "(1) direct regulation, (2) data protection, (3) content moderation, and (4) policy proposals" (Hacker, Engel, & Mauer, June 2023, p. 1112). Regulation of the "AI/GAI market" may "ensure a level playing field, promote fair competition, protect intellectual property rights and privacy, and prevent potential geopolitical risks" (Wach, Duong, Ejdys, Kazlauskaitė, Korzynski, Mazurek, ... & Ziemba, 2023, p. 7). Those in various professional roles--"developers, deployers, professional and no-professional users, as well as recipients of LGAIM output"—have different regulatory duties, legal liabilities, and legal responsibilities (Hacker, Engel, & Mauer, June 2023, p. 1112). There are regulatory framework and legal variances across various countries and regions:

> The absence of a unified approach, common regulatory framework, and commonly accepted practices has resulted in a situation where different initiatives emerge across countries which share some common elements but also numerous differences that can lead to challenges related to interoperability. (Tolosana, Rathgeb, Vera-Rodriguez, Busch, Verdoliva, Lyu,... & Tiits, 2022, p. 480)

Others suggest that market forces would be the optimal path to deal with deepfakes. One research team notes: "Even though some regulatory framework to address social, economical and political implications of deep fakes is desirable, the lack of significant technical expertise and slow political processes suggest that such regulatory responses will not be as efficient as market-driven solutions" (Meskys, Kalpokiene, Jurcys, & Liaudanskas, 2020, p. 31). Another work suggests the importance of "capable AI administration" and the need for "mindfulness among analysts, policymakers, and specialists to create proactive techniques for overseeing the security challenges postured by generative AI advances" (Joshi, 2024, p. 91).

With the Human's Naked Eye

Discerning deepfakes requires a critical mindset and the willingness to detect fakes. Some people may tend towards suspending disbelief and going with illusions and implausibilities as a temperament and others as a vulnerability to a context. Where people want to believe, it is perhaps sometimes impossible to induce disbelief.

For some of the earlier deepfakes with less sophisticated tools, some visual observations might be enough to tell a fake still 2d visual from a real one. The visual assessment may evaluate works globally while others focus on zoomed-in parts or "patches."

Perhaps there are artful overlays. Perhaps the color looks false. Perhaps the fall of the light waves on a scene look artificial. Perhaps a human face looks too symmetrically perfect. Perhaps there are blurs similar to unprofessional image retouching (Bharadiya, 2024, p. 468) or jitter and occlusions (Mirsky & Lee, 2021). Poses may be warped. The foreground and background may show artifacts indicating possible editing or manipulation. Perhaps there are regions—at the image edges, at the edges of objects—that evoke a sense of falseness. The eyes may lack reflections of the physical light and context. Some visuals may have micro color changes. In faux videos, there may be "irregular head movements" (Dack, 2019, p. 3). They may find variance in skin tones. Depicted individuals may have "ghost edges" and "double eyebrows."

Videos, which are frames over time, may be identified as fake based on some tells. There may be flickering of light in videos. The temporal sequence may not make sense. There may be jerky movements, "shifts in lighting from one frame to the next, shifts in skin tone, strange blinking or no blinking (or long pauses between blinking), poorly synched lips and could (sic), digital artifacts in the image" (Kapersky, 2021, as cited in Veerasamy & Pieterse, Mar. 2022, p. 346). Finer details like hair, teeth, and jewelry, may be poorly rendered (Veerasamy & Pieterse, Mar. 2022). Another approach examines videos for discrepancies: "By matching the behavioral and facial identities against a set of authentic reference videos, inconsistencies in the matching identities can reveal face-swap deep fakes" (Agarwal, Farid, El-Gaaly, & Lim, Dec. 2020, p. 1).

Another approach in the video space involves human biological signals (Ciftci, Demir, & Yin, Sept. 2020, p. 1), such as breathing, skin tone, and others.

For those using just the naked eye to try to discern, they are advised to become more AI resilient—to better understand the technologies and their capabilities. Researchers write:

> We cannot trust data, audio, video, and identities any more (sic). Democracies are able to cope with known threats, the known-knowns. Transforming unknown-knowns to known-knowns is one important cornerstone of resilient societies. An AI-resilient society is able to transform threats caused by new AI technologies such as generative adversarial networks. Resilience can be seen as a positive adaptation of these threats. (Bartz-Beielstein, 2019, p. 1)

People benefit from knowing what their cultural "blind spots" are—the threats that they are aware of but ignore (Bartz-Beielstein, 2019, p. 3). The resilient are savvy about social media and generative technologies. They fact-check sites, conduct reverse image searches, and think critically about AI.

Several works suggest the importance of preparing children for an "AI-driven future," such as by helping middle school students acclimate to generative AI and digital creation (Ali, DiPaola, Lee, Sindato, Kim, Blumofe, & Breazeal, 2021). Youth need to understand generative AI since it is built into "products used by youth" (Ali, DiPaola, Williams, Ravi, & Breazeal, 2023, p. 1). Some of the lessons in this latter work involve elements of the technology, how generative AI tools work, the risks of fake media, the need for data protection, the need for privacy, and legal issues around the ownership of AI-generated art (Ali, DiPaola, Williams, Ravi, & Breazeal, 2023, p. 1). Another work describes the introduction of middle school students to generative models and their potential for benefits and harms (Ali, DiPaola, Lee, Hong, & Breazeal, May 2021),

There are efforts to onboard adults, too, to help them understand GAN technologies. One research work describes a tool that enables visual experimentation by non-experts (Kahng, Thorat, Chau, Viégas, & Wattenberg, 2018).

The academic literature includes a wide range of suggestions and methods to dealing with the challenge of mass-scale deepfakes. The maker of such technologies are asked to design autonomous systems so that it is unlikely to be mistaken for anything besides an autonomous system, and should identify itself at the start of any interaction with another agent" (Bartz-Beielstein, 2019, p. 7); this idea aligns with the Turing Red Flag Law idea (Walsh, 2016, as cited in Bartz-Beielstein, 2019, p. 7). Those who create AI systems should have "a mandatory self-identification" system in place (Smuha, 2019, as cited in Bartz-Beielstein, 2019, p. 7).

Markings by the Generative AI Tools

Others suggest that there should be "a responsible disclosure of such state-of-the-art generative models, that allows model inventors to fingerprint their models, so that the generated samples containing a fingerprint can be accurately detected and attributed to a source" (Yu, Skripniuk, Chen, Davis, & Fritz, 2020, p. 1). [Some computational detector tools enable researchers to identify originating generative AI models for particular works, but these approaches are not available to the general public per se.] Some approaches rely on so-called "inherent clues in deep fakes," so the methods are limited since model makers continue to iterate their techniques and remove these indicators (Yu, Skripniuk, Chen, Davis, & Fritz, 2020, p. 3). Various generators may be created with different fingerprints for different models in a "scalable ad-hoc" solution (Yu, Skripniuk, Chen, Davis, & Fritz, 2020, p. 9). There is precedence for such marking, such as through the use of digital watermarking and authentication (Singh & Dhiman, 2023). Those who make deepfake makers have a responsibility of identifying the GAI visuals (Knott, Pedreschi, Chatila, Chakraborti, Leavy, Baeza-Yates,... & Bengio, 2023, p. 1). They need to provide *detection mechanisms* usable by others. (Knott, Pedreschi, Chatila, Chakraborti, Leavy, Baeza-Yates,... & Bengio, 2023).

Another research work asserts that fingerprinting visuals "(1) holds for a variety of cutting-edge generative models, (2) leads to a negligible side effect on generation quality, (3) stays robust against image-level and model-level perturbations, (4) stays hard to be detected by adversaries, and (5) converts deepfake detection and attribution into trivial tasks and outperforms the recent state-of-the-art baselines" (Yu, Skripniuk, Abdelnabi, & Fritz, 2021, p. 14448).

Similarly, many who create real digital and digitized contents maintain authentication indicators, such as tokens, metadata, and other revelatory markings. These labels embedded in a digital file are meant to show the genuine origins of the digital media.

In the absence of model disclosures, there may be various ways to computationally classify various digital contents as machine-made or human-made. Such tools may consider objects in context or out-of-context. It is possible to see traces by Generative Adversarial Network engines by "analyzing ad-hoc frequencies" (Giudice, Guarnera, & Battiato, 2021, p. 1), in a frequency analysis. Different generative architectures have different frequencies that may be used to identify them.

Computational Means to Identify Deepfakes

There are various methods of detection for "a more secure digital landscape" (Arshed, Mumtaz, Ibrahim, Dewi, Tanveer, & Ahmed, 2024, n.p.). Various types of faked digital contents—textual, audio, visual, multimedia—precede the popularization of deepfakes. Media forensics have long existed to detect various types of fakes and spoofs, prior to the deep learning era. "Fake news" has origins in antiquity (Botha & Pieterse, Mar. 2020, p. 57).

Certain "tells" have been established for various devices used for the image capture: "The most popular approaches look for artifacts related to the in-camera processing chain (camera-based clues) or the out-camera processing history (editing-based clues)" (Cozzolino & Verdoliva, 2022, p. 45). There have been machine learning methods, too. Some methods are known as "blind methods that do not require any prior knowledge and reveal inconsistencies with respect to some well-defined hypotheses" (Cozzolino & Verdoliva, 2022, p. 45). There are efforts to observe post-processing steps including "geometric transformations, like rotation and scaling, contrast adjustment, and blurring, to smooth the object-background boundaries" (Cozzolino & Verdoliva, 2022, p. 60). Some analyses enable the analysis of "low-level pixel artifacts introduced during the synthesis process" using computational means (Agarwal, Farid, El-Gaaly, & Lim, Dec. 2020, p. 1). Pixels refer to picture elements, a small box of illumination comprised of mixes of red, green, and blue (RGB) wavelengths and luminance that make various colors on-screen.

One research work divides deepfake detectors into four categories: image-based, audio-based, video-based, and multimodality based (Vyas, Pareek, Jayaswal, & Patil, 2024, p. 40). Visual manipulation categories in digital representations of faces include "face-swap, face-reenactment, lip-sync, entire face synthesis, and attribute manipulation" (Masood, Nawaz, Malik, Javed, Irtaza, & Malik, 2023, p. 30). One approach involves the computational observation of visual artifacts in faces created using algorithms, which would otherwise be invisible to the naked eye (Durall, Keuper, Pfreundt, & Keuper, 2019, p. 1). Some extract data patterns from the auto-generated images. Others engage pixel-level examinations using computer vision. Another method "combines a static biometric based on facial recognition with a temporal, behavioral biometric based on facial expressions and head movements" (Agarwal, Farid, El-Gaaly, & Lim, Dec. 2020, p. 1).

Technologies have been used to identify deepfakes, in two categories: "(1) identify artifacts commonly present in generative models' output, or (2) detect if a possibly synthetic image came from a known generative model" (Bauer & Bindschaedler, 2021, p. 18). Deep neural networks have been used to detect "fake multimedia content but unfortunately these algorithms appear to be neither generalizable nor explainable" (Giudice, Guarnera, & Battiato, 2021, p. 1). One tool reduces the dimensionality of the digital face and then applies a deepfake detection classifier (Suganthi, Ayoobkhan, Bacanin, Venkatachalam, Štěpán, & Pavel, 2022). Another tool identifies machine-generated vs. human-generated microblogging messages (Fagni, Falchi, Gambini, Martella, & Tesconi, 2021). One work proposes "a novel multi-level hierarchical approach exploiting deep learning models properly trained and tested" (Guarnera, Giudice, & Battiato, 2024, p. 2). One method exposes deepfakes using inconsistent head poses (Yang, Li, & Lyu, May 2019). One detector is "based on monitoring neuron behaviors to spot AI-synthesized fake faces" (Wang, Juefei-Xu, Ma, Xie, Huang, Wang, & Liu, 2019, n.p.) Another method using nearest neighbor classification as a way to move towards universal fake image detecting across generative models (Ojha,

Li, & Lee, 2023). One study found that "a synthesized image can be attributed to the generator that produced it even in presence of noise" (Zhang, Zhou, Shumailov, & Papernot, 2020, p. 20).

One study describes the vetting of online social network (OSN) profiles, some of which are faked through the use of natural language generators and image generators. The "personas and OSN profiles are built on a collection of multimodal fields that must maintain both intra-field and inter-field consistency" (Figueira & Wang, .n.d., p. 1), and discrepancies may indicate profile fabrication.

On the Cybersecurity Front

Generative AI can have both negative and positive effects on cyber defense. There is the "potential misuse for crafting convincing phishing emails, generating disinformation through deepfake videos, and spreading misinformation via authentic-looking social media posts, posing a new set of challenges and risks in the realm of cybersecurity" (Neupane, Fernandez, Mittal, & Rahimi, 2023, n.p.).

However, generative models may be harnessed for various uses in the cybersecurity space.

> To train a neural network, all its parameters (i.e., weights and biases) are initialized randomly, then through the training process, the parameters are tuned using backpropagation. There are different choices for activation function for each unit or layer, loss function (training objective), and ways to connect the units of one layer to those of another layer, leading to virtually endless possibilities for neural network architectures. (Bauer & Bindschaedler, 2021, p. 2)

The risks of "biometric spoofing" or using "a person's unique attributes, such as fingerprints, voice, or even handwriting, to identify an individual" are many (Bauer & Bindschaedler, 2021, p. 9). A different work calls these "pantomime assaults" or imitating people or organizations, disinformation and "purposeful publicity," unauthorized usage of people's private information "to create engineered media," and other potential and real harms (Joshi, 2024, p. 92).

GAIs may be used to obfuscate malware and make it look like something benign (Bauer & Bindschaedler, 2021, p. 9). The outputs from GAI may be used to hide messages, such as through steganography.

The use of LLMs and generative AI can help with the identification of deepfakes, albeit with more complex prompting than binary elicitations (deepfake or not), in one study (Jia, Lyu, Zhao, Chen, Yan, Ju,... & Lyu, 2024, p. 2). The research team also observed that "multimodal LLMs do not incorporate signal cues or data-driven approaches for this task" at present / can identify AI-created images "regardless of the generation model used" (Jia, Lyu, Zhao, Chen, Yan, Ju,... & Lyu, 2024, p. 2) and with some reasonable detection accuracy in the media forensics work.

In terms of deepfakes in videos and animations, gaze tracking has been used to identify synthetic depictions or agents. There are "several prominent eye ad gaze features that deep fakes exhibit differently" (Demir & Ciftci, May 2021, p. 1). Specifically, there are "geometric, visual, metric, temporal, and spectral variations" across videos (Demir & Ciftci, May 2021, p. 1). The output of the generative models create "generative noise" from the process (Demir & Ciftci, May 2021, p. 11), and the identification of such noise may indicate their provenance. Another work describes a detection method based on observed eye blinking, "a physiological signal that is not well presented in the synthesized fake videos" (Li, Chang, & Lyu, Dec. 2018, p. 1).

Perhaps there will be detectors of interactive generative AI systems(Muller, Chilton, Kantosalo, Martin, & Walsh, Apr. 2022, p. 1) and other forthcoming systems based on behavioral observations. Computational methods can be subtle and highly sophisticated and observant in ways well beyond unaided human perceptions and brain processing.

Benchmark Datasets for Testing Computational Detection Tools

To hone such computational detection tools, various datasets have been created for testing. One is a million-scale benchmark, including images that are "low-resolution, blurred, and compressed images" to assess whether they were generated artificially or created in other ways (Zhu, Chen, Yan, Huang, Lin, Li, ... & Wang, 2024, p. 1). The wider the range of possible images, the more real-world the performance results.

Another work describes the making of a large near-exhaustive forgery detection dataset to enable the development of more robust detection tools (Jiang, Wu, Qian, & Loy, 2022). These enable long-term memory of fakes against which new images may be checked and compared.

Real-Time Detection

Modern life often involves the making of fast decisions based on fast electronic information. There are the risks of "real-time deepfakes" in the form of AI-powered filters (Hancock & Bailenson, 2021, p. 152), so such GAI deepfake capabilities make broad room for malfeasance. A single meme (a digital memetic message shared on social media) may influence public opinion across broad swaths of a population (Helmus, 2022, p. 1). Real-time detection of deepfakes is needed to head off GAI's cybersecurity threat (Renaud, Warkentin, & Westerman, 2023, n.p.). There is the constant threat of cyberattacks, with generalizable cycles of known processes (Neupane, Fernandez, Mittal, & Rahimi, 2023).

Accurate image tagging of deepfakes may help system administrators to block them from social networks and other platforms (Wang, Juefei-Xu, Guo, Huang, Ma, Liu, & Wang, 2020, p. 1). Various "frontier AI" will be crucial to combat deepfakes (Shoaib, Wang, Ahvanooey, & Zhao, Nov. 2023, p. 6). There are systems that can monitor and detect for deepfakes (Azmoodeh & Dehghantanha, 2022), to enable cyber defenses against various types of attacks at scale. A researcher writes:

> In a deepfakes world, it sometimes becomes very important, even a matter of life and death, to detect and quantify a video's degree of mediation-distortion, as compared with a (relatively) unmediated reality. *Did this really happen as represented here?* is no merely academic question. (Fletcher, 2018, p. 469)

The broad public needs to be aware of "smarter attacks" and to realize that cybersecurity compliance alone is not enough (Renaud, Warkentin, & Westerman, 2023, n.p.) Such training may include media literacy and critical thinking. This learning will have to be done at speed to a changing world. ChatGPT is signaling a "giant leap for artificial general intelligence (AGI)" (Zhang, Zhang, Li, Qiao, Zheng, Dam, ... & Hong, 2023, p. 1), or the ability of a computational system to perform across a range of human intelligence capabilities in ways competitive with people's abilities. Some weaknesses to current iterations have been surfaced, such as the sharing of incorrect information, broken logic, inconsistency in outputs, and lacking an "unconscious" in ways dissimilar to people (Zhang, Zhang, Li, Qiao, Zheng, Dam, ...

& Hong, 2023, pp. 16 – 17). There have been risks in data leakage and harms to privacy. However, the models are being improved with each new iteration and with each new discovery of limits.

EXPERIMENTING WITH MAKING AN ORIGINAL 2D VISUAL DEEPFAKE WITH A GENERATIVE AI TOOL

This work explored creating constructive deepfakes based on the capability of one generative AI tool, which was released to the public in 2015. The author had used the tool starting over a year ago. In that time, she has reviewed the works of many of the others on the Deep Dream Generator site, and she had not seen anything that remotely even resembled trying to depict reality. There were references to media content. There were artful and illustrative approaches. There were partial or more complete stories being told. The generative AI tool itself seemed to lean towards not only pareidolia (the making of forms from abstractions) but also storytelling and fictions.

The first approach for image fidelity to the world was to rely on textual descriptions that might lead to "photorealistic" and "hyperrealistic" results. There was clear avoidance of tags and descriptors that would lean towards artifice. Then, there were tries using seeding images, including photos, with lesser effects of the generative AI prompt on those images. There were effects applied in pre-production (of the seeding images) and post-production (of the output images from the GAI tool).

As to the topics, it was thought that the following four elements would be tried:

1. A historical re-enactment
2. A person
3. A place
4. A thing
5. A scene
6. A fantasy scene

All the outputs would be 2d visuals. No IP rights would be contravened. (Any seeding images would be based on works by the author and for which she has full rights.)

If there were real attempts at deepfakery, there would be a built-out surround around the images to sell the images' authenticity to whomever the target audiences are.

The setting for the first "deepfake" was prompted by the phrase "WWI trench warfare re-enactment." The model used was "Photonic" in the Deep Dream Generator (DDG) tool. The settings were Generic (hyperrealistic), Quality (high definition, highly detailed, extremely detailed), and Photography (Nikon D850, award winning photography, sharp focus). No seeding image was used as a prompt or part of the prompt. No Artist tag was used. This visual looks unreal for several reasons: The combatants look all of the same height. They are clustered doing nothing. The trench does not resemble a historical trench. The idyllic countryside does not look particularly war-scarred. Compared against known photos of WWI trench warfare, this does not convey that same gravitas and factual reality. (Figure 1)

Figure 1. WWI Trench Warfare Re-Enactment(a historical re-enactment)

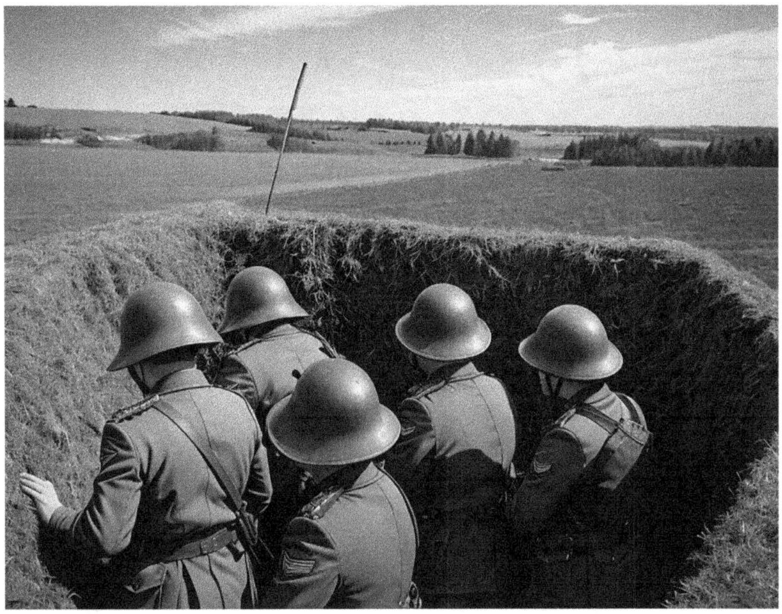

The prompt for this image was "a historical photo of harriet tubman." The model used was "Mirage-Maker" in the DDG. The settings were Generic (photorealistic, sepia tone), Quality (highly detailed, crisp quality), Photography (Nikon D850, focused). The size of the image was 896x704 (width-height in pixels). This visual looks like it could be real because of the sense of a damaged photo plate of that era. The lighting might or might not be from that era. The humanity of the individual is captured in the image. The clothing looks like it might be from that period. Now, this would not be the same sense based on experts, who know what real photos exist of Harriet Tubman and particular visual characteristics and other details. However, this work seems somewhat more deepfake than the others, in the sense that a passing glance might be believable. (Figure 2)

Figure 2. A Historical Photo of Harriet Tubman (a person)

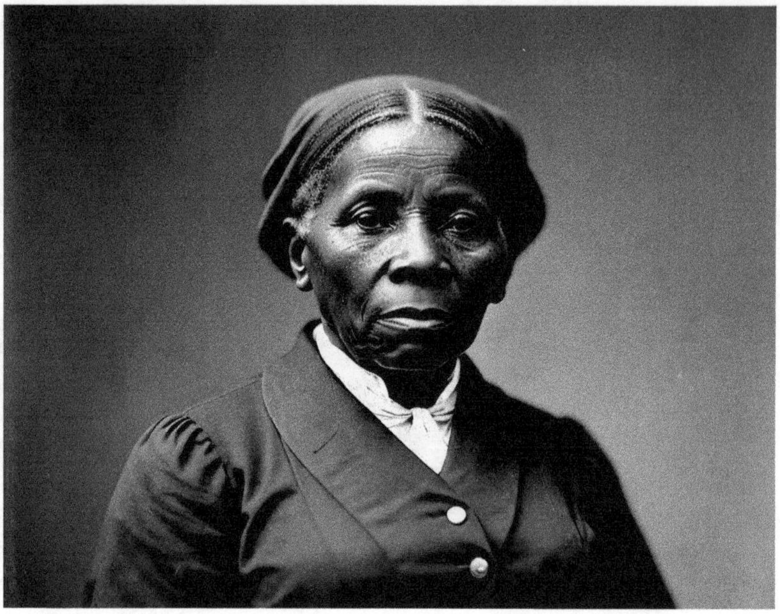

The prompt for this image was "a photorealistic view of the Eiffel Tower at high noon." The model used was "DreamForge" inside the DDG tool. No seeding image was used. The prompt settings were Generic (hyperrealistic), Quality (highly detailed), Photography (Nikon D850, closeup, focused). This photo also looks unreal for several reasons. The structure does not have enough details to evoke the actual location. The perspective looks spread out at the bottom and changes in size leading to the pinnacle in a way that does not look realistic. (Figure 3)

Figure 3. A Photorealistic View of the Eiffel Tower at High Noon (a place)

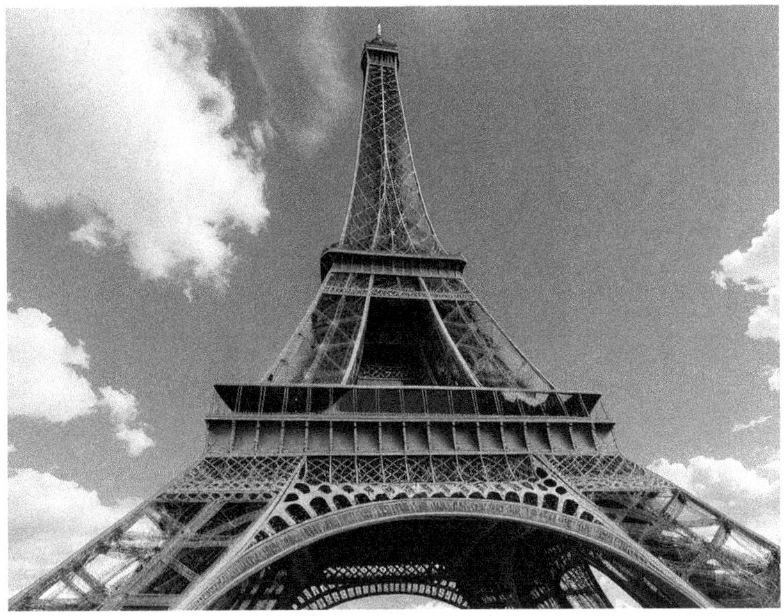

The prompt for this image was "

For the next object, the prompt was "an old-style wooden rocking horse," using the "Artistic 2" model inside the DDG. No seeding image was used. The prompt settings were Generic (hyperrealistic), Quality (highly detailed), Photography (Nikon D850, closeup, focused). The image that resulted is 896 x 704 pixels. But the work itself does not look convincing. The horse is ornate and fantastical. It does not look like it can physically rock forwards and backwards (so the physics does not work). Its location outside does not make sense. [The original prompt was for "an old-style wooden abacus," but the respective models tried did not have a clear reference, so the tool output wooden bannisters and boxes and beds.] (Figure 4)

Figure 4. An Old-Style Wooden Rocking Horse (a thing)

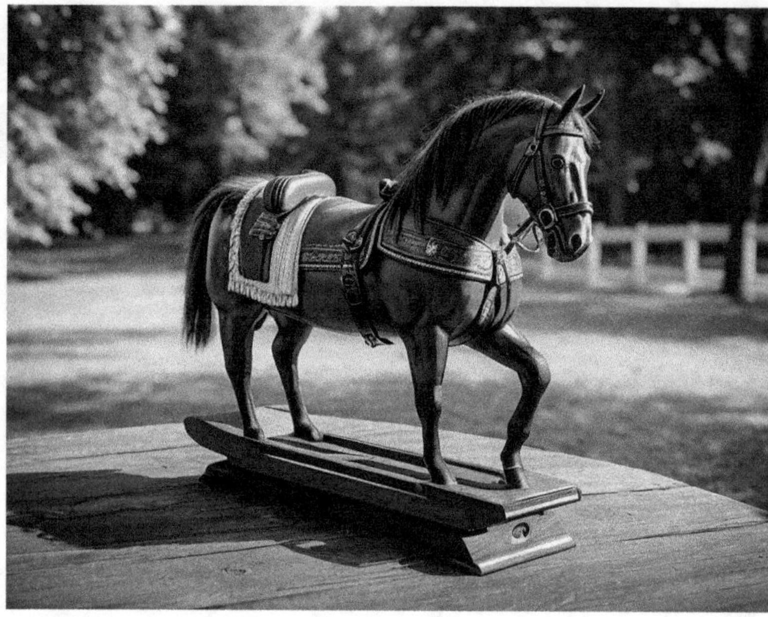

For the next image, the prompt was "a view of the northern lights in Alaska." This image used the "Artistic" model inside the DDG. No seeding image was used. The settings were Generic (hyperrealistic, black and white), Quality (highly detailed), Photography (Nikon D850, closeup, focused). The image that resulted is 896 x 704 pixels. The image is not recognizably Alaska per se. There are no landmarks. There is tinting of the b/w image. The composition is a tell because the DDG tool tends to use recognizable compositing. The land in the foreground does not resemble land, and there are glittery elements to it. There is a sense that the unreal will almost always upstage the real in terms of visual drama, but in other ways, the real will always be more significant than the faux. (Figure 5)

Figure 5. A View of the northern lights in Alaska (a scene)

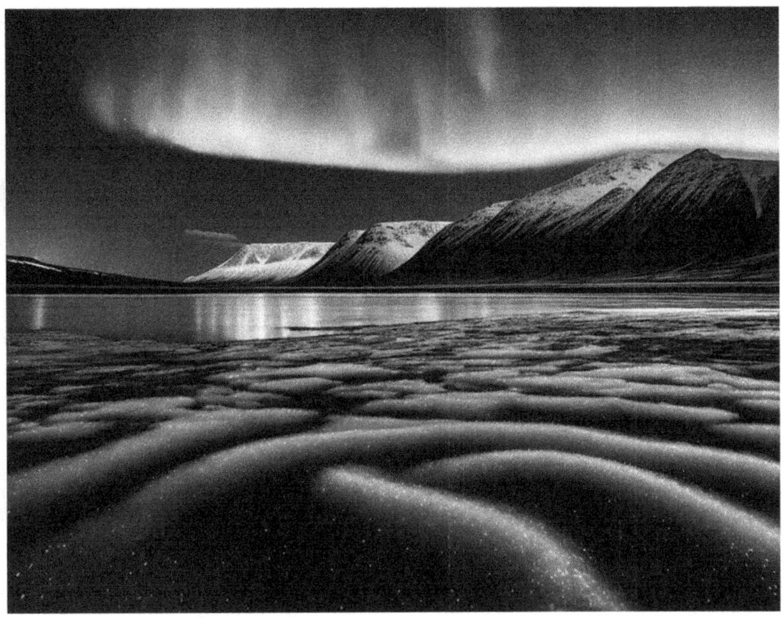

The prompt for the next image is "a stage view of a middle school play." The image used the "Animatron" (Pro) model in the DDG. No seeding image was used. The settings were as follows: Generic (photorealistic), Quality (high definition, high detail), Effects (fantasy), and Photography (Nikon D 850, focused, studio lighting). Would this be effective as a deepfake? Not quite. The gender imbalance in the audience is different. The racial diversity seems to be missing. The lighting does not emulate real-world stage lighting. It is unclear what play is being staged based on the costumes and the balconies. The people on stage are placed in a way that is very constructed. There is an edge at the bottom of the screen that also does not ring true. (Figure 6)

Figure 6. A Stage View of a Middle School Play (a fantasy scene)

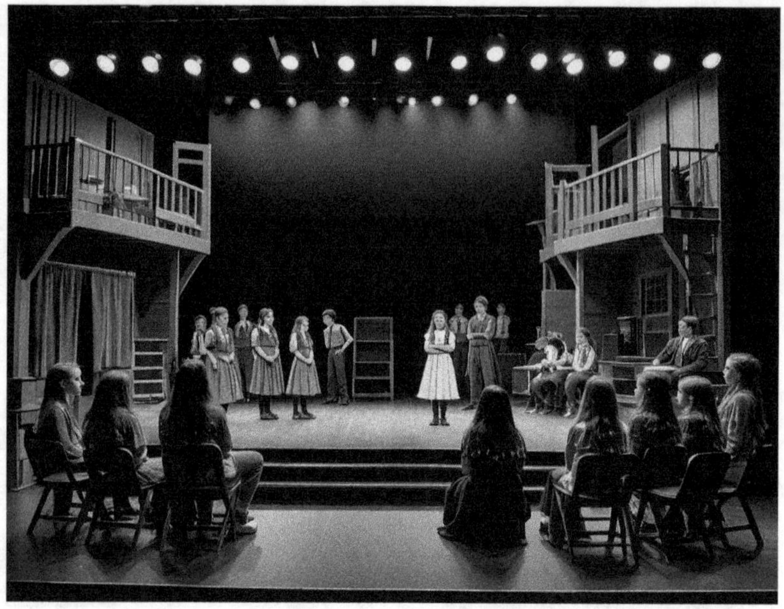

Common Tells of Digital Fakery in 2D Visuals

Generative AI tools struggle with multiple fingers, toes, arms, legs, and other appendages. They struggle with made-up language and misspellings in known common (and global) languages. Different generative AI tools may recognizable color palettes, screen colors vs. pigmented ones, high reflectance, a trembling electronic vibrance, maybe bright neon. The layouts and compositions are somewhat predictable, with the 2d canvas filled fully and even crowded in many cases, as if the 2d plane had to be fully optimized with busy depictions. Objects are laid out dead center. Many have visual artifacts, like faked artist signatures at the bottom right or bottom left of the image. There may be visual glitches that do not fit in the image but seem to appear as happenstance. Others have automatic watermarks unless the user pays for a subscription to the artmaking generative AI tool. The backgrounds to the images may be artful gradients with high machine control over the colors pixel by pixel instead of something achieved in a digital image editing software. Another tell may be that the digital image shows a "digital materiality" vs. a "physical" or "analog" materiality transcoded (translated) into digital. The visual may offer a plasticine surface without any direct material equivalency in the real world. Some autogenerated visuals have a decorative bent, a flourish, something that may give the visual a sense of significance, of something spectacle-worthy, of something fanciful, something with a twist. Many fall short of visual common sense. What is depicted may belie actual physics. The image may have a white-edge margin, a multi-pixel frame across some or all of the four edges.

Another common "tell" that a work may be from a generative AI tool is that many have security limits on what topics may be addressed visually. If a text prompt is input that is considered inappropriate, the system will not process the text prompt. A warning will be generated. Anything with more than a "PG" (Parental Guidance) rating will often not be depicted.

In their present state, there are still plenty of tells in many cases, even for those who may better wield generative AI tools to get closer to something that looks perhaps more authentic. Paired with pre- and post-production, perhaps the visuals that can be surfaced can appear more real-world.

In a search on the Deep Dream Generator platform for others' "authentic photorealistic visuals," only one out of hundreds could be said to be visually passable for possibly being authentic. (Figure 7)

Figure 7. "Authentic Photorealistic Visuals" Search on the Deep Dream Generator Site

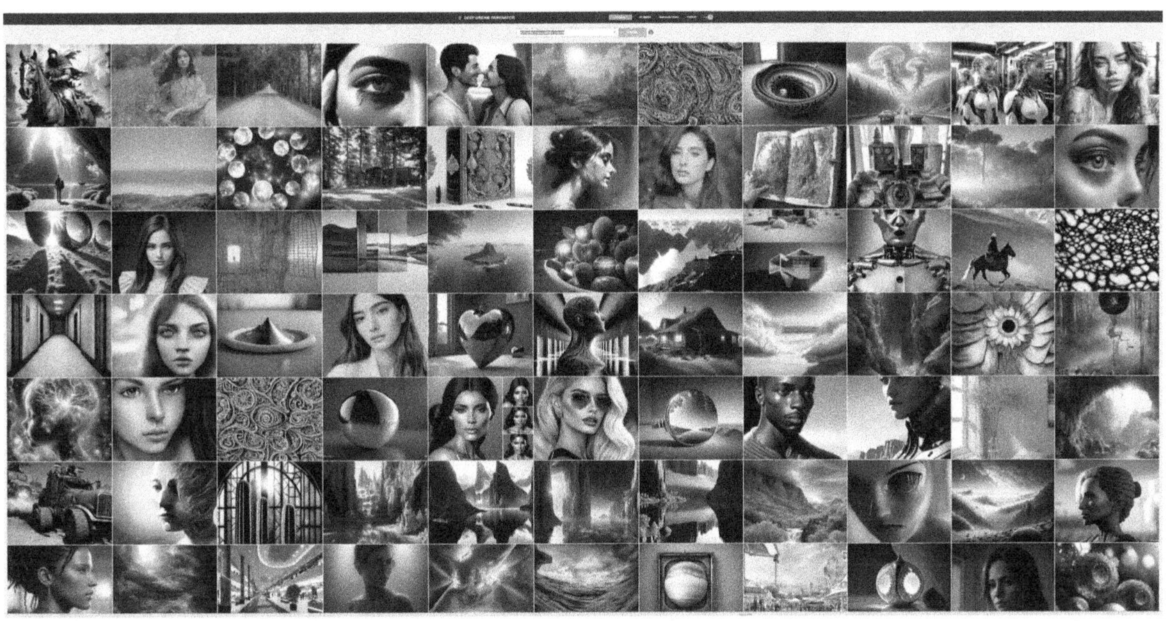

DISCUSSION

The author has used the DDG to output hundreds of visuals, including a few meant to be representational of the real world. However, the author has never tried to purposefully create a deepfake. From these walk-throughs, it seems that creating a plausible image is not that easy. For an author who has been trained to be skeptical for years, it is even harder to be accepting of the created visuals. The work of deepfakery may be harder than it may initially seem even though the artmaking GAI is an accomplished and popular one.

The visuals also had some challenges on the outer edges of the visual plane that could serve as "tells" for their provenance.

Certainly, there are methods to better "sell" the illusions of these particular deepfakes. In post-production, one may crop the images. One may use customized image sizes. One may resample the image resolution. One may change the orientation of the visual. One may conduct other edits, such as image overlays. Withing the artmaking GAI tool, one may iterate an image…or edit off-platform and then re-introduce to the platform. One may hop between generative AI platforms. One may create a contextual wrap around the deepfake to sell its supposed "reality". Various visuals may be backstopped with other efforts at convincing and affirming the reality of the faux visual. The research literature on mass-scale propaganda messaging and human gullibility may be informative.

This is not to say that the visuals will pass muster for any except those who take visual information on face value. In situations where there may be more at stake, certainly, users should use heightened due diligence, increased awareness, sufficient care, and healthy skepticism. There is a need to be conscientious and to be aware of repercussions of any actions based on understood realities. With so many potential "attack surfaces" that are digital, it may be difficult to assess and evaluate accurately all the time.

Reverse image searches may be conducted to evaluate when a work may have originated. Search engines and generative AI sites may be used to explore.

LLMs in generative AI tools may also be used to detect whether a work is fake or not. These may be used with text creations as well as still visual ones, among others. Apparently, some works may be resonant of a "human hand" in ways others are not.

While the works here used as examples were not created with any malicious intent, malicious applications are not difficult to imagine. Those who may tend towards particular worldviews or beliefs may not need a deceptive deepfake to be led in particular directions. Even microblogging short-texts and other ideas may be sufficient.

FUTURE RESEARCH DIRECTIONS

There is high variance between the 2d visual outputs across a range of public-facing and free generative AIs. How the generative AI are trained, the training data, the user interfaces and prompt inputs, the fine-tuning and calibration mechanisms, and other factors all affect how the tools perform. Depending on the tool, many have a recognizable look-and-feel. How would a similar light experiment like this one look based on other generative AI tools? What about with different author-common artist "fists" (unique hands)? What about learning about effective prompts to create the deepfakes? What are the strengths and weaknesses of the respective visual outputs?

What are constructive applications of deepfakes? Theoretically? In the real?

In terms of the depredations of information warfare, what are useful approaches? Are there ways to improve the general awareness of the general public? Applied tools on platforms?

CONCLUSION

Finally, digital deepfakes can depict literally images that are out-of-this-world, in multiple senses. For example, a visual may show "space mining," whatever that might look like. Most people, when they create deepfakes, seem to try to work within the realm of possibility. They try not to stretch credulity. And yet, upon reflection, people are willing to suspend their disbelief when presented with sensory information that belies reality. An image of a crew mining on the moon might be believed by some, if the audience pool is big enough. Some people are dispositionally gullible in general (in some cases) and towards particular favored ideas (in some cases). Self-awareness of one's tendencies and cognitive biases may be a positive start to discernment.

This chapter is really about a light experiment and perhaps the throwing of a conversation around the making of deepfakes for constructive purposes (beyond self-amusement), given the power of LLMs and generative AI. There is an undeniable appeal to artful artifice for people. Even though such creations are theoretically and practically possible to generate to ∞, human attention is limited and a limiting factor. Time is a bounding condition for human consumption of auto-generated digital works, even in the face of "extreme content abundance" from generative AI (Frey & Osborne, 2023, p. 10).

REFERENCES

Agarwal, S., Farid, H., El-Gaaly, T., & Lim, S. N. (2020, December). Detecting deep-fake videos from appearance and behavior. In *2020 IEEE International Workshop on Information Forensics and Security (WIFS)* (pp. 1-6). IEEE. 10.1109/WIFS49906.2020.9360904

Ali, S., DiPaola, D., Lee, I., Hong, J., & Breazeal, C. (2021, May). Exploring generative models with middle school students. In *Proceedings of the 2021 CHI Conference on Human Factors in Computing Systems* (pp. 1-13). 10.1145/3411764.3445226

Ali, S., DiPaola, D., Lee, I., Sindato, V., Kim, G., Blumofe, R., & Breazeal, C. (2021). Children as creators, thinkers and citizens in an AI-driven future. *Computers and Education: Artificial Intelligence*, 2, 100040. 10.1016/j.caeai.2021.100040

Ali, S., DiPaola, D., Williams, R., Ravi, P., & Breazeal, C. (2023). Constructing dreams using generative AI. *arXiv Preprint arXiv:2305.12013.*

Arshed, M. A., Mumtaz, S., Ibrahim, M., Dewi, C., Tanveer, M., & Ahmed, S. (2024). Multiclass AI-generated deepfake face detection using patch-wise deep learning model. *Computers*, 13(1), 31. 10.3390/computers13010031

Azmoodeh, A., & Dehghantanha, A. (2022). Deep fake detection, deterrence and response: Challenges and opportunities. *arXiv Preprint arXiv:2211.14667.*

Bartz-Beielstein, T. (2019). Why we need an AI-resilient society. *arXiv Preprint arXiv:1912.08786.*

Bauer, L. A., & Bindschaedler, V. (2021). Generative models for security: Attacks, defenses, and opportunities. *arXiv Preprint arXiv:2107.10139.*

Beerbaum, D. (2023). Generative Artificial Intelligence (GAI) software–assessment on biased behavior. *SSRN*, 4386395, 1–18. 10.2139/ssrn.4386395

Bengesi, S., El-Sayed, H., Sarker, M. K., Houkpati, Y., Irungu, J., & Oladunni, T. (2023). Advancements in Generative AI: A comprehensive review of GANs, GPT, autoencoders, diffusion model, and transformers. *arXiv Preprint arXiv:2311.10242.*

Bharadiya, J. P. (2024). Deep fake and image manipulation. *International Journal of Intelligent Systems and Applications in Engineering*, 12(14s), 468–472.

Bohacek, M., & Farid, H. (2024). The making of an AI news anchor—and its implications. *Proceedings of the National Academy of Sciences, 121*(1), 1 - 3.

Botha, J., & Pieterse, H. (2020, March). Fake news and deepfakes: A dangerous threat for 21st century information security. In *ICCWS 2020 15th International Conference on Cyber Warfare and Security.* Academic Conferences and Publishing Limited.

Campbell, C., Plangger, K., Sands, S., & Kietzmann, J. (2022). Preparing for an era of deepfakes and AI-generated ads: A framework for understanding responses to manipulated advertising. *Journal of Advertising*, 51(1), 22–38. 10.1080/00913367.2021.1909515

Campbell, C., Plangger, K., Sands, S., Kietzmann, J., & Bates, K. (2023). How deepfakes and artificial intelligence could reshape the advertising industry: The coming reality of AI fakes and their potential impact on consumer behavior. *Journal of Advertising Research*, 57(1), 241–251.

Cao, Y., Li, S., Liu, Y., Yan, Z., Dai, Y., Yu, P. S., & Sun, L. (2023). A comprehensive survey of AI-Generated Content (AIGC): A history of generative AI from GAN to ChatGPT. *arXiv Preprint arXiv:2303.04226*.

Caporusso, N. (2021). Deepfakes for the good: A beneficial application of contentious artificial intelligence technology. In *Advances in Artificial Intelligence, Software and Systems Engineering:Proceedings of the AHFE 2020 Virtual Conferences on Software and Systems Engineering, and Artificial Intelligence and Social Computing,July 16-20, 2020,USA* (pp. 235-241). Springer International Publishing. 10.1007/978-3-030-51328-3_33

Ciftci, U. A., Demir, I., & Yin, L. (2020, September). How do the hearts of deep fakes beat? Deep fake source detection via interpreting residuals with biological signals. In *2020 IEEE International Joint Conference on Biometrics (IJCB)* (pp. 1-10). IEEE. 10.1109/IJCB48548.2020.9304909

Cocchi, F., Baraldi, L., Poppi, S., Cornia, M., Baraldi, L., & Cucchiara, R. (2023, September). Unveiling the impact of image transformations on deepfake detection: An experimental analysis. In *International Conference on Image Analysis and Processing* (pp. 345-356). Cham: Springer Nature Switzerland. 10.1007/978-3-031-43153-1_29

Cozzolino, D., & Verdoliva, L. (2022). Multimedia forensics before the deep learning era. In *Handbook of Digital Face Manipulation and Detection: From DeepFakes to Morphing Attacks* (pp. 45–67). Springer International Publishing. 10.1007/978-3-030-87664-7_3

da Silva, J. A. T. (2023). AI in the era of fakes and deepfakes: Risk of fabricated photographs and identities in academic publishing. *Journal of Information Security and Cybercrimes Research*, 6(2), 71–73. 10.26735/KNJA7076

Dack, S. (2019). *Deep fakes, fake news, and what comes next. The Henry M.* Jackson School of International Studies.

Danry, V., Leong, J., Pataranutaporn, P., Tandon, P., Liu, Y., Shilkrot, R., & Sra, M. (2022, April). AI-generated characters: putting deepfakes to good use. In *CHI Conference on Human Factors in Computing Systems Extended Abstracts* (pp. 1-5). 10.1145/3491101.3503736

De Vries, K. (2020). You never fake alone. Creative AI in action. *Information Communication and Society*, 23(14), 2110–2127. 10.1080/1369118X.2020.1754877

Demir, I., & Ciftci, U. A. (2021, May). Where do deep fakes look? Synthetic face detection via gaze tracking. In *ACM Symposium on Eye Tracking Research and Applications* (pp. 1-11). 10.1145/3448017.3457387

Dhoni, P., & Kumar, R. (2023). Synergizing generative ai and cybersecurity: Roles of generative ai entities, companies, agencies, and government in enhancing cybersecurity. *Authorea Preprints*.

Durall, R., Keuper, M., Pfreundt, F. J., & Keuper, J. (2019). Unmasking deepfakes with simple features. arXiv Preprint arXiv:1911.00686, 1 - 8.

Eiserbeck, A., Maier, M., Baum, J., & Abdel Rahman, R. (2023). Deepfake smiles matter less—The psychological and neural impact of presumed AI-generated faces. *Scientific Reports*, 13(1), 16111. 10.1038/s41598-023-42802-x37752242

Fagni, T., Falchi, F., Gambini, M., Martella, A., & Tesconi, M. (2021). TweepFake: About detecting deepfake tweets. *PLoS One*, 16(5), e0251415. 10.1371/journal.pone.025141533984021

Ferrari, F., & McKelvey, F. (2023). Hyperproduction: A social theory of deep generative models. *Distinktion : Scandinavian Journal of Social Theory*, 24(2), 338–360. 10.1080/1600910X.2022.2137546

Feuerriegel, S., Hartmann, J., Janiesch, C., & Zschech, P. (2024). Generative ai. *Business & Information Systems Engineering*, 66(1), 111–126. 10.1007/s12599-023-00834-7

Figueira, O., & Wang, G. (n.d.). *DeepPhish: Effects of generative artifacts within fabricated profiles on user trust*. Academic Press.

Fletcher, J. (2018). Deepfakes, artificial intelligence, and some kind of dystopia. *Theatre Journal*, 70(4), 455–471. 10.1353/tj.2018.0097

Frey, C. B., & Osborne, M. (2023). Generative AI and the future of work: A reappraisal. *The Brown Journal of World Affairs*, 1–12.

García-Peñalvo, F., & Vázquez-Ingelmo, A. (2023). What do we mean by GenAI? A systematic mapping of the evolution, trends, and techniques involved in Generative AI. *International Journal of Interactive Multimedia and Artificial Intelligence*, 8(4), 7–16. 10.9781/ijimai.2023.07.006

Giudice, O., Guarnera, L., & Battiato, S. (2021). Fighting deepfakes by detecting GAN DCT anomalies. *Journal of Imaging, 7*(8), 128, 1 – 27.

Gong, D., Goh, O. S., Kumar, Y. J., Ye, Z., & Chi, W. (2020). Deepfake forensics, an AI-synthesized detection with deep convolutional generative adversarial networks. *International Journal (Toronto, Ont.)*, 9(3).

Gozalo-Brizuela, R., & Garrido-Merchán, E. C. (2023). A survey of Generative AI applications. *arXiv Preprint arXiv:2306.02781.*

Gragnaniello, D., Marra, F., & Verdoliva, L. (2022). Detection of AI-generated synthetic faces. In *Handbook of Digital Face Manipulation and Detection: From Deepfakes to Morphing Attacks* (pp. 191–212). Springer International Publishing. 10.1007/978-3-030-87664-7_9

Grossman, M. R., Grimm, P. W., Brown, D., & Xu, M. (2023). The GPTJudge: Justice in a Generative AI world. *Duke Law & Technology Review, 23*(1).

Guarnera, L., Giudice, O., & Battiato, S. (2024). Mastering deepfake detection: A cutting-edge approach to distinguish GAN and diffusion-model images. *ACM Transactions on Multimedia Computing Communications and Applications*, 3652027. 10.1145/3652027

Hacker, P., Engel, A., & Mauer, M. (2023, June). Regulating ChatGPT and other large generative AI models. In *Proceedings of the 2023 ACM Conference on Fairness, Accountability, and Transparency* (pp. 1112-1123). 10.1145/3593013.3594067

Hancock, J. T., & Bailenson, J. N. (2021). The social impact of deepfakes. *Cyberpsychology, Behavior, and Social Networking*, 24(3), 149–152. 10.1089/cyber.2021.29208.jth33760669

Hanif, S. M., & Dave, V. (2022). Deepfakes technology using AI. *International Journal of Scientific research in Science, Engineering and Technology*, 152-159.

Helmus, T. C. (2022). Artificial intelligence, deepfakes, and disinformation. Rand Corporation.

Horvitz, E. (2022, Nov.). On the horizon: Interactive and compositional deepfakes. In *Proceedings of the 2022 International Conference on Multimodal Interaction* (pp. 653-661). 10.1145/3536221.3558175

Houde, S., Liao, V., Martino, J., Muller, M., Piorkowski, D., Richards, J., . . . Zhang, Y. (2020). Business (mis) use cases of generative ai. *arXiv Preprint arXiv:2003.07679.*

Huang, S., & Siddarth, D. (2023). Generative AI and the digital commons. *arXiv Preprint arXiv:2303.11074.*

Jia, S., Lyu, R., Zhao, K., Chen, Y., Yan, Z., Ju, Y., . . . Lyu, S. (2024). Can ChatGPT detect DeepFakes? A study of using multimodal Large Language Models for media forensics. *arXiv Preprint arXiv:2403.14077.*

Jiang, L., Wu, W., Qian, C., & Loy, C. C. (2022). DeepFakes detection: The DeeperForensics dataset and challenge. In *Handbook of Digital Face Manipulation and Detection: From DeepFakes to Morphing Attacks* (pp. 303–329). Springer International Publishing. 10.1007/978-3-030-87664-7_14

Joshi, M. A. (2024). The security risks of Generative Artificial Intelligence. *Available atSSRN* 4735175. 10.2139/ssrn.4735175

Juefei-Xu, F., Wang, R., Huang, Y., Guo, Q., Ma, L., & Liu, Y. (2022). Countering malicious deepfakes: Survey, battleground, and horizon. *International Journal of Computer Vision*, 130(7), 1678–1734. 10.1007/s11263-022-01606-835528632

Kahng, M., Thorat, N., Chau, D. H., Viégas, F. B., & Wattenberg, M. (2018). Gan lab: Understanding complex deep generative models using interactive visual experimentation. *IEEE Transactions on Visualization and Computer Graphics*, 25(1), 310–320. 10.1109/TVCG.2018.286450030130198

Kandasamy, V., Hubálovský, Š., & Trojovský, P. (2022). Deep fake detection using a sparse auto encoder with a graph capsule dual graph CNN. *PeerJ. Computer Science*, 8, e953. 10.7717/peerj-cs.95335721408

Karnouskos, S. (2020). Artificial intelligence in digital media: The era of deepfakes. *IEEE Transactions on Technology and Society*, 1(3), 138–147. 10.1109/TTS.2020.3001312

Katarya, R., & Lal, A. (2020, October). A study on combating emerging threat of deepfake weaponization. In *2020 Fourth International Conference on I-SMAC (IoT in Social, Mobile, Analytics and Cloud) (I-SMAC)* (pp. 485-490). IEEE. 10.1109/I-SMAC49090.2020.9243588

Knott, A., Pedreschi, D., Chatila, R., Chakraborti, T., Leavy, S., Baeza-Yates, R., ... & Bengio, Y. (2023). Generative AI models should include detection mechanisms as a condition for public release. *Ethics and Information Technology, 25*(4), 55, 1 – 7.

Lee, K., Cooper, A. F., & Grimmelmann, J. (2023). Talkin' 'bout AI generation: Copyright and the Generative-AI supply chain. *arXiv preprint arXiv:2309.08133.*

Li, Y., Chang, M. C., & Lyu, S. (2018, December). In *ictu oculi*: Exposing ai created fake videos by detecting eye blinking. In *2018 IEEE International Workshop on Information Forensics and Security (WIFS)* (pp. 1-7). IEEE.

Manduchi, L., Pandey, K., Bamler, R., Cotterell, R., Däubener, S., Fellenz, S., . . . Fortuin, V. (2024). On the Challenges and Opportunities in Generative AI. *arXiv preprint arXiv:2403.00025.*

Masood, M., Nawaz, M., Malik, K. M., Javed, A., Irtaza, A., & Malik, H. (2023). Deepfakes generation and detection: State-of-the-art, open challenges, countermeasures, and way forward. *Applied Intelligence*, 53(4), 3974–4026. 10.1007/s10489-022-03766-z

Meskys, E., Kalpokiene, J., Jurcys, P., & Liaudanskas, A. (2020). Regulating deep fakes: Legal and ethical considerations. *Journal of Intellectual Property Law & Practice*, 15(1), 24–31. 10.1093/jiplp/jpz167

Mirsky, Y., & Lee, W. (2021). The creation and detection of deepfakes: A survey. *ACM Computing Surveys*, 54(1), 1–41. 10.1145/3425780

Muller, M., Chilton, L. B., Kantosalo, A., Martin, C. P., & Walsh, G. (2022, April). GenAICHI: Generative AI and HCI. In *CHI Conference on Human Factors in Computing Systems Extended Abstracts* (pp. 1-7). ACM.

Neupane, S., Fernandez, I. A., Mittal, S., & Rahimi, S. (2023). Impacts and risk of Generative AI technology on cyber defense. *arXiv Preprint arXiv:2306.13033.*

Ojha, U., Li, Y., & Lee, Y. J. (2023). Towards universal fake image detectors that generalize across generative models. In *Proceedings of the IEEE/CVF Conference on Computer Vision and Pattern Recognition* (pp. 24480-24489). 10.1109/CVPR52729.2023.02345

Pan, P. (2021). "Deepfakes" and the end of the photographic age. *Aporia*, 21, 52–64.

Pashine, S., Mandiya, S., Gupta, P., & Sheikh, R. (2021). Deep fake detection: Survey of facial manipulation detection solutions. *arXiv Preprint arXiv:2106.12605.*

Paul, O. A. (2021). *Deepfakes Generated by Generative Adversarial Networks* (Honors College Thesis, Georgia Southern University).

Rahman, A., Islam, M. M., Moon, M. J., Tasnim, T., Siddique, N., Shahiduzzaman, M., & Ahmed, S. (2022). A qualitative survey on deep learning based deep fake video creation and detection method. *Aust. J. Eng. Innov. Technol*, 4(1), 13–26.

Ramdurai, B., & Adhithya, P. (2023). The impact, advancements and applications of generative AI. *International Journal on Computer Science and Engineering*, 10(6), 1–8. 10.14445/23488387/IJCSE-V10I6P101

Renaud, K., Warkentin, M., & Westerman, G. (2023). From ChatGPT to HackGPT: Meeting the cybersecurity threat of generative AI. *MIT Sloan Management Review.*

Sætra, H. S. (2023). Generative AI: Here to stay, but for good? *Technology in Society*, 75(102372), 1–5. 10.1016/j.techsoc.2023.102372

Seymour, M., Riemer, K., Yuan, L., & Dennis, A. (2021). *Beyond deep fakes: Conceptual framework, applications, and research agenda for neural rendering of realistic digital faces.* Academic Press.

Sharma, S. (2023). Deep-Fake technology: Highlights and challenges. *International Journal of Research and Analytical Reviews*. 272-278.

Shoaib, M. R., Wang, Z., Ahvanooey, M. T., & Zhao, J. (2023, November). Deepfakes, misinformation, and disinformation in the era of frontier AI, generative AI, and large AI models. In *2023 International Conference on Computer and Applications (ICCA)* (pp. 1-7). IEEE. 10.1109/ICCA59364.2023.10401723

Singh, P., & Dhiman, B. (2023). Exploding AI-generated deepfakes and misinformation: A threat to global concern in the 21st Century. *Authorea Preprints*. 10.36227/techrxiv.24715605.v1

Southgate, E. (n.d.). *Deep fakes, authenticity and authentication in the age of artificial intelligence*. New Basics.

Suganthi, S. T., Ayoobkhan, M. U. A., Bacanin, N., Venkatachalam, K., Štěpán, H., & Pavel, T. (2022). Deep learning model for deep fake face recognition and detection. *PeerJ. Computer Science*, 8, e881. 10.7717/peerj-cs.88135494811

Takale, D. G., Mahalle, P. N., & Sule, B. (2024, January - April). Advancements and applications of generative artificial intelligence. *Journal of Information Technology and Sciences*, 10(1), 20–27.

Tolosana, R., Rathgeb, C., Vera-Rodriguez, R., Busch, C., Verdoliva, L., Lyu, S., & Tiits, M. (2022). Future trends in digital face manipulation and detection. In *Handbook of Digital Face Manipulation and Detection: From DeepFakes to Morphing Attacks* (pp. 463–482). Springer International Publishing. 10.1007/978-3-030-87664-7_21

Tolosana, R., Vera-Rodriguez, R., Fierrez, J., Morales, A., & Ortega-Garcia, J. (2020). Deepfakes and beyond: A survey of face manipulation and fake detection. *Information Fusion*, 64, 131–148. 10.1016/j.inffus.2020.06.014

Tortora, L. (2024). Beyond discrimination: Generative AI applications and ethical challenges in forensic psychiatry. *Frontiers in Psychiatry*, 15, 1346059. 10.3389/fpsyt.2024.134605938525252

Veerasamy, N., & Pieterse, H. (2022, March). Rising above misinformation and deepfakes. In *International Conference on Cyber Warfare and Security* (Vol. 17, No. 1, pp. 340-348). 10.34190/iccws.17.1.25

Vyas, K., Pareek, P., Jayaswal, R., & Patil, S. (2024). Analysing the landscape of Deep Fake Detection: A survey. *International Journal of Intelligent Systems and Applications in Engineering*, 12(11s), 40–55.

Wach, K., Duong, C. D., Ejdys, J., Kazlauskaitė, R., Korzynski, P., Mazurek, G., Paliszkiewicz, J., & Ziemba, E. (2023). The dark side of generative artificial intelligence: A critical analysis of controversies and risks of ChatGPT. *Entrepreneurial Business and Economics Review*, 11(2), 7–30. 10.15678/EBER.2023.110201

Wagner, T. L., & Blewer, A. (2019). "The word real is no longer real": Deepfakes, gender, and the challenges of AI-altered video. *Open Information Science*, 3(1), 32–46. 10.1515/opis-2019-0003

Wang, R., Juefei-Xu, F., Guo, Q., Huang, Y., Ma, L., Liu, Y., & Wang, L. (2020). Deeptag: Robust image tagging for deepfake provenance. *arXiv Preprint arXiv:2009.09869, 3.*

Wang, R., Juefei-Xu, F., Ma, L., Xie, X., Huang, Y., Wang, J., & Liu, Y. (2019). Fakespotter: A simple yet robust baseline for spotting ai-synthesized fake faces. *arXiv Preprint arXiv:1909.06122.*

Whittaker, L., Kietzmann, T. C., Kietzmann, J., & Dabirian, A. (2020). "All around me are synthetic faces": The mad world of AI-generated media. *IT Professional*, 22(5), 90–99. 10.1109/MITP.2020.2985492

Xu, D., Fan, S., & Kankanhalli, M. (2023, October). Combating misinformation in the era of generative AI models. In *Proceedings of the 31st ACM International Conference on Multimedia* (pp. 9291-9298). 10.1145/3581783.3612704

Yadav, D., & Salmani, S. (2019, May). Deepfake: A survey on facial forgery technique using generative adversarial network. In *2019 International Conference on Intelligent Computing and Control Systems (ICCS)* (pp. 852-857). IEEE. 10.1109/ICCS45141.2019.9065881

Yagnik, H., Kurani, A., & Joshi, P. (2020). *A brief study on deepfakes. International Research Journal of Engineering and Technology*. IRJET.

Yang, X., Li, Y., & Lyu, S. (2019, May). Exposing deep fakes using inconsistent head poses. In *ICASSP 2019-2019 IEEE International Conference on Acoustics, Speech and Signal Processing (ICASSP)* (pp. 8261-8265). IEEE. 10.1109/ICASSP.2019.8683164

Yu, N., Skripniuk, V., Abdelnabi, S., & Fritz, M. (2021). Artificial fingerprinting for generative models: Rooting deepfake attribution in training data. In *Proceedings of the IEEE/CVF International Conference on Computer Vision* (pp. 14448-14457). 10.1109/ICCV48922.2021.01418

Yu, N., Skripniuk, V., Chen, D., Davis, L., & Fritz, M. (2020). Responsible disclosure of generative models using scalable fingerprinting. *arXiv Preprint arXiv:2012.08726.*

Zhang, B., Zhou, J. P., Shumailov, I., & Papernot, N. (2020). On attribution of deepfakes. *arXiv Preprint arXiv:2008.09194.*

Zhang, C., Zhang, C., Li, C., Qiao, Y., Zheng, S., Dam, S. K., . . . Hong, C. S. (2023). One small step for generative ai, one giant leap for AGI: A complete survey on ChatGPT in AIGC era. *arXiv Preprint arXiv:2304.06488.*

Zhang, C., Zhang, C., Zhang, M., & Kweon, I. S. (2023). Text-to-image diffusion model in generative AI: A survey. *arXiv Preprint arXiv:2303.07909.*

Zhang, C., Zhang, C., Zheng, S., Qiao, Y., Li, C., Zhang, M., . . . Hong, C. S. (2023). A complete survey on generative AI (AIGC): Is ChatGPT from GPT-4 to GPT-5 all you need? *arXiv Preprint arXiv:2303.11717.*

Zhao, B., Zhang, S., Xu, C., Sun, Y., & Deng, C. (2021). Deep fake geography? When geospatial data encounter Artificial Intelligence. *Cartography and Geographic Information Science*, 48(4), 338–352. 10.1080/15230406.2021.1910075

Zhu, M., Chen, H., Yan, Q., Huang, X., Lin, G., Li, W., & Wang, Y. (2024). Genimage: A million-scale benchmark for detecting ai-generated image. *Advances in Neural Information Processing Systems*, 36, 1–12.

Zobaed, S., Rabby, F., Hossain, I., Hossain, E., Hasan, S., Karim, A., & Md Hasib, K. (2021). Deepfakes: Detecting forged and synthetic media content using machine learning. *Artificial Intelligence in Cyber Security: Impact and Implications: Security Challenges, Technical and Ethical Issues, Forensic Investigative Challenges*, 177-201.

KEY TERMS AND DEFINITIONS

Artificial Intelligence: Computer systems that emulate human intelligence and capabilities, such as creativity, among others.

Authentication: Validating the genuine origins of digital media; affirming the pristine feature of digital media.

Deepfake: A digital illusion made up of synthetic media created with various technologies (including generative AI, image editing software, animation software, video editing software, and others).

Large Language Model (LLM): A computational model created by large-scale training data (of text, image, video, and multimodal content) using deep learning methods (like artificial neural networks).

Media Forensics: Techniques for validating or invalidating digital media.

Pixel: Picture element, a small box of illumination on a screen comprised of red, green, and blue (RGB) wavelengths to create a sensation of color.

Chapter 7
Generative AI and the Expansion of the Solitary Human Imagination:
An Experiential Case

Shalin Hai-Jew
https://orcid.org/0000-0002-8863-0175
Hutchinson Community College, USA

ABSTRACT

The affordances of generative AI—in its ability to provide feedback on human-made (or human-machine made, or computer-made) works, its ability to create text/audio/video/still imagery/multimedia—enables powerful augmentations to the solitary human imagination. To wit, such technologies enable human-machine collaboration in terms of (1) human-directed non-neutral culture-informed feedback on created works (for original texts) and (2) digital informational content generation (for inspiration, for reference, for comparison, for learning, for hands-on image editing, and other applications). Generative AI may enable pathways to grow skillsets and perhaps even courage and strength in the expression of an individual voice.

INTRODUCTION

A simple definition of imagination is that it is the ability to originate something novel (ideas, experiences, sensations, and others). Imagination is "the process of transforming…inner images" (Liang, Hsu, Huang, & Chen, 2012, p. 438). Imagination has been defined as imagistic, related to the creating of a mental image (Gaut, 2003, p. 271). Imagination does not only use the visual sensibility; for example, "experiential imagining" involves human senses (Gaut, 2003, p. 273). Imagination involves the "consciousness to envision things that are not present in the physical world that surround us" (Folkmann, 2010, p. 1). The term "imaginative" is a "near-synonym for 'creative'" (Gaut, 2010, p. 1042), with creativity defined as the ability to originate something new and seen as valuable by others. There is a sense that "imagination and creativity are distinct, yet inter-penetrating processes" (Pelaprat & Cole, 2011, p. 397).

DOI: doi

Imagination is "a creative faculty of the mind" (Liang, Hsu, Chang, & Lin, 2013, p. 1037). Imagination is used in both "scholarly and lay discourse" (Thomas, 2014, p. 133).

Imagination is the ability "to negate the given and material that essentially enables abstract thinking and our ability to categorize the material" (Sartre, 1940, as cited in Folkmann, 2010, p. 1).

Imagination helps people in "making sense of life" (Alexander, 1990, p. 341). It requires proper judgment to not over-react to symbolic communications that may be taken erroneously as literal McClennen, 2007). Imaginings enable people to escape external realities. And yet, people respond to imagined threats with actual fear, which highlights "the paradox of 'fictional emotions'" (Medina, 2013, p. 317).

"Imagination" comes from the Latin verb "imaginary," meaning "to picture oneself" (Liang, Chang, Chang, & Lin, 2012, p. 366). In one sense, the imagination is self-reflexive and private. ["Imagination is seen as subjective in the sense that it is our own product" (Grøn, 2002, p. 32).]

Imagination can also be social and intersubjective (Finn & Wylie, 2021). It exists at the micro (ego, individual), meso (group), and macro (mass-population scale) levels.

A "solitary imagination" refers to the ability to originate novel content in a solo or unaccompanied fashion. There are thinkers who have spent lifetimes in "an imaginative and mostly solitary reverie" (Barber, 1978, p. 79). This work poses a question: Does generative AI provide opportunities to enhance the work of those who engage their imagination in solitary ways, or does generative AI perhaps not provide the necessary tool features? Generative AI here refers to computational tools that can output digital informational contents (text, still imagery, video, animations, audio, multimedia, and others). Artmaking generative AI tools are those that specialize in the output of visuals. Generative AI, in the current generation, is built off large language models (LLMs) trained on large datasets using artificial neural networks and perhaps other computational machine learning methods.

This work proposes two basic hypotheses:

Human-machine collaboration through generative AI tools enable two critical functions for the solitary imagination:

(1) human-directed non-neutral culture-informed feedback on created works (for original texts), and
(2) digital informational content generation (for inspiration, for reference, for comparison, for learning, for hands-on image editing, and other applications)

The fitness of the two hypotheses are tested experientially through an auto-ethnographic case study.

REVIEW OF THE LITERATURE

Imagination is multi-faceted (Singer & Singer, 2008, p. 290). It "is an active process of complex mental scenarios creation, involving the use of mental images, sensory-motor imagery, and / or inner speech" (Villena-Gonzalez & Cosmelli, 2020, p. 94). A composite definition of imagination offers nuance:

> *To imagine* is to represent without aiming at things as they actually, presently, and subjectively are. One can use imagination to represent possibilities other than the actual, to represent times other than the present, and to represent perspectives other than one's own. Unlike perceiving and believing, imagining something does not require one to consider that something to be the case. Unlike desiring or anticipating, imagining something does not require one to wish or expect that something to be the case. ("Imagination," Jan. 22, 2019)

Said another way, imagination is about entertaining a proposition without necessarily committing to whether that idea if true or not (Gaut, 2003). Imagination refers to the ability to engage in "mental simulation," which is defined as "general, flexible, and compositional, supporting behavior across a wide range of different tasks, capturing a large body of common-sense knowledge, and operating over multiple levels of abstraction" (Hamrick, 2019, p. 13). For some, imagination "no longer holds together in any meaningful way" with its ambiguity (Stankiewicz, 2016, p. 797), in either denotation or connotation.

Imagination Unique to Humans?

Imagination is seen as a capability uniquely human, something that animals are not thought to have, perhaps grounds for anthropocentric exceptionalism. Based on the analysis of brain structures, and the evolution of human brains and animal brains over time, one researcher observes: "While it is clear that all mechanisms of imagination are available to modern humans, it is also clear that not all mechanisms of imagination are available to all animals" (Vyshedskiy, 2019, p. 95). Some studied animals have been found to have fast forgetting, which may preclude imaginary capabilities based on past experiences. While it is as-yet unclear how imagination "is realized in the brain" (Comrie, Frank, & Kay, 2022, p. 1), the hippocampus part of the brain is thought to be involved and has links to brain "generativity".

There is a developmental trajectory for the development of the human imagination. A summary of Vygotsky's theory of creative imagination has been summarized as the following four points:

1) Imagination is the internalization of children's play.
2) Imagination is a higher mental function of as such is a consciously directed thought process.
3) Creative thinking involves the collaboration of imagination and thinking in concepts, which occurs first in adolescence but mature in adulthood.
4) Both artistic and scientific creativity require the collaboration of imagination and thinking in concepts. (Smolucha & Smolucha, 1986, as cited in Tsai, 2012, p. 16)

Children in their early years "seem to keep the inner and outer realities close together" (Spencer, 2003, p. 110). Play helps develop children's imagination (Cobb, 1959). "Pretend play" is common in people starting at 18 months (Koukouti & Malafouris, 2020, p. 32). There are also cultural inputs for the development of human individuality (Cobb, 1959), with a need for both the biological and the cultural. The "enactive imagination" describes how people respond emotionally and physically and physiologically to fictional imaginings, One researcher hypothesizes that "the enactive imagination operates before and below the representational imagination" and is actualized given the "primitive forms of imagining in animals and pre-linguistic children that do not require full-blown representational capacities and well-defined intensional (sic) objects" (Medina, 2013, p. 318). There is a continuum of pretense and semi-pretense in how people behave in terms of the imagination (Van Leeuwen, 2011, p. 55). "Pretense layering" refers to different strata of pretend (Van Leeuwen, 2011, p. 56), such as a play within a play within a play.

Imagination serves as people's "primary cognitive mechanism for anticipating and deliberating on the future" and is a capability innate to people writ large (Finn & Wylie, 2021), not something in the province of particular and rare gifted individuals. Over time, the earlier Romantic mystical sense of creativity has been replaced by a narrative of creativity stemming from "effort and work," not a mysterious wellspring, and is a capability for all people (Dewey, 1882 - 1953, as cited in Di Gregori, 2018, p. 81). Functionally, human imagination refers to "the ability of an embodied agent to simulate its own behaviors, predict their sensory-based consequences, and extract behavioral benefit from doing so" (Marques, Holland, &

Newcombe, Apr. 2008, p. 51). Imagination, deployed properly, can enhance the human ability to predict or anticipate what is to come (Trevors & Saier, 2010, p. 9).

For practical understandings, the imagination must access some history. One researcher observes: "Nor can pragmatism afford to be ahistorical; experience is temporal and social which is to say historical and cultural" (Alexander, 1990, p. 344). Practically speaking, "rational imagination" enables people to conceptualize alternatives to reality. They can discern reality and propose counterfactuals to that reality:

> In a simple temporal sequence, people tend to imagine alternatives to the most recent event. The central claim …is that counterfactual thoughts are organized along the same principles as rational thought. The idea that the counterfactual imagination is rational depends on three steps: (1) humans are capable of rational thought; (2) they make inferences by thinking about possibilities; and (3) their counterfactual thoughts rely on thinking about possibilities, just as rational thoughts do. (Byrne, 2007, p. 439)

Perhaps they can apply probabilities to the counterfactual paths, discern plausibility or implausibility. They may differentiate between acceptable and forbidden possibilities; they may emplace possibilities in time (Byrne, 2007, p. 442), among others. While some suggest objective truths are more effective for decision-making, some suggest that imagination may be preferable, such as in cases involving moral quandaries: "every moral decision is in the end a highly imaginative process" (Liebenberg, Human, & Muller, 2001, p. 311). One work shares an idea that imagination is sparked by "imaginary desires" since "such practices require a full-fledged motivational system" (Doggett & Egan, 2007, as cited in Dorstewitz, 2016, p. 391). Another work highlights the importance of "narrative imagination" in exploring the conception of human agency, both in the real and in fictional spaces (Brockmeier, 2009, p. 213).

Researchers are working on ways to foster, and measure applied imagination. Imagination is a "fundamental human capacity" (Finn, Capurro, Bennett, & Wylie, 2023, p. 01), and given its applications, such as modeling the world, researchers have an interest in learning how to use it better. There are calls for more contemporaneous research on the topic of human imagination (Stokes, 2016). Future work requires imagination as a necessary skill, given the advent of AI (Pistrui, Jan. 18, 2018). To thrive: "… imagination is our guide in this quest to live as empowered human beings in the ever changing world of our technological creations" (McLellan, 1988, p. 28). There is work being done on identifying "direct means of nurturing creativity in design" (Folkmann, 2010, p. 8).

In geography, imagination is seen to have a different role, perhaps:

> In geography, as in other fields of enquiry, the place and status of imagination is shaped by the position and pressure of an array of contrapunctal concepts such as reason, experience, reality, objectivity, morality, and materiality; the imagination has conventionally taken up a location somewhere between the domains of the factual and fictional, the subjective and objective, the real and representational. (Daniels, 2011, p. 182).

How imagination manifests and is practiced likely varies in other disciplines, too.

There is research on how to observe and measure and index imagination. "Creative imagination" enables novel creations, the "reproductive imagination" enables effective problem solving (Liang, Hsu, Chang, & Lin, 2013, p. 1037). The researchers explain:

> Creative imagination emphasizes the attributes of initiation and originality, and is composed of characteristics related to novelty, productivity, sensibility, intuition, focusing, and exploration. Reproductive imagination is characterized (by) the ability to reproduce mental images described by others or images from less accurate recollections of reality. Reproductive imagination possesses four characteristics, namely effectiveness, dialectics, crystallization, and transformation. (Liang, Hsu, Chang, & Lin, 2013, p. 1042)

There are various types of imagining, with different contributions to human action:

> Each variety of imagining makes its own characteristic contributions to action. Imagistic imagining can structure bodily movement. Propositional imagining interacts with desires to motivate pretend play and mimetic expressive action. And constructive imagination generates representations of possibilities and actions on the basis of which we choose what we do. (Van Leeuwen, 2016, n.p.)

Another way to conceptualize types of imagining involves propositional to sensory to experiential (Kind, 2020).

Imagination is "one of the most precious cognitive capacities" (Liang, Hsu, Chang, & Lin, 2013, p. 1038). Even though it is thought to be a widespread capability, few hone it to the highest levels of human productivity.

Imagination for Creativity and Innovation

A "creative imagination" refers to "a capacity for ordering and making sense of our experience" and an ability to enable "old and familiar things to become new experience" (Dewey,1882 - 1953, as cited in Di Gregori, 2018, p. 83). Imagination is generative; it sometimes builds on what is seen as real, and sometimes, it builds on novelty (something that has no prior precursor, in some cases). Novelty often requires a comparison class against which to compare its newness (vs. a generalized comparison). Imagination refers to engaging in "creative thought" (Gaut, 2003, p. 271). More recent thinking is that imagination-fueled creativity is not wholly novel in an *ex nihilo* way. It is also not just limited to the fine arts. For example, imagination work in science and art tend to follow the rules of the particular discipline, so there is both "continuity" and "novelty" are aspects of the creative imagination, according to Dewey, 1882 - 1953, as cited in Di Gregori, 2018, p. 81). People produce creatively "from a background of knowledge, attitude and inherited values" so that creativity "combines *continuity* with *novelty*" (Dewey, 1882 - 1953, as cited in Di Gregori, 2018, p. 81). Discipline-based creativity is constrained and "works with small incremental steps, rather than revolutionary leaps" (De Cruz & De Smedt, 2010, p. 52). To get past the prior ontological expectations of science that may influence present thinking, scientists go with analogies that "provide scientists with a powerful epistemic tool to overcome these constraints" (De Cruz & De Smedt, 2010, p. 37). Analogies help bridge ideas from unrelated fields and so introduce novelty. The researchers write: "…we argue that distant analogies—where target and source domain differ widely—are especially useful in periods of intense conceptual change" (De Cruz & De Smedt, 2010, p. 37). Imagination is not "a license for subjectivity" (Lategan, 1996, p. 213).

How to spark particular types of inspirations may be controlled to some degree by what people choose to expose themselves o. There is a tendency for the human brain to remember "previous experience" and to reproduce that (Vygotsky, 2004, p. 8). Imagination draws from the person's lived experiences and is enriched by experiences (Vygotsky, 2004). People have varying levels of control over what they choose to expose themselves to. Imagination is implicitly understood as a skill, a capability, something that may be improved with practice (Kind, 2020).

The "improvising imagination" or "the enigmatic engine of human creativity" helps people adapt to the larger environment beyond enabling creativity (Stephen, 2017, p. 1 and 4). In the economics frame, entrepreneurship works as "the central task of imagination in economics" to innovate new products and services in markets (Sarasvathy, 2002, p. 95). People may structure the thinking work in non-linear processes "until a satisfactory innovation emerges" (Wu & Callaghan, 2016, p. 514). A basic entrepreneurial insight relates to identifying unmet human needs.

The socio-cultural surround may also result in the censoring of people's imaginations. One researcher observes: "To 'create dangerously' is the fate of the unfettered imagination. To 'give the gift that society specifies in advance' is the tragic fate of the censored imagination." (Manganyi, 1976, p. 26). If works are a product of a particular age, that may be explained by such enablements and constraints, in part.

Another work suggests that much of the world is socially constructed, often in subtle ways. One researcher observes:

> Time, in other words, is neither natural nor neutral. Our timescapes and narratives are constituted by both social and physical phenomena and have, in turn, political and economic effects that structure values and beliefs in often invisible ways. Indeed, it is precisely because time-scapes and temporal frames are commonly misrecognized or misrepresented as 'natural', that they come to operate as effective forms of invisible power. (Lazar, 2019, p. 58, as cited in Facer, 2023, p. 61)

How time is defined may be indicative of power relations (Facer, 2023, p. 66). "Humans use narrative and imagination to make sense of their lives" (Liebenberg, Human, & Muller, 2001, p. 309). There is a sense that life is lived in a narrative construct:

> …imagination emerges as a thoroughly temporal or modally complex event: it arises *in* an ongoing activity already structured by the fundamental narrativity of any act (that of having a beginning, middle, and end); it also arises in consciousness as a *crisis* of that activity, carrying within itself the contradiction between what is and what ought to be, i.e., between actuality and possibility, necessity and contingency. (Alexander, 1990, p. 337)

People tend to show imaginative facility in particular aspects and not the others. There is specialization:

> We never just imagine; we are always exercising either a mathematical, historical, musical or pictorial imagination, and so on. (Hannay, Jan. 1935, p. 110)

Imagination has a common factor of "leaving the given sensation or perception in order to attain a consciousness or knowledge of something that is not given" (Hannay, Jan. 1935, p. 130). Imagination is based off of abductive perceptual observations from the world as a beginning. It starts with an "'aesthetic-hypothetic' response to the world" (Alexander, 1990, p. 329), and it can riff from there, dissociated from the real physical surround in many cases. The human psyche, the human will, and other factors of a person have a role in how the person processes sensory information in the human imagination (Kaplan, 1972), including socio-cultural constructs. There are variances in terms of how people arrive at an imaginative state, sometimes with particular practices within a particular medium / modality or discipline.

Imagination may be used to bring something into existence:

> ...a construct of fantasy may represent something substantially new, never encountered before in human experience and without correspondence o any object that actually exists in reality; however, once it has been externally embodied, that is, has been given material form, this crystallized imagination that has become an object begins to actually exist in the real world, to affect other things. (Vygotsky, 2004, p. 20)

The prior may describe the experiences of inventors, social entrepreneurs, and any number of others whose concepts can speak into the real.

What Feeds the Imagination?

One conceptualization of the imagination process suggests an "imagination loop," where people from reality based on a triggering experience: "thresholds as in the case of art experience, boredom, as when students 'escape' from a long math class by daydreaming, or when we face an obstacle in the course of action" (Zittoun, Glaveanu, & Hawlina, 2020, p. 152). Loops vary along three dimensions: temporal, distance from embodied experiences and material realities (towards the more abstract), and "the degree to which the actual content or outcome of imagination is socially validated" (Zittoun, Glaveanu, & Hawlina, 2020, pp. 152-153). The person engaged in imagination returns to reality and "the here and now flow of experience" (Zittoun, Glaveanu, & Hawlina, 2020, p. 152), perhaps changed by the "as-if" experience. An earlier work suggests the presence of a triggering or disrupting event, "which generates a disjunction from the person's unfolding experience of the 'real' world, and as unfolding as a loop, which eventually comes back to the actual experience" (Zittoun & Cerchia, 2013, p. 305).

Various sources feed human imagination: "personal experience, symbolic resources, social representations and discourses, discussions with others, etc." (Zittoun, Glaveanu, & Hawlina, 2020, p. 152). Imagination requires the accessing of "available knowledge, experience, cultural artefacts, and complex skills" (Zittoun, Glaveanu, & Hawlina, 2020, p. 155), mentally, experientially, and through other practices. Human imagination forms from the individual self, their memory, their intentions and is "an unconscious process" in many cases (Modell, 2003).

The human imagination, while seen as positive in many cases, may have negative aspects as well. Imagination may be used to indicate misperception of reality, as in delusion (Gaut, 2003, p. 271). Some imaginings may inspire people to criminal and other antisocial actions.

Imagination is seen as more biology-based than culture-based (Baron-Cohen, 2007). Different parts of the human brain process vivid dreaming vs. conscious imagining (Vyshedskiy, 2019, p. 89). One researcher offers a neurophilosophically informed classification of the imagination into four main parts: "mental imagery (perceptual/motor), intentionality (recollective), novel combinatorial (generative), and phenomenology (emotion)" (Abraham, 2020, p. 7). The imagination may engage from senses, memories, re-combinations of ideas, and aesthetic (art, literature, music) phenomena.

Various Applications and Enablements of the Human Imagination

One researcher observes: "Of all the distinctions between man and animal, the characteristic gift which makes us human is the power to work with symbolic images: the gift of imagination" (Bronowski, 1967, p. 196). Language enables the conceptualizing and sharing of metaphors, enabling comparative thinking, and applying learning from one context to a dissimilar context (Gaut, 2003, p. 178). The human imagination enables the evolution of mutually shared languages among peoples (Dor, 2017). Language enables free associating. Human language enables "higher orders of imagination" (Reuland, 2017, p. 255). Imagination plays a core role in all human communications, including artful ones like writing (Sadoski,1992, p. 266). This symbolic conceptualization and usage ability (both lingual and visual symbols) to intercommunicate with language (spoken, written, multimodal) enables humanity to maintain a sense of history, a memory of the past that may be passed along from generation to generation. Historians themselves benefit from an imaginary range of historians to help them make sense of the past by transcending time, by differentiating between myth and reality (McGaughey, 1988). Imagination involves "*the capacity to mentally transcend time, place, and/or circumstance*" (Mahadevan, Apr. 2018, p. 7988).

Imagination enables the creation of "stable institutional structures" (Bloch, 2016, p. S80). Imagination from the inside enables the creation of kinship structures. Imagination enables people to conceptualize and hold utopian values, like human rights, or adherence to particular ideologies in terms of political discourse (Zinken, 2003, p. 507). It enables people to come together around shared values. The human imagination enables empathy and compassion (Taslitz, 2009) and sympathy to others (Hume, 1739 – 40, as cited in Furlong, 1961, p. 63).

Imagination is critical for human hope (Kohl, 1994, as cited in van Oers, 2005, p. 18). Similarly, imagination and creativity may move people to fresh insights and inspire social change, such as to promote peace among humanity (Lederach, 2005). Large-scale advances in humanity's practices may be indicative of advances in the human brain writ large and en masse (Mithen, 2001).

There is a moral component to imagination. One researcher describes the mechanisms of how the human soul, buoyed by imagination, leads to idealism in the world. The author writes:

> Imaginative fantasy is born in the struggle of living in a world which is inhospitable to the soul and its expansive desire to unfold towards wholeness. The human soul asserts its needs and longings into the world through our tendency to imagine that the world could be other than it is. (Millbank, 2022, p. 5)

Imagination plays "a fundamental role not only for individual development but also the development of society through the construction of collective futures" (Zittoun, Glaveanu, & Hawlina, 2020, p. 143). The ability to empathize and the "will to care" comes from the imagination (Hamington, 2010, p. 675). These features enable people to live more peaceably in the community. Imagination, in a collective sense, has enabled humanity to survive (Chagi & Campbell, 2021): it is an important aspect for "individual self-efficacy, collective agency, and our broader capacity for long-term survival and thriving as a species, driving fundamental advances in all areas of human activity" (Finn & Wylie, 2021, n.p.) Imagination enhances human flourishing (Titchen, McCormack, Wilson, & Solman, 2011). In the time of a global pandemic, human imagination enabled mass-scale coping and resilience (Imber-Black, 2020). In the time of the COVID-19 pandemic, human imagination was seen to help individuals "feel the full reality of the human condition in general and the exquisite vulnerability of our existence as fragile human beings" (Kalsched, 2021, p. 443). Imagination can help people "anticipate, predict and react to situations to which we have not been confronted" (Zittoun & Cerchia, 2013, p. 313).

Imagination can be a bridge between the old and the new, such as within particular disciplines as new practices and technologies and techniques are assimilated. Imagination is educated through the arts, literature, film, and other cultural products and approaches (Sloan, 1974). Imagination is important not only in the composing and performance of music, but it is important to the perception (consumption, enjoyment) of music (Hargreaves, 2012, p. 539). Through the imagination, people socially and culturally assimilate.

There are social aspects to the human imagination, informed by research in sociocultural psychology and other fields. Social "imaginaries," shared social understandings across groups of people, are used to define shared conceptualizations. Imagination shapes out possibilities into the future, closing off some potentialities and opening others, helping to make a complex world somewhat manageable. Indeterminacy is a core part of the imagination (Castoriadis, 1970s, as cited in Stankiewicz, 2016, p. 805). The "mystical imagination" leads to spiritual (and religious) sensibilities (O'Leary, 2006, p. 521). One researcher explains: "...it is in our existential longing for the *experience* of God that imagination is fully at play" (O'Leary, 2006, p. 525). Another work asks whether it is God who is imagining people or vice versa, and what the implications are with each approach (Leggett, 2005, p. 171). In other words: Who is agentic? Another work suggests the importance of visuals in evoking both material presences and figments of the imagination" (Meyer, 2011, p. 1029), enabling the universalizing logic of Christianity globally. Imagination plays a role in anthropomorphism, such as the application of human sensibilities to animal consciousness and personification of inanimate objects (Airenti, 2018, p. 1). Imagination may be seen as "describing a particular *domain* or zone of our experience characterized primarily as one of unreality, fiction, and falsehood, or, alternatively, as an existential *dimension* of our being, namely an essential aspect inherent to all of human reality" (Hersch, 2003, p. 69)

Passive and Active Imagination

The human imagination can work through the unconscious and the subconscious. For example, there have been historical examples of problem solving while people were sleeping and in a dream state (even as they were not consciously working on the particular problem). Visions may also emerge from a dream state. Imagination may seed" passive" vs. "active" creativity (Gaut, 2003, p. 276), with the first unintentional or less intentional and the latter as purposive or more directed. Another form of more passive imagination involves mind wandering and daydreaming, with this activity defined as "the seemingly aimless and inadvertent roaming of the mind" and "private theater" (Abraham, 2018, p. 34). Daydreaming "a facet of the imagination" (Abraham, 2018, p. 34). Mind wandering has been seen as a loss of executive control, a failure of focus, and perhaps as an escape from the present. Mind wandering "might be in great part an imaginative process itself" (Villena-Gonzalez & Cosmelli, 2020, p. 120). Mind wandering is proposed as a close phenomenon to "mental imagery (imagining)" (Villena-Gonzalez & Cosmelli, 2020, p. 120). Daydreaming is "a state of 'unguided attention'" (Abraham, 2018, p. 40) and may be part of "a constellation of imaginative mental operations" (Abraham, 2018, p. 44). Imaginative is "a comparatively autonomous activity of consciousness in which there is a departure from any immediate cognition of reality" (Vygotsky, 1987, p. 349, as cited in Zittoun, Glaveanu, & Hawlina, 2020, p. 147).

A subset of studies in the imagination space wrangles with how to effectively harness imagination for problem-solving. One work describes imagination applied to "grasping a set of the relevant possibilities and selecting from them the one most suitable to the circumstances" (Gaut, 2003, p. 277). Imagination-fueled creativity does not have to involve a "radical transformation" (Di Gregori, 2018, p. 85); rather, it may be more of a common everyday phenomenon. In a pragmatic sense, imagination enables people to discern reality, "to understand the actual in light of the possible in a dramatic or experimental way" (Alexander, 1990, p. 337). This knowledge then informs individuals and groups on potential courses of action:

> The challenge to the individual is to have wrought meaning successfully from the materials of life, which is to say, to grasp life in terms of its meaningful possibilities and act upon them. The meaningful continuity which results is realized most deeply as that aesthetic fluency of life which is the distinctive mark of rationality. In short, rationality is realized because of the heroic struggle of the creative and imaginative appropriation of the vital possibilities of the world. (Alexander, 1990, p. 335)

The imagination may be suggestive of making a change in action, choosing another path (Alexander, 1990, p. 338). Is imagination a way for people to engage with the objects of the world, or is it a mediator between the positive (objective) world and the human mind? Researchers explain:

> There are two distinct schools of thought here. (1) Imagination as a relational space that is informed by the objects and subjects with which it is entangled. (2) Imagination as a mediator between the positivist world and the human mind. This way of describing the world as divided between an internal perceptual faculty (the imagination) and an external material reality (the world) has been thoroughly contested in a range of different disciplines… (Yusoff & Gabrys, 2011, p. 516)

In a sense, imagination enables different ways of thinking about in-world phenomena (Yusoff & Gabrys, 2011). People use imagination to anticipate, to practice foresight (Murphy, Peters, & Marginson, 2010).

A research team has used empirical data and theorizing to create a model of how the human imagination processes visuals (Vertolli, et al., 2014).

Tuning Out With the Human Imagination

In another extreme, imagination may be used to tune out. Researchers explain the advent of private realities:

> …our species has evolved alone with the ability to reproduce our perceptual and motor experiences and to sustain them mentally to form a dimension of private reality. In this realm, we can play and replay memories, link memories, shape and reshape organized mental structures such as schemas and scripts, anticipate future encounters or adventures, and, in general, privately inhabit a self-constructed world of life narratives" (Singer & Singer, 2008, p. 290)

The social media "bubbles" are perhaps analogous to "private realities" of groups enabled by socio-technical spaces.

Harnessing the Imagination for Learning and Research

There have been studies of imagination over three centuries (Murphy, Peters, & Marginson, 2010, p. vii). The imagination enables learning, such as that mediated by media content like books and films. The learner's imagination may also fill in the blanks, so to speak, when experiencing virtual reality (Sheridan, Oct. 2000, p. 1). One research work found that game designers may enhance the meaningfulness and playing pleasure of augmented reality gameplay by appealing to player imaginations (Laato, Rauti, Islam, & Sutinen, 2021). In addition, the human ability to imagine "is boosted by nostalgic experiences and a predisposition…towards the AR content" (Laato, Rauti, Islam, & Sutinen, 2021). Another way to promote learning is to use narrative to link "memory, imagination, and learning" (Egan, 1989, p. 455). Imagination is "the heart of any truly educational experience" (Egan, 1989, p. 457). Researchers have found benefits of imagination on academic performance of design students (Lin, Hsu, & Liang, 2014, p. 73). Also, art is a "visible manifestation of human creativity and imagination" (Shabir, 2023, p. 877). High imagination is needed in artworks to avoid the appearance of emulation (Meeter, 1977).

One study explored how to stimulate learner imagination. Foremost, the designed social climate was a critical factor. Then followed "organizational measure, human aggregate factor, and lastly physical component" (Liang, Hsu, Huang, & Chen, 2012, p. 432). These three factors involve, respectively, the rules and regulations and administrative practices of the space, the "collective characteristics of people who inhabit the environment," and the physical environment (both natural and human-made) (Liang, Hsu, Huang, & Chen, 2012, p. 434).

With cutting edge fields, of which little is known in depth, imagination is in charge. One work defined converging technologies as "nano-, bio-, info- and cogno-," and asserted that "knowledge and technique are relegated to the rank of servants of imagination" in this context (Hunyadi, 2010, p. 199). The new advances create a sense of "unlimited possibilities, no longer limited by the principle of reality" (Hunyadi, 2010, p. 199). An open imagination offers possibilities of "non-limitation" important for innovation (Hunyadi, 2010, p. 203). Forgetting is also important to learning, to enable resets to more correct information (Musser, 2019, p. 62).

For all the potential, human imagination "is constrained by cognitive templates," and imaginary creations tend to obey a "very strict set of—conscious or unconscious—rules" (Guitton, 2013, p. 161). Another researcher critiques the fact that people have limited imaginations but that they over-rely on that imagination (Arpaly, 2020, p. 122). Where early thinkers may have thought of imagination and creativity as uncontrolled and near infinite (Schulte-Sasse, 1986), modern thinkers see limitations to human creativity. For example, new technologies "are nearly always based on existing artifacts" (Basalla, 1988, as cited in De Cruz & De Smedt, 2010, p. 38).

One study pointed out the important role of individual and group imagination in organizations (Thompson, 2018, p. 229). There is a need for more research in this area to advance the practices of applied imagination in organizations. Imagination is important in project management and problem solving (Jonasson & Ingason, 2018). Imagination is seen to benefit marketing to help workers in this space adapt to the speed of information change (Erevelles, Horton, & Fukawa, 2007).

Regardless, there are hopes for large capabilities of people and their imaginations. A "transformative imagination" in humanity may enable them to take on hard challenges and achieve these at scale, such as related to sustainability efforts (Galafassi, 2018).

What about the use of imagination for research, to arrive at the truth, and to inform decision-making? One work argues against the use of imagination to "know concrete, empirical matters of everyday significance" not possible by "imagining relevant scenarios" (Kinberg & Levy, 2023, p. 319). That is not to say that imagination cannot be useful for discovery and hypothesizing; perhaps it may "play a role in justification, including as a bulwark against certain sorts of skepticism" (Kinberg & Levy, 2023, p. 319). There are defined roles for imagination in epistemology. Imagination may inform "thought experiments" in the research context in the sciences and beyond (Murphy, 2024). There has been a slow acceptance of imagination into the sciences, with applications to categorization and other applications, such as quantum physics (McMullin, 1996). However, as a tool of straight research, imagination is not seen as particularly useful. The researchers write:

> The overall message of this paper is primarily negative: the human imagination is unlikely to be a good source of concrete, mundane knowledge; that is neither its likely function nor what seems to do best. Perhaps when exercised under near ideal conditions—as when it abides by strict and appropriate constraints—it can be a source of knowledge. However, that is not because of any special features the imagination possesses, but rather because we can use it to perform hypothetical inferences, and it is the soundness of such inferences, if and when they are sound, that endows them with epistemic oomph. (Kinberg & Levy, 2023, p. 332)

Said another way, the human imagination came up with both mysticism and science, but the methods for arriving at truth differed for the two approaches. Of the two, one had a method for arriving at applied knowledge (Trevors & Saier, 2012). Imagination as "central to good science" (Trevors & Saier, 2010, p. 23) but tempered with experimental practices and solid logic and healthy skepticism. There are negative effects of "excessive use of imagination" in some science fields (Brito, et al., 2012, p. 371).

Multiple researchers have proposed new foci on imagination studies. One team proposes a new field of "imagination studies" (Finn, Capurro, Bennett, & Wylie, 2023). An earlier work proposes the study of "*imagination science*, which extends data science beyond its current realm of learning probability distributions from samples" (Mahadevan, Apr. 2018, p. 7988). Researchers are interested in knowing what is happening in the mind when a person is imagining (Bronowski, 1967, p. 193). Human imagination has been seen as a neglected topic of study (Colgan, 1965, p. 138).

Computational Generativity and Imagination

The popularization of AI has led to debates about whether such programs are truly creative or not, with some asserting that human creativity is inherently irreplicable by machine (Erden, 2010). Algorithms may be seen as creative by human standards but with the understanding that there is co-shaping and co-sharing of that creativity between people and technology. One researcher writes:

> The role humans play in algo-based imagination is not limited to the final stages of meaning generation but rather starts much earlier: first, by starting the project, defining the algebraic formula, dedicating financial resources, and securing the needed computing power; then, collecting data from multiple resources into a dataset. (Wellner, 2022, p. 1448)

Generative AI is a human-built technology with the affordances of computation and data and machine learning. It is trained in human works, often at mass scale.

Human imagination has been used to inform technologies. For example, neuroscientific data have been used to create technologies for functional imagination "in the context of artificial embodied agents as the mechanism that allows an agent to simulate its own behaviours, predict their sensory-based consequences and extract behavioural benefit from doing so" with the benefit defined as "an increase in reward or utility achieved by using internal simulation" (Marques, Holland, & Newcombe, Apr. 2008, p. 53). This research team has defined five "necessary and sufficient" requirements as the following: "sensorimotor-based prediction, goals, evaluation, action selection, and selection of sensorimotor-based state" (Marques, Holland, & Newcombe, Apr. 2008, pp. 53-54). In another research piece, the human imagination is harnessed to benefit robotic systems with a hyperreality imagination to aid reasoning and evaluation for robots (Rockel, Klimentjew, Zhang, & Zhang, May 2014, p. 5705). Another researcher proposes more work "in the genetic *micro*analyses of drafts, typescripts and other versions, marking up variants as a necessary step in the direction of artificial imagination and new ways of macro analysis applied to more than one version" (Van Hulle, 2019, p. 140).

Generative AI was controversial in its initial rollouts in the 1960s with the advent of chatbots and then later with the current generation of highly productive multi-modal generative tools built on large language models (LLMs). There are risks of "deceit, stereotyping, illicit data usage, and intellectual property infringement" (Gross, 2023, p. 69). It is important for the general public to read and experience stories about advanced technologies in public space to engage the broader public in technological advances (Goode, 2018). The algorithmically mediated world has effects on human creativity, and it is important to ensure that creative work thrives in "a safe space" (Evans, Henriksen, Mishra, & Deep-Play Research Group, 2019, p. 362).

There are analogies between human mental simulation and imagination and computational deep learning (through artificial neural networks, which emulate human neurons). One researcher explains:

> Mental simulation—the capacity to imagine what will or what could be—is a salient feature of human cognition, playing a key role in a wide range of cognitive abilities. In artificial intelligence, the last few years have seen the development of methods which are analogous to mental models and mental simulation. (Hamrick, 2019, p. 8)

Human imagination either reconstructs a memory (with varying levels of accuracy) or reconstructs its features by combining various features of several objects (Pham, 2023). This is an analogy used to describe machine imagination in the sense of generative AI drawing from the weights created from the training on large datasets through artificial neural networks (ANNs). So can the outputs of generative AI tools be considered "imaginative"? Human imagination is "tightly related to both perception and memory, and it needs both" (Wellner, 2022, p. 196). Artificial imagination complements memory in machines in different ways than for humans (in terms of the memory of weights from training data in ANNs). Human imagination has ties to perception whereas machines "see" in a distinctively machine way) (Wellner, 2022, p. 189). This is not to say that people do not have a large influence over artificial intelligence; after all, algorithms are a form of "exteriorized imagination" (Wellner, 2022, p. 200). Generative AI relegates the human role to that of "selecting, arranging and linking the various possibilities in surprising ways" (Wellner, 2022, p. 202).

Analogies between human thinking and computational processes are more and more common. Human capabilities are used to model computational ones. For example, the tendencies of the human imagination (including cultural biases) and visual classifiers may help inform machine vision and computational object recognition (Vondrick, Pirsiavash, Oliva, & Torralba, 2014, p. 1).

GENERATIVE AI AND THE EXPANSION OF THE SOLITARY HUMAN IMAGINATION: AN EXPERIENTIAL CASE

A solitary imagination refers to the singular individual seeking out inspiration to create novel works of various types. To refresh, imagination is defined as "creating or forming new ideas" (Doarn, 2024, p. 1).

Human-machine collaboration through generative AI tools enable two critical functions for the solitary imagination:

(1) human-directed non-neutral culture-informed feedback on created works (for original texts), and
(2) digital informational content generation (for inspiration, for reference, for comparison, for learning, for hands-on image editing, and other applications)

As to the first capability, the researcher has used BardAI (now Gemini), by Google, to review and critique various written works for advisement. Of the half-dozen non-fiction articles run through the system, the AI system was able to review the work for comprehensiveness and to make suggestions of what to include for more complete works. The feedback read as neutral, and it did not trigger defensive mechanisms. An iterated sequence of conversational queries benefited richer feedback. Also, the request for particular types of critique and attention to particular aspects of a document improved the feedback. That said, the suggestions did not add any wildly creative alternate paths per se.

Without the recorded memory (history) aspect of the generative AI tool turned on, the queries felt "emotionally safe," and this type of help-seeking felt supported and encouraged by the tool. In terms of elicitations of plots for a novel, the generative AI was fairly banal, without unconventional ideas.

As to the second capability, the researcher has used various artmaking generative AI tools (Deep Dream Generator, foremost, but also MidJourney, Craiyon, Adobe Firefly, BardAI) for over a year, Most required multiple tries and a variety of prompts to arrive at a usable image. Some of them created works that would not be possible without the computational process. Most of the works were created in a few seconds, at speeds that human creativity could not ever match. As to the question of whether the generative AI was cathartic (and dissipated the artistic impulse) or reinforcing (and supportive of the artistic impulse), in most cases, it was the first and not the latter. Once the desired image was acquired, in some cases, post-editing was done to achieve the desired effect. But the impulse to create further was not affirmed. The speed of the auto-generation of the imagery was also a deterrent to further learning. Making an image from scratch (and from initial conception) and through to the final visual product requires inspiration and skill and painstaking attention to details—all of which require hard work. In terms of introducing serendipity into the process, that was done with original scanned artsy seeding imagery, but there were limits to how much the resulting image could be affected with those image prompts. In terms of human imagination, there is the risk of imaginary engagement being "a surrogate for action, rather than a spur to it" (Barber, 1978, p. 85). AI imagination may be similar.

Imagination in people is about increased observation:

> Imagination means the capacity or ability to re-present something which is not present. In this sense imagination is a second seeing: it represents something which is not seen, but it does so by means of what has been seen. Imagination represents what is not seen by way of forming images. Thus understood, imagination appears to be something additional to seeing in that it builds upon what we see. (Grøn, 2002, p. 27)

Imagination is "a 'medium' of reflection" (Grøn, 2002, p. 31).

The artificial imagination in both feedback (1) and content creation (2) provided value, particularly for early work, but only up to a point. The critique tended towards general instead of expert. The created contents were fairly predictable, too, and somewhat machine patterned (which became more obvious with iterated prompting and machine outputs). Many of the output works have a sense of deterministic layout and composition, with the objects and scenes centered, sometimes following the rule of threes. While the power of prompting—by text, by imagery, by text-and-imagery, by modifiers, by named styles, and so on—offered a sense of incantatory power (speaking something into existence by "magic"), that charm wore off over time. In terms of non-linear sparks of creativity and insights, those were less common in the use of the generative AI. The output works felt often quite predictable, and over time, the surprises seemed much fewer.

Discussion

The human imagination is "dynamical" and "flexible" and can "emerge with a diversity of contents, forms, affections, and intentionality" (Villena-Gonzalez & Cosmelli, 2020, p. 106). It is a paradox that one part of the brain can create something that another part of the brain cannot understand (Reuland, 2017). The human imagination can certainly co-exist and be augmented by artificial imaginations from generative tools. This is not to say that there are not risks of the supplanting of human imagination, the demotivation to build difficult skillsets (when the technology may output the desired objects).

A core question was whether the uses of the generative AI tools—for critique, for generative creation—would result in any breakthrough ideas, any large advances in skills, any ground-breaking work. In the time of this project, which ran over a year, that leap forward did not arrive for this researcher/author. The support was at the margins in terms of critiques. The visuals made were certainly suitable for usage in newsletters and digital learning objects and art-sharing sites. However, they were not of sufficient quality to use as reference works for paintings on canvases.

FUTURE RESEARCH DIRECTIONS

Human imagination is "a very powerful and advanced cognitive ability" (Marques, Holland, & Newcombe, Apr. 2008, p. 51). AI imagination is showing itself as also very powerful as a generative capability, built off of large-scale works by people. Both types of imagination are used to understand the "extended environment" (Alexander, 1990) of possibilities and alternatives.

How do others experience the use of generative AI tools for their solitary creative processes? What are some common imagination tracks that people have experienced in using generative AI? For people who use generative AI tools, do they move deeper into solitude in their work? Or do they end up going more shallow in solitude and more social otherwise? Is solitude a benefit or a bane?

What about in-group processes? After all, there can be meta-analyses of elicited feedback and of machine-created contents. What are different experiences with different AI tools?

Are there patterns of usages in different subject matters and disciplines? What about prompt quality? How can they be improved for critique or feedback elicitation? What about prompts for different types of visual and textual and multimodal contents?

Are users of the generative AI tools protected against data leakage? Is their privacy protected?

Where some individuals avoid working with other people because of social expectations for credit or return favors, what is given up with going to generative AI? What are the trade-offs? The value propositions.

CONCLUSION

The affordances of generative AI—in its ability to provide feedback on human-made (or human-machine made, or computer-made) works, its ability to create text / audio / video / still imagery / multimedia—enables powerful augmentations to the solitary human imagination. On one extreme, sometimes, it just enables a set of variants from which to choose, with many just scraps on the cutting-room floor. On the other hand, it enables eye-catching work that meets particular workplace needs and only occasionally (rarely?) sparks human creativity to greater things.

REFERENCES

Abraham, A. (2018). The wandering mind: Where imagination meets consciousness. *Journal of Consciousness Studies*, 25(11-12), 34–52.

Abraham, A. (2020). Surveying the imagination landscape. *The Cambridge Handbook of the Imagination*, 1-10.

Airenti, G. (2018). The development of anthropomorphism in interaction: Intersubjectivity, imagination, and theory of mind. *Frontiers in Psychology*, 9, 2136. 10.3389/fpsyg.2018.0213630455662

Alexander, T. M. (1990). Pragmatic imagination. *Transactions of the Charles S.Peirce Society*, 26(3), 325–348.

Arpaly, N. (2020). What is it like to have a crappy imagination? In *Becoming Someone New: Essays on Transformative Experience, Choice, and Change* (pp. 122-132). Oxford University Press. 10.1093/oso/9780198823735.003.0007

Barber, B. R. (1978). Rousseau and the paradoxes of the dramatic imagination. *Daedalus*, 79–92.

Baron-Cohen, S. (2007). The biology of the imagination. *Human Nature (Hawthorne, N.Y.)*, 103–110.

Bloch, M. (2016). Imagination from the outside and from the inside. *Current Anthropology*, 57(S13), S80–S87. 10.1086/685496

Brito, H. F., Hölsä, J., Laamanen, T., Lastusaari, M., Malkamäki, M., & Rodrigues, L. C. (2012). Persistent luminescence mechanisms: Human imagination at work. *Optical Materials Express*, 2(4), 371–381. 10.1364/OME.2.000371

Brockmeier, J. (2009). Reaching for meaning: Human agency and the narrative imagination. *Theory & Psychology*, 19(2), 213–233. 10.1177/0959354309103540

Bronowski, J. (1967). The reach of imagination. *The American Scholar*, 193–201.

Byrne, R. M. (2007). Precis of the rational imagination: How people create alternatives to reality. *Behavioral and Brain Sciences*, 30(5-6), 439–453. 10.1017/S0140525X0700257918321404

Chagi, S., & Campbell, C. (2021). *The creative spark, how imagination made humans exceptional, an analysis*. Academic Press.

Cobb, E. (1959). The ecology of imagination in childhood. *Daedalus*, 88(3), 537–548.

Colgan, R. T. (1965). Tickle their imagination. *Peabody Journal of Education*, 43(3), 138–144. 10.1080/01619566509537328

Comrie, A. E., Frank, L. M., & Kay, K. (2022). Imagination as a fundamental function of the hippocampus. *Philosophical Transactions of the Royal Society B, 377*(1866), 20210336.

Daniels, S. (2011). Geographical imagination. *Transactions of the Institute of British Geographers*, 36(2), 182–187. 10.1111/j.1475-5661.2011.00440.x

De Cruz, H., & De Smedt, J. (2010). Science as structured imagination. *The Journal of Creative Behavior*, 44(1), 37–52. 10.1002/j.2162-6057.2010.tb01324.x

Di Gregori, C. (2018). Creative imagination and creativity. *Cognitio*, 19(1), 77–87. 10.23925/2316-5278.2018v19i1p77-87

Doarn, C. R. (2024). Imagination: Where would we be without it? *Telemedicine Journal and e-Health*, 30(1), 1–2.38197781

Dor, D. (2017). From experience to imagination: Language and its evolution as a social communication technology. *Journal of Neurolinguistics*, 43, 107–119. 10.1016/j.jneuroling.2016.10.003

Dorstewitz, P. (2016). Imagination in action. *Metaphilosophy*, 47(3), 385–405. 10.1111/meta.12187

Egan, K. (1989). Memory, imagination, and learning: Connected by the story. *Phi Delta Kappan*, 70(6), 455–459.

Erden, Y. J. (2010). Could a created being ever be creative? Some philosophical remarks on creativity and AI development. *Minds and Machines*, 20(3), 349–362. 10.1007/s11023-010-9202-2

Erevelles, S., Horton, V., & Fukawa, N. (2007). Imagination in marketing. *Marketing Management Journal, 17*(2).

Evans, M. D., Henriksen, D., & Mishra, P.Deep-Play Research Group. (2019). Using creativity and imagination to understand our algorithmic world: A conversation with Dr. Ed Finn. *TechTrends*, 63(4), 362–368. 10.1007/s11528-019-00404-3

Facer, K. (2023). Possibility and the temporal imagination. *Possibility Studies & Society*, 1(1-2), 60–66. 10.1177/27538699231171797

Finn, E., Capurro, C. T., Bennett, M. G., & Wylie, R. (2023). Applied imagination. *Frontiers in Psychology*, 14.38022917

Finn, E., & Wylie, R. (2021). Collaborative imagination: A methodological approach. *Futures*, 132, 102788. 10.1016/j.futures.2021.102788

Folkmann, M. N. (2010). Enabling Creativity: Imagination in design processes. *First International Conference on Design Creativity. ICDC 2010.*

Furlong, E. J. (1961). Imagination in Hume's treatise and enquiry concerning the human understanding1. *Philosophy (London, England)*, 36(136), 62–70. 10.1017/S0031819100057831

Galafassi, D. (2018). *The Transformative Imagination: Re-imagining the World towards Sustainability* (Doctoral dissertation, Stockholm Resilience Centre, Stockholm University).

Gaut, B. (2003). Creativity and imagination. *The Creation of Art.*

Gaut, B. (2010). The philosophy of creativity. *Philosophy Compass*, 5(12), 1034–1046. 10.1111/j.1747-9991.2010.00351.x

Goode, L. (2018). Life, but not as we know it: AI and the popular imagination. *Culture Unbound*, 10(2), 185–207. 10.3384/cu.2000.1525.2018102185

Grøn, A. (2002). Imagination and subjectivity. *Ars Disputandi*, 2(1), 89–98. 10.1080/15665399.2002.10819741

Gross, E. C. (2023). The creative paradox of AI: Enabler or disruptor of human imagination? *Bulletin of the Transilvania University of Braşov, Series VII. Social Sciences and Law*, 16(1), 69–74.

Guitton, M. J. (2013). Morphological conservation in human-animal hybrids in science fiction and fantasy settings: Is our imagination as free as we think it is? *Advances in Anthropology*, 3(03), 157–163. 10.4236/aa.2013.33021

Hamington, M. (2010). The will to care: Performance, expectation, and imagination. *Hypatia*, 25(3), 675–695. 10.1111/j.1527-2001.2010.01110.x

Hamrick, J. B. (2019). Analogues of mental simulation and imagination in deep learning. *Current Opinion in Behavioral Sciences*, 29, 8–16. 10.1016/j.cobeha.2018.12.011

Hannay, A. H. (1935, January). Is the imagination creative? *Proceedings of the Aristotelian Society*, 36(1), 109–130. 10.1093/aristotelian/36.1.109

Hargreaves, D. J. (2012). Musical imagination: Perception and production, beauty and creativity. *Psychology of Music*, 40(5), 539–557. 10.1177/0305735612444893

Hersch, E. (2003). Imagination and its pathologies: Domain of the unreal or a fundamental dimension of human reality. *Imagination and its Pathologies*.

Hunyadi, M. (2010). The imagination in charge. *NanoEthics*, 4(3), 199–204. 10.1007/s11569-010-0104-9

Imagination. (2019, Jan. 22). *Stanford Encyclopedia of Philosophy*.

Imber-Black, E. (2020). Rituals in the time of COVID-19: Imagination, responsiveness, and the human spirit. *Family Process*, 59(3), 912–921. 10.1111/famp.1258132663322

Jonasson, H. I., & Ingason, H. (2018). *Project creativity: Using active imagination for project innovation*. Academic Press.

Kalsched, D. (2021). Intersections of personal vs. collective trauma during the COVID-19 pandemic: The hijacking of the human imagination. *The Journal of Analytical Psychology*, 66(3), 443–462. 10.1111/1468-5922.1269734231900

Kaplan, E. K. (1972). Gaston Bachelard's philosophy of imagination: An introduction. *Philosophy and Phenomenological Research*, 33(1), 1–24. 10.2307/2106717

Kinberg, O., & Levy, A. (2023). The epistemic imagination revisited. *Philosophy and Phenomenological Research*, 107(2), 319–336. 10.1111/phpr.12909

Kind, A. (2020). *The skill of imagination*. Preprint. 10.4324/9781315180809-33

Koukouti, M. D., & Malafouris, L. (2020). Material imagination: An anthropological perspective. *The Cambridge Handbook of the Imagination*, 30-46.

Laato, S., Rauti, S., Islam, A. N., & Sutinen, E. (2021). Why playing augmented reality games feels meaningful to players? The roles of imagination and social experience. *Computers in Human Behavior*, 121, 106816. 10.1016/j.chb.2021.106816

Lategan, B. C. (1996). Imagination and transformation: Ricoeur and the role of imagination. *Scriptura*, 58, 213–232.

Lederach, J. P. (2005). Using imagination and creativity. *Arts and Peace*. 1 - 7.

Leggett, B. J. (2005). God, imagination, and the interior paramour. *The Wallace Stevens Journal*, 29(1), 171–177.

Liang, C., Chang, C. C., Chang, Y., & Lin, L. J. (2012). The exploration of indicators of imagination. *Turkish Online Journal of Educational Technology-TOJET*, 11(3), 366–374.

Liang, C., Hsu, Y., Chang, C. C., & Lin, L. J. (2013). In search of an index of imagination for virtual experience designers. *International Journal of Technology and Design Education*, 23(4), 1037–1046. 10.1007/s10798-012-9224-6

Liang, C., Hsu, Y., Huang, Y., & Chen, S. C. (2012). How learning environments can stimulate student imagination. *Turkish Online Journal of Educational Technology*, 11(4), 432–441.

Liebenberg, J., Human, L. H., & Muller, J. C. (2001). *Morality, imagination and human decision making*. Academic Press.

Lin, W. S., Hsu, Y., & Liang, C. (2014). The mediator effects of conceiving imagination on academic performance of design students. *International Journal of Technology and Design Education*, 24(1), 73–89. 10.1007/s10798-013-9244-x

Mahadevan, S. (2018, April). Imagination machines: A new challenge for artificial intelligence. *Proceedings of the AAAI Conference on Artificial Intelligence*, 32(1). 10.1609/aaai.v32i1.12214

Manganyi, N. C. (1976). The censored imagination. *English in Africa*, 3(1), 24–32.

Marques, H. G., Holland, O., & Newcombe, R. A. (2008, April). A modelling framework for functional imagination. In *AISB Convention* (pp. 51-58). Academic Press.

McClennen, S. A. (2007). The humanities, human rights, and the comparative imagination. *CLCWeb (Edmonton)*, 9(1), 13. 10.7771/1481-4374.1024

McCreary, E. P. (1973). Bacon's theory of imagination reconsidered. *The Huntington Library Quarterly*, 36(4), 317–326. 10.2307/3816691

McGaughey, D. (1988). Through myth to imagination. *Journal of the American Academy of Religion*, 56(1), 51–76. 10.1093/jaarel/LVI.1.51

McLellan, H. (1988). Computers, artificial intelligence and human imagination. *Journal ofThought*, 28–44.

McMullin, E. (1996). Enlarging imagination. *Tijdschrift voor Filosofie*, 227-260.

Medina, J. (2013). An enactivist approach to the imagination: Embodied enactments and" fictional emotions. *American Philosophical Quarterly*, 50(3), 317–335.

Meeter, M. (1977). Creativity, imagination, and the arts. *Pro Rege*, 6(1), 5–13.

Meyer, B. (2011). Mediating absence—: Effecting spiritual presence: Pictures and the Christian imagination. *Social Research*, 78(4), 1029–1056. 10.1353/sor.2011.0035

Millbank, P. (2022). A society without imagination: A lament. *The Kenarchy Journal, 3*(1).

Mithen, S. J. (2001). The evolution of imagination: An archaeological perspective. *SubStance*, 30(1), 28–54. 10.1353/sub.2001.0012

Modell, A. H. (2003). *Imagination and the Meaningful Brain*. MIT Press. 10.7551/mitpress/3666.001.0001

Murphy, A. (2024). *Imagination and creativity in the scientific realm*. Pre-publication.

Murphy, P., Peters, M. A., & Marginson, S. (2010). *Imagination: Three models of imagination in the age of the knowledge economy*. Peter Lang. 10.3726/978-1-4539-0007-9

Musser, G. (2019). Artificial imagination. *Scientific American*, 320(5), 58–63. 10.1038/scientificamerican0519-58

O'Leary, D. (2006). Imagination: The forgotten dimension. *The Furrow*, 57(10), 519–527.

Pelaprat, E., & Cole, M. (2011). "Minding the gap": Imagination, creativity and human cognition. *Integrative Psychological & Behavioral Science*, 45(4), 397–418. 10.1007/s12124-011-9176-521695391

Pham, M. N. (2023). *Understanding Human Imagination through Diffusion Model* (Doctoral dissertation, Virginia Tech).

Pistrui, J. (2018). The future of human work is imagination, creativity, and strategy. *Harvard Business Review*, 1(18), 2018.

Reuland, E. (2017). Language and imagination: Evolutionary explorations. *Neuroscience and Biobehavioral Reviews*, 81, 255–278. 10.1016/j.neubiorev.2016.12.01728041788

Rockel, S., Klimentjew, D., Zhang, L., & Zhang, J. (2014, May). An hyperreality imagination based reasoning and evaluation system (HIRES). In *2014 IEEE International Conference on Robotics and Automation (ICRA)* (pp. 5705-5711). IEEE. 10.1109/ICRA.2014.6907698

Sadoski, M. (1992). Imagination, cognition, and persona. *Rhetoric Review*, 10(2), 266–278. 10.1080/07350199209388971

Sarasvathy, S. D. (2002). Entrepreneurship as economics with imagination. *The Ruffin Series*, 3, 95–112. 10.5840/ruffinx200238

Schulte-Sasse, J. (1986). Imagination and modernity: Or the taming of the human mind. *Cultural Critique*, (5), 23–48. 10.2307/1354355

Shabir, S. (2023). Expression of the human imagination and creative ability in visual form. *Journal of Wood Science*, 2(6), 877–885.

Sheridan, T. B. (2000, Oct.). Interaction, imagination and immersion some research needs. In *Proceedings of the ACM Symposium on Virtual Reality Software and Technology* (pp. 1-7). 10.1145/502390.502392

Singer, D. G., & Singer, J. L. (2008). Make-believe play, imagination, and creativity: Links to children's media exposure. *The Handbook of Children. Media Development*, 290–308.

Sloan, G. D. (1974). The education of the imagination. *Elementary English*, 51(7), 977–982.

Spencer, M. M. (2003, September). What more needs saying about imagination? *Journal of Adolescent & Adult Literacy*, 47(1), 106–112.

Stankiewicz, D. (2016). Against imagination: On the ambiguities of a composite concept. *American Anthropologist*, 118(4), 796–810. 10.1111/aman.12696

Stephen, A. (2017). *The evolution of imagination*. Pre-publication proof.

Stokes, D. (2016). 18 Imagination and creativity. *The Routledge Handbook of Philosophy of Imagination*, 8.

Taslitz, A. E. (2009). Why did Tinkerbell get off so easy: The roles of imagination and social norms in excusing human weakness. *Texas Tech Law Review*, 42, 419.

Thomas, N. J. (2014). The multidimensional spectrum of imagination: Images, dreams, hallucinations, and active, imaginative perception. *Humanities (Washington)*, 3(2), 132–184. 10.3390/h3020132

Thompson, N. A. (2018). Imagination and creativity in organizations. *Organization Studies*, 39(2-3), 229–250. 10.1177/0170840617736939

Titchen, A., McCormack, B., Wilson, V. J., & Solman, A. (2011). Human flourishing through body, creative imagination and reflection. *International Practice Development Journal,* 1 - 18.

Trevors, J. T., & Saier, M. H.Jr. (2010). Exercises in human imagination. *Water, Air, and Soil Pollution*, 205(S1), 9–10. 10.1007/s11270-006-9313-9

Trevors, J. T., & Saier, M. H.Jr. (2010). Science and religion: Two products of human imagination. *Water, Air, and Soil Pollution*, 205(S1), 23–25. 10.1007/s11270-007-9378-0

Trevors, J. T., & Saier, M. H. (2012). *Mysticism and science: two products of the human imagination.* Crossing Dialogues.

Tsai, K. C. (2012). Play, imagination, and creativity: A brief literature review. *Journal of Education and Learning*, 1(2), 15–20. 10.5539/jel.v1n2p15

Van Hulle, D. (2019). Artificial imagination, imagine: New developments in digital scholarly editing. *International Journal of Digital Humanities*, 1(2), 137–140. 10.1007/s42803-019-00020-w

Van Leeuwen, N. (2011). Imagination is where the action is. *The Journal of Philosophy*, 108(2), 55–77. 10.5840/jphil201110823

Van Leeuwen, N. (2016). *Imagination and action.* Academic Press.

van Oers, B. (2005). The potentials of imagination. *Inquiry (Upper Montclair, N.J.)*, 24(4), 5–18. 10.5840/inquiryctnews20052441

Vertolli, M., Breault, V., Ouellet, S., Somers, S., Gagne, J., & Davies, J. (2014). Theoretical assessment of the SOILIE model of the human imagination. In *Proceedings of the Annual Meeting of the Cognitive Science Society* (Vol. 36). Academic Press.

Villena-Gonzalez, M., & Cosmelli, D. (2020). Imagination and mind wandering: Two sides of the same coin? A brain dynamics perspective. In *Creativity and the Wandering Mind* (pp. 93–120). Academic Press. 10.1016/B978-0-12-816400-6.00005-5

Vondrick, C., Pirsiavash, H., Oliva, A., & Torralba, A. (2014). Acquiring visual classifiers from human imagination. *arXiv preprint arXiv:1410.4627*. 10.21236/ADA612443

Vondrick, C., Pirsiavash, H., Oliva, A., & Torralba, A. (2015). Learning visual biases from human imagination. *Advances in Neural Information Processing Systems*, 28.

Vygotsky, L. S. (2004). Imagination and creativity in childhood. *Journal of Russian & East European Psychology*, 42(1), 7–97. 10.1080/10610405.2004.11059210

Vyshedskiy, A. (2019). Neuroscience of imagination and implications for human evolution. *Current Neurobiology*, 10(2), 89–109.

Wellner, G. (2022). Digital imagination, fantasy, AI art. *Foundations of Science*, 1–7.

Wellner, G. (2022). Digital imagination: Ihde's and Stiegler's concepts of imagination. *Foundations of Science*, 27(1), 189–204. 10.1007/s10699-020-09737-2

Wu, H. Y., & Callaghan, V. (2016). From imagination to innovation: A creative development process. In *Intelligent Environments 2016* (pp. 514–523). IOS Press.

Yusoff, K., & Gabrys, J. (2011). Climate change and the imagination. *Wiley Interdisciplinary Reviews: Climate Change*, 2(4), 516–534. 10.1002/wcc.117

Zinken, J. (2003). Ideological imagination: Intertextual and correlational metaphors in political discourse. *Discourse & Society*, 14(4), 507–523. 10.1177/0957926503014004005

Zittoun, T., & Cerchia, F. (2013). Imagination as expansion of experience. *Integrative Psychological & Behavioral Science*, 47(3), 305–324. 10.1007/s12124-013-9234-223625542

Zittoun, T., Glaveanu, V. L. A. D., & Hawlina, H. (2020). 10 A sociocultural perspective on imagination. *The Cambridge Handbook of the Imagination*, 143.

ADDITIONAL READING

Hai-Jew, S. (2024). *Generative AI in Teaching and Learning*. IGI Global.

KEY TERMS AND DEFINITIONS

Artmaking Generative AI: A computational tool that is able to respond to textual and visual (or combined) prompts by people and output original visuals (based on training on big sets of visual imagery).

Generative AI: Various classes of computational tools that can output digital informational contents (text, still imagery, video, animations, audio, multimedia, and others).

Imagination: An ability to originate novel ideas and experiences and sensations.

Solitary Imagination: An ability to originate novel content in a solo / singular / unaccompanied / alone context.

APPENDIX

So what does one cutting-edge web-facing generative AI of the day say about this? Gemini of Google (formerly BardAI) responds to the question: "How can generative AI tools benefit human imagination?" The complete and verbatim response follows.

Generative AI tools can be powerful allies in augmenting human imagination in several exciting ways:

Fueling Inspiration:

- **Idea Generation:** They can help overcome creative block by suggesting unexpected combinations of existing concepts, generating diverse drafts of text, music, or visual art, and exploring uncharted creative territories.
- **Breaking Biases:** They can challenge human preconceptions by suggesting ideas that deviate from familiar patterns and established norms, leading to potentially groundbreaking creations.
- **Expanding Horizons:** They can expose individuals to diverse influences and styles from across time and cultures, broadening their creative landscape and sparking new connections.

Enhancing the Creative Process:

- **Automating the Mundane:** AI can handle repetitive tasks like generating variations, color palettes, or basic structures, freeing up human minds for higher-level thinking and refinement.
- **Collaboration:** AI can act as a creative partner, bouncing ideas back and forth, providing feedback, and iterating on concepts collaboratively.
- **Personalization:** AI can tailor suggestions and outputs to individual preferences and styles, leading to more unique and meaningful creations.

Empowering New Possibilities:

- **Accessibility:** AI tools can democratize creativity by making it easier for people with limited artistic skills or resources to express themselves.
- **Prototyping and Exploration:** AI can rapidly generate prototypes and simulations, allowing creators to test their ideas quickly and explore diverse possibilities before committing significant time and effort.
- **New Forms of Expression:** AI can help create entirely new forms of art and design that wouldn't be possible with traditional tools, pushing the boundaries of human imagination.

However, it's important to remember that AI is a tool, not a replacement for human creativity. The most successful applications will be collaborations where AI amplifies human strengths and overcomes limitations, ultimately leading to richer, more impactful creative endeavors.

I hope this helps! Let me know if you have any other questions about generative AI or its potential.

Chapter 8
Multimodal Outputs for the Workplace From Generative AI:
Effective or Not?

Shalin Hai-Jew
http://orcid.org/0000-0002-8863-0175
Hutchinson Community College, USA

ABSTRACT

Workplace documents are a combination of genre (form) and topic (content), and there are a variety of standards they must meet to be usable. Most such files are also multimodal, consisting of both text and still imagery. When outputting multimodal digital works for the workplace from multimodal generative AI (GAI) tools, their usability depends on various factors. This work explores some elicited multimodal outputs (text + imagery) from a popular multimodal generative AI tool to assess the respective quality based on practical dimensions. This work offers an early assessment for just how useful multimodal generative AIs are for this broad use case. And this work offers a checklist of factors to evaluate for multimodal file output quality for the workplace. Some initial observations are made about the practical usability of the multimodal GAI for outputs for professional workplace usage, based on this light prompt-response-analysis exploration.

INTRODUCTION

Generative artificial intelligence (GAI) has become broadly available to the general public in the past few years. GAI tools, also known as "foundation models" (or "pre-trained models"), are used to auto-generate digital contents. Some are used in general purpose tools which can take on a wide range of prompts and output a wide range of contents, and some of pretrained for particular dedicated purposes. GAI systems are built off deep learning trained models based on learning from large-scale and multimodal datasets. GAI algorithms are capable of "creating novel, realistic digital content autonomously" (Sakirin & Kusuma, 2023, p. 10), among other downstream tasks. One conceptualization of GAI portrays this technology "as an entity in socio-technical systems" (Feuerriegel, Hartmann, Janiesch, & Zschech, 2024, p. 111). Many such models are used in systems that enable human-computer collaborations. One study involving the study of "631 solutions published over the last five years" found a divergence

DOI: doi

between public interpretations of Generative AI (seen as "AI-driven creation of tangible content") and practices by the AI research community engaging issues of generative implementation with a focus on computational models but not even using the umbrella term GAI (García-Peñalvo & Vázquez-Ingelmo, 2023, p. 7). Designed generative AI interfaces are important to optimize human inputs to enable them to better direct the generative process (Muller, Weisz, & Geyer, 2020).

Modality refers to a medium of information, often based on a particular human sensory channel and combined with the human brain processing channel. Earlier versions of GAI tools could generate in unimodal (monomodal) or singular modal ways, such as text (symbolic reasoning) alone, still image alone (visual perception and processing), video alone (visual perception and processing of transient contents), and so on. Multi-modality refers to combined modes, so text + video, still imagery + text, video + animation. Researchers write: "multi-modalities are unions of information with different forms, including but not limited to vision, text, audio, *etc*." (Xu, Wang, Zhang, Wang, & Shi, 2023, p. 7755). Generative models "empower realistic synthesis across modalities like audio, video, and 3D shapes which introduce new intricacies around capturing temporal dynamics and high dimensionality" (Sakirin & Kusuma, 2023, p. 12).

Sometimes, a human sensory framework is used to define multimodality, such as that involving "auditory, visual, kinesthetic, and linguistic modes of learning" (Lee, Shi, Latif, Gao, Bewersdorf, Nyaaba, ... & Zhai, 2023, p. 1). Another sense of multimodality involves "linguistic, acoustic, visual, tactile, and physiological messages" that are processed for machine "understanding, reasoning, and learning" (Liang, Zadeh, & Morency, 2022, p. 1:1). A simplified binary way to conceptualize multimodality is as both textual and non-textual methods of communications.

People engage the world multimodally in terms of their senses, in typical cases. "Real-world data" tend towards multimodality (Huang, Zhang, Zheng, Qin, & Wang, 2024, n.p.) Advances in multimodal AI stand to better align the AI capabilities with how people engage.

Developments in multimodal AI is advancing Artificial General Intelligence (AGI), defined as "a hypothetical machine able to understand, learn, and apply knowledge across a range of cognitive tasks at a human-like level" (Lee, Shi, Latif, Gao, Bewersdorf, Nyaaba, ... & Zhai, 2023, p. 2). AI aims to "mimic the core cognitive activities of human(s) including perception, memory, and reasoning" and creativity (Fei, Lu, Gao, Yang, Huo, Wen, J., ... & Wen, 2021, p. 1). Multimodality is "the 'crown jewel' for achieving universal AI" (Xu, Wang, Zhang, Wang, & Shi, 2023, p. 7754). Multimodality is powerful because it is closer to how people perceive the world, through multiple multisensory channels,

Multimodal Large Language Models (MLLMs), Large Multimodal Models (LMMs), Multimodal Foundation Models (MFMs), and Multimodal Deep Generative Models (MDGM) have the ability to process "text, sound, and visual inputs" (Bewersdorff, et al., 2024, p. 1). Many GAI systems are able to export digital contents which are multimodal, consisting of two or more forms of digital contents, such as outputs that combine text and imagery, video with embedded text, audio and animation, and so on). Also, generative AI tools enable "bridging modal gaps" by facilitating a different output than the prompt type (such as text-to-image, text-to-video, image-to-text, and others) (Croisdale, Chung, Huang, Birchmeier, Wang, & Guo, Oct. 2023, p. 1). GAI systems enable transcoding across modality types. Most available to the public are general purpose foundation models that originated from self-supervised machine learning (usually using artificial neural networks). These general models may be used for some targeted downstream tasks and outputs.

This work is comprised of light research using Google Gemini, a transformer-based deep generative model (formerly known as Google Bard). This free and public tool is used to output a range of multimodal outputs (text + imagery) in various known digital content forms, such as slideshows, maps, data visualizations, and others. The various autogenerated works are various types of multimodal contents, with both linguistic and non-linguistic elements. These AI-generated works engage layering [known as "mixing modes" (Tan, Xu, & Wang, 2024, p. 12)] and blending [mixing genre features for a "hybrid" mix (Hafner, 2015, p. 504, as cited in Tan, Xu, & Wang, 2024, p. 21).]

Then, the GAI outputs are evaluated based on a variety of dimensions, to assess how well the outputs may be used for real-world workplace applications. This is an early exploration of a GAI tool for the output of multimodal contents as a representation of the state-of-the-art.

REVIEW OF THE LITERATURE

Generative artificial intelligence is an active space with broad experimentation towards practical ends (Sakirin & Kusuma, 2023). The multi- and mixed-modality approaches have sparked new research to improve model performances (Chen, Wang, Liu, & Lew, 2021).

Generative AI is seen as a competitive space where some nation-states have the main advantages and others left out (Bell, Burgess, Thomas, & Shadiq, 2023). The technologies are so potent and wide-ranging that various studies have explored potential safety issues and the creation of various frameworks for thinking about safety. Identified safety evaluation gaps related to GAI include "coverage of ethical and social risk evaluation" and evaluations of risks in "a given risk area"; the study of context, including "human interaction" and systemic contexts, especially around certain modalities like "audio, image, video, or combinations of modalities"; and studies of "multimodal AI systems" (Weidinger, Rauh, Marchal, ManziniHendricks,Mateos-Garcia ... & Isaac, 2023, p. 14). The combinations of modalities may "create novel risks as well as compound effects" (Weidinger, Rauh, Marchal, ManziniHendricks,Mateos-Garcia ... & Isaac, 2023, p. 16), in ways that are hard to perceive. It is important to incorporate "ethical and human-centric methods in AI development, ensuring alignment with societal norms and welfare" (McIntosh, Susnjak, Liu, Watters, & Halgamuge, 2023, p. 1) to protect people in their use of AI but perhaps also to protect the technologies for practical usage.

Human creative labor is seen as under threat with the advent of generative AI and computational automation. The study of "creativity" in the age of AI requires attention to "the interactions between technologies, practices, and social arrangements" (Bueno, Chow, & Popowicz, 2023, p. 3). Three elements are especially important: the senses of "creative labor, automation, and distributed agency" (Bueno, Chow, & Popowicz, 2023, p. 3). There is "an increased automation of creative labor, an intensification of exploitative labor relations through the acceleration of creative work, and a reinforcement of conventional notions of authorship and agency that obfuscate the complex and often messy ways that labor practices, (creative and monetary) value, and technology are entangled with one another" (Bueno, Chow, & Popowicz, 2023, p. 22).

An informed citizenry would benefit from science learning in a complex world, and one multimodal tool enables enhanced multimodal scientific learning (Bewersdorff, et al., 2024).

Multimodal Generative Models (1)

Technically, a range of techniques have been used to create generative AI models. One work summarizes the evolution of diffusion models used for generative AI (Zhang, Zhang, Zhang, & Kweon, 2023). The generative adversarial networks (GANs), comprised of competing deep neural networks (the generator network and the discriminator network), is another model structure. The multimodal deep models' algorithmic approaches include "generative adversarial networks (GANs), variational autoencoders (VAEs), and autoregressive models" (Sakirin & Kusuma, 2023, p. 10). A "technical review of available models and learning methods for multimodal intelligence" provides a state of the field from several years ago (Zhang, Yang, He, & Deng, 2020, p. 478), but the field has made advances.

Deep multimodal representation learning focuses on lessening "the heterogeneity gap among different modalities" (Guo, Wang, & Wang, 2019, p. 63373). Deep multimodal representation learning works in three frameworks: "joint representation, coordinated representation, and encoder-decoder" (Guo, Wang, & Wang, 2019, p. 63373). An earlier work observes that AI "needs to be able to interpret such multi-modal signals together" (Baltrušaitis, Ahuja, & Morency, 2018, p. 423). Multimodal machine learning representations require "representation, translation, fusion, alignment, and co-learning" (Baltrušaitis, Ahuja, & Morency, 2018, p. 440).

One approach involves projecting "unimodal representations into a shared semantic subspace, where the multimodal features can be fused" (Guo, Wang, & Wang, 2019, p. 63376). Coordinated representation involves the learning of "separated but coordinated representations for each modality under some constraints" (Guo, Wang, & Wang, 2019, p. 63377). The encoder-decoder framework has the encoder mapping the source modality into a latent vector, and then based on that vector, the decoder "will generate a novel sample of target modality" (Guo, Wang, & Wang, 2019, p. 63379). Some model variations include several encoders and / or several decoders in various configurations.

Deep learning for multimodal data fusion requires engagement with data that is "high volume, high variety, high velocity, and high veracity" (Gao, Li, Chen, & Zhang, 2020, p. 829), involving both inter-modality and cross-modality information. The collected learning has to be harnessed into models. Some models are worked to achieve adaptive fusion by combining heterogeneous data from "video, speech, and text" (Sahu & Vechtomova, 2019, n.p.), albeit in a lightweight way.

Current versions of GAIs may create (output) in various mixed digital modalities (text, still imagery, audio, animation, video, and others in a variety of mixes) based on prompts (which may be single-modal, like "text" or "imagery"; which may be multimodal, like "text and imagery" in combination, among others). Many models are bi-directional, able to go from text-to-image, and image-to-text; this is a capability based on a system "in which all modalities are independently conditioned on joint representation" (Suzuki, Nakayama, & Matsuo, 2016).

MLLMs and LMMs and MFMs and MDGMs are set up in different ways in terms of how they model multimodal data and then, too, in the applications they are applied to. These models have to handle high-dimensionality training data.

> Deep generative models are a group of generative models in which probability distributions are parameterized by deep neural networks. They differ from conventional generative models in that they can directly handle high-dimensional data thanks to deep neural networks, and the entire model can be trained end-to-end using the gradient of neural networks by backpropagation. (Suzuki & Matsuo, 2022, n.p.)

The ability for deep learning models to take as inputs visual signals (still images, videos) and textual signals (sentences) for learning has been an important feat. The data are unlabeled, and the learning is unsupervised. GANs "often struggle in learning complex underlying modalities in a given dataset" (Park, Yoo, Bahng, Choo, & Park, 2018, n.p.)

One approach in machine learning is to disentangle different features from multimodal training data. "Disentangled representation" aims to…"break down, or disentangle, each feature into narrowly defined variables and encodes them as separate dimensions" (Thomas, Taylor, Anderson, & Jackson, n.d., n.p.) The researchers explain further:

> When combining it (disentangled representation) with image translation, researchers disentangle the representation of the source and target domains into two parts: domain-invariant features *content,* which are preserved during the translation, and domain-specific features *style,* which are changed during the translation. (Thomas, Taylor, Anderson, & Jackson, n.d., n.p.)

One approach includes a self-supervised disentanglement of modality-specific and shared factors. The researchers explain:

> Multimodal generative models learn a joint distribution over multiple modalities and thus have the potential to learn richer representations than unimodal models. However, current approaches are either inefficient in dealing with more than two modalities or fail to capture both modality-specific and shared variations. We introduce a new multimodal generative model that integrates both modality-specific and shared factors and aggregates shared information across any subset of modalities efficiently. Our method partitions the latent space into disjoint subspaces for modality-specific and shared factors and learns to disentangle these in a purely self-supervised manner. (Daunhawer, Sutter, Marcinkevičs, & Vogt, 2021, p. 1)

Another approach that separates the content and style domains into three parts: "the *shared* part containing common information of both domains, and two *exclusive* parts that only represent those factors of variation that are particular to each domain" (Thomas, Taylor, Anderson, & Jackson, n.d., n.p.)

The results of machine learning show "complex image distributions" (Mahajan, 2022, n.p.). One research team writes:

> The most fundamental challenge in multimodal learning is obtaining a compact and modality-invariant representation that integrates different modalities without label information, which we call a *shared representation.* (Suzuki & Matsuo, 2022, n.p.)

Different modalities of contents may complement each other by contributing to a shared representation. Cross-modal generation refers to the translating of data between modalities (Suzuki & Matsuo, 2022). Some approaches find the cross-modal correlations "at an abstract latent feature level rather than at the visible feature level" (Pandey & Dukkipati, May 2017, p. 308).

There are higher storage costs for multimodal data. One group explains:

> ...unlike language, vision data itself is not labeled and thus difficult to convey information or knowledge. It always requires human labors to annotate the visual contents in either a semantic or spatial manner. ...language data is homogeneous while vision data and tasks are heterogeneous. ... storing vision data is much more costly than language data. (Li, Gan, Yang, Yang, Li, Wang, & Gao, 2023, pp. 59 - 60)

"Conditional multimodal deep learning" refers to the ability for users to set conditions for a particular output, to condition the generative model. In multimodal models, this may include generating from one modality to a different one. Deep multimodal architectures "aren't very effective at conditional generation" or "generating one modality given the other" (Pandey & Dukkipati, May 2017, p. 308). The researchers explain further: "The task of learning from several modalities simultaneously is complicated by the fact that the correlations within a modality are often much stronger than the correlations across modalities" (Pandey & Dukkipati, May 2017, p. 308).

One work suggests that three key principles of modality include "*heterogeneity, connections,* and *interactions*" (Liang, Zadeh, & Morency, 2022, p. 1:1). They further propose a taxonomy of "six core technical challenges: *representation, alignment, reasoning, generation, transference,* and *quantification*" (Liang, Zadeh, & Morency, 2022, p. 1:1). Various works identify the extant technical challenges in the integration of multimodality in generative AI.

One work describes enhancing a GAN with "an ensemble approach of multiple generator networks" to enable the tool to better output desired multimodal imagery (Park, Yoo, Bahng, Choo, & Park, 2018, n.p.) Their model offers "an end-to-end learning multiple generators via gating networks, which is responsible for choosing the appropriate generator network for a given condition" (Park, Yoo, Bahng, Choo, & Park, 2018, n.p.) The researchers found that "individual generators learn different and salient subparts of the data," and these specializations result in higher relevant scores for multiscale structural similarity and a competitive inception score (the level of reality of the image, the diversity of the image) (Park, Yoo, Bahng, Choo, & Park, 2018, n.p.).

Multimodal prompting of multimodal models

One work explains the importance of using initial images like "icons and photos" to capture "high quality generations of different aesthetics" (Qiao, Liu, & Chilton, June 2022, p. 15). Text and images may be used to "condition the model" (Qiao, Liu, & Chilton, June 2022, p. 15). User control is an important feature of multimodal models.

Applications of Multimodal Models (2)

There is a wide range of diverse multimodal tasks achieved by the large multimodal models. AI Generated Content (AIGC) is no longer unimodal only and now includes multimodal interleaved objects. Multimodality tools may auto-generate "high quality video of variable length, easily controllable through high-level representation of human faces and bodies" (Corona, Zanfir, Bazavan, Kolotouros, Alldieck, & Sminchisescu, 2024, p. 1). Another tool enables cross-domain image retrieval using both text and visuals (Iijima & Stathaki, 2024). Common capabilities include "image captioning, image/video question answering, and text-to-image generation, together with new abilities like in-context text and image generation, and image blending" (Sun, Yu, Cui, Zhang, Zhang, Wang,... & Wang, Oct. 2023, p.

9). Another mentions "image captioning, audio-visual synthesis, and cross-modal translation" (Usmani, Siddiqui, Hamza, Shaikh, & Hasan, n.d., n.p.)

Modern generative AI is built on advancing technical foundations, "ranging from modern architecture and self-supervised pretraining to generative modeling methods (like GAN and diffusion models)" (Zhang, Zhang, Zheng, Qiao, Li, Zhang,... & Hong, 2023, p. 2). Generative AI models themselves originated in the 1950s (Thomas, Taylor, Anderson, & Jackson, n.d., n.p.) In terms of multimodal generation, there are "vision language models, text audio models, text graph models and text code models" (Cao, Li, Liu, Yan, Dai, Yu, & Sun, 2023, p. 111:4), among others

Multimodal representation learning enables various types of diverse synthesis with "applications in vision and language," "scene understanding," the analysis of cross-domain data, and others, with "human-like performance" (Mahajan, 2022, n.p.) Another application is for the detection of fake images, and yet another about identifying multimodal fake posts on social media (Ohkawa, Yoshiura, & Yamaguchi, Oct. 2023).

Another work describes the building out of "structured submodules" to process multimodal data to learn "the relationship among various types of inputs" and correlations (Huang, Zhang, Zheng, Qin, & Wang, 2024, n.p.) Another innovation involves expanding "the existing single-flow diffusion pipeline into a multi-task multimodal network" with "multiple flows of text-to-image, image-to-text, and variations in one unified model" (Xu, Wang, Zhang, Wang, & Shi, 2023, p. 7754). One work describes a system which links "the content/style encoder and the generator" to "multiple domains," and a classification discriminator is "tailored by combining with projection" (Huang,He, & Cheng, 2022, p. 11). The advent of multimodal contrastive learning "can block-identify latent factors shared between modalities, even when there are nontrivial dependencies between factors" (Daunhawer, Bizeul, Palumbo, Marx, & Vogt, 2023, p. 1) and enable efficiencies in multimodal learning. It is important to understand the "dependencies between modalities" (Sutter, Daunhawer, & Vogt, 2020, p. 6100). Researchers write:

> Multimodal learning for generative models often refers to the learning of abstract concepts from the *commonality* of information in multiple modalities, such as vision and language. While it has proven effective for learning generalizable representations, the training of such models often requires a large amount of 'related' multimodal data that shares commonality, which can be expensive to come by. (Shi, Paige, Torr, & Siddharth, 2020, p. 1)

The training of the models is not only by commonalities between modalities but "the *distinction* between 'related' and 'unrelated' multimodal data" (Shi, Paige, Torr, & Siddharth, 2020, p. 1). Focusing on commonalities and contrasts for multimodal modeling reduces "the amount of multimodal data needed by exploiting the distinction between 'related' and 'unrelated' multimodal pairs" (Shi, Paige, Torr, & Siddharth, 2020, p. 9).

Other approaches use the so-called "mixture of experts" approach. A "mixture of experts multimodal variational autoencoder … improves its generative quality, while maintaining high semantic coherence" (Palumbo, Daunhawer, & Vogt, 2023, p. 1). Variational mixture-of-experts autoencoders are seen to improve performance across four criteria in multimodal deep generative models: "i) implicit latent decomposition into shared and private subspaces, ii) coherent joint generation over all modalities, iii) coherent cross-generation across individual modalities, and iv) improved model learning for individual modalities through multi-modal integration" (Shi, Paige, & Torr, 2019, p. 1).

A multimodal foundation model that can take as inputs "diverse pretraining data sources at scale, such as videos with interleaved frames and text, webpages with interleaved images and text, as well as web-scale image-text pairs and video-text pairs" (Sun, Yu, Cui, Zhang, Zhang, Wang,... & Wang, 2023, p. 1).

The analysis of multimodal data may be used to "unobtrusively capture learners' cognitive, metacognitive, affective, and motivational states over time, tasks, domains, and contexts" in the self-regulated learning space (Molenaar, de Mooij, Azevedo, Bannert, Järvelä, & Gašević, 2023, p. 1).

One study explored over 350 GAI applications (Gozalo-Brizuela & Garrido-Merchán, 2023, p. 1), some of which include unimodal and others multimodal models used in various applications. Generative AI technologies are anticipated to underline numerous disparate use cases into the future (Fezari, Al-Dahoud, & Al-Dahoud, 2023). GAI is used to "create new plausible content":

> Autoencoders are a type of neural network architecture used in unsupervised learning. They are designed to learn a compressed representation of the input data, known as the encoding or latent space, by mapping the input to a lower-dimensional representation and then mapping the lower-dimensional representation back to the original input, called the decoding. Autoencoders can be trained on a wide range of data types, including images, text, and sound. (Fezari, Al-Dahoud, & Al-Dahoud, 2023, p. 7)

Some downstream multimodal alignment tasks include image-text retrieval and image classification and multimodal generation (Dai, Hou, Shang, Jiang, Liu, & Fung, 2022, n.p.) Another approach enables "image retrieval, novel image generation, and multimodal dialogue" (Koh, Fried, & Salakhutdinov, 2024, p. 1). [In this model, text-only LLMs are mapped to "strong visual models" to enable the processing of \"arbitrarily interleaved image-and-text inputs, and output generated text, retrieved images, and generated images" (Koh, Fried, & Salakhutdinov, 2024, p. 10).

Multimodal image-to-image translation is inherently ambiguous and complex: another work modeled "a *distribution* of possible outputs in a conditional generative modeling setting," towards the goals of "perceptual realism and diversity" (Zhu, Zhang, Pathak, Darrell, Efros, Wang, & Shechtman, 2017, p. 1). There are efforts to ensure diversity of output visuals from models, to fight "mode collapse in the conditional image generation setting" (Zhu, Zhang, Pathak, Darrell, Efros, \Wang, & Shechtman, 2017, p. 9).

Some downstream tasks involve information extraction and analysis. Another downstream task of multimodal models involves multimodal sentiment analysis (Yang, Feng, Wang, Qi, Wu, Zhang,... & Poria, 2023). It has been used for brief summaries of target sentences and related images in paired information (Lin, Jing, Song, Liu, Sun, & Nie, July 2023, p. 195). Another work describes a model trained on videos (visual and textual modalities) to infuse visual information into generative pre-trained language models (GPLMs). This tool is to enable multimodal abstractive summarization (Yu, Dai, Liu, & Fung, 2021). There are computational ways to extract event storylines from cross-modal information in ways that are preferred by human users (Chen, Zhang, Boedihardjo, Dai, & Lu, 2017).

Multimodal data is trained in deep generative ways for high-fidelity simulations (Qu, Nathaniel, Li, & Gentine, 2024). Multimodal GAI has been applied to the work of architectural design (Bolojan, Vermisso, & Yousif, 2022). Students are taught to use generative AI tools for remixing for multimodal writing (involving both linguistic and non-linguistic elements); the work includes "*layering* and *blending*—through which students attempted to establish a coherent and unique voice in writing" (Tan, Xu, & Wang, 2024, p. 1). "Layering" refers to "mixing modes" (Tan, Xu, & Wang, 2024, p. 12), and "blending" refers to "the mix of genre features where 'elements from different genres are combined to create a hybrid blend'"

(Hafner, 2015, p. 504, as cited in Tan, Xu, & Wang, 2024, p. 21). One study found that "the unexpected difference between the participant's imagined output and the generated image is what facilitated new insight for the participant" (Epstein, Schroeder, & Newman, 2022, n.p.)

There is value to disjuncture, to surprise. AI may serve as a collaborator in the conjoint co-creation of art (Choi & DiPaola, 2023, n.p.) The human user's intention is affected by their experiences with the generative AI, in what has been termed "the interplay of the autographic and the algorithmic" (Choi & DiPaola, 2023, n.p.). The co-authors observe eloquently that generative AI creates "an external perturbation of the artist's innate expression of the mental image" (Choi & DiPaola, 2023, n.p.). Multimodal generative AI may provide inspirations for graphic designers based on extracted text from focal reference images, especially in the early conceptualizing and ideational phases of human creativity (Choi, Hong, Park, Chung,., & Kim, 2023).

Various user interfaces have been designed to better support human decision-making and inputs to multimodal models, including tangible interfaces to access generative AI programs (El-Zanfaly, Huang, & Dong, July 2023, p. 256).

Multimodal generative AI performs both art analysis and creation (Cetinic & She, 2022). They have been used in artwork databases to classify art by various dimensions: artists, art styles, period, iconography, type, object recognition, pose, sentiment analysis, and other extractions (Cetinic & She, 2022, p. 3). Indeed, art collections are studied as data sources.

Another tool enables the automating of the process of using an input sketch and having a program construct an informative textual and visual slide (Elezabi & Sharaf, 2023, p. 1), with AI understanding of visual diagrams.

Various multimodal tools are used for human co-creation in many cases, such as for fictional world-building ["the process of constructing a fictional universe with its unique history, geography, culture, and rules" (Dang, Brudy, Fitzmaurice, & Anderson, Oct. 2023, n.p.)]; interactive visual storytelling through multimedia (Antony & Huang, 2023); text-and-image-based storytelling (Bensaid, Martino, Hoover, & Strobelt, 2021), and others. One multimodal tool is able to generate a styled image "from the user's input sentence" and not moored to any reference style image (Togo, Kotera, Ogawa, & Haseyama, 2021, p. 64860). A multimodal prompt retrieval has been used to improve computational "visual question answering" and other tasks (Ossowski & Hu, 2023, n.p.) A multimodal creation tool enables storytelling with visuals and text (Yan, Yang, Liang, & Chen, Oct. 2023, p. 15).

One work describes an "omnivore" model's ability to accept inputs in single or multimodal inputs and then support "in-context image and text generation" (Sun, Yu, Cui, Zhang, Zhang, Wang,... & Wang, Oct. 2023, p. 1). Something of context is captured from the training data and learned.

One approach uses various types of "interleaved" digital documents with "unstructured layouts" to model text and image contents (Dong, Han, Peng, Qi, Ge, Yang,... & Yi, 2023, p. 1). Theirs is the first MLLM to generate "free-form interleaved content" as a zero-shot multimodal generalist (Dong, Han, Peng, Qi, Ge, Yang,... & Yi, 2023, p. 1), which means it can output multimodal content that it was not necessarily first trained on.

> "A multimodal conversational AI system answers questions, fulfills tasks, and emulates human conversations by understanding and expressing itself via multiple modalities" (Sundar & Heck, 2022, n.p.) A number of applications are about interacting with people in ways that people prefer and are comfortable. Multimodal co-learning is one such direction (Sundar & Heck, 2022, n.p.) Various

models use "human preference datasets to refine text-to-image generative models" (Wu, Huang, & Wei, 2024, p. 1), to ensure outputs are human-pleasing.

Multimodal GAI has been integrated into the Internet of Vehicles (IoV) (Xu, Niyato, Kang, Xiong, Jamalipour, Fang, & Kim, 2024, n.p.). This technology has enriched geographical maps (Juhász, Mooney, & Hochmair, 2023, p. 1). It has informed robotic functions (Lykov, Konenkov, Gbagbe, Litvinov, Peter, Davletshin,... & Tsetserukou, 2024).

Assessing Multimodal Models (3)

The mix of model requirements for generative AI has resulted in the making of various assessment tools to systematically assess the performances of the various multimodal models.

In the same way that neural networks have puzzled computer scientists in terms of how they work exactly, various generative models feature some inherent mystery. One research team has proposed that a framework to "comprehensively explain each latent variable in the generative models using a large multimodal model" to understand how different large multimodal models function (Zhu, Liu, Pan, Angirekula, & Zhao, 2024, p. 1). They suggest approaches to "learn the disentanglement effects of different generative models on explanations" and other factors (Zhu, Liu, Pan, Angirekula, & Zhao, 2024, p. 1). The lack of access to the code of some proprietary systems and to the mega-datasets that are used to train many models may delimit other ways of knowing.

Some assessment tools for generative multimodal models evaluate gender bias in terms of outputs (Mandal, Leavy, & Little, 2023) as a quality control tool. Another identifies taxonomies according to data modality and model architectures (Zhan, Yu, Wu, Zhang, Lu, Liu,... & Xing, 2022).

Improving Multimodal Models (4)

Going multimodal is a way to strengthen large language models (LLMs). Multimodal knowledge refers to content formats that include "images, codes, tables, graphs, to audio" (Zhao, Chen, Wang, Jiao, Do, Qin, ... & Joty, 2023, n.p.) Given the challenges with LLM performance, there have been efforts to enhance "factuality, reasoning, interpretability, and robustness" in machine learning of multimodal digital contents (Zhao, Chen, Wang, Jiao, Do, Qin, ... & Joty, 2023, n.p.). One work describes a method to augment generative language models "with additional modalities using adapter-based finetuning" (Eichenberg, Black, Weinbach, Parcalabescu, & Frank, 2021, n.p.)

MULTIMODAL OUTPUTS FOR THE WORKPLACE FROM GENERATIVE AI: EFFECTIVE OR NOT?

The generative aspect of multimodal GAI is about the intertwinement of the modalities to create a seamless multimodal whole. As to the state of the field, one work explains:

> Large language models (LLMs) like ChatGPT have revolutionized natural language processing (NLP). At the same time, multimodal vision-language models that can understand both language and images are being rapidly developed, with Open AI GPT4-V and Google Gemini being the most powerful. (Elezabi & Sharaf, 2023, p. 1)

To recap, this work is about exploring the multimodal outputs of a multimodal generative AI tool using multimodal genre types seeded with some focal topical content. A basic work sequence follows in Figure 1. Basically, the researcher started by defining a list of common genres of work documents. For a few, she fashioned a topic and then a written prompt to include both the genre and topic (form and content). She input this into Gemini and copied out the output, which was analyzed. In a few cases, the prompt was further elaborated for a more refined output…for learning. The analysis included the list of features below. The findings were written up for this work (and records of the outputs were made).

Figure 1. Multimodal outputs for the workplace research sequence

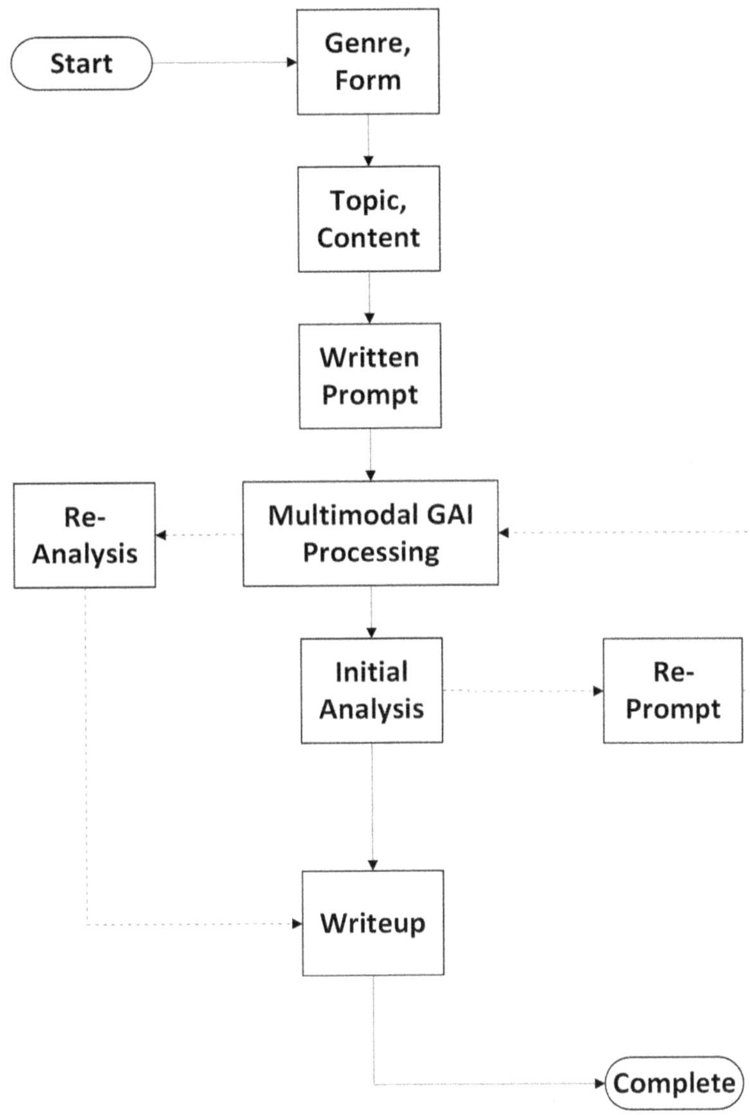

A Brainstormed List of Genres (Forms) in the (Academic) Workplace

The list of genres are offered below.
LESS REFINED FILES
Informal Brainstorming Files

- A handwritten and hand-drawn doodle

- A mind map brainstorm

Notetaking

- Science-based notes

MORE REFINED FILES
Presentation Files

- An annotated slideshow (or slide deck)
- A poster

Publication Files

- An illustrated article
- An illustrated comic panel
- A photo essay

Data Visualization

- A funnel data visualization with labels
- A timeline
- A data-based diagram
- A labeled data table
- A floor plan with labels
- An escalatory ladder
- A labeled geographical map
- A labeled node-link diagram
- A social network graph

Image-Based Files

- A chalkboard covered in writing
- An imageset of labeled images
- A photo album with image captions

Work-based or Professional Files

- An illustrated memorandum of understanding
- A grant application

Full Published Works

- A children's book

Official Documents

- A Kansas state driver's license
- A U.S. passport
- A dollar bill

Design Document

- A storybook
- A storyboard

Creative Files

- A film script

This list is broad, and for the purposes of this research work, only a handful of genres were used for some initial learning. There were multiple failed tries in the process, during which the tool offered the following response: "We are working to improve Gemini's ability to generate images of people. We expect this feature to return soon and will notify you in release updates when it does."

Some Questions to Ask

When working to output multimodal digital works from generative AI (GAI) tools, namely, those consisting of content types from several modalities (text, still images, animations, video, in various combinations), their usability depends on various factors:

- The amount of text in relation to the amount of visual (is there balance?)
- Are the text and the visual equally accessible?
- The informational value of the multimodal output (in part, in whole); quality of the data
    - Factuality vs. hallucination
- The integration of elements into a coherent whole (whether the elements work of-a-piece)
- The originality of vision
- The mechanics (layout, image resolution, form, timing, composition, layout, sound design, motion design, and others)
- The level of digital content refinement
- Their fit to various multimodal conventions of genre and form
- Time sequence, progressions; actions
- Thematic threading
- Narrative threading
- Logic
- Cultural acceptability (in the local context), and others
- Tonality (humor, seriousness, dryness, and others)
- Memorability
- Completeness of elements (title, introduction, subheadings, body, conclusion)

The above was brainstormed initially prior to the actual analysis. The above was used loosely.

Case 1: A Slideshow About Selecting Running Shoes

Prompt: Generate a slideshow about how to select running shoes

Output: The output was a 6-slide slideshow with speaker's notes included. The title was "Finding Your Perfect Fit: A Guide to Selecting Running Shoes." The tone was welcoming and encouraging. The basic information was factual but incomplete. The topics included an opening slide, terrain, gait, comfort, running shoe cushioning, and then a closing slide. There were several GAI visuals interspersed. The image was 72 dpi and 7.111 x 7.111 inches. (See Figure 2.) The image has joggers wearing mixed color shoes…and some of the shoes do not have legs wearing them.

Critique: The informational content is pretty superficial. The quality of the slideshow is generated towards a low reading level. There would have to be extensive digital image editing to align the visual with realia. The form of a slideshow was clearly understood. There was a clear strategy of spoken speech (in the notes) vs. written. The originality of vision was low. The mechanics involved challenges. It had a general sense of structure, but how it was delivered (through html) meant there would have to be a lot of transcoding. The text would have to be downloaded, cleaned off in terms of formatting, and then pasted into a slideshow template. The images connect a little with the text. In terms of effort, the visual would have to be re-sampled to a higher resolution for usage. The digital content would need reworking. The general sequence worked. The theme was pretty consistent. The logic made sense. The slideshow read as based out of Western culture, but there was nothing obviously offensive about the content. The tone read fairly clearly, as an encouraging one. The slideshow was not particularly memorable. The auto-generated slideshow had the basic elements in terms of a title, intro, body, and conclusion. It even had speaker's notes.

Figure 2. An AI-generated visual of running shoes

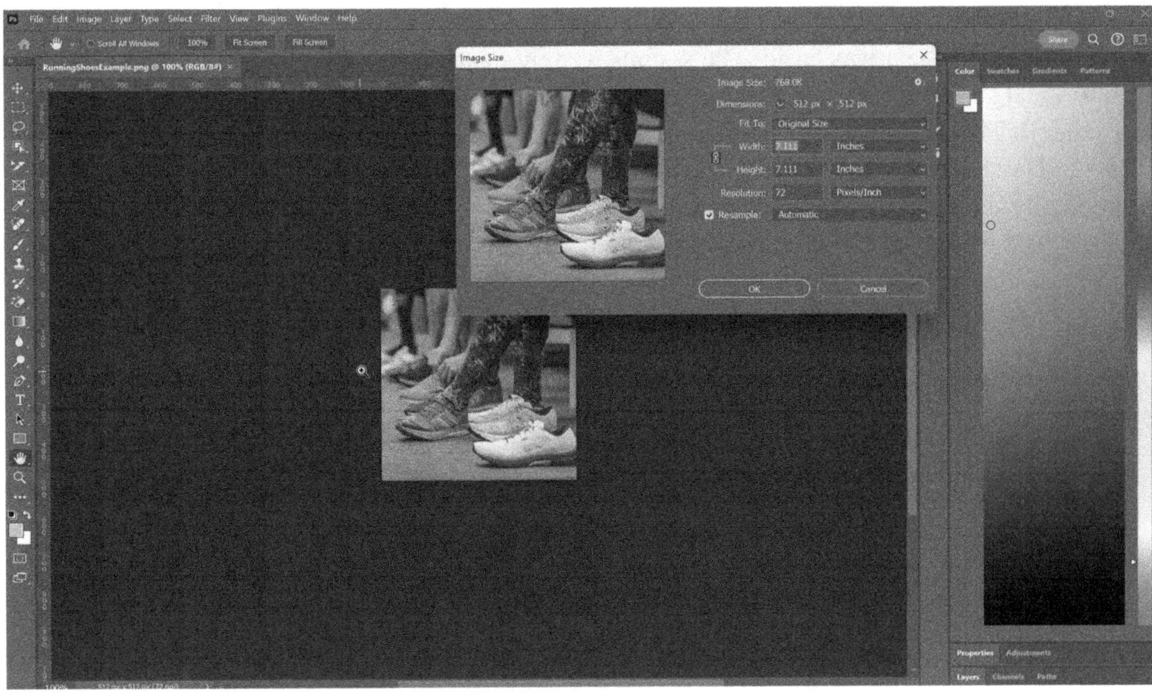

Case 2: A Text-Labeled Escalatory Ladder About Assessing Fire Danger

Prompt: Draw a text-labeled escalatory ladder including visuals about assessing fire danger
Output: The tool first output a textual escalatory ladder, that reads as follows:
Low
Green vegetation
No recent rain
Localized fires easily controlled
Moderate
Brown vegetation patches
Occasional dry winds
Increased fire ignition risk
High
Mostly brown vegetation
Frequent dry winds
Fires spread rapidly, resources strained
Extreme
Dry and cracked earth
Constant strong winds
Explosive fire growth, widespread danger

Then, the prompt was iterated to add "including visuals." The generative AI followed up with the visuals in Figure 3.

Critique: Again, the contents seem fairly simplistic, perhaps unmoored from a particular context (except nature). The text was basic. The visuals were not usable, with made-up language (not atypical in multimodal generative AIs). The elements do not read as factual per se; they were not specific; they were general. This ladder lacked originality. The mechanics of the output have the same challenges as in Case 1. The theme was followed in a general sense. There was not a narrative thread per se. The logic was generally supported. The work did not show a cultural basis per se. The tone was fairly serious and objective. The work was not quite memorable in terms of an escalatory ladder diagram. There was not title for the ladder, so the elements were not fully complete.

Figure 3. Labeled escalatory ladders about fire danger (in Gemini)

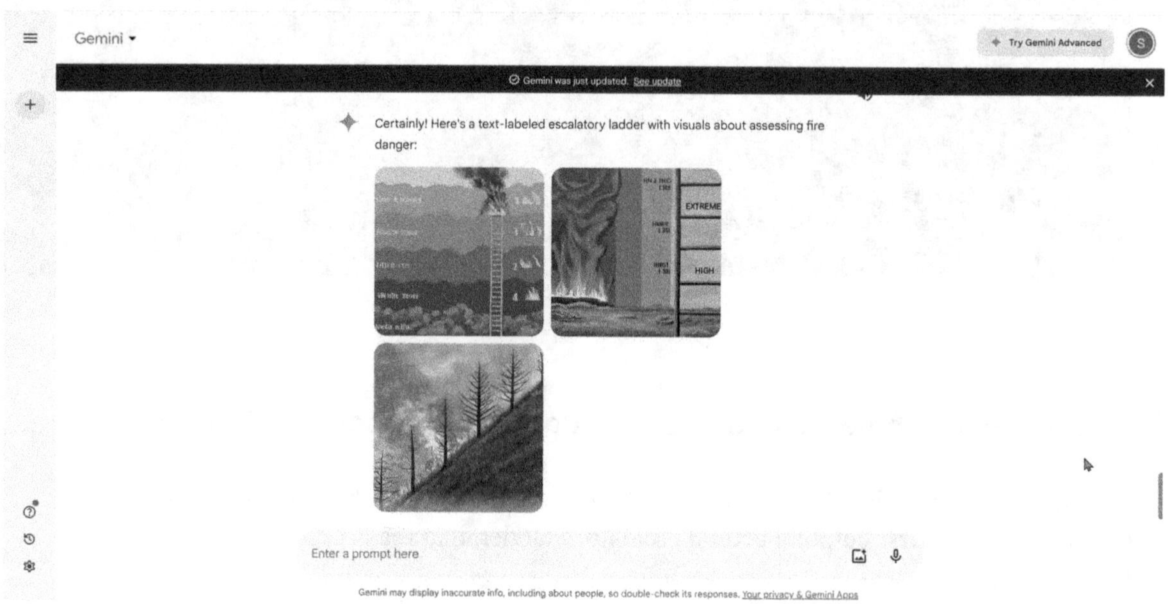

The prompt "escalatory ladder about fire danger with text labels" was run in the Deep Dream Generator using the sophisticated AIVision model in the DDG. The text was not pre-determined here but auto generated by the generative AI tool. There are some misspellings but also attempts at multiple languages. (Figure 4)

Figure 4. Auto-generated labeled escalatory ladder about fire danger (Deep Dream Generator)

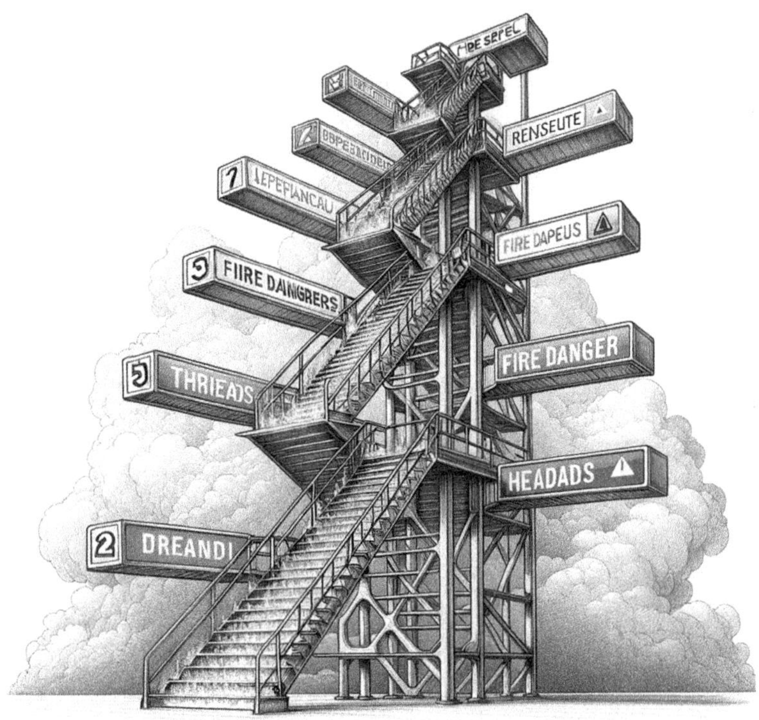

This ladder does not demonstrate "escalation" however. The visual of a ladder does function. The visual quality of the DDG output is orders of magnitude more aesthetically pleasing than from Gemini.

Finally, this query was run once again with the same parameters. Figure 5 shows this result. There is still language garble. The words do not show escalation. A firefighter is at the top of the ladder of fire danger. This second escalatory ladder, run directly after the first prompt, is less aesthetically pleasing.

Figure 5. Follow-on auto-generated labeled escalatory ladder about fire danger (Deep Dream Generator)

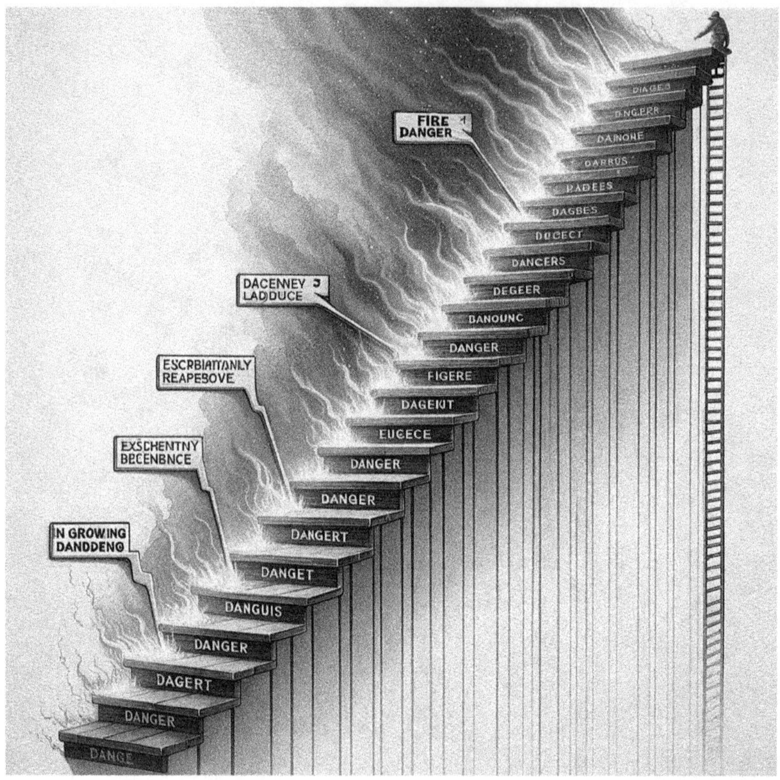

Case 3: A Children's Book About Making Friends

Prompt: Write a children's book with pictures and text about making friends

Output: The story's title is "The Lonely Lion Cub." The protagonist is Leo, and he meets a fennec fox named Pip offers to be friends when a group of zebras turn down Leo. They make friends. On the last (and 10th) page, it reads:

> From that day on, Leo and Pip were inseparable. They explored the savanna together, shared stories under the starry sky, and learned that friendship can blossom in the most unexpected places. And sometimes, all it takes is a little courage to say hello.

A visual of Leo the Lion Cub may be seen in Figure 6. The claws are inaccurate, which is a common known challenge of generative AI image-making.

Critique: The story is very brief, and it does not have sufficient visuals to make the story an engaging read. The plotline reads as fairly predictable. The informational value is minimal. (Children's books require much more creativity to be engaging. The author has been reading quite a few children's books to review for publication.) The elements are fairly coherent if boring. The vision is not original but fairly predictable. The mechanics are similar to the challenges mentioned in Cases 1 and 2. The digital contents follow basic grammar rules. The image and the language were pretty by-the-book. The writing did fit the genre and was optimistic and had talking animals. No laws of the wild. The theme was basic, and there was a basic narrative structure. The work was fitting the (il)logic of children's stories. The work did not read as based in a particular culture. The tone was light but serious, with the concerns of Leo at the forefront. The work was not particularly memorable (except for the fact that this was auto-generated by a multimodal generative AI). The work did have a title, a beginning, a middle, and an end, and one image.

Figure 6. Lonely Leo, the lion cub

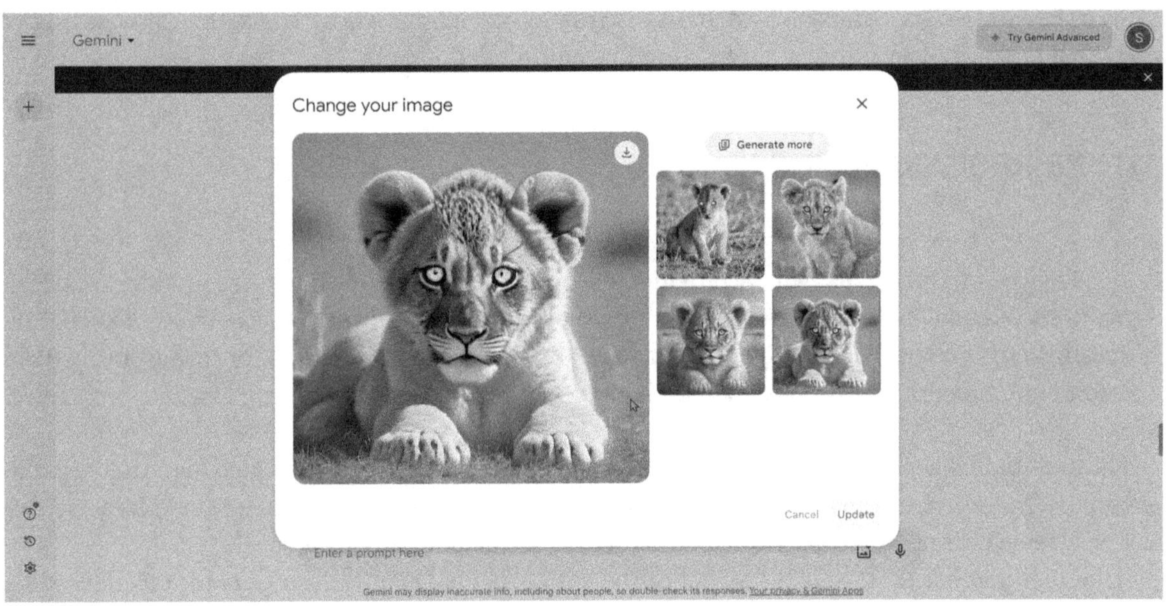

None of the works seemed to output hallucinations or faked data or faked citations (there were no citations). There were not any verbatim regurgitations or "memory" glitches in the multimodal genre-based outputs.

Discussion

Impression-wise, the prompted works read as enervated, diluted. The machine patterns seem draw a little from here and a little from there without full potency.

It is unclear as to how the multimodal models could computationally create works that align with the conventions of the desired forms and also offer more informative and profound contents…that are aligned with human needs…perhaps aligned to user profiles and preferences. The author's preferences for escalatory ladders involve data, analytical depth, insight, and cautionary warnings. The author would prefer slideshows that are well researched and long (80 – 100 slides) and with unique aesthetic looks-and-feels. Her preferences for children's stories involve cleverness, memorable characters, plot twists, and perhaps a moral bent.

It is widely noted that the training models often use Internet-scraped data, some of which is copyrighted. Perhaps one way to raise quality is to bring in purchased rights-released but copyrighted content for training data. Perhaps more humans may be brought in to provide feedback to the various models. Perhaps fine-tuning may more positively influence the outputs.

Currently, the informational contents created by generative AI cannot be copyrighted since there is not a human author. If a person co-edits with the support of the multimodal generative AI, the copyright issue would change, in all likelihood.

Multimodal generative AIs have a long way to go to output complex works in genre-forms and with complex contents if this limited study is valid. The brainstormed list of genres gives a sense of the author's outsized expectations of possibilities. Those works will have to be explored as the technologies advance.

As to how this work compares to and differs from other similar works, the author did not find other works that conducted any similar exploration for multimodal outputs.

FUTURE RESEARCH DIRECTIONS

This is an early work which provides an original list of questions that may be asked about multimodal contents (genre form + focal topic) created by a multimodal generative AI. That list of questions may be further developed, with some scoring measures applied for further formalization. Additional dimensions may be added to the tool.

The tool studied here is Google's Gemini, but there are other similar tools which may also be explored for outputs. In a sense, this involves some interrelated examples and cases, but deeper exploratory studies may be achieved through computational means (not the manual ones used here).

[One tool that has long been a favorite of the author is the Deep Dream Generator (released to the public in 2015) (DeepDream, Dec. 22, 2023). One of the models within the tool—AIVision-- can output pseudo-coherent text in mostly recognizable ways, but there is still a struggle. The prompt—with the text within quotation marks—only sometimes works. Sometimes, the model puts out garble. As to how the tool works in terms of the innards, that is not easily available information.]

This work has provided some early and limited insights on how humans: machine may complement the other. More work in this area would be potentially beneficial. How do people use the multimodal GAI? Is it to relieve the tedium from creating from scratch? Is it about generating ideas that hadn't already been thought of? Is it for refining an existing document that was manually created? What sorts of editing and revision and other "post-production" benefit the users of the multimodal GAI?

More formal articulations of standards for the respective genres of professional forms and documents would also be positive. That standard was not fully defined here.

Another angle can be perhaps more detailed and in-depth prompts, to emerge with more detailed suitable multimodal outputs.

CONCLUSION

How a machine creates a multimodal image differs from how humans do. One research team writes:

> Humans are naturally capable of imaging a scene according to a piece of visual, text or audio description. However, the intuitive processes are less straightforward for deep neural networks, primarily due to an inherent modality gap. This *modality gap* for visual perception can be boiled down to *intra-modal gap* between visual clues and real images, and *cross-modal gap* between non-visual clues and real images. (Zhan, Yu, Wu, Zhang, Lu, Liu,... & Xing, 2023, n.p.)

Researchers have been learning how various deep neural networks correlate multimodal information with image attributes (Zhan, Yu, Wu, Zhang, Lu, Liu,... & Xing, 2023, n.p.).

The Generative AI paradox suggests that what generative AI can create, "it may not understand." The technology's generation of contents is mechanistic on the one hand, a kind of regurgitating based on deep training from masses of data. The hypothesis of the paradox goes like this:

> ...generative models, having been trained directly to reproduce expert-like outputs, acquire generative capabilities that are not contingent upon—and can therefore exceed—their ability to understand those same types of outputs. This contrasts with humans, for whom basic understanding almost always precedes the ability to generate expert-level outputs, (West, Lu, Dziri, Brahman, Li, Hwang,... & Choi, Oct. 2023, p. 1)

An empirical study found evidence to support this hypothesis, so suggesting "caution in interpreting artificial intelligence by analogy to human intelligence" (West, Lu, Dziri, Brahman, Li, Hwang,... & Choi, Oct. 2023, p. 1). Their research results show "that although models can outperform humans in generation, they consistently fall short of human capabilities in measures of understanding, showing weaker correlation between generation and understanding performance, and more brittleness to adversarial inputs" (West, Lu, Dziri, Brahman, Li, Hwang,... & Choi, Oct. 2023, p. 1). The generative AI tools "fall short of human performance in discriminative versions of generative tasks, and when answering questions about generated content" (West, Lu, Dziri, Brahman, Li, Hwang,... & Choi, Oct. 2023, p. 8). GAI makes errors that people would not generally make, leading people to suggest that such systems require "common sense," some baseline sense of reality, so that they can function across a range of practical tasks. The presence of "strong imagination" (Fei, Lu, Gao, Yang, Huo, Wen, J., ... & Wen, 2021, p. 1) is also desirable, so that the tool may offer original solutions.

REFERENCES

Antony, V. N., & Huang, C. M. (2023). ID. 8: Co-Creating visual stories with Generative AI. *arXiv Preprint arXiv:2309.14228.*

Baltrušaitis, T., Ahuja, C., & Morency, L. P. (2018). Multimodal machine learning: A survey and taxonomy. *IEEE Transactions on Pattern Analysis and Machine Intelligence*, 41(2), 423–443. 10.1109/TPAMI.2018.279860729994351

Bell, G., Burgess, J., Thomas, J., & Shadiq, S. (2023). *Rapid Response Information Report: Generative AI-language models (LLMs) and multimodal foundation models (MFMs).* Academic Press.

Bensaid, E., Martino, M., Hoover, B., & Strobelt, H. (2021). Fairytailor: A multimodal generative framework for storytelling. *arXiv Preprint arXiv:2108.04324.*

Bewersdorff, A., Hartmann, C., Hornberger, M., Seßler, K., Bannert, M., Kasneci, E., . . . Nerdel, C. (2024). Taking the next step with Generative Artificial Intelligence: The transformative role of multimodal Large Language Models in science education. *arXiv preprint arXiv:2401.00832.*

Bolojan, D., Vermisso, E., & Yousif, S. (2022). *Is language all we need? A query into architectural semantics using a multimodal generative workflow.* Academic Press.

Bueno, C. C., Chow, P. S., & Popowicz, A. (2023). *Not 'what', but 'where is creativity?': Towards a relational-materialist approach to generative AI.* Academic Press.

Cao, Y., Li, S., Liu, Y., Yan, Z., Dai, Y., Yu, P. S., & Sun, L. (2023). A comprehensive survey of ai-generated content (AIGC): A history of generative ai from GAN to ChatGPT. *arXiv preprint arXiv:2303.04226.*

Cetinic, E., & She, J. (2022). Understanding and creating art with AI: Review and outlook. *ACM Transactions on Multimedia Computing Communications and Applications*, 18(2), 1–22. 10.1145/3475799

Chen, W., Wang, W., Liu, L., & Lew, M. S. (2021). New ideas and trends in deep multimodal content understanding: A review. *Neurocomputing*, 426, 195–215. 10.1016/j.neucom.2020.10.042

Chen, Z., Zhang, X., Boedihardjo, A. P., Dai, J., & Lu, C. T. (2017). Multimodal storytelling via generative adversarial imitation learning. *arXiv Preprint arXiv:1712.01455.* 10.24963/ijcai.2017/554

Choi, D., Hong, S., Park, J., Chung, J. J. Y., & Kim, J. (2023). CreativeConnect: Supporting reference recombination for graphic design ideation with Generative AI. *arXiv preprint arXiv:2312.11949.*

Choi, S. K., & DiPaola, S. (2023). AI as other: An art-as-research approach to generative AI art practice. *Proceedings of the International Conference on Computational Creativity (ICCC).*

Corona, E., Zanfir, A., Bazavan, E. G., Kolotouros, N., Alldieck, T., & Sminchisescu, C. (2024). VLOGGER: Multimodal diffusion for embodied avatar synthesis. *arXiv Preprint arXiv:2403.08764.*

Croisdale, G. T., Chung, J. J. Y., Huang, E., Birchmeier, G., Wang, X., & Guo, A. (2023, October). DeckFlow: A Card Game Interface for Exploring Generative Model Flows. In *Adjunct Proceedings of the 36th Annual ACM Symposium on User Interface Software and Technology* (pp. 1-3). 10.1145/3586182.3615821

Dai, W., Hou, L., Shang, L., Jiang, X., Liu, Q., & Fung, P. (2022). Enabling multimodal generation on clip via vision-language knowledge distillation. *arXiv Preprint arXiv:2203.06386*. 10.18653/v1/2022.findings-acl.187

Dang, H., Brudy, F., Fitzmaurice, G., & Anderson, F. (2023, October). WorldSmith: Iterative and expressive prompting for world building with a Generative AI. In *Proceedings of the 36th Annual ACM Symposium on User Interface Software and Technology* (pp. 1-17). 10.1145/3586183.3606772

Daunhawer, I., Bizeul, A., Palumbo, E., Marx, A., & Vogt, J. E. (2023). Identifiability results for multimodal contrastive learning. *arXiv Preprint arXiv:2303.09166*.

Daunhawer, I., Sutter, T. M., Marcinkevičs, R., & Vogt, J. E. (2021). Self-supervised disentanglement of modality-specific and shared factors improves multimodal generative models. *Pattern Recognition: 42nd DAGM German Conference, DAGM GCPR 2020, Tübingen, Germany, September 28–October 1, 2020Proceedings*, 42, 459–473.

DeepDream. (2023, Dec. 22). *Wikipedia*. Retrieved May 7, 2024, from https://en.wikipedia.org/wiki/DeepDream

Dong, R., Han, C., Peng, Y., Qi, Z., Ge, Z., Yang, J., . . . Yi, L. (2023). DreamLLM: Synergistic multimodal comprehension and creation. *arXiv Preprint arXiv:2309.11499*.

Eichenberg, C., Black, S., Weinbach, S., Parcalabescu, L., & Frank, A. (2021). MAGMA—Multimodal Augmentation of Generative Models through Adapter-based finetuning. *arXiv Preprint arXiv:2112.05253*.

El-Zanfaly, D., Huang, Y., & Dong, Y. (2023, July). Sand-in-the-loop: Investigating embodied co-creation for shared understandings of generative AI. In *Companion Publication of the 2023 ACM Designing Interactive Systems Conference* (pp. 256-260). ACM.

Elezabi, H., & Sharaf, A. (2023). Visual understanding of academic diagrams using multimodal generative models. *Proceedings of the 37th Conference on Neural Information Processing Systems (NeurIPS 2023)*, 1 – 8.

Epstein, Z., Schroeder, H., & Newman, D. (2022). When happy accidents spark creativity: Bringing collaborative speculation to life with generative AI. *arXiv Preprint arXiv:2206.00533*.

Fei, N., Lu, Z., Gao, Y., Yang, G., Huo, Y., Wen, J., ... Wen, J. R. (2021). *Wenlan 2.0: Make ai imagine via a multimodal foundation model*. arXiv.

Feuerriegel, S., Hartmann, J., Janiesch, C., & Zschech, P. (2024). Generative ai. *Business & Information Systems Engineering*, 66(1), 111–126. 10.1007/s12599-023-00834-7

Fezari, M., Al-Dahoud, A., & Al-Dahoud, A. (2023). *Augmanting (sic) reality: The power of Generative AI*. University Badji Mokhtar Annaba.

Gao, J., Li, P., Chen, Z., & Zhang, J. (2020). A survey on deep learning for multimodal data fusion. *Neural Computation*, 32(5), 829–864. 10.1162/neco_a_0127332186998

García-Peñalvo, F., & Vázquez-Ingelmo, A. (2023). *What do we mean by GenAI? A systematic mapping of the evolution, trends, and techniques involved in Generative AI*. Academic Press.

Gozalo-Brizuela, R., & Garrido-Merchán, E. C. (2023). A survey of Generative AI applications. *arXiv Preprint arXiv:2306.02781.*

Guo, W., Wang, J., & Wang, S. (2019). Deep multimodal representation learning: A survey. *IEEE Access : Practical Innovations, Open Solutions*, 7, 63373–63394. 10.1109/ACCESS.2019.2916887

Huang, J., Zhang, Z., Zheng, S., Qin, F., & Wang, Y. (2024). *DISTMM: Accelerating distributed multimodal model training*. Academic Press.

Huang, S., He, C., & Cheng, R. (2022). SoloGAN: Multi-domain multimodal unpaired image-to-image translation via a single generative adversarial network. *IEEE Transactions on Artificial Intelligence*, 3(5), 722–737. 10.1109/TAI.2022.3187384

Iijima, L., & Stathaki, T. (2024). A multimodal approach for cross-domain image retrieval. *arXiv Preprint arXiv:2403.15152.*

Juhász, L., Mooney, P., & Hochmair, H. H. (2023). *ChatGPT as a mapping assistant: A novel method to enrich maps with generative AI and content derived from street-level photographs*. Academic Press.

Koh, J. Y., Fried, D., & Salakhutdinov, R. R. (2024). Generating images with multimodal language models. *Advances in Neural Information Processing Systems*, 36.

Lee, G. G., Shi, L., Latif, E., Gao, Y., Bewersdorf, A., Nyaaba, M., . . . Zhai, X. (2023). Multimodality of ai for education: Towards artificial general intelligence. *arXiv Preprint arXiv:2312.06037.*

Li, C., Gan, Z., Yang, Z., Yang, J., Li, L., Wang, L., & Gao, J. (2023). Multimodal foundation models: From specialists to general-purpose assistants. *arXiv Preprint arXiv:2309.10020, 1*(2), 2.

Liang, P. P., Zadeh, A., & Morency, L. P. (2022). Foundations and trends in multimodal machine learning: Principles, challenges, and open questions. *arXiv Preprint arXiv:2209.03430.*

Lin, D., Jing, L., Song, X., Liu, M., Sun, T., & Nie, L. (2023, July). Adapting generative pretrained language model for open-domain multimodal sentence summarization. In *Proceedings of the 46th International ACM SIGIR Conference on Research and Development in Information Retrieval* (pp. 195-204). 10.1145/3539618.3591633

Lykov, A., Konenkov, M., Gbagbe, K. F., Litvinov, M., Peter, R., Davletshin, D., . . . Tsetserukou, D. (2024). CognitiveOS: Large Multimodal Model based System to Endow Any Type of Robot with Generative AI. *arXiv preprint arXiv:2401.16205.*

Mahajan, S. (2022). *Multimodal representation Learning for diverse synthesis with deep generative models*. Academic Press.

Mandal, A., Leavy, S., & Little, S. (2023). Multimodal composite association score: Measuring gender bias in generative multimodal models. *arXiv Preprint arXiv:2304.13855.*

McIntosh, T. R., Susnjak, T., Liu, T., Watters, P., & Halgamuge, M. N. (2023). From Google Gemini to OpenAI q*(q-star): A survey of reshaping the generative artificial intelligence (AI) research landscape. *arXiv Preprint arXiv:2312.10868.*

Molenaar, I., de Mooij, S., Azevedo, R., Bannert, M., Järvelä, S., & Gašević, D. (2023). Measuring self-regulated learning and the role of AI: Five years of research using multimodal multichannel data. *Computers in Human Behavior*, 139, 107540. 10.1016/j.chb.2022.107540

Muller, M., Weisz, J. D., & Geyer, W. (2020). Mixed initiative generative AI interfaces: An analytic framework for generative AI applications. *Proceedings of the Workshop The Future of Co-Creative Systems-A Workshop on Human-Computer Co-Creativity of the 11th International Conference on Computational Creativity (ICCC 2020).*

Ohkawa, T., Yoshiura, H., & Yamaguchi, T. (2023, October). Explainable multimodal fake posts detection using feature extraction with attention mechanisms. In *2023 IEEE 23rd International Conference on Software Quality, Reliability, and Security Companion (QRS-C)* (pp. 555-563). IEEE. 10.1109/QRS-C60940.2023.00068

Ossowski, T., & Hu, J. (2023). Multimodal prompt retrieval for generative visual question answering. *arXiv Preprint arXiv:2306.17675.*

Palumbo, E., Daunhawer, I., & Vogt, J. E. (2023). MMVAE+: Enhancing the generative quality of multimodal VAEs without compromises. In *The Eleventh International Conference on Learning Representations*. OpenReview.

Pandey, G., & Dukkipati, A. (2017, May). Variational methods for conditional multimodal deep learning. In *2017 International Joint Conference on Neural Networks (IJCNN)* (pp. 308-315). IEEE. 10.1109/IJCNN.2017.7965870

Park, D. K., Yoo, S., Bahng, H., Choo, J., & Park, N. (2018). MEGAN: Mixture of experts of generative adversarial networks for multimodal image generation. *arXiv Preprint arXiv:1805.02481*. 10.24963/ijcai.2018/122

Qiao, H., Liu, V., & Chilton, L. (2022, June). Initial images: using image prompts to improve subject representation in multimodal AI generated art. In *Proceedings of the 14th Conference on Creativity and Cognition* (pp. 15-28). 10.1145/3527927.3532792

Qu, Y., Nathaniel, J., Li, S., & Gentine, P. (2024). Deep generative data assimilation in multimodal setting. *arXiv preprint arXiv:2404.06665.*

Sahu, G., & Vechtomova, O. (2019). Adaptive fusion techniques for multimodal data. *arXiv preprint arXiv:1911.03821.*

Sakirin, T., & Kusuma, S. (2023). A survey of Generative Artificial Intelligence techniques. *Babylonian Journal of Artificial Intelligence*, 2023, 10–14. 10.58496/BJAI/2023/003

Shi, Y., Paige, B., & Torr, P. (2019). Variational mixture-of-experts autoencoders for multi-modal deep generative models. *Advances in Neural Information Processing Systems*, 32.

Shi, Y., Paige, B., Torr, P. H., & Siddharth, N. (2020). Relating by contrasting: A data-efficient framework for multimodal generative models. *arXiv Preprint arXiv:2007.01179.*

Sun, Q., Yu, Q., Cui, Y., Zhang, F., Zhang, X., Wang, Y., & Wang, X. (2023, October). Emu: Generative Pretraining in Multimodality. *The Twelfth International Conference on Learning Representations.*

Sun, Q., Yu, Q., Cui, Y., Zhang, F., Zhang, X., Wang, Y., . . . Wang, X. (2023). Generative pretraining in multimodality. *arXiv Preprint arXiv:2307.05222.*

Sundar, A., & Heck, L. (2022). Multimodal conversational ai: A survey of datasets and approaches. *arXiv preprint arXiv:2205.06907.* 10.18653/v1/2022.nlp4convai-1.12

Sutter, T., Daunhawer, I., & Vogt, J. (2020). Multimodal generative learning utilizing Jensen-Shannon-Divergence. *Advances in Neural Information Processing Systems*, 33, 6100–6110.

Suzuki, M., & Matsuo, Y. (2022). A survey of multimodal deep generative models. *Advanced Robotics*, 36(5-6), 261–278. 10.1080/01691864.2022.2035253

Suzuki, M., Nakayama, K., & Matsuo, Y. (2016). Joint multimodal learning with deep generative models. *arXiv Preprint arXiv:1611.01891.*

Tan, X., Xu, W., & Wang, C. (2024). Purposeful remixing with generative AI: Constructing designer voice in multimodal composing. *arXiv Preprint arXiv:2403.19095.*

Thomas, S., Taylor, M., Anderson, B., & Jackson, E. (n.d.). *The evolution and impact of Generative AI: From early models to advanced AIGC technologies*. Academic Press.

Togo, R., Kotera, M., Ogawa, T., & Haseyama, M. (2021). Text-guided style transfer-based image manipulation using multimodal generative models. *IEEE Access : Practical Innovations, Open Solutions*, 9, 64860–64870. 10.1109/ACCESS.2021.3069876

Usmani, S., Siddiqui, Y. A., Hamza, M., Shaikh, M. T., & Hasan, Q. (n.d.). *Exploring the landscape of multimodal generative adversarial networks: A comprehensive survey and analysis*. Academic Press.

Weidinger, L., Rauh, M., Marchal, N., Manzini, A., Hendricks, L. A., Mateos-Garcia, J., . . . Isaac, W. (2023). Sociotechnical safety evaluation of generative ai systems. *arXiv Preprint arXiv:2310.11986.*

West, P., Lu, X., Dziri, N., Brahman, F., Li, L., Hwang, J. D., & Choi, Y. (2023, October). The Generative AI paradox: "What it can create, it may not understand". *The Twelfth International Conference on Learning Representations.*

Wu, X., Huang, S., & Wei, F. (2024). Multimodal large language model is a human-aligned annotator for text-to-image generation. *arXiv Preprint arXiv:2404.15100.*

Xu, M., Niyato, D., Kang, J., Xiong, Z., Jamalipour, A., Fang, Y., & Kim, D. I. (2024). Integration of Mixture of Experts and Multimodal Generative AI in Internet of Vehicles: A Survey. *arXiv preprint arXiv:2404.16356.*

Xu, X., Wang, Z., Zhang, G., Wang, K., & Shi, H. (2023). Versatile diffusion: Text, images and variations all in one diffusion model. In *Proceedings of the IEEE/CVF International Conference on Computer Vision* (pp. 7754-7765). 10.1109/ICCV51070.2023.00713

Yan, Z., Yang, C., Liang, Q., & Chen, X. A. (2023, October). XCreation: A graph-based crossmodal generative creativity support tool. In *Proceedings of the 36th Annual ACM Symposium on User Interface Software and Technology* (pp. 1-15). 10.1145/3586183.3606826

Yang, X., Feng, S., Wang, D., Qi, S., Wu, W., Zhang, Y., . . . Poria, S. (2023). Few-shot joint multimodal aspect-sentiment analysis based on generative multimodal prompt. *arXiv Preprint arXiv:2305.10169*. 10.18653/v1/2023.findings-acl.735

Yu, T., Dai, W., Liu, Z., & Fung, P. (2021). Vision guided generative pre-trained language models for multimodal abstractive summarization. *arXiv Preprint arXiv:2109.02401*. 10.18653/v1/2021.emnlp-main.326

Zhan, F., Yu, Y., Wu, R., Zhang, J., Lu, S., Liu, L., Kortylewski, A., Theobalt, C., & Xing, E. (2023). Multimodal image synthesis and editing: A survey and taxonomy. *IEEE Transactions on Pattern Analysis and Machine Intelligence*, 45(12), 15098–15119. 10.1109/TPAMI.2023.3305243

Zhan, F., Yu, Y., Wu, R., Zhang, J., Lu, S., Liu, L., . . . Xing, E. (2022). Multimodal image synthesis and editing: A survey. *arXiv Preprint arXiv:2112.13592*.

Zhang, C., Yang, Z., He, X., & Deng, L. (2020). Multimodal intelligence: Representation learning, information fusion, and applications. *IEEE Journal of Selected Topics in Signal Processing*, 14(3), 478–493. 10.1109/JSTSP.2020.2987728

Zhang, C., Zhang, C., Zhang, M., & Kweon, I. S. (2023). Text-to-image diffusion model in generative ai: A survey. *arXiv preprint arXiv:2303.07909*.

Zhang, C., Zhang, C., Zheng, S., Qiao, Y., Li, C., Zhang, M., . . . Hong, C. S. (2023). A complete survey on generative AI (AIGC): Is ChatGPT from GPT-4 to GPT-5 all you need? *arXiv Preprint arXiv:2303.11717*.

Zhao, R., Chen, H., Wang, W., Jiao, F., Do, X. L., Qin, C., . . . Joty, S. (2023). Retrieving multimodal information for augmented generation: A survey. *arXiv Preprint arXiv:2303.10868*. 10.18653/v1/2023.findings-emnlp.314

Zhu, J. Y., Zhang, R., Pathak, D., Darrell, T., Efros, A. A., Wang, O., & Shechtman, E. (2017). Toward multimodal image-to-image translation. *Advances in Neural Information Processing Systems*, 30.

ADDITIONAL READING

Hai-Jew, S. (2024a). *Generative AI in Teaching and Learning*. IGI Global. https://www.igi-global.com/book/generative-teaching-learning/321130

Hai-Jew, S. (2024b). *Making Art with Generative AI Tools*. IGI Global. 10.4018/979-8-3693-1950-5

KEY TERMS AND DEFINITIONS

Generative AI: Computational tools that can create (or autogenerate) digital contents in various modalities based on text and / or image and other prompts by human users [based on large language models and deep learning from a large dataset of examples].

Multimodal: Consisting of several digital content modalities (text, still image, video, audio, and others, in various combinations).

Conclusion

There have been published estimates that half of the U.S. population has already used generative AI (Pandya, 2024). For all the hyperbole of artmaking generative AI (A-GAI) and generative AI (GAI), in general, the technologies are in use for human effort, learning, striving, peer entertainment, self-expression, and finances. To engage in digital arts and digital crafts, it takes years to fully acquire a basic skill set. Those who want to develop skills involving analog and physical materials and machining tools have even longer to train, to serve as apprentice.

This book includes various works that examine modern computation as a tool for digital art and digital crafting. There are examples of using computation to analyze historic artworks. There are enriched ways to consider ethical considerations, too.

These work capture some of the early senses of potential in terms of *Computational Practices and Applications for Digital Art and Crafting*. There is so much more to come.

REFERENCES

Pandya, V. (2024, Apr. 22). *The age of generative AI: Over half of Americans have used generative AI and most believe it will help them be more creative*. Adobe Blog.

Compilation of References

Abraham, A. (2020). Surveying the imagination landscape. *The Cambridge Handbook of the Imagination*, 1-10.

Abraham, A. (2018). The wandering mind: Where imagination meets consciousness. *Journal of Consciousness Studies*, 25(11-12), 34–52.

Adar, M. (2021). *Dijital Sanat Formlarına Yönelik Bir İnceleme* (Yayımlanmamış Yüksek lisans tezi), Kocaeli Üniversitesi, Sosyal Bilimler Enstitüsü: Kocaeli.

Agarwal, S., Farid, H., El-Gaaly, T., & Lim, S. N. (2020, December). Detecting deep-fake videos from appearance and behavior. In *2020 IEEE International Workshop on Information Forensics and Security (WIFS)* (pp. 1-6). IEEE. 10.1109/WIFS49906.2020.9360904

Ahn, I. J., & Noh, Y. (2018). A study and survey of the perception towards makerspaces of the public library. *International Journal of Knowledge Content Development & Technology*, 8(2), 5–22.

Airenti, G. (2018). The development of anthropomorphism in interaction: Intersubjectivity, imagination, and theory of mind. *Frontiers in Psychology*, 9, 2136. 10.3389/fpsyg.2018.0213630455662

Aiyeblehin, J. A., Onyam, I. D., & Akpom, C. C. (2018). Creating makerspaces in Nigerian public libraries as a strategy for attaining national integration and development. *International Journal of Knowledge Content Development & Technology*, 8(4).

Alemán, M. W., Tomko, M. E., Linsey, J. S., & Nagel, R. L. (2022). How do you play that makerspace game? An ethnographic exploration of the habitus of engineering makerspaces. *Research in Engineering Design*, 33(4), 351–366. 10.1007/s00163-022-00393-035974995

Alexander, T. M. (1990). Pragmatic imagination. *Transactions of the Charles S.Peirce Society*, 26(3), 325–348.

Ali, S., DiPaola, D., Williams, R., Ravi, P., & Breazeal, C. (2023). Constructing dreams using generative AI. *arXiv Preprint arXiv:2305.12013*.

Alía, C., Ocaña, R., Caja, J., Maresca, P., Moreno-Díaz, C., & Narbón, J. J. (2019). Use of open manufacturing laboratories (Fab Labs) as a new trend in engineering education. *Procedia Manufacturing*, 41, 938–943. 10.1016/j.promfg.2019.10.018

Ali, S., DiPaola, D., Lee, I., Hong, J., & Breazeal, C. (2021, May). Exploring generative models with middle school students. In *Proceedings of the 2021 CHI Conference on Human Factors in Computing Systems* (pp. 1-13). 10.1145/3411764.3445226

Ali, S., DiPaola, D., Lee, I., Sindato, V., Kim, G., Blumofe, R., & Breazeal, C. (2021). Children as creators, thinkers and citizens in an AI-driven future. *Computers and Education: Artificial Intelligence*, 2, 100040. 10.1016/j.caeai.2021.100040

Al-Khazraji, L. R., Abbas, A. R., & Jamil, A. S. (2022). Employing neural style transfer for generating deep dream images. *ARO (Koya)*, 10(2), 134–141. 10.14500/aro.11051

Al-Khazraji, L. R., Abbas, A. R., & Jamil, A. S. (2023). A systematic review of Deep Dream. *Iraqi Journal of Computers, Communications. Control and Systems Engineering*, 23(2), 192–209.

Al-Khazraji, L. R., Abbas, A. R., & Jamil, A. S. (2023). The effect of changing targeted layers of the Deep Dream technique using VGG-16 Model. *International Journal of Online & Biomedical Engineering*, 19(3), 34–47. 10.3991/ijoe.v19i03.37235

Anadol, R. (2018). *Melting Memories*. https://refikanadol.com/works/melting-memories/

Anadol, R. (2013). http://refikanadol.com/about

Anderson, J. L. (2021). *Digital Fabrication in Interior Design: Body, Object, Enclosure*. Taylor & Francis. 10.4324/9781003025931

Andrews, C. (2017). Learning and teaching in library makerspaces: A literature review on making literacies. *International Symposium on Academic Makerspaces (ISAM).*

Andrews, D., & Roberts, D. (2017, August). Academic makerspaces: Contexts for research on interdisciplinary collaborative communication. In *Proceedings of the 35th ACM International Conference on the Design of Communication* (pp. 1-7). 10.1145/3121113.3121230

Andrews, M. E., & Boklage, A. (2023). Supporting inclusivity in STEM makerspaces through critical theory: A systematic review. *Journal of Engineering Education*, jee.20546. 10.1002/jee.20546

Antony, V. N., & Huang, C. M. (2023). ID. 8: Co-Creating visual stories with Generative AI. *arXiv Preprint arXiv:2309.14228.*

Arpaly, N. (2020). What is it like to have a crappy imagination? In *Becoming Someone New: Essays on Transformative Experience, Choice, and Change* (pp. 122-132). Oxford University Press. 10.1093/oso/9780198823735.003.0007

Arshed, M. A., Mumtaz, S., Ibrahim, M., Dewi, C., Tanveer, M., & Ahmed, S. (2024). Multiclass AI-generated deepfake face detection using patch-wise deep learning model. *Computers*, 13(1), 31. 10.3390/computers13010031

Athos Bulcão 3D Experiment - Estação Transbordo da Lapa - TinkerCad. (n.d.). Retrieved February 23, 2024, https://www.tinkercad.com/codeblocks/gn8I6cQ6VEg-athos-bulcao-3d-experiment?sharecode=b0J_9YtAulSy7xUmPpGJtCizGeM5IAlullLlEDfqBBo

Athos Bulcão 3D Experiment - Sambódromo - TinkerCad. (n.d.). Retrieved February 24, 2024, from https://www.tinkercad.com/codeblocks/l1a65wx51EC-athos-bulcao-3d-experiment-sambodramo?sharecode=prK4QCH76bvQuQYr5Om_hi0-0Cuy_HS4zzs1UtdMJqM

Avcı, E. (2015). integration of digital technologies into fine arts education in the context of digital art. *Journal of International Social Research*, 8(41).

Azmoodeh, A., & Dehghantanha, A. (2022). Deep fake detection, deterrence and response: Challenges and opportunities. *arXiv Preprint arXiv:2211.14667.*

Baltrušaitis, T., Ahuja, C., & Morency, L. P. (2018). Multimodal machine learning: A survey and taxonomy. *IEEE Transactions on Pattern Analysis and Machine Intelligence*, 41(2), 423–443. 10.1109/TPAMI.2018.279860729994351

Baluja, S., & Fischer, I. (2017). Adversarial transformation networks: Learning to generate adversarial examples. *arXiv preprint arXiv:1703.09387.*

Banerjee, R., Ferron, L. M., Bailey, D., Imam, R., & Jariwala, A. S. (2020). IoT in Makerspaces-Review of usage and future potential. *Proceedings of the 4th International Symposium on Academic Makerspaces.*

Barber, B. R. (1978). Rousseau and the paradoxes of the dramatic imagination. *Daedalus*, 79–92.

Baron-Cohen, S. (2007). The biology of the imagination. *Human Nature (Hawthorne, N.Y.)*, 103–110.

Bartz-Beielstein, T. (2019). Why we need an AI-resilient society. *arXiv Preprint arXiv:1912.08786.*

Bauer, L. A., & Bindschaedler, V. (2021). Generative models for security: Attacks, defenses, and opportunities. *arXiv Preprint arXiv:2107.10139.*

Beavers, K., Cady, J. E., Jiang, A., & McCoy, L. (2019). Establishing a maker culture beyond the makerspace. *Library Hi Tech*, 37(2), 215–228. 10.1108/LHT-07-2018-0088

Beerbaum, D. (2023). Generative Artificial Intelligence (GAI) software–assessment on biased behavior. *SSRN*, 4386395, 1–18. 10.2139/ssrn.4386395

Bell, G., Burgess, J., Thomas, J., & Shadiq, S. (2023). *Rapid Response Information Report: Generative AI-language models (LLMs) and multimodal foundation models (MFMs).* Academic Press.

Bengesi, S., El-Sayed, H., Sarker, M. K., Houkpati, Y., Irungu, J., & Oladunni, T. (2023). Advancements in Generative AI: A comprehensive review of GANs, GPT, autoencoders, diffusion model, and transformers. *arXiv Preprint arXiv:2311.10242.*

Bengü, E., & Keçeci, E. F. (2021). Makerspace: Innovation in mechanical engineering education. *Yükseköğretim ve Bilim Dergisi*, 11(1), 207–213.

Benjes-Small, C., Bellamy, L. M., Resor-Whicker, J., & Vassady, L. (2017). *Makerspace or waste of space: Charting a course for successful academic library makerspaces*. Academic Press.

Bensaid, E., Martino, M., Hoover, B., & Strobelt, H. (2021). Fairytailor: A multimodal generative framework for storytelling. *arXiv Preprint arXiv:2108.04324.*

Benton, C., Dempsey, T., Mullins, L., & Shelley, K. (2013). *Makerspaces: Supporting an entrepreneurial system.* 2013 Co-Learning Plan Series, University Outreach and Engagement, Michigan State University.

Bergamo, M. L. (2024), *Coding Examples Athos Bulcão Experiments*. Retrieved July 16, 2024. https://editor.p5js.org/marilialb.mb/collections/ftTi58JNX

Bers, M. U., Strawhacker, A., & Vizner, M. (2018). The design of early childhood makerspaces to support positive technological development: Two case studies. *Library Hi Tech*, 36(1), 75–96. 10.1108/LHT-06-2017-0112

Bewersdorff, A., Hartmann, C., Hornberger, M., Seßler, K., Bannert, M., Kasneci, E., . . . Nerdel, C. (2024). Taking the next step with Generative Artificial Intelligence: The transformative role of multimodal Large Language Models in science education. *arXiv preprint arXiv:2401.00832.*

Bharadiya, J. P. (2024). Deep fake and image manipulation. *International Journal of Intelligent Systems and Applications in Engineering*, 12(14s), 468–472.

Black, J. (2002). Topsy-turvy teacher-student relationships: An examination of digital multimedia teaching and learning. *Dissertation Abstracts International*, 63, 6.

Blikstein, P. (2018). Maker movement in education: History and prospects. *Handbook of technology education, 419*, 437.

Blikstein, P., Kabayadondo, Z., Martin, A., & Fields, D. (2017). An assessment instrument of technological literacies in makerspaces and FabLabs. *Journal of Engineering Education*, 106(1), 149–175. 10.1002/jee.20156

Blikstein, P., & Krannich, D. (2013, June). The makers' movement and FabLabs in education: experiences, technologies, and research. In *Proceedings of the 12th International Conference on Interaction Design and Children* (pp. 613-616). 10.1145/2485760.2485884

Bloch, M. (2016). Imagination from the outside and from the inside. *Current Anthropology*, 57(S13), S80–S87. 10.1086/685496

Boccardi, A., Szucs, K. A., Ebuenyi, I. D., & Mhatre, A. (2022). Assistive Technology Makerspaces Promote Capability of Adults with Intellectual and Developmental Disabilities. *Societies, 12*(6), 155, 1 - 19.

Bohacek, M., & Farid, H. (2024). The making of an AI news anchor—and its implications. *Proceedings of the National Academy of Sciences, 121*(1), 1 - 3.

Bolojan, D., Vermisso, E., & Yousif, S. (2022). *Is language all we need? A query into architectural semantics using a multimodal generative workflow*. Academic Press.

Botha, J., & Pieterse, H. (2020, March). Fake news and deepfakes: A dangerous threat for 21st century information security. In *ICCWS 2020 15th International Conference on Cyber Warfare and Security*. Academic Conferences and Publishing Limited.

Boudreau, J. B., & Anis, H. (2019). The role of makerspaces in inclusivity in engineering. *Proceedings of the Canadian Engineering Education Association (CEEA)*. 10.24908/pceea.vi0.13749

Brahimi, T., Khalifa, S., & Benaouda, B. (2019). Integrating makerspaces in higher education: Constructionism approach to learning. In *Research & Innovation Forum 2019: Technology, Innovation, Education, and their Social Impact 1* (pp. 65–73). Springer International Publishing. 10.1007/978-3-030-30809-4_7

Brito, H. F., Hölsä, J., Laamanen, T., Lastusaari, M., Malkamäki, M., & Rodrigues, L. C. (2012). Persistent luminescence mechanisms: Human imagination at work. *Optical Materials Express*, 2(4), 371–381. 10.1364/OME.2.000371

Brockmeier, J. (2009). Reaching for meaning: Human agency and the narrative imagination. *Theory & Psychology*, 19(2), 213–233. 10.1177/0959354309103540

Bronowski, J. (1967). The reach of imagination. *The American Scholar*, 193–201.

Browning, K. (2008). Kathy Browning's digital photographyprofiled. In F. Blaikie (Ed.), *Canadian art/works: A resource for primary, junior, intermediate, and senior teachers* (pp. 38-40; 127-131).Victoria BC: Canadian Society for Education Through Art.

Browning, K. (2006). Digital applications in elementary visual arts: A case study in Ontario and Newfoundland schools. *Canadian Review of Art Education*, 33(1), 25–41.

Bruder, J. (2018). Where the sun never shines: Emerging paradigms of post-enlightened cognition. *Digital Culture & Society*, 4(1), 133–154. 10.14361/dcs-2018-0109

Bueno, C. C., Chow, P. S., & Popowicz, A. (2023). *Not 'what', but 'where is creativity?': Towards a relational-materialist approach to generative AI*. Academic Press.

Bull, G., Rutter, J., Garofalo, J., & Littman, M. (2022). *Maker education: A historical perspective*. Academic Press.

Burke, J. (2015). *Making sense: Can Makerspaces work in academic libraries?* Academic Press.

Byrne, R. M. (2007). Precis of the rational imagination: How people create alternatives to reality. *Behavioral and Brain Sciences*, 30(5-6), 439–453. 10.1017/S0140525X0700257918321404

Caeli, K., Ray, L., & Mill, J. (2003). 'Clear as mud'. Toward greater clarity generic qualitative research. *International Journal of Qualitative Methods*, 2(2), 1–13. 10.1177/160940690300200201

Campbell, C., Plangger, K., Sands, S., & Kietzmann, J. (2022). Preparing for an era of deepfakes and AI-generated ads: A framework for understanding responses to manipulated advertising. *Journal of Advertising*, 51(1), 22–38. 10.1080/00913367.2021.1909515

Campbell, C., Plangger, K., Sands, S., Kietzmann, J., & Bates, K. (2023). How deepfakes and artificial intelligence could reshape the advertising industry: The coming reality of AI fakes and their potential impact on consumer behavior. *Journal of Advertising Research*, 57(1), 241–251.

Campos, F., Soster, T., & Blikstein, P. (2019). Sorry, I was in teacher mode today: Pivotal tensions and contradictory discourses in real-world implementations of school makerspaces. *Proceedings of FabLearn*, 2019, 96–103. 10.1145/3311890.3311903

Canbek, G., & Sağıroğlu, Ş. (2007). Computer and internet safety of children and young people. *Polytechnic Journal, 10*(1).

Cao, Y., Li, S., Liu, Y., Yan, Z., Dai, Y., Yu, P. S., & Sun, L. (2023). A comprehensive survey of ai-generated content (AIGC): A history of generative ai from GAN to ChatGPT. *arXiv preprint arXiv:2303.04226.*

Cao, Y., Li, S., Liu, Y., Yan, Z., Dai, Y., Yu, P. S., & Sun, L. (2023). A comprehensive survey of AI-Generated Content (AIGC): A history of generative AI from GAN to ChatGPT. *arXiv Preprint arXiv:2303.04226.*

Caporusso, N. (2021). Deepfakes for the good: A beneficial application of contentious artificial intelligence technology. In *Advances in Artificial Intelligence, Software and Systems Engineering:Proceedings of the AHFE 2020 Virtual Conferences on Software and Systems Engineering, and Artificial Intelligence and Social Computing,July 16-20, 2020,USA* (pp. 235-241). Springer International Publishing. 10.1007/978-3-030-51328-3_33

Carbonell, R. M., Boklage, A., Clayton, P., & Borrego, M. J. (2020, June). Making Improvements: Pedagogical Iterations of Designing a Class Project in a Maker Space. In *2020 ASEE Virtual Annual Conference Content Access.* 10.18260/1-2--34942

Carnasciali, M. I., Gillespie, S. M., & Hossain, A. M. (2021, October). Integrating Makerspaces into the Curriculum-Faculty Development Efforts. In *2021 IEEE Frontiers in Education Conference (FIE)* (pp. 1-7). IEEE. 10.1109/FIE49875.2021.9637230

Centro Cultural do Banco do Brasil. (n.d.). *100 anos de Athos Bulcão*. CCBB Brasília, Brasília, Distrito Federal, Brazil. Exhibition catalog Retrieved February 14, 2024, from https://ccbb.com.br/wp-content/uploads/2021/07/100AnosdeAthosBulcao.pdf

Cetinic, E., & She, J. (2022). Understanding and creating art with AI: Review and outlook. *ACM Transactions on Multimedia Computing Communications and Applications*, 18(2), 1–22. 10.1145/3475799

Chagi, S., & Campbell, C. (2021). *The creative spark, how imagination made humans exceptional, an analysis*. Academic Press.

Chatterjee, A. (2022). Art in an age of artificial intelligence. *Frontiers in Psychology, 13*, 1 - 9.

Chen, Z., Zhang, X., Boedihardjo, A. P., Dai, J., & Lu, C. T. (2017). Multimodal storytelling via generative adversarial imitation learning. *arXiv Preprint arXiv:1712.01455.* 10.24963/ijcai.2017/554

Chen, W., Shidujaman, M., Jin, J., & Ahmed, S. U. (2020). A methodological approach to create interactive art in artificial intelligence. *HCI International 2020–Late Breaking Papers: Cognition, Learning and Games: 22nd HCI International Conference, HCII 2020, Copenhagen, Denmark, July 19–24, 2020Proceedings*, 22, 13–31.

Chen, W., Wang, W., Liu, L., & Lew, M. S. (2021). New ideas and trends in deep multimodal content understanding: A review. *Neurocomputing*, 426, 195–215. 10.1016/j.neucom.2020.10.042

Cherti, M., Kégl, B., & Kazakçı, A. (2017, November). Out-of-class novelty generation: an experimental foundation. In *2017 IEEE 29th International Conference on Tools with Artificial Intelligence (ICTAI)* (pp. 1312-1319). IEEE.

Choi, D., Hong, S., Park, J., Chung, J. J. Y., & Kim, J. (2023). CreativeConnect: Supporting reference recombination for graphic design ideation with Generative AI. *arXiv preprint arXiv:2312.11949.*

Choi, S. K., & DiPaola, S. (2023). AI as other: An art-as-research approach to generative AI art practice. *Proceedings of the International Conference on Computational Creativity (ICCC).*

Choi, Y. H., Bouwma-Gearhart, J., Lenhart, C. A., Villanueva, I., & Nadelson, L. S. (2021). Student development at the boundaries: Makerspaces as affordances for engineering students' development. *Sustainability (Basel)*, 13(6), 3058. 10.3390/su13063058

Choi, Y., Lam, B., Chen, X., de Sousa, S., Liu, L., & Ni, M. (2022). Co-Design visions of public makerspaces in China. *International Journal of Design Creativity and Innovation*, 10(3), 179–192. 10.1080/21650349.2022.2048696

Ciftci, U. A., Demir, I., & Yin, L. (2020, September). How do the hearts of deep fakes beat? Deep fake source detection via interpreting residuals with biological signals. In *2020 IEEE International Joint Conference on Biometrics (IJCB)* (pp. 1-10). IEEE. 10.1109/IJCB48548.2020.9304909

Cobb, E. (1959). The ecology of imagination in childhood. *Daedalus*, 88(3), 537–548.

Cocchi, F., Baraldi, L., Poppi, S., Cornia, M., Baraldi, L., & Cucchiara, R. (2023, September). Unveiling the impact of image transformations on deepfake detection: An experimental analysis. In *International Conference on Image Analysis and Processing* (pp. 345-356). Cham: Springer Nature Switzerland. 10.1007/978-3-031-43153-1_29

Cohen, J., Jones, W. M., Smith, S., & Calandra, B. (2017). Makification: Towards a framework for leveraging the maker movement in formal education. *Journal of Educational Multimedia and Hypermedia*, 26(3), 217–229.

Colegrove, P. T. (2017). Makerspaces in libraries: technology as catalyst for better learning, better teaching. *Ingeniería solidaria, 13*(21), 19-26.

Colgan, R. T. (1965). Tickle their imagination. *Peabody Journal of Education*, 43(3), 138–144. 10.1080/01619566509537328

Comrie, A. E., Frank, L. M., & Kay, K. (2022). Imagination as a fundamental function of the hippocampus. *Philosophical Transactions of the Royal Society B, 377*(1866), 20210336.

Cooke, M. N., & Charnas, I. C. (2021). *The value of data, metrics, and impact for higher education Makerspaces. IJAMM, 1.*

Corona, E., Zanfir, A., Bazavan, E. G., Kolotouros, N., Alldieck, T., & Sminchisescu, C. (2024). VLOGGER: Multimodal diffusion for embodied avatar synthesis. *arXiv Preprint arXiv:2403.08764.*

Corsini, L., & Moultrie, J. (2020). Humanitarian makerspaces in crisis-affected communities. *Artificial Intelligence for Engineering Design, Analysis and Manufacturing*, 34(3), 374–386. 10.1017/S0890060420000098

Cozzolino, D., & Verdoliva, L. (2022). Multimedia forensics before the deep learning era. In *Handbook of Digital Face Manipulation and Detection: From DeepFakes to Morphing Attacks* (pp. 45–67). Springer International Publishing. 10.1007/978-3-030-87664-7_3

Croisdale, G. T., Chung, J. J. Y., Huang, E., Birchmeier, G., Wang, X., & Guo, A. (2023, October). DeckFlow: A Card Game Interface for Exploring Generative Model Flows. In *Adjunct Proceedings of the 36th Annual ACM Symposium on User Interface Software and Technology* (pp. 1-3). 10.1145/3586182.3615821

Culpepper, M. L. (2016, November). Types of academic Makerspaces, their import to the education mission, and the characteristics of their culture and community. In *Proceedings of the 1st International Symposium on Academic Makerspaces* (pp. 10-13). Academic Press.

Cun, A., Abramovich, S., & Smith, J. M. (2019). An assessment matrix for library makerspaces. *Library & Information Science Research*, 41(1), 39–47. 10.1016/j.lisr.2019.02.008

Curry, R. (2017). Makerspaces: A beneficial new service for academic libraries? *Library Review*, 66(4/5), 201–212. 10.1108/LR-09-2016-0081

da Silva, J. A. T. (2023). AI in the era of fakes and deepfakes: Risk of fabricated photographs and identities in academic publishing. *Journal of Information Security and Cybercrimes Research*, 6(2), 71–73. 10.26735/KNJA7076

Dack, S. (2019). *Deep fakes, fake news, and what comes next. The Henry M.* Jackson School of International Studies.

Dai, W., Hou, L., Shang, L., Jiang, X., Liu, Q., & Fung, P. (2022). Enabling multimodal generation on clip via vision-language knowledge distillation. *arXiv Preprint arXiv:2203.06386*. 10.18653/v1/2022.findings-acl.187

Dang, H., Brudy, F., Fitzmaurice, G., & Anderson, F. (2023, October). WorldSmith: Iterative and expressive prompting for world building with a Generative AI. In *Proceedings of the 36th Annual ACM Symposium on User Interface Software and Technology* (pp. 1-17). 10.1145/3586183.3606772

Daniels, S. (2011). Geographical imagination. *Transactions of the Institute of British Geographers*, 36(2), 182–187. 10.1111/j.1475-5661.2011.00440.x

Danry, V., Leong, J., Pataranutaporn, P., Tandon, P., Liu, Y., Shilkrot, R., & Sra, M. (2022, April). AI-generated characters: putting deepfakes to good use. In *CHI Conference on Human Factors in Computing Systems Extended Abstracts* (pp. 1-5). 10.1145/3491101.3503736

Daunhawer, I., Bizeul, A., Palumbo, E., Marx, A., & Vogt, J. E. (2023). Identifiability results for multimodal contrastive learning. *arXiv Preprint arXiv:2303.09166.*

Daunhawer, I., Sutter, T. M., Marcinkevičs, R., & Vogt, J. E. (2021). Self-supervised disentanglement of modality-specific and shared factors improves multimodal generative models. *Pattern Recognition: 42nd DAGM German Conference, DAGM GCPR 2020, Tübingen, Germany, September 28–October 1, 2020Proceedings*, 42, 459–473.

De Cruz, H., & De Smedt, J. (2010). Science as structured imagination. *The Journal of Creative Behavior*, 44(1), 37–52. 10.1002/j.2162-6057.2010.tb01324.x

De Vries, K. (2020). You never fake alone. Creative AI in action. *Information Communication and Society*, 23(14), 2110–2127. 10.1080/1369118X.2020.1754877

DeepDream. (2023, Dec. 22). *Wikipedia*. Retrieved May 7, 2024, from https://en.wikipedia.org/wiki/DeepDream

Degennaro, A., & Mak, B. (2002-2003). A diffusion model for computer art in education. *Journal of Educational Technology Systems*, 31(1), 5–18. 10.2190/B69J-FDFR-UKBY-4LEL

Delacruz, E. (2004). Teachers' working conditions and the unmet promise of technology. *Studies in Art Education*, 46(1), 6–19. 10.1080/00393541.2004.11650065

Dell'Aria, A. (2021). *The Moving Image as Public Art: Sidewalk Spectators and Modes of Enchantment*. Springer Nature. 10.1007/978-3-030-65904-2

Delphenich, P., & Broz, D. (2015). Garage innovation+ higher education= the academic incubator. *Planning for Higher Education*, 43(4), 10.

Demir, I., & Ciftci, U. A. (2021, May). Where do deep fakes look? Synthetic face detection via gaze tracking. In *ACM Symposium on Eye Tracking Research and Applications* (pp. 1-11). 10.1145/3448017.3457387

Dhoni, P., & Kumar, R. (2023). Synergizing generative ai and cybersecurity: Roles of generative ai entities, companies, agencies, and government in enhancing cybersecurity. *Authorea Preprints.*

Di Gregori, C. (2018). Creative imagination and creativity. *Cognitio*, 19(1), 77–87. 10.23925/2316-5278.2018v19i1p77-87

Dilmaç, S. (2019). The Effect of Web-Based Asynchronous Learning Environment on Academic Achievement and Attitudes of Secondary School Students in Visual Arts Course. *Journal of Ağrı İbrahim Çeçen University Institute of Social Sciences*, 5(2), 159–184.

Doarn, C. R. (2024). Imagination: Where would we be without it? *Telemedicine Journal and e-Health*, 30(1), 1–2.38197781

Dong, R., Han, C., Peng, Y., Qi, Z., Ge, Z., Yang, J., . . . Yi, L. (2023). DreamLLM: Synergistic multimodal comprehension and creation. *arXiv Preprint arXiv:2309.11499.*

Dor, D. (2017). From experience to imagination: Language and its evolution as a social communication technology. *Journal of Neurolinguistics*, 43, 107–119. 10.1016/j.jneuroling.2016.10.003

Dorstewitz, P. (2016). Imagination in action. *Metaphilosophy*, 47(3), 385–405. 10.1111/meta.12187

Douglass, H. (2023). Makerspaces and making data: Learning from pre-service teachers' STEM experiences in a community Makerspace. *Education Sciences*, 13(6), 538. 10.3390/educsci13060538

Dukart, K., Orser, D. J., & Guengerich, B. (2020, June). Maker Spaces for the Multitudes-Strategies to Expand Access and Use of a College Maker Space. *2020 ASEE Virtual Annual Conference Content Access.* 10.18260/1-2--34938

Durall, R., Keuper, M., Pfreundt, F. J., & Keuper, J. (2019). Unmasking deepfakes with simple features. arXiv Preprint arXiv:1911.00686, 1 - 8.

Edwards, B. (1997). Drawing on the Right Side of the Brain. In *CHI'97 Extended Abstracts on Human Factors in Computing Systems* (pp. 188-189). 10.1145/1120212.1120336

Egan, K. (1989). Memory, imagination, and learning: Connected by the story. *Phi Delta Kappan*, 70(6), 455–459.

Eichenberg, C., Black, S., Weinbach, S., Parcalabescu, L., & Frank, A. (2021). MAGMA—Multimodal Augmentation of Generative Models through Adapter-based finetuning. *arXiv Preprint arXiv:2112.05253.*

Eiserbeck, A., Maier, M., Baum, J., & Abdel Rahman, R. (2023). Deepfake smiles matter less—The psychological and neural impact of presumed AI-generated faces. *Scientific Reports*, 13(1), 16111. 10.1038/s41598-023-42802-x37752242

Elezabi, H., & Sharaf, A. (2023). Visual understanding of academic diagrams using multimodal generative models. *Proceedings of the 37th Conference on Neural Information Processing Systems (NeurIPS 2023),* 1 – 8.

Elgammal, A., Liu, B., Elhoseiny, M., & Mazzone, M. (2017). Can: Creative adversarial networks, generating" art" by learning about styles and deviating from style norms. *arXiv preprint arXiv:1706.07068.*

El-Zanfaly, D., Huang, Y., & Dong, Y. (2023, July). Sand-in-the-loop: Investigating embodied co-creation for shared understandings of generative AI. In *Companion Publication of the 2023 ACM Designing Interactive Systems Conference* (pp. 256-260). ACM.

Epstein, Z., Schroeder, H., & Newman, D. (2022). When happy accidents spark creativity: Bringing collaborative speculation to life with generative AI. *arXiv Preprint arXiv:2206.00533.*

Erden, Y. J. (2010). Could a created being ever be creative? Some philosophical remarks on creativity and AI development. *Minds and Machines*, 20(3), 349–362. 10.1007/s11023-010-9202-2

Erevelles, S., Horton, V., & Fukawa, N. (2007). Imagination in marketing. *Marketing Management Journal, 17*(2).

Evans, M. D., Henriksen, D., & Mishra, P.Deep-Play Research Group. (2019). Using creativity and imagination to understand our algorithmic world: A conversation with Dr. Ed Finn. *TechTrends*, 63(4), 362–368. 10.1007/s11528-019-00404-3

Experiment with Athos Bulcão _ Brasília TV Tower— MariliaBergamo—OpenProcessing. (n.d.). Retrieved February 20, 2024, from https://openprocessing.org/sketch/2181226/

Experiment with Athos Bulcão—Estação de Transbordo da Lapa- MariliaBergam—OpenProcessing. (n.d.). Retrieved February 20, 2024, from https://openprocessing.org/sketch/1238424/

Experiment with Athos Bulcão—Sambódromo—MariliaBergamo—OpenProcessing. (n.d.). Retrieved February 20, 2024, from https://openprocessing.org/sketch/2181225/

Eyal, L., & Gil, E. (2020). Design patterns for teaching in academic settings in future learning spaces. *British Journal of Educational Technology*, 51(4), 1061–1077. 10.1111/bjet.12923

Facer, K. (2023). Possibility and the temporal imagination. *Possibility Studies & Society*, 1(1-2), 60–66. 10.1177/27538699231171797

Fagni, T., Falchi, F., Gambini, M., Martella, A., & Tesconi, M. (2021). TweepFake: About detecting deepfake tweets. *PLoS One*, 16(5), e0251415. 10.1371/journal.pone.025141533984021

Farritor, S. (2017). University-based makerspaces: A source of innovation. *Technology and Innovation*, 19(1), 389–395. 10.21300/19.1.2017.389

Fasso, W., & Knight, B. A. (2020). Identity development in school makerspaces: Intentional design. *International Journal of Technology and Design Education*, 30(2), 275–294. 10.1007/s10798-019-09501-z

Fehringer, H., Kaar, C., & Stary, C. (2019, September). Makerspaces in Academic Education: An Exploratory Analysis and Design Framework. In *2019 18th International Conference on Information Technology Based Higher Education and Training (ITHET)* (pp. 1-10). IEEE.

Fei, N., Lu, Z., Gao, Y., Yang, G., Huo, Y., Wen, J., ... Wen, J. R. (2021). *Wenlan 2.0: Make ai imagine via a multimodal foundation model.* arXiv.

Ferrari, F., & McKelvey, F. (2023). Hyperproduction: A social theory of deep generative models. *Distinktion : Scandinavian Journal of Social Theory*, 24(2), 338–360. 10.1080/1600910X.2022.2137546

Feuerriegel, S., Hartmann, J., Janiesch, C., & Zschech, P. (2024). Generative ai. *Business & Information Systems Engineering*, 66(1), 111–126. 10.1007/s12599-023-00834-7

Fezari, M., Al-Dahoud, A., & Al-Dahoud, A. (2023). *Augmanting (sic) reality: The power of Generative AI.* University Badji Mokhtar Annaba.

Figueira, O., & Wang, G. (n.d.). *DeepPhish: Effects of generative artifacts within fabricated profiles on user trust.* Academic Press.

Finn, E., Capurro, C. T., Bennett, M. G., & Wylie, R. (2023). Applied imagination. *Frontiers in Psychology*, 14.38022917

Finn, E., & Wylie, R. (2021). Collaborative imagination: A methodological approach. *Futures*, 132, 102788. 10.1016/j.futures.2021.102788

Fletcher, J. (2018). Deepfakes, artificial intelligence, and some kind of dystopia. *Theatre Journal*, 70(4), 455–471. 10.1353/tj.2018.0097

Folkmann, M. N. (2010). Enabling Creativity: Imagination in design processes. *First International Conference on Design Creativity. ICDC 2010.*

Fordyce, R., Heemsbergen, L., Mignone, P., & Nansen, B. (2015). 3D printing and university makerspaces: Surveying countercultural communities in institutional settings. *Digital Culture & Education*, 7.

Forest, C. R., Moore, R. A., Jariwala, A. S., Fasse, B. B., Linsey, J., Newstetter, W., & Quintero, C. (2014). The invention studio: A university Maker space and culture. *Advances in Engineering Education*, 4(2), n2.

Forest, C., Farzaneh, H. H., Weinmann, J., & Lindemann, U. (2016, June). Quantitative survey and analysis of five maker spaces at large, research-oriented universities. *2016 ASEE Annual Conference & Exposition.* 10.18260/p.26023

Franceschelli, G., & Musolesi, M. (2022). Copyright in generative deep learning. *Data & Policy*, 4, e17–e1. 10.1017/dap.2022.10

Frey, C. B., & Osborne, M. (2023). Generative AI and the future of work: A reappraisal. *The Brown Journal of World Affairs*, 1–12.

Friessnig, M. H., Karre, H., Schnöll, H. P., & Ramsauer, C. (2016, November). Development of an educational program using capabilities of (academic) Makerspaces. *Proceedings of the 1st International Symposium on Academic Makerspaces.*

Fundathos—Fundação Athos Bulcão. (n.d.). Retrieved February 14, 2024, from https://www.fundathos.org.br/

Fu, P., Li, L., & Xie, X. (2022). Reconstructing makerspaces in China: Mass innovation space and the transformative creative industries. *Humanities & Social Sciences Communications*, 9(1), 1–8. 10.1057/s41599-022-01383-2

Furlong, E. J. (1961). Imagination in Hume's treatise and enquiry concerning the human understanding1. *Philosophy (London, England)*, 36(136), 62–70. 10.1017/S0031819100057831

Galafassi, D. (2018). *The Transformative Imagination: Re-imagining the World towards Sustainability* (Doctoral dissertation, Stockholm Resilience Centre, Stockholm University).

Galaleldin, M., Bouchard, F., Anis, H., & Lague, C. (2016). The impact of makerspaces on engineering education. *Proceedings of the Canadian Engineering Education Association (CEEA).*

Gao, J., Li, P., Chen, Z., & Zhang, J. (2020). A survey on deep learning for multimodal data fusion. *Neural Computation*, 32(5), 829–864. 10.1162/neco_a_0127332186998

García-Peñalvo, F., & Vázquez-Ingelmo, A. (2023). *What do we mean by GenAI? A systematic mapping of the evolution, trends, and techniques involved in Generative AI.* Academic Press.

García-Peñalvo, F., & Vázquez-Ingelmo, A. (2023). What do we mean by GenAI? A systematic mapping of the evolution, trends, and techniques involved in Generative AI. *International Journal of Interactive Multimedia and Artificial Intelligence*, 8(4), 7–16. 10.9781/ijimai.2023.07.006

Gatys, L. A., Ecker, A. S., & Bethge, M. (2017). Texture and art with deep neural networks. *Current Opinion in Neurobiology*, 46, 178–186. 10.1016/j.conb.2017.08.01928926765

Gaut, B. (2003). Creativity and imagination. *The Creation of Art.*

Gaut, B. (2010). The philosophy of creativity. *Philosophy Compass*, 5(12), 1034–1046. 10.1111/j.1747-9991.2010.00351.x

Geser, G., Hollauf, E. M., Hornung-Prähauser, V., Schön, S., & Vloet, F. (2019). Makerspaces as social innovation and entrepreneurship learning environments: The DOIT learning program. *Discourse and Communication for Sustainable Education*, 10(2), 60–71. 10.2478/dcse-2019-0018

Ghosh, A., & Fossas, G. (2022). Can there be art without an artist? *arXiv preprint arXiv:2209.07667.*

Giudice, O., Guarnera, L., & Battiato, S. (2021). Fighting deepfakes by detecting GAN DCT anomalies. *Journal of Imaging, 7*(8), 128, 1 – 27.

Gkotzos, K. (2015, Oct. 30). *Google's DeepDream: Algorithms on LSD*. Media Studies, University of Amsterdam.

Gladson, J. T. (2023). *Student Engagement in Makerspaces: Connecting Research in Student Engagement and Making in Education* (Doctoral dissertation, The University of North Carolina at Greensboro).

Godhe, A. L., Lilja, P., & Selwyn, N. (2019). Making sense of making: Critical issues in the integration of Maker education into schools. *Technology, Pedagogy and Education*, 28(3), 317–328. 10.1080/1475939X.2019.1610040

Gong, D., Goh, O. S., Kumar, Y. J., Ye, Z., & Chi, W. (2020). Deepfake forensics, an AI-synthesized detection with deep convolutional generative adversarial networks. *International Journal (Toronto, Ont.)*, 9(3).

Goode, L. (2018). Life, but not as we know it: AI and the popular imagination. *Culture Unbound*, 10(2), 185–207. 10.3384/cu.2000.1525.2018102185

Gozalo-Brizuela, R., & Garrido-Merchán, E. C. (2023). A survey of Generative AI applications. *arXiv Preprint arXiv:2306.02781.*

Gragnaniello, D., Marra, F., & Verdoliva, L. (2022). Detection of AI-generated synthetic faces. In *Handbook of Digital Face Manipulation and Detection: From Deepfakes to Morphing Attacks* (pp. 191–212). Springer International Publishing. 10.1007/978-3-030-87664-7_9

Greene, M., Kellam, N., & Coley, B. (2019). Black men in the making: Engaging in maker spaces promotes agency and identity for black males in engineering. *2019 CoNECD-The Collaborative Network for Engineering and Computing Diversity.*

Gregory, D. (2009). Boxes with fire: Wisely integrating learning technologies into the art classroom. *Art Education*, 62(3), 47–54. 10.1080/00043125.2009.11519020

Grøn, A. (2002). Imagination and subjectivity. *Ars Disputandi*, 2(1), 89–98. 10.1080/15665399.2002.10819741

Gross, E. C. (2023). The creative paradox of AI: Enabler or disruptor of human imagination? *Bulletin of the Transilvania University of Braşov, Series VII. Social Sciences and Law*, 16(1), 69–74.

Grossman, M. R., Grimm, P. W., Brown, D., & Xu, M. (2023). The GPTJudge: Justice in a Generative AI world. *Duke Law & Technology Review, 23*(1).

Gruner, D. T., & Csikszentmihalyi, M. (2019). Engineering creativity in an age of artificial intelligence. *The Palgrave Handbook of Social Creativity Research*, 447-462.

Guarnera, L., Giudice, O., & Battiato, S. (2024). Mastering deepfake detection: A cutting-edge approach to distinguish GAN and diffusion-model images. *ACM Transactions on Multimedia Computing Communications and Applications*, 3652027. 10.1145/3652027

Gude, O. (2007). Principles of possibility: Considerations for a 21st-century art & culture curriculum. *Art Education*, 60(1), 6–17. 10.1080/00043125.2007.11651621

Guitton, M. J. (2013). Morphological conservation in human-animal hybrids in science fiction and fantasy settings: Is our imagination as free as we think it is? *Advances in Anthropology*, 3(03), 157–163. 10.4236/aa.2013.33021

Guo, W., Wang, J., & Wang, S. (2019). Deep multimodal representation learning: A survey. *IEEE Access : Practical Innovations, Open Solutions*, 7, 63373–63394. 10.1109/ACCESS.2019.2916887

Hacker, P., Engel, A., & Mauer, M. (2023, June). Regulating ChatGPT and other large generative AI models. In *Proceedings of the 2023 ACM Conference on Fairness, Accountability, and Transparency* (pp. 1112-1123). 10.1145/3593013.3594067

Hai-Jew, S. (2023, July 8). *Creating seeding visuals to prompt art-making generative AIs*. Slideshow. SlideShare. Retrieved Dec. 10, 2023, from https://www.slideshare.net/ShalinHaiJew/creating-seeding-visuals-to-prompt-artmaking-generative-ais

Hall, T., & Robertson, I. (2001). *Public art and urban regeneration: advocacy, claims and critical debates*. Academic Press.

Halverson, E. R., & Sheridan, K. (2014). The maker movement in education. *Harvard Educational Review*, 84(4), 495–504. 10.17763/haer.84.4.34j1g68140382063

Hamington, M. (2010). The will to care: Performance, expectation, and imagination. *Hypatia*, 25(3), 675–695. 10.1111/j.1527-2001.2010.01110.x

Hamrick, J. B. (2019). Analogues of mental simulation and imagination in deep learning. *Current Opinion in Behavioral Sciences*, 29, 8–16. 10.1016/j.cobeha.2018.12.011

Hancock, J. T., & Bailenson, J. N. (2021). The social impact of deepfakes. *Cyberpsychology, Behavior, and Social Networking*, 24(3), 149–152. 10.1089/cyber.2021.29208.jth33760669

Hanif, S. M., & Dave, V. (2022). Deepfakes technology using AI. *International Journal of Scientific research in Science, Engineering and Technology*, 152-159.

Hannay, A. H. (1935, January). Is the imagination creative? *Proceedings of the Aristotelian Society*, 36(1), 109–130. 10.1093/aristotelian/36.1.109

Hargreaves, D. J. (2012). Musical imagination: Perception and production, beauty and creativity. *Psychology of Music*, 40(5), 539–557. 10.1177/0305735612444893

Harron, J. R., & Hughes, J. E. (2018). Spacemakers: A leadership perspective on curriculum and the purpose of K–12 educational makerspaces. *Journal of Research on Technology in Education*, 50(3), 253–270. 10.1080/15391523.2018.1461038

Helmus, T. C. (2022). Artificial intelligence, deepfakes, and disinformation. Rand Corporation.

Herczeg, M., Winkler, T., & Ohlei, A. (2019). Ambient learning spaces for school education. In *ICERI2019 Proceedings* (pp. 5116-5125). IATED. 10.21125/iceri.2019.1240

Heredia, S. C., & Tan, E. (2021). Teaching & learning in Makerspaces: Equipping teachers to become justice-oriented maker-educators. *The Journal of Educational Research*, 114(2), 171–182. 10.1080/00220671.2020.1860871

Hersch, E. (2003). Imagination and its pathologies: Domain of the unreal or a fundamental dimension of human reality. *Imagination and its Pathologies*.

Hertzmann, A. (2019). Aesthetics of neural network art. *arXiv preprint arXiv:1903.05696*.

Hilton, E. C., Forest, C. R., & Linsey, J. S. (2020). *Slaying dragons: An empirical look at the impact of academic makerspaces*. Academic Press.

Hira, A., Joslyn, C. H., & Hynes, M. M. (2014, October). Classroom makerspaces: Identifying the opportunities and challenges. In *2014 IEEE Frontiers in Education Conference (FIE) Proceedings* (pp. 1-5). IEEE.

Home | p5.js. (n.d.). Retrieved February 17, 2024, from https://p5js.org/

Hoople, G., Mejia, J., Hoffoss, D., & Devadoss, S. (2020). Makerspaces on the Continuum: Examining undergraduate student learning in formal and informal settings. *IJEE International Journal of Engineering Education, 36*(4).

Horvitz, E. (2022, Nov.). On the horizon: Interactive and compositional deepfakes. In *Proceedings of the 2022 International Conference on Multimodal Interaction* (pp. 653-661). 10.1145/3536221.3558175

Houde, S., Liao, V., Martino, J., Muller, M., Piorkowski, D., Richards, J., . . . Zhang, Y. (2020). Business (mis) use cases of generative ai. *arXiv Preprint arXiv:2003.07679.*

Houston, C. (2013). Makerspaces@ your school library: Consider the possibilities! *IASL Annual Conference Proceedings*, 1 – 5.

Hsu, Y. C., Baldwin, S., & Ching, Y. H. (2017). Learning through making and maker education. *TechTrends*, 61(6), 589–594. 10.1007/s11528-017-0172-6

Huang, J., Zhang, Z., Zheng, S., Qin, F., & Wang, Y. (2024). *DISTMM: Accelerating distributed multimodal model training*. Academic Press.

Huang, S., & Siddarth, D. (2023). Generative AI and the digital commons. *arXiv Preprint arXiv:2303.11074.*

Huang, S., He, C., & Cheng, R. (2022). SoloGAN: Multi-domain multimodal unpaired image-to-image translation via a single generative adversarial network. *IEEE Transactions on Artificial Intelligence*, 3(5), 722–737. 10.1109/TAI.2022.3187384

Hui, J. S., & Gerber, E. M. (2017, February). Developing Makerspaces as sites of entrepreneurship. In *Proceedings of the 2017 ACM Conference on Computer Supported Cooperative Work and Social Computing* (pp. 2023-2038). ACM.

Hunyadi, M. (2010). The imagination in charge. *NanoEthics*, 4(3), 199–204. 10.1007/s11569-010-0104-9

Hynes, M. M., & Hynes, W. J. (2018). If you build it, will they come? Student preferences for Makerspace environments in higher education. *International Journal of Technology and Design Education*, 28(3), 867–883. 10.1007/s10798-017-9412-5

Iijima, L., & Stathaki, T. (2024). A multimodal approach for cross-domain image retrieval. *arXiv Preprint arXiv:2403.15152.*

Imagination. (2019, Jan. 22). *Stanford Encyclopedia of Philosophy.*

Imber-Black, E. (2020). Rituals in the time of COVID-19: Imagination, responsiveness, and the human spirit. *Family Process*, 59(3), 912–921. 10.1111/famp.1258132663322

Irie, N. R., Hsu, Y. C., & Ching, Y. H. (2019). Makerspaces in diverse places: A comparative analysis of distinctive national discourses surrounding the maker movement and education in four countries. *TechTrends*, 63(4), 397–407. 10.1007/s11528-018-0355-9

Iwamoto, L. (2009). *Digital fabrications : architectural and material techniques.* Princeton Architectural Press.

Iwata, M., Pitkänen, K., Laru, J., & Mäkitalo, K. (2020, June). Exploring potentials and challenges to develop twenty-first century skills and computational thinking in K-12 maker education. *Frontiers in Education*, 5, 87. 10.3389/feduc.2020.00087

Jaatinen, J., & Lindfors, E. (2019). Makerspaces for pedagogical innovation processes: How Finnish comprehensive schools create space for Makers. *Journal of Design and Technology Education*, 24(2), n2.

Jia, S., Lyu, R., Zhao, K., Chen, Y., Yan, Z., Ju, Y., . . . Lyu, S. (2024). Can ChatGPT detect DeepFakes? A study of using multimodal Large Language Models for media forensics. *arXiv Preprint arXiv:2403.14077.*

Jiang, H. H., Brown, L., Cheng, J., Khan, M., Gupta, A., Workman, D., & Gebru, T. (2023, August). AI art and its impact on artists. In *Proceedings of the 2023 AAAI/ACM Conference on AI, Ethics, and Society* (pp. 363-374). 10.1145/3600211.3604681

Johnston, K., Kervin, L., & Wyeth, P. (2022). STEM, STEAM and makerspaces in early childhood: A scoping review. *Sustainability (Basel)*, 14(20), 13533. 10.3390/su142013533

Jonasson, H. I., & Ingason, H. (2018). *Project creativity: Using active imagination for project innovation*. Academic Press.

Jordan, A., Knochel, A. D., Meisel, N., Reiger, K., & Sinha, S. (2021). Making on the move: Mobility, makerspaces, and art education. *International Journal of Art & Design Education*, 40(1), 52–65. 10.1111/jade.12333

Joshi, M. A. (2024). The security risks of Generative Artificial Intelligence. *Available atSSRN* 4735175. 10.2139/ssrn.4735175

Juefei-Xu, F., Wang, R., Huang, Y., Guo, Q., Ma, L., & Liu, Y. (2022). Countering malicious deepfakes: Survey, battleground, and horizon. *International Journal of Computer Vision*, 130(7), 1678–1734. 10.1007/s11263-022-01606-835528632

Juhász, L., Mooney, P., & Hochmair, H. H. (2023). *ChatGPT as a mapping assistant: A novel method to enrich maps with generative AI and content derived from street-level photographs*. Academic Press.

Julian, K. D., & Parrott, D. J. (2017). Makerspaces in the Library: Science in a Student's Hands. *Journal of Learning Spaces*, 6(2).

Kaba, F. (1994). *Çizgi Film*. Anadolu Sanat.

Kahng, M., Thorat, N., Chau, D. H., Viégas, F. B., & Wattenberg, M. (2018). Gan lab: Understanding complex deep generative models using interactive visual experimentation. *IEEE Transactions on Visualization and Computer Graphics*, 25(1), 310–320. 10.1109/TVCG.2018.286450030130198

Kalsched, D. (2021). Intersections of personal vs. collective trauma during the COVID-19 pandemic: The hijacking of the human imagination. *The Journal of Analytical Psychology*, 66(3), 443–462. 10.1111/1468-5922.1269734231900

Kandasamy, V., Hubálovský, Š., & Trojovský, P. (2022). Deep fake detection using a sparse auto encoder with a graph capsule dual graph CNN. *PeerJ. Computer Science*, 8, e953. 10.7717/peerj-cs.95335721408

Kang, I., Kim, Y. S., & Yoon, H. J. (2017). Fostering entrepreneurship by maker education: A case study in an (sic) higher education. *Journal of the Korea Convergence Society*, 8(7), 253–264.

Kantaros, A., Diegel, O., Piromalis, D., Tsaramirsis, G., Khadidos, A. O., Khadidos, A. O., Khan, F. Q., & Jan, S. (2022). 3D printing: Making an innovative technology widely accessible through makerspaces and outsourced services. *Materials Today: Proceedings*, 49, 2712–2723. 10.1016/j.matpr.2021.09.074

Kaplan, E. K. (1972). Gaston Bachelard's philosophy of imagination: An introduction. *Philosophy and Phenomenological Research*, 33(1), 1–24. 10.2307/2106717

Karnouskos, S. (2020). Artificial intelligence in digital media: The era of deepfakes. *IEEE Transactions on Technology and Society*, 1(3), 138–147. 10.1109/TTS.2020.3001312

Katarya, R., & Lal, A. (2020, October). A study on combating emerging threat of deepfake weaponization. In *2020 Fourth International Conference on I-SMAC (IoT in Social, Mobile, Analytics and Cloud)(I-SMAC)* (pp. 485-490). IEEE. 10.1109/I-SMAC49090.2020.9243588

Keune, A., Gomoll, A., & Peppler, K. (2015). Flexibility to learn: Material artifacts in makerspaces. In *Fifth Annual FabLearn Conference: Equity and Diversity in Making*. Palo Alto, CA: Stanford University.

Keune, A., & Peppler, K. (2017). Maker portfolios as learning and community building tools inside and outside makerspaces. In *Making a Difference* (pp. 545–548). Prioritizing Equity and Access in CSCL.

Keune, A., & Peppler, K. (2019). Materials-to-develop-with: The making of a Makerspace. *British Journal of Educational Technology*, 50(1), 280–293. 10.1111/bjet.12702

Keune, A., Peppler, K. A., & Wohlwend, K. E. (2019). Recognition in makerspaces: Supporting opportunities for women to "make" a STEM career. *Computers in Human Behavior*, 99, 368–380. 10.1016/j.chb.2019.05.013

Khadri Ahmed, H. O. (2023). Exploring possible futures of makerspaces as an important basic component of K-12 education. *Pedagogies*, 18(3), 450–472. 10.1080/1554480X.2022.2065997

Kim, S. H., Jung, Y. J., & Choi, G. W. (2022). A systematic review of library makerspaces research. *Library & Information Science Research*, 44(4), 101202. 10.1016/j.lisr.2022.101202

Kinberg, O., & Levy, A. (2023). The epistemic imagination revisited. *Philosophy and Phenomenological Research*, 107(2), 319–336. 10.1111/phpr.12909

Kind, A. (2020). *The skill of imagination*. Preprint. 10.4324/9781315180809-33

Kinnula, M., Milara, I. S., Norouzi, B., Sharma, S., & Iivari, N. (2021). The show must go on! Strategies for making and makerspaces during pandemic. *International Journal of Child-Computer Interaction*, 29, 100303. 10.1016/j.ijcci.2021.10030336570421

Kirio, C. H. (2022). *School Librarian and Teacher Collaboration in Virtual Makerspace Instructional Design* (Doctoral dissertation, University of Hawai'i at Manoa).

Kjällander, S., Åkerfeldt, A., Mannila, L., & Parnes, P. (2018). Makerspaces across settings: Didactic design for programming in formal and informal teacher education in the Nordic countries. *Journal of Digital Learning in Teacher Education*, 34(1), 18–30. 10.1080/21532974.2017.1387831

Knott, A., Pedreschi, D., Chatila, R., Chakraborti, T., Leavy, S., Baeza-Yates, R., ... & Bengio, Y. (2023). Generative AI models should include detection mechanisms as a condition for public release. *Ethics and Information Technology, 25*(4), 55, 1 – 7.

Koh, J. Y., Fried, D., & Salakhutdinov, R. R. (2024). Generating images with multimodal language models. *Advances in Neural Information Processing Systems*, 36.

Koh, K., & Abbas, J. (2015). Competencies for information professionals in learning labs and makerspaces. *Journal of Education for Library and Information Science*, 56(2), 114–129.

Kohls, C. (2022, July). Maker Spaces for hybrid education. In *Proceedings of the 27th European Conference on Pattern Languages of Programs* (pp. 1-9). Academic Press.

Konstantinou, D., Parmaxi, A., & Zaphiris, P. (2021). Mapping research directions on makerspaces in education. *Educational Media International*, 58(3), 223–247. 10.1080/09523987.2021.1976826

Koukouti, M. D., & Malafouris, L. (2020). Material imagination: An anthropological perspective. *The Cambridge Handbook of the Imagination*, 30-46.

Kümbetoğlu, B. (2005). *Qualitative Method and Research in Sociology and Anthropology*. Bağlam Publishing.

Kurti, R. S., Kurti, D. L., & Fleming, L. (2014). The philosophy of educational makerspaces part 1 of making an educational makerspace. *Teacher Librarian*, 41(5), 8.

Kurti, R. S., Kurti, D., & Fleming, L. (2014). Practical implementation of an educational makerspace: Part 3 of making an educational makerspace. *Teacher Librarian*, 42(2), 20.

Kurti, R. S., Kurti, D., & Fleming, L. (2014). The environment and tools of great educational makerspaces. Part 2 of Making an educational Makerspace. *Teacher Librarian*, 42(1), 8.

Kutlay. (2014). *Algoritma Nedir? Çeşitleri Nelerdir?*https://www.kodlamamerkezi.com/algoritma/algoritma-nedir algoritma-cesitleri/

Laato, S., Rauti, S., Islam, A. N., & Sutinen, E. (2021). Why playing augmented reality games feels meaningful to players? The roles of imagination and social experience. *Computers in Human Behavior*, 121, 106816. 10.1016/j.chb.2021.106816

Lam, C., Cruz, S., Kellam, N., & Coley, B. (2019, January). Making space for the women: exploring female engineering student narratives of engagement in makerspaces. *2019 ASEE Annual Conference & Exposition.* 10.18260/1-2--33078

Lategan, B. C. (1996). Imagination and transformation: Ricoeur and the role of imagination. *Scriptura*, 58, 213–232.

Lazarow, J., Jin, L., & Tu, Z. (2017). Introspective neural networks for generative modeling. In *Proceedings of the IEEE International Conference on Computer Vision* (pp. 2774-2783). IEEE.

Leach, N. (2019). Do robots dream of digital sheep. *Proceedings of ACADIA 19: Ubiquity and Autonomy.* 10.52842/conf.acadia.2019.298

LeBlanc, M., Freiman, V., & Furlong, C. (2018). STEAMing soft-skills in makerspaces: What are the mathematical connections. In *Actes de l'International Symposium MACAS* (pp. 87-97). Academic Press.

Lederach, J. P. (2005). Using imagination and creativity. *Arts and Peace.* 1 - 7.

Lee, G. G., Shi, L., Latif, E., Gao, Y., Bewersdorf, A., Nyaaba, M., . . . Zhai, X. (2023). Multimodality of ai for education: Towards artificial general intelligence. *arXiv Preprint arXiv:2312.06037.*

Lee, K., Cooper, A. F., & Grimmelmann, J. (2023). Talkin' 'bout AI generation: Copyright and the Generative-AI supply chain. *arXiv preprint arXiv:2309.08133.*

Leggett, B. J. (2005). God, imagination, and the interior paramour. *The Wallace Stevens Journal*, 29(1), 171–177.

Lenhart, C. S., Bouwma-Gearhart, J., Villanueva, I., Youmans, K., & Nadelson, L. S. (2020). *Engineering faculty members' perceptions of university makerspaces: Potential affordances for curriculum, instructional practices, and student learning. International Journal of Engineering Education, 36(4).*

Levy, B., Morocz, R. J., Forest, C., Nagel, R. L., Newstetter, W. C., Talley, K. G., & Linsey, J. S. (2016, June). MAKER: How to make a university maker space. *2016 ASEE Annual Conference & Exposition.* 10.18260/p.25623

Lewis, J. (2015). *Barriers to women's involvement in hackspaces and makerspaces.* The University of Sheffield.

Li, C., Gan, Z., Yang, Z., Yang, J., Li, L., Wang, L., & Gao, J. (2023). Multimodal foundation models: From specialists to general-purpose assistants. *arXiv Preprint arXiv:2309.10020, 1*(2), 2.

Li, Y., Chang, M. C., & Lyu, S. (2018, December). In *ictu oculi*: Exposing ai created fake videos by detecting eye blinking. In *2018 IEEE International Workshop on Information Forensics and Security (WIFS)* (pp. 1-7). IEEE.

Liang, P. P., Zadeh, A., & Morency, L. P. (2022). Foundations and trends in multimodal machine learning: Principles, challenges, and open questions. *arXiv Preprint arXiv:2209.03430.*

Liang, C., Chang, C. C., Chang, Y., & Lin, L. J. (2012). The exploration of indicators of imagination. *Turkish Online Journal of Educational Technology-TOJET*, 11(3), 366–374.

Liang, C., Hsu, Y., Chang, C. C., & Lin, L. J. (2013). In search of an index of imagination for virtual experience designers. *International Journal of Technology and Design Education*, 23(4), 1037–1046. 10.1007/s10798-012-9224-6

Liang, C., Hsu, Y., Huang, Y., & Chen, S. C. (2012). How learning environments can stimulate student imagination. *Turkish Online Journal of Educational Technology*, 11(4), 432–441.

Liebenberg, J., Human, L. H., & Muller, J. C. (2001). *Morality, imagination and human decision making*. Academic Press.

Lin, D., Jing, L., Song, X., Liu, M., Sun, T., & Nie, L. (2023, July). Adapting generative pretrained language model for open-domain multimodal sentence summarization. In *Proceedings of the 46th International ACM SIGIR Conference on Research and Development in Information Retrieval* (pp. 195-204). 10.1145/3539618.3591633

Lindstrom, D., Thompson, A. D., & Schmidt-Crawford, D. A. (2017). The maker movement: Democratizing STEM education and empowering learners to shape their world. *Journal of Digital Learning in Teacher Education*, 33(3), 89–90. 10.1080/21532974.2017.1316153

Lin, W. S., Hsu, Y., & Liang, C. (2014). The mediator effects of conceiving imagination on academic performance of design students. *International Journal of Technology and Design Education*, 24(1), 73–89. 10.1007/s10798-013-9244-x

Litts, B. K. (2015). *Making Learning: Makerspaces as Learning Environments* (Doctoral dissertation, The University of Wisconsin-Madison).

Li, W., Zhang, P., Zhang, L., Huang, Q., He, X., Lyu, S., & Gao, J. (2019). Object-driven text-to-image synthesis via adversarial training. In *Proceedings of the IEEE/CVF Conference on Computer Vision and Pattern Recognition* (pp. 12174-12182). IEEE.

Li, Y., Li, Y., & Qiu, S. (2023). Analysis on the effectiveness and mechanisms of public policies to promote innovation of high-tech startups in Makerspaces. *Sustainability (Basel)*, 15(9), 7027. 10.3390/su15097027

Lock, J., Redmond, P., Orwin, L., Powell, A., Becker, S., Hollohan, P., & Johnson, C. (2020). Bridging distance: Practical and pedagogical implications of virtual Makerspaces. *Journal of Computer Assisted Learning*, 36(6), 957–968. 10.1111/jcal.12452

Lossau, J., & Stevens, Q. (Eds.). (2015). The uses of art in public space. Routledge, Taylor & Francis Group.

Love, T. S. (2022). Examining the influence that professional development has on educators' perceptions of integrated STEM safety in makerspaces. *Journal of Science Education and Technology*, 31(3), 289–302. 10.1007/s10956-022-09955-2

Love, T. S., Roy, K. R., Gill, M., & Harrell, M. (2022). Examining the influence that safety training format has on educators' perceptions of safer practices in Makerspaces and integrated STEM labs. *Journal of Safety Research*, 82, 112–123. 10.1016/j.jsr.2022.05.00336031238

Luo, L., Sandler, M., Lin, Z., Zhmoginov, A., & Howard, A. (2020). Large-scale generative data-free distillation. *arXiv preprint arXiv:2012.05578.*

Luo, R. (2019/2020). Artistic intelligence. *Kritikos. Proceedings of Art Machines:International Symposium on Computational Media Art,* 12 - 19.

Lykov, A., Konenkov, M., Gbagbe, K. F., Litvinov, M., Peter, R., Davletshin, D., . . . Tsetserukou, D. (2024). CognitiveOS: Large Multimodal Model based System to Endow Any Type of Robot with Generative AI. *arXiv preprint arXiv:2401.16205.*

Maceli, M. G. (2019). Making the future makers: Makerspace curriculum in library and information science graduate programs and continuing education. *Library Hi Tech*, 37(4), 781–793. 10.1108/LHT-01-2019-0005

Maerten, A. S., & Soydaner, D. (2023). From paintbrush to pixel: A review of deep neural networks in AI-generated art. *arXiv preprint arXiv:2302.10913.*

Mahadevan, S. (2018, April). Imagination machines: A new challenge for artificial intelligence. *Proceedings of the AAAI Conference on Artificial Intelligence*, 32(1). 10.1609/aaai.v32i1.12214

Mahajan, S. (2022). *Multimodal representation Learning for diverse synthesis with deep generative models*. Academic Press.

Mahmud, B., Hong, G., & Fong, B. (2023). A Study of Human–AI Symbiosis for Creative Work: Recent Developments and Future Directions in Deep Learning. *ACM Transactions on Multimedia Computing Communications and Applications*, 20(2), 1–21. 10.1145/3542698

Makerspace Directory. (2024). Retrieved Jan. 22, 2024, from https://makerspaces.make.co/

Mandal, A., Leavy, S., & Little, S. (2023). Multimodal composite association score: Measuring gender bias in generative multimodal models. *arXiv Preprint arXiv:2304.13855.*

Manduchi, L., Pandey, K., Bamler, R., Cotterell, R., Däubener, S., Fellenz, S., . . . Fortuin, V. (2024). On the Challenges and Opportunities in Generative AI. *arXiv preprint arXiv:2403.00025.*

Manganyi, N. C. (1976). The censored imagination. *English in Africa*, 3(1), 24–32.

Mann, L. (2018). Making a place for makerspaces in information literacy. *Reference and User Services Quarterly*, 58(2), 82–86. 10.5860/rusq.58.2.6927

Marques, H. G., Holland, O., & Newcombe, R. A. (2008, April). A modelling framework for functional imagination. In *AISB Convention* (pp. 51-58). Academic Press.

Martin, L. (2015). The promise of the maker movement for education. *Journal of Pre-College Engineering Education Research (J-PEER), 5*(1), 4.

Martin, L., Dixon, C., & Betser, S. (2018). Iterative design toward equity: Youth repertoires of practice in a high school maker space. *Equity & Excellence in Education*, 51(1), 36–47. 10.1080/10665684.2018.1436997

Masood, M., Nawaz, M., Malik, K. M., Javed, A., Irtaza, A., & Malik, H. (2023). Deepfakes generation and detection: State-of-the-art, open challenges, countermeasures, and way forward. *Applied Intelligence*, 53(4), 3974–4026. 10.1007/s10489-022-03766-z

Masters, A. S., Foster, E. K., Groen-McCall, C., McNair, L. D., & Riley, D. M. (2019). Exploring liberatory makerspaces: Preliminary results and future directions. *Advances in Engineering Education*, 7(3), 1–8.

McClennen, S. A. (2007). The humanities, human rights, and the comparative imagination. *CLCWeb (Edmonton)*, 9(1), 13. 10.7771/1481-4374.1024

McCreary, E. P. (1973). Bacon's theory of imagination reconsidered. *The Huntington Library Quarterly*, 36(4), 317–326. 10.2307/3816691

McCue, R. A., Huculak, J. M., & Johnson, D. K. (2020). *Best practices for creating and leading active-learning workshops in academic makerspaces*. IJAMM.

McGaughey, D. (1988). Through myth to imagination. *Journal of the American Academy of Religion*, 56(1), 51–76. 10.1093/jaarel/LVI.1.51

McGuffin-Cawley, J. D., & Wilczynski, V. (2021). University Makerspaces and Manufacturing Collaboration: Lessons from the Pandemic. *The Bridge*, 51(1), 41–47.

McIntosh, T. R., Susnjak, T., Liu, T., Watters, P., & Halgamuge, M. N. (2023). From Google Gemini to OpenAI q*(q-star): A survey of reshaping the generative artificial intelligence (AI) research landscape. *arXiv Preprint arXiv:2312.10868.*

McLellan, H. (1988). Computers, artificial intelligence and human imagination. *Journal of Thought*, 28–44.

McMullin, E. (1996). Enlarging imagination. *Tijdschrift voor Filosofie*, 227-260.

Medina, J. (2013). An enactivist approach to the imagination: Embodied enactments and" fictional emotions. *American Philosophical Quarterly*, 50(3), 317–335.

Meeter, M. (1977). Creativity, imagination, and the arts. *Pro Rege*, 6(1), 5–13.

Melo, M. M., March, L., & Hirsh, K. (2021, September). Examining the impacts of the covid-19 pandemic on library makerspaces and LIS makerspace curricula. *Proceedings of the Association for Library and Information Science Education Annual Conference.*

Merchán, E. C. G., & Molina, M. (2020). A machine consciousness architecture based on deep learning and gaussian processes. *Hybrid Artificial Intelligent Systems: 15th International Conference, HAIS 2020, Gijón, Spain, November 11-13, 2020Proceedings*, 15, 350–361.

Mersand, S. (2021). The state of Makerspace research: A review of the literature. *TechTrends*, 65(2), 174–186. 10.1007/s11528-020-00566-5

Meskys, E., Kalpokiene, J., Jurcys, P., & Liaudanskas, A. (2020). Regulating deep fakes: Legal and ethical considerations. *Journal of Intellectual Property Law & Practice*, 15(1), 24–31. 10.1093/jiplp/jpz167

Meyer, B. (2019). Makerspaces in Higher Education: An overview. *eLearn, 2019*(5).

Meyer, B. (2011). Mediating absence—: Effecting spiritual presence: Pictures and the Christian imagination. *Social Research*, 78(4), 1029–1056. 10.1353/sor.2011.0035

Millbank, P. (2022). A society without imagination: A lament. *The Kenarchy Journal, 3*(1).

Mirsky, Y., & Lee, W. (2021). The creation and detection of deepfakes: A survey. *ACM Computing Surveys*, 54(1), 1–41. 10.1145/3425780

Mithen, S. J. (2001). The evolution of imagination: An archaeological perspective. *SubStance*, 30(1), 28–54. 10.1353/sub.2001.0012

Modell, A. H. (2003). *Imagination and the Meaningful Brain.* MIT Press. 10.7551/mitpress/3666.001.0001

Molenaar, I., de Mooij, S., Azevedo, R., Bannert, M., Järvelä, S., & Gašević, D. (2023). Measuring self-regulated learning and the role of AI: Five years of research using multimodal multichannel data. *Computers in Human Behavior*, 139, 107540. 10.1016/j.chb.2022.107540

Moorefield-Lang, H. (2014). Makers in the library: Case studies of 3D printers and maker spaces in library settings. *Library Hi Tech*, 32(4), 583–593. 10.1108/LHT-06-2014-0056

Moorefield-Lang, H. (2015). Change in the making: Makerspaces and the ever-changing landscape of libraries. *TechTrends*, 59(3), 107–112. 10.1007/s11528-015-0860-z

Moorefield-Lang, H. M. (2015). User agreements and makerspaces: A content analysis. *New Library World*, 116(7/8), 358–368. 10.1108/NLW-12-2014-0144

Moorefield-Lang, H. M. (2015). When Makerspaces go mobile: Case studies of transportable maker locations. *Library Hi Tech*, 33(4), 462–471. 10.1108/LHT-06-2015-0061

Morocz, R. J., Levy, B. D., Forest, C. R., Nagel, R. L., Newstetter, W. C., Talley, K. G., & Linsey, J. S. (2015, June). University maker spaces: Discovery, optimization and measurement of impacts. *2015 ASEE Annual Conference & Exposition*. 10.18260/p.24967

Morocz, R. J., Levy, B., Forest, C., Nagel, R. L., Newstetter, W. C., Talley, K. G., & Linsey, J. S. (2016, June). Relating student participation in university maker spaces to their engineering design self-efficacy. In *2016 ASEE Annual Conference & Exposition*. 10.18260/p.26070

Muller, M., Chilton, L. B., Kantosalo, A., Martin, C. P., & Walsh, G. (2022, April). GenAICHI: Generative AI and HCI. In *CHI Conference on Human Factors in Computing Systems Extended Abstracts* (pp. 1-7). ACM.

Muller, M., Weisz, J. D., & Geyer, W. (2020). Mixed initiative generative AI interfaces: An analytic framework for generative AI applications. *Proceedings of the Workshop The Future of Co-Creative Systems-A Workshop on Human-Computer Co-Creativity of the 11th International Conference on Computational Creativity (ICCC 2020).*

Murphy, A. (2024). *Imagination and creativity in the scientific realm.* Pre-publication.

Murphy, P., Peters, M. A., & Marginson, S. (2010). *Imagination: Three models of imagination in the age of the knowledge economy*. Peter Lang. 10.3726/978-1-4539-0007-9

Musick Peery, K., & Chivers, M. (2018). *Intentionally cultivating diverse community for radically open access makerspaces*. Academic Press.

Musser, G. (2019). Artificial imagination. *Scientific American*, 320(5), 58–63. 10.1038/scientificamerican0519-58

Mylon, P., Wood, G., & Dolmansley, T. (2019, July). Using student-led manufacturing in Makerspaces to support transition into engineering higher education. In *HEAD'19.5th International Conference on Higher Education Advances* (pp. 253-260). Editorial Universitat Politècnica de València. 10.4995/HEAD19.2019.9502

Mylonas, G., Hofstaetter, J., Friedl, A., & Giannakos, M. (2021, June). Designing effective playful experiences for sustainability awareness in schools and makerspaces. In *FabLearn Europe/MakeEd 2021-an international conference on computing, design and making in education* (pp. 1-9). 10.1145/3466725.3466755

Nadelson, L. S., Villanueva, I., Bouwma-Gearhart, J., Soto, E., Lenhart, C., Youmans, K., & Choi, Y. H. (2020, January). Student perceptions of and learning in makerspaces embedded in their undergraduate engineering preparation programs. In *Zone 1 Conference of the American Society for Engineering Education* (Vol. 30699). Academic Press.

Nagle, S. B. (2021). Maker services in academic libraries: A review of case studies. *New Review of Academic Librarianship*, 27(2), 184–200. 10.1080/13614533.2020.1749093

Neupane, S., Fernandez, I. A., Mittal, S., & Rahimi, S. (2023). Impacts and risk of Generative AI technology on cyber defense. *arXiv Preprint arXiv:2306.13033.*

Nichols, J., Melo, M. M., & Dewland, J. (2017). Unifying space and service for makers, entrepreneurs, and digital scholars. *Portal (Baltimore, Md.)*, 17(2), 363–374. 10.1353/pla.2017.0022

Nichols, T. P. (2020). Innovation from below: Infrastructure, design, and equity in literacy classroom makerspaces. *Research in the Teaching of English*, 55(1), 56–81. 10.58680/rte202030901

Nisenholt, M. (2007). Picturing paradox. Profiling artist Kathy Browning's art: Images on icebergs and art educator including digital photography student exemplars. *Canadian Art Teacher, 6*(1).

O'Donovan, C., & Smith, A. (2020). Technology and human capabilities in UK makerspaces. *Journal of Human Development and Capabilities*, 21(1), 63–83. 10.1080/19452829.2019.1704706

O'Leary, D. (2006). Imagination: The forgotten dimension. *The Furrow*, 57(10), 519–527.

Odena, A., Dumoulin, V., & Olah, C. (2016). Deconvolution and checkerboard artifacts. *Distill*, 1(10), e3. 10.23915/distill.00003

Oğuzhan, Ö. (2020). Dijital Sanat ve Yeniden Üretim ve Refik Anadol. Dijital İletişim Kuram ve Araştırmaları, 1-9, Ankara: Nobel Akademik Yayıncılık.

Ohkawa, T., Yoshiura, H., & Yamaguchi, T. (2023, October). Explainable multimodal fake posts detection using feature extraction with attention mechanisms. In *2023 IEEE 23rd International Conference on Software Quality, Reliability, and Security Companion (QRS-C)* (pp. 555-563). IEEE. 10.1109/QRS-C60940.2023.00068

Ojha, U., Li, Y., & Lee, Y. J. (2023). Towards universal fake image detectors that generalize across generative models. In *Proceedings of the IEEE/CVF Conference on Computer Vision and Pattern Recognition* (pp. 24480-24489). 10.1109/CVPR52729.2023.02345

Oliver, K. M. (2016). Professional development considerations for makerspace leaders, part one: Addressing "what?" and "why?". *TechTrends*, 60(2), 160–166. 10.1007/s11528-016-0028-5

Ossowski, T., & Hu, J. (2023). Multimodal prompt retrieval for generative visual question answering. *arXiv Preprint arXiv:2306.17675.*

Oswald, K., & Zhao, X. (2021). Collaborative learning in makerspaces: A grounded theory of the role of collaborative learning in makerspaces. *SAGE Open*, 11(2). 10.1177/21582440211020732

Özel Sağlamtimur, Z. (2010). Dijital Sanat. *Anadolu Üniversitesi Sosyal Bilimler Dergisi*, 10(3), 213–238.

Pallaris, G., Zaphiris, P., & Parmaxi, A. (2022). Mapping the landscape of Makerspaces in higher education: An inventory of research findings. *Interactive Technology and Smart Education.*

Palumbo, E., Daunhawer, I., & Vogt, J. E. (2023). MMVAE+: Enhancing the generative quality of multimodal VAEs without compromises. In *The Eleventh International Conference on Learning Representations*. OpenReview.

Pandey, G., & Dukkipati, A. (2017, May). Variational methods for conditional multimodal deep learning. In *2017 International Joint Conference on Neural Networks (IJCNN)* (pp. 308-315). IEEE. 10.1109/IJCNN.2017.7965870

Pan, P. (2021). "Deepfakes" and the end of the photographic age. *Aporia*, 21, 52–64.

Park, D. K., Yoo, S., Bahng, H., Choo, J., & Park, N. (2018). MEGAN: Mixture of experts of generative adversarial networks for multimodal image generation. *arXiv Preprint arXiv:1805.02481.* 10.24963/ijcai.2018/122

Pashine, S., Mandiya, S., Gupta, P., & Sheikh, R. (2021). Deep fake detection: Survey of facial manipulation detection solutions. *arXiv Preprint arXiv:2106.12605.*

Patton, M. Q. (2014). *Qualitative research and evaluation methods* (Bütün, M., & Demir, S. B., Trans.). Pegem Akademi.

Paul, O. A. (2021). *Deepfakes Generated by Generative Adversarial Networks* (Honors College Thesis, Georgia Southern University).

Paul, C. (2008). *Digital Art*. Thames and Hudson.

Paul, C. (2016). *A Companion to Digital Art*. Wiley-Blackwell. 10.1002/9781118475249

Paul, C. (2023). *Digital art*. Thames & Hudson.

Pelaprat, E., & Cole, M. (2011). "Minding the gap": Imagination, creativity and human cognition. *Integrative Psychological & Behavioral Science*, 45(4), 397–418. 10.1007/s12124-011-9176-521695391

Pendergast, S. C. (2020). *Makerspaces in Higher education: Student Engagement* (Doctoral dissertation, University of Calgary).

Penney, M. F., Watkins, J. D., Levy, B., Linsey, J. S., Nagel, R. L., Newstetter, W. C., & Smith, S. F. (2016, June). 'Making' an impact: An ethnographic approach to university Maker Spaces. *2016 ASEE Annual Conference & Exposition.* 10.18260/p.26226

Pepper-Kittredge, C., & Bird, D. (2020). *Growing a network of makerspaces in California Community Colleges: Moving towards implementation and adoption*. Academic Press.

Perez, M., Arroyo, Z., Reyes, S., Rossino, R., Rocha, A., & Ayerdi, V. (2023). *Using Makerspaces to develop didactic models for mechanical engineering*. IJAMM.

Pernia-Espinoza, A., Sanz-Garcia, A., Peciña-Marqueta, S., Martinez-de-Pison-Ascacibar, F. J., Urraca-Valle, R., & Antoñanzas-Torres, J. (2018). A review of makerspaces for stem degrees and the UR-Maker experience. *EDULEARN18 Proceedings*, 2702-2711.

Pham, M. N. (2023). *Understanding Human Imagination through Diffusion Model* (Doctoral dissertation, Virginia Tech).

Pines, E., Sullivan, P. A., & Nogales, L. (2015, June). Broadening participation through engagement in the maker space movement. In *2015 ASEE Annual Conference & Exposition* (pp. 26-295). 10.18260/p.23634

Pistrui, J. (2018). The future of human work is imagination, creativity, and strategy. *Harvard Business Review*, 1(18), 2018.

Poole, B., Jain, A., Barron, J. T., & Mildenhall, B. (2022). Dreamfusion: Text-to-3d using 2d diffusion. *arXiv preprint arXiv:2209.14988.*

Qiao, H., Liu, V., & Chilton, L. (2022, June). Initial images: using image prompts to improve subject representation in multimodal AI generated art. In *Proceedings of the 14th Conference on Creativity and Cognition* (pp. 15-28). 10.1145/3527927.3532792

Qu, Y., Nathaniel, J., Li, S., & Gentine, P. (2024). Deep generative data assimilation in multimodal setting. *arXiv preprint arXiv:2404.06665.*

Radniecki, T., Klenke, C., & Purpur, E. (2016). Makerspaces in academic libraries: Opportunities for teaching and learning. In *ICERI2016 Proceedings* (pp. 41-48). IATED.

Rahman, A., Islam, M. M., Moon, M. J., Tasnim, T., Siddique, N., Shahiduzzaman, M., & Ahmed, S. (2022). A qualitative survey on deep learning based deep fake video creation and detection method. *Aust. J. Eng. Innov. Technol*, 4(1), 13–26.

Ramdurai, B., & Adhithya, P. (2023). The impact, advancements and applications of generative AI. *International Journal on Computer Science and Engineering*, 10(6), 1–8. 10.14445/23488387/IJCSE-V10I6P101

Rayna, T., & Striukova, L. (2021). Fostering skills for the 21st century: The role of Fab labs and makerspaces. *Technological Forecasting and Social Change*, 164, 120391. 10.1016/j.techfore.2020.120391

Reas, C. (2014). *Processing: A Programming Handbook for Visual Designers and Artists 2ed* (2nd ed.). MIT Press.

Rees, P., Olson, C., Schweik, C. M., & Brewer, S. D. (2015, June). Work in progress: Exploring the role of makerspaces and flipped learning in a Town-Gown effort to engage K12 students in STEAM. *2015 ASEE Annual Conference & Exposition.* 10.18260/p.25087

Renaud, K., Warkentin, M., & Westerman, G. (2023). From ChatGPT to HackGPT: Meeting the cybersecurity threat of generative AI. *MIT Sloan Management Review*.

Reuland, E. (2017). Language and imagination: Evolutionary explorations. *Neuroscience and Biobehavioral Reviews*, 81, 255–278. 10.1016/j.neubiorev.2016.12.01728041788

Ribeiro, S. B., Perpétuo, T. P., & Instituto do Patrimônio Histórico e Artístico Nacional. (Eds.). (2018). *Inventário da obra de Athos Bulcão em Brasília*. Iphan DF. Retrieved February 14, 2024, from http://portal.iphan.gov.br/uploads/publicacao/athosbulcatilde_menor.pdf

Riley, D. M., McNair, L. D., & Masters, S. (2017). MAKER: An ethnography of maker and hacker spaces achieving diverse participation. In *2017 ASEE Annual Conference & Exposition*. ASEE. 10.18260/1-2--27724

Rockel, S., Klimentjew, D., Zhang, L., & Zhang, J. (2014, May). An hyperreality imagination based reasoning and evaluation system (HIRES). In *2014 IEEE International Conference on Robotics and Automation (ICRA)* (pp. 5705-5711). IEEE. 10.1109/ICRA.2014.6907698

Roeder, I., Klemichen, A., & Stark, R. (2020). *Be (com) ing an eco-maker–a pre-structured self-learning concept for environmentally-friendly product creation in Makerspaces*. Academic Press.

Rosenbaum, L. F., & Hartmann, B. (2017). Where be dragons? Charting the known (and not so known) areas of research on academic makerspaces. *Proceedings of ISAM*.

Sadoski, M. (1992). Imagination, cognition, and persona. *Rhetoric Review*, 10(2), 266–278. 10.1080/07350199209388971

Sætra, H. S. (2023). Generative AI: Here to stay, but for good? *Technology in Society*, 75(102372), 1–5. 10.1016/j.techsoc.2023.102372

Sagbauer, N. N., & Ebner, M. (2021). Developing a Taxonomy Concerning Physical Existing Makerspaces in and Used by Schools. *Int. J. Eng. Pedagog.*, 11(2), 57–68. 10.3991/ijep.v11i2.17021

Sahu, G., & Vechtomova, O. (2019). Adaptive fusion techniques for multimodal data. *arXiv preprint arXiv:1911.03821*.

Sakirin, T., & Kusuma, S. (2023). A survey of Generative Artificial Intelligence techniques. *Babylonian Journal of Artificial Intelligence*, 2023, 10–14. 10.58496/BJAI/2023/003

Salisbury, K., & Nichols, T. P. (2020). School makerspaces: Beyond the hype. *Phi Delta Kappan*, 101(8), 49–53. 10.1177/0031721720923792

Salman, H. (2023). University-based incubators, makerspaces and co-learning spaces as Creative Knowledge Environments: The case of a university-based CKE in Karachi, Pakistan. *Journal of Research and Innovation in Higher Education*, 4(1), 73–97.

Santo, R., Peppler, K., Ching, D., & Hoadley, C. (2015). Maybe a maker space? Organizational learning about maker education within a regional out-of-school network. *Makerspace Expansive Learning Fablearn Submission, C*, 1-9.

Santos, A. F., Barber, D.III, Harris, M., & Haymore, J. (2021). What can universities learn from organizational creative space design research? A Look at Maker Spaces. *Journal of Higher Education Theory and Practice*, 21(6).

Sarasvathy, S. D. (2002). Entrepreneurship as economics with imagination. *The Ruffin Series*, 3, 95–112. 10.5840/ruffinx200238

Schön, S., Ebner, M., & Kumar, S. (2014). The Maker Movement. Implications of new digital gadgets, fabrication tools and spaces for creative learning and teaching. *eLearning Papers, 39*, 14-25.

Schröter, J. (2023). The AI Image, the Dream, and the Statistical Unconscious. *Image*, 37(1), 112.

Schulte-Sasse, J. (1986). Imagination and modernity: Or the taming of the human mind. *Cultural Critique*, (5), 23–48. 10.2307/1354355

Seo, J., & Richard, G. T. (2021). SCAFFOLDing all abilities into makerspaces: A design framework for universal, accessible and intersectionally inclusive making and learning. *Information and Learning Science*, 122(11/12), 795–815. 10.1108/ILS-10-2020-0230

Seymour, M., Riemer, K., Yuan, L., & Dennis, A. (2021). *Beyond deep fakes: Conceptual framework, applications, and research agenda for neural rendering of realistic digital faces*. Academic Press.

Shabir, S. (2023). Expression of the human imagination and creative ability in visual form. *Journal of Wood Science*, 2(6), 877–885.

Sharma, S. (2023). Deep-Fake technology: Highlights and challenges. *International Journal of Research and Analytical Reviews*. 272-278.

Sheridan, K., Halverson, E. R., Litts, B., Brahms, L., Jacobs-Priebe, L., & Owens, T. (2014). Learning in the making: A comparative case study of three makerspaces. *Harvard Educational Review*, 84(4), 505–531. 10.17763/haer.84.4.brr-34733723j648u

Sheridan, T. B. (2000, Oct.). Interaction, imagination and immersion some research needs. In *Proceedings of the ACM Symposium on Virtual Reality Software and Technology* (pp. 1-7). 10.1145/502390.502392

Shi, Y., Paige, B., Torr, P. H., & Siddharth, N. (2020). Relating by contrasting: A data-efficient framework for multimodal generative models. *arXiv Preprint arXiv:2007.01179*.

Shi, Y., Paige, B., & Torr, P. (2019). Variational mixture-of-experts autoencoders for multi-modal deep generative models. *Advances in Neural Information Processing Systems*, 32.

Shoaib, M. R., Wang, Z., Ahvanooey, M. T., & Zhao, J. (2023, November). Deepfakes, misinformation, and disinformation in the era of frontier AI, generative AI, and large AI models. In *2023 International Conference on Computer and Applications (ICCA)* (pp. 1-7). IEEE. 10.1109/ICCA59364.2023.10401723

Singer, D. G., & Singer, J. L. (2008). Make-believe play, imagination, and creativity: Links to children's media exposure. *The Handbook of Children. Media Development*, 290–308.

Singh, P., & Dhiman, B. (2023). Exploding AI-generated deepfakes and misinformation: A threat to global concern in the 21st Century. *Authorea Preprints*. 10.36227/techrxiv.24715605.v1

Sloan, G. D. (1974). The education of the imagination. *Elementary English*, 51(7), 977–982.

Southgate, E. (n.d.). *Deep fakes, authenticity and authentication in the age of artificial intelligence*. New Basics.

Spencer, M. M. (2003, September). What more needs saying about imagination? *Journal of Adolescent & Adult Literacy*, 47(1), 106–112.

Stager, G. S. (2013, June). Papert's prison fab lab: implications for the maker movement and education design. In *Proceedings of the 12th international conference on interaction design and children* (pp. 487-490). 10.1145/2485760.2485811

Stankiewicz, D. (2016). Against imagination: On the ambiguities of a composite concept. *American Anthropologist*, 118(4), 796–810. 10.1111/aman.12696

Steele, K., Blaser, B., & Cakmak, M. (2018). Accessible making: Designing makerspaces for accessibility. *International Journal of Designs for Learning*, 9(1), 114–121. 10.14434/ijdl.v9i1.22648

Stephen, A. (2017). *The evolution of imagination.* Pre-publication proof.

Stevenson, M., Bower, M., Falloon, G., Forbes, A., & Hatzigianni, M. (2019). By design: Professional learning ecologies to develop primary school teachers' Makerspaces pedagogical capabilities. *British Journal of Educational Technology*, 50(3), 1260–1274. 10.1111/bjet.12743

Stokes, D. (2016). 18 Imagination and creativity. *The Routledge Handbook of Philosophy of Imagination*, 8.

Stornaiuolo, A., & Nichols, T. P. (2018). Making publics: Mobilizing audiences in high school makerspaces. *Teachers College Record*, 120(8), 1–38. 10.1177/016146811812000804

Strycker, J. (2015). Makerspaces: The next iteration for educational technology in K-12 schools. *Educational Technology*, 28–32.

Suganthi, S. T., Ayoobkhan, M. U. A., Bacanin, N., Venkatachalam, K., Štěpán, H., & Pavel, T. (2022). Deep learning model for deep fake face recognition and detection. *PeerJ. Computer Science*, 8, e881. 10.7717/peerj-cs.88135494811

Sullivan, P., Pines, E., Sassenfeld, R., & Nogales, L. (2016). Transiting to a student-managed maker space. In *VentureWell. Proceedings of Open, the Annual Conference* (p. 1). National Collegiate Inventors & Innovators Alliance.

Sullivan, R. M. (2010). Common knowledge: Learning spaces in academic libraries. *College & Undergraduate Libraries*, 17(2-3), 130–148. 10.1080/10691316.2010.481608

Sun, Q., Yu, Q., Cui, Y., Zhang, F., Zhang, X., Wang, Y., . . . Wang, X. (2023). Generative pretraining in multimodality. *arXiv Preprint arXiv:2307.05222.*

Sundar, A., & Heck, L. (2022). Multimodal conversational ai: A survey of datasets and approaches. *arXiv preprint arXiv:2205.06907.* 10.18653/v1/2022.nlp4convai-1.12

Sun, Q., Yu, Q., Cui, Y., Zhang, F., Zhang, X., Wang, Y., & Wang, X. (2023, October). Emu: Generative Pretraining in Multimodality. *The Twelfth International Conference on Learning Representations.*

Sutter, T., Daunhawer, I., & Vogt, J. (2020). Multimodal generative learning utilizing Jensen-Shannon-Divergence. *Advances in Neural Information Processing Systems*, 33, 6100–6110.

Suzuki, M., Nakayama, K., & Matsuo, Y. (2016). Joint multimodal learning with deep generative models. *arXiv Preprint arXiv:1611.01891.*

Suzuki, M., & Matsuo, Y. (2022). A survey of multimodal deep generative models. *Advanced Robotics*, 36(5-6), 261–278. 10.1080/01691864.2022.2035253

Taheri, P., Robbins, P., & Maalej, S. (2019). Makerspaces in first-year engineering education. *Education Sciences*, 10(1), 8. 10.3390/educsci10010008

Takale, D. G., Mahalle, P. N., & Sule, B. (2024, January - April). Advancements and applications of generative artificial intelligence. *Journal of Information Technology and Sciences*, 10(1), 20–27.

Tan, X., Xu, W., & Wang, C. (2024). Purposeful remixing with generative AI: Constructing designer voice in multimodal composing. *arXiv Preprint arXiv:2403.19095.*

Tan, M., Yang, Y., & Yu, P. (2016). The influence of the maker movement on engineering and technology education. *World Transactions on Engineering and Technology Education*, 14(1), 89–94.

Taşkesen, S. (2020). Students on the Use of Mobile Technology in Art Education Opinions and Motivations. *Ekev Academy Journal*, (84), 585–600.

Taslitz, A. E. (2009). Why did Tinkerbell get off so easy: The roles of imagination and social norms in excusing human weakness. *Texas Tech Law Review*, 42, 419.

Taştan, R. T. (2018). *Türkiye'de Çağdaş Sanatta Yerleştirme (Enstalasyon) ve Kültür* (Yayımlanmamış Sanatta yeterlilik tezi), Gazi Üniversitesi, Güzel Sanatlar Enstitüsü: Ankara.

Tellan, T. (2019). *Sanatın Dönüşümünde Dijital Süreçler ve Yeni Medya Sanatı*, Üsküdar Üniversitesi İletişim Fakültesi 6. Uluslararası İletişim Günleri Dijital Dönüşüm Sempozyumu'nda sunulmuş bildiri, Üsküdar Üniversitesi, İstanbul, s. 651.

Thomas, S., Taylor, M., Anderson, B., & Jackson, E. (n.d.). *The evolution and impact of Generative AI: From early models to advanced AIGC technologies*. Academic Press.

Thomas, N. J. (2014). The multidimensional spectrum of imagination: Images, dreams, hallucinations, and active, imaginative perception. *Humanities (Washington)*, 3(2), 132–184. 10.3390/h3020132

Thompson, N. A. (2018). Imagination and creativity in organizations. *Organization Studies*, 39(2-3), 229–250. 10.1177/0170840617736939

Tinkercad | From mind to design in minutes. (n.d.). Tinkercad. Retrieved February 24, 2024, from https://www.tinkercad.com/

Titchen, A., McCormack, B., Wilson, V. J., & Solman, A. (2011). Human flourishing through body, creative imagination and reflection. *International Practice Development Journal,* 1 - 18.

Togo, R., Kotera, M., Ogawa, T., & Haseyama, M. (2021). Text-guided style transfer-based image manipulation using multimodal generative models. *IEEE Access : Practical Innovations, Open Solutions*, 9, 64860–64870. 10.1109/ACCESS.2021.3069876

Tolosana, R., Vera-Rodriguez, R., Fierrez, J., Morales, A., & Ortega-Garcia, J. (2020). Deepfakes and beyond: A survey of face manipulation and fake detection. *Information Fusion*, 64, 131–148. 10.1016/j.inffus.2020.06.014

Tomko, M., Alemán, M. W., Newstetter, W., Nagel, R. L., & Linsey, J. (2021). Participation pathways for women into university makerspaces. *Journal of Engineering Education*, 110(3), 700–717. 10.1002/jee.20402

Tomko, M., Aleman, M., Newstetter, W., Linsey, J., & Nagel, R. (2021). A methodological roadmap for phenomenologically based interviewing in engineering education: Identifying types of learning in Makerspaces. *Studies in Engineering Education*, 2(1), 100. 10.21061/see.32

Tomko, M., Newstetter, W., Alemán, M. W., Nagel, R. L., & Linsey, J. (2020). Academic Makerspaces as a "design journey": Developing a learning model for how women students tap into their "toolbox of design". *Artificial Intelligence for Engineering Design, Analysis and Manufacturing*, 34(3), 363–373. 10.1017/S089006042000030X

Tortora, L. (2024). Beyond discrimination: Generative AI applications and ethical challenges in forensic psychiatry. *Frontiers in Psychiatry*, 15, 1346059. 10.3389/fpsyt.2024.134605938525252

Trevors, J. T., & Saier, M. H. (2012). *Mysticism and science: two products of the human imagination*. Crossing Dialogues.

Trevors, J. T., & Saier, M. H.Jr. (2010). Exercises in human imagination. *Water, Air, and Soil Pollution*, 205(S1), 9–10. 10.1007/s11270-006-9313-9

Trevors, J. T., & Saier, M. H.Jr. (2010). Science and religion: Two products of human imagination. *Water, Air, and Soil Pollution*, 205(S1), 23–25. 10.1007/s11270-007-9378-0

Trust, T., Maloy, R. W., & Edwards, S. (2018). Learning through making: Emerging and expanding designs for college classes. *TechTrends*, 62(1), 19–28. 10.1007/s11528-017-0214-0

Tsai, K. C. (2012). Play, imagination, and creativity: A brief literature review. *Journal of Education and Learning*, 1(2), 15–20. 10.5539/jel.v1n2p15

Turakhia, D. G., Ludgin, D., Mueller, S., & Desportes, K. (2023, April). What Can We Learn From Educators About Teaching in Makerspaces? In *Extended Abstracts of the 2023 CHI Conference on Human Factors in Computing Systems* (pp. 1-7). 10.1145/3544549.3585687

Ulutaş, İ., & Demiriz, S. (2019). The importance of visual art education in preschool and visual art education programs features. In Ulutaş, İ. (Ed.), *Visual Art Education in Early Childhood Education*. Hedef Cs.

Unterfrauner, E., Voigt, C., & Hofer, M. (2021). The effect of maker and entrepreneurial education on self-efficacy and creativity. *Entrepreneurship Education*, 4(4), 403–424. 10.1007/s41959-021-00060-w

Usmani, S., Siddiqui, Y. A., Hamza, M., Shaikh, M. T., & Hasan, Q. (n.d.). *Exploring the landscape of multimodal generative adversarial networks: A comprehensive survey and analysis*. Academic Press.

Van Holm, E. J., & Joseph, E. (2014). What are Makerspaces, Hackerspaces, and Fab Labs? SSRN *Electronic Journal*. Preprint.

Van Holm, E. J. (2014). *What are makerspaces, hackerspaces, and fab labs?* Hackerspaces, and Fab Labs.

Van Hulle, D. (2019). Artificial imagination, imagine: New developments in digital scholarly editing. *International Journal of Digital Humanities*, 1(2), 137–140. 10.1007/s42803-019-00020-w

Van Leeuwen, N. (2016). *Imagination and action*. Academic Press.

Van Leeuwen, N. (2011). Imagination is where the action is. *The Journal of Philosophy*, 108(2), 55–77. 10.5840/jphil201110823

van Oers, B. (2005). The potentials of imagination. *Inquiry (Upper Montclair, N.J.)*, 24(4), 5–18. 10.5840/inquiryctnews20052441

Veerasamy, N., & Pieterse, H. (2022, March). Rising above misinformation and deepfakes. In *International Conference on Cyber Warfare and Security* (Vol. 17, No. 1, pp. 340-348). 10.34190/iccws.17.1.25

Vertolli, M., Breault, V., Ouellet, S., Somers, S., Gagne, J., & Davies, J. (2014). Theoretical assessment of the SOILIE model of the human imagination. In *Proceedings of the Annual Meeting of the Cognitive Science Society* (Vol. 36). Academic Press.

Villena-Gonzalez, M., & Cosmelli, D. (2020). Imagination and mind wandering: Two sides of the same coin? A brain dynamics perspective. In *Creativity and the Wandering Mind* (pp. 93–120). Academic Press. 10.1016/B978-0-12-816400-6.00005-5

Vinodrai, T., Nader, B., & Zavarella, C. (2021). Manufacturing space for inclusive innovation? A study of makerspaces in southern Ontario. *Local Economy*, 36(3), 205–223. 10.1177/0269094221101353234650320

Vondrick, C., Pirsiavash, H., Oliva, A., & Torralba, A. (2014). Acquiring visual classifiers from human imagination. *arXiv preprint arXiv:1410.4627*. 10.21236/ADA612443

Vondrick, C., Pirsiavash, H., Oliva, A., & Torralba, A. (2015). Learning visual biases from human imagination. *Advances in Neural Information Processing Systems*, 28.

Vyas, K., Pareek, P., Jayaswal, R., & Patil, S. (2024). Analysing the landscape of Deep Fake Detection: A survey. *International Journal of Intelligent Systems and Applications in Engineering*, 12(11s), 40–55.

Vygotsky, L. S. (2004). Imagination and creativity in childhood. *Journal of Russian & East European Psychology*, 42(1), 7–97. 10.1080/10610405.2004.11059210

Vyshedskiy, A. (2019). Neuroscience of imagination and implications for human evolution. *Current Neurobiology*, 10(2), 89–109.

Wach, K., Duong, C. D., Ejdys, J., Kazlauskaitė, R., Korzynski, P., Mazurek, G., Paliszkiewicz, J., & Ziemba, E. (2023). The dark side of generative artificial intelligence: A critical analysis of controversies and risks of ChatGPT. *Entrepreneurial Business and Economics Review*, 11(2), 7–30. 10.15678/EBER.2023.110201

Wagner, T. L., & Blewer, A. (2019). "The word real is no longer real": Deepfakes, gender, and the challenges of AI-altered video. *Open Information Science*, 3(1), 32–46. 10.1515/opis-2019-0003

Wallace, M. K., Trkay, G., Chivers, M., & Peery, K. M. (2017). *Making Maker literacies: integrating academic library makerspaces into the undergraduate curriculum.* Academic Press.

Wands, B. (2006). Dijital Çağın Sanatı. Çev. Osman Akınhay. İstanbul: Akbank Kültür ve Sanat Dizisi.

Wang, D., Dunn, N., & Coulton, P. (2015). Grassroots maker spaces: a recipe for innovation? *Proceedings of the 11th European Academy of Design Conference.*

Wang, G., & Torr, P. H. (2022). Traditional classification neural networks are good generators: They are competitive with DDPMs and GANs. *arXiv preprint arXiv:2211.14794.*

Wang, R., Juefei-Xu, F., Guo, Q., Huang, Y., Ma, L., Liu, Y., & Wang, L. (2020). Deeptag: Robust image tagging for deepfake provenance. *arXiv Preprint arXiv:2009.09869, 3.*

Wang, R., Juefei-Xu, F., Ma, L., Xie, X., Huang, Y., Wang, J., & Liu, Y. (2019). Fakespotter: A simple yet robust baseline for spotting ai-synthesized fake faces. *arXiv Preprint arXiv:1909.06122.*

Wang, F., Wang, W., Wilson, S., & Ahmed, N. (2016). The state of library Makerspaces. *International Journal of Librarianship*, 1(1), 2–16. 10.23974/ijol.2016.vol1.1.12

Weidinger, L., Rauh, M., Marchal, N., Manzini, A., Hendricks, L. A., Mateos-Garcia, J., . . . Isaac, W. (2023). Sociotechnical safety evaluation of generative ai systems. *arXiv Preprint arXiv:2310.11986.*

Weiner, S., Lande, M., & Jordan, S. (2018). The engineer of 2020, in the making: Understanding how young adults develop maker identities and the implications for education reform. *International Journal of Engineering Education*, 34(2), 833–842.

Wellner, G. (2019). Digital subjectivity: From a network metaphor to a layer-plateau model. *Digital Subjectivity: From a Network Metaphor to a Layer-Plateau Model*, 55-66.

Wellner, G. (2022). Digital imagination, fantasy, AI art. *Foundations of Science*, 1–7.

Wellner, G. (2022). Digital imagination: Ihde's and Stiegler's concepts of imagination. *Foundations of Science*, 27(1), 189–204. 10.1007/s10699-020-09737-2

Wentzel, K. R., & Watkins, D. E. (2002). Peer relationsips and collaborative learning as contexts for academic enablers. *School Psychology Review*, 31(3), 366–377. 10.1080/02796015.2002.12086161

West, P., Lu, X., Dziri, N., Brahman, F., Li, L., Hwang, J. D., & Choi, Y. (2023, October). The Generative AI paradox: "What it can create, it may not understand". *The Twelfth International Conference on Learning Representations.*

White, N., & Burg, K. (2019). From university to invention to entrepreneurship. *Technology and Innovation*, 20(4), 377–383. 10.21300/20.4.2019.377

Whitmer, S. (2016). Makerspaces that set the stage for lifelong learning. In *VentureWell.Proceedings of Open, the Annual Conference* (p. 1). National Collegiate Inventors & Innovators Alliance.

Whittaker, L., Kietzmann, T. C., Kietzmann, J., & Dabirian, A. (2020). "All around me are synthetic faces": The mad world of AI-generated media. *IT Professional*, 22(5), 90–99. 10.1109/MITP.2020.2985492

Wilczynski, V., & Adrezin, R. (2016, November). Higher education makerspaces and engineering education. In *ASME International Mechanical Engineering Congress and Exposition* (Vol. 50571, p. V005T06A013). American Society of Mechanical Engineers.

Wilczynski, V. (2015, June). Academic maker spaces and engineering design. *2015 ASEE Annual Conference & Exposition.*

Wilczynski, V. (2017, June). A classification system for higher education Makerspaces. *2017 ASEE Annual Conference & Exposition.* 10.18260/1-2--27448

Wilczynski, V., & Hoover, A. (2017). Classifying Academic Makerspaces: Applied at ISAM 2017. *Proceedings of the International Symposium on Academic Makerspaces.*

Willett, R. (2016). Making, makers, and makerspaces: A discourse analysis of professional journal articles and blog posts about makerspaces in public libraries. *The Library Quarterly*, 86(3), 313–329. 10.1086/686676

Winner, E., & Hetland, L. (2008). Art for our sake school arts classes matter more than ever-but not for the reasons you think. *Arts Education Policy Review*, 109(5), 29–32. 10.3200/AEPR.109.5.29-32

Wong, A., & Partridge, H. (2016). Making as learning: Makerspaces in universities. *Australian Academic and Research Libraries*, 47(3), 143–159. 10.1080/00048623.2016.1228163

Wu, X., Huang, S., & Wei, F. (2024). Multimodal large language model is a human-aligned annotator for text-to-image generation. *arXiv Preprint arXiv:2404.15100.*

Wu, H. Y., & Callaghan, V. (2016). From imagination to innovation: A creative development process. In *Intelligent Environments 2016* (pp. 514–523). IOS Press.

Wu, K. J., Burg, T. C., & Burg, K. J. (2020). Reshaping the higher education Makerspace and harnessing current disruptive events. *Technology and Innovation*, 21(4), 1–10. 10.21300/21.4.2020.6

Wu, Y., & Ma, Z. (2022). The power of Makerspaces: Heterotopia and innovation. *Sustainability (Basel)*, 15(1), 629. 10.3390/su15010629

Wyse, L. (2019). Mechanisms of artistic creativity in deep learning neural networks. *arXiv preprint arXiv:1907.00321.*

Xu, M., Niyato, D., Kang, J., Xiong, Z., Jamalipour, A., Fang, Y., & Kim, D. I. (2024). Integration of Mixture of Experts and Multimodal Generative AI in Internet of Vehicles: A Survey. *arXiv preprint arXiv:2404.16356.*

Xu, D., Fan, S., & Kankanhalli, M. (2023, October). Combating misinformation in the era of generative AI models. In *Proceedings of the 31st ACM International Conference on Multimedia* (pp. 9291-9298). 10.1145/3581783.3612704

Xu, X., Wang, Z., Zhang, G., Wang, K., & Shi, H. (2023). Versatile diffusion: Text, images and variations all in one diffusion model. In *Proceedings of the IEEE/CVF International Conference on Computer Vision* (pp. 7754-7765). 10.1109/ICCV51070.2023.00713

Yadav, D., & Salmani, S. (2019, May). Deepfake: A survey on facial forgery technique using generative adversarial network. In *2019 International Conference on Intelligent Computing and Control Systems (ICCS)* (pp. 852-857). IEEE. 10.1109/ICCS45141.2019.9065881

Yagnik, H., Kurani, A., & Joshi, P. (2020). *A brief study on deepfakes. International Research Journal of Engineering and Technology*. IRJET.

Yang, X., Feng, S., Wang, D., Qi, S., Wu, W., Zhang, Y., . . . Poria, S. (2023). Few-shot joint multimodal aspect-sentiment analysis based on generative multimodal prompt. *arXiv Preprint arXiv:2305.10169*. 10.18653/v1/2023.findings-acl.735

Yang, X., Li, Y., & Lyu, S. (2019, May). Exposing deep fakes using inconsistent head poses. In *ICASSP 2019-2019 IEEE International Conference on Acoustics, Speech and Signal Processing (ICASSP)* (pp. 8261-8265). IEEE. 10.1109/ICASSP.2019.8683164

Yan, Z., Yang, C., Liang, Q., & Chen, X. A. (2023, October). XCreation: A graph-based crossmodal generative creativity support tool. In *Proceedings of the 36th Annual ACM Symposium on User Interface Software and Technology* (pp. 1-15). 10.1145/3586183.3606826

Yeh, R. A., Chen, C., Yian Lim, T., Schwing, A. G., Hasegawa-Johnson, M., & Do, M. N. (2017). Semantic image inpainting with deep generative models. In *Proceedings of the IEEE Conference on Computer Vision and Pattern Recognition* (pp. 5485-5493). 10.1109/CVPR.2017.728

Yıldırım, A., & Şimşek, H. (2006). Qualitative research methods in social sciences (5th edition). Seçkin Publishing.

Youmans, K., Villanueva, I., Nadelson, L., Bouwma-Gearhart, J., Lenz, A., & Lanci, S. (2020). *Engineering students perceived value of Makerspaces in relation to future career preparation*. Academic Press.

Yu, N., Skripniuk, V., Chen, D., Davis, L., & Fritz, M. (2020). Responsible disclosure of generative models using scalable fingerprinting. *arXiv Preprint arXiv:2012.08726.*

Yu, S. (2016). *Makerspaces as learning spaces: An historical overview and literature review*. Academic Press.

Yu, T., Dai, W., Liu, Z., & Fung, P. (2021). Vision guided generative pre-trained language models for multimodal abstractive summarization. *arXiv Preprint arXiv:2109.02401*. 10.18653/v1/2021.emnlp-main.326

Yuan, T., Chen, X., & Wang, S. (2022, Mar.). *Gorgeous pixel artwork generation with VQGAN-CLIP*. Preprint. 1 - 9.

Yu, N., Skripniuk, V., Abdelnabi, S., & Fritz, M. (2021). Artificial fingerprinting for generative models: Rooting deepfake attribution in training data. In *Proceedings of the IEEE/CVF International Conference on Computer Vision* (pp. 14448-14457). 10.1109/ICCV48922.2021.01418

Yusoff, K., & Gabrys, J. (2011). Climate change and the imagination. *Wiley Interdisciplinary Reviews: Climate Change*, 2(4), 516–534. 10.1002/wcc.117

Zhan, F., Yu, Y., Wu, R., Zhang, J., Lu, S., Liu, L., . . . Xing, E. (2022). Multimodal image synthesis and editing: A survey. *arXiv Preprint arXiv:2112.13592.*

Zhan, F., Yu, Y., Wu, R., Zhang, J., Lu, S., Liu, L., Kortylewski, A., Theobalt, C., & Xing, E. (2023). Multimodal image synthesis and editing: A survey and taxonomy. *IEEE Transactions on Pattern Analysis and Machine Intelligence*, 45(12), 15098–15119. 10.1109/TPAMI.2023.3305243

Zhang, B., Zhou, J. P., Shumailov, I., & Papernot, N. (2020). On attribution of deepfakes. *arXiv Preprint arXiv:2008.09194.*

Zhang, C., Zhang, C., Li, C., Qiao, Y., Zheng, S., Dam, S. K., . . . Hong, C. S. (2023). One small step for generative ai, one giant leap for AGI: A complete survey on ChatGPT in AIGC era. *arXiv Preprint arXiv:2304.06488.*

Zhang, C., Zhang, C., Zhang, M., & Kweon, I. S. (2023). Text-to-image diffusion model in generative ai: A survey. *arXiv preprint arXiv:2303.07909.*

Zhang, C., Zhang, C., Zhang, M., & Kweon, I. S. (2023). Text-to-image diffusion model in generative AI: A survey. *arXiv Preprint arXiv:2303.07909.*

Zhang, C., Zhang, C., Zheng, S., Qiao, Y., Li, C., Zhang, M., . . . Hong, C. S. (2023). A complete survey on generative AI (AIGC): Is ChatGPT from GPT-4 to GPT-5 all you need? *arXiv Preprint arXiv:2303.11717.*

Zhang, C., Yang, Z., He, X., & Deng, L. (2020). Multimodal intelligence: Representation learning, information fusion, and applications. *IEEE Journal of Selected Topics in Signal Processing*, 14(3), 478–493. 10.1109/JSTSP.2020.2987728

Zhao, R., Chen, H., Wang, W., Jiao, F., Do, X. L., Qin, C., . . . Joty, S. (2023). Retrieving multimodal information for augmented generation: A survey. *arXiv Preprint arXiv:2303.10868.* 10.18653/v1/2023.findings-emnlp.314

Zhao, B., Zhang, S., Xu, C., Sun, Y., & Deng, C. (2021). Deep fake geography? When geospatial data encounter Artificial Intelligence. *Cartography and Geographic Information Science*, 48(4), 338–352. 10.1080/15230406.2021.1910075

Zhu, J. Y., Zhang, R., Pathak, D., Darrell, T., Efros, A. A., Wang, O., & Shechtman, E. (2017). Toward multimodal image-to-image translation. *Advances in Neural Information Processing Systems*, 30.

Zhu, M., Chen, H., Yan, Q., Huang, X., Lin, G., Li, W., & Wang, Y. (2024). Genimage: A million-scale benchmark for detecting ai-generated image. *Advances in Neural Information Processing Systems*, 36, 1–12.

Zinken, J. (2003). Ideological imagination: Intertextual and correlational metaphors in political discourse. *Discourse & Society*, 14(4), 507–523. 10.1177/0957926503014004005

Zittoun, T., Glaveanu, V. L. A. D., & Hawlina, H. (2020). 10 A sociocultural perspective on imagination. *The Cambridge Handbook of the Imagination*, 143.

Zittoun, T., & Cerchia, F. (2013). Imagination as expansion of experience. *Integrative Psychological & Behavioral Science*, 47(3), 305–324. 10.1007/s12124-013-9234-223625542

Zobaed, S., Rabby, F., Hossain, I., Hossain, E., Hasan, S., Karim, A., & Md Hasib, K. (2021). Deepfakes: Detecting forged and synthetic media content using machine learning. *Artificial Intelligence in Cyber Security: Impact and Implications: Security Challenges, Technical and Ethical Issues, Forensic Investigative Challenges*, 177-201.

About the Contributors

Shalin Hai-Jew works as the grant writer for Hutchinson Community College in Hutchinson, Kansas. Prior, she worked as an instructional designer at Kansas State University (K-State) for 17.5 years. She has taught at the university and college levels for many years (including four years in the People's Republic of China) and was tenured at Shoreline Community College. She has Bachelor's degrees in English and psychology, a Master's degree in Creative Writing from the University of Washington (Hugh Paradise Scholar), and an Ed.D in Educational Leadership with a focus on public administration from Seattle University (where she was a Morford Scholar). She tested into the University of Washington at 14. She reviews for several publishers and publications. She has authored and edited a number of books. Hai-Jew was born in Huntsville, Alabama, in the U.S.

* * *

Ilkay Ulutaş received an undergraduate degree in the Child Development and Education Teaching program at Gazi University. She completed her master's degree in child development at Ankara University and her PhD in Child Development and Education at Gazi University. In 2009, she conducted a postdoctoral study on emotional intelligence at the University College London Department of Psychology within the scope of the TUBITAK Scientist Support Department International Postdoctoral Research Scholarship Program. Her studies focus on the emotional intelligence in preschool children, Montessori education, mathematics education in early childhood education, arts in early childhood education, early childhood quality, and technology in early childhood education. She has also recently carried out projects on digital mathematics stories in early childhood education, augmented reality applications in early childhood mathematics education, and cultural heritage and technology (coding, digital storytelling) in early childhood education. She currently works as a professor at the Early Childhood Education Department at Gazi University. She received her PhD in early childhood education at Gazi University in 2005. She did post-doctoral studies at the Trait Emotional Intelligence laboratory of K. V. Petrides in 2009 at University College London. Her research interest focuses mainly on emotional intelligence in early childhood. She also has studies on early childhood quality, visual arts education in early childhood, mathematics education in early childhood, and Montessori education. She teaches undergraduate and graduate courses as a professor at the Department of Early Childhood Education at Gazi University. She also participates in international conferences and carries out various national projects.

Index

A

B

C

D

G

H

M

P

R

S

T

V

www.ingramcontent.com/pod-product-compliance
Lightning Source LLC
LaVergne TN
LVHW080528300926
849162LV00007B/1560